# The Way of Music

# THE WAY of MUSIC

## WILLIAM E. BRANDT
### WASHINGTON STATE UNIVERSITY

ALLYN AND BACON, INC.

BOSTON

First Printing . . . May, 1963
Second Printing . . . December, 1963
Third Printing . . . December, 1964
Fourth Printing . . . August, 1965
Fifth Printing . . . August, 1966
Sixth Printing . . . February, 1967

# Preface

What is the purpose of a study of music literature? To learn amusing anecdotes about composers? To hear a variety of music? To learn to recognize the orchestral instruments by the sounds they produce? Or is it to learn how the music functions, how it is put together, how the composer was affected by his times and how he expresses his time as well as himself in the music? I feel that the last question most nearly states the requirements necessary to allow the serious listener to penetrate the music, become involved in it and to examine it "from the inside." For that reason, this book spends considerable time upon the constructive elements of the art — melody, harmony, rhythm, form and style — so that the person with curiosity and interest in the great music of Europe and America may better understand the universality and importance of these works.

The listener is probably aware that there are many different ways of responding to compositions. We may daydream when certain pieces are played, or become excited. We may "see" in our mind scenes or landscapes, or we may feel our blood tingling in response to the force or the grandeur or the rhythm of the music. Or again, we may follow the drama unfolding in sound in much the same way as we attend a play in the theater, with intellectual and emotional satisfaction over the dynamic progression of events, penetration into the "message" of the work, and appreciation of the structural balance. All of these ways are legitimate, but some yield more profound enjoyment than others. In general, the more one knows about the processes of a work, the more intensely he understands the final accomplishment, whether it be a skyscraper, a round of golf, a piano recital or a symphony.

And, best of all, the addition of new ways of understanding does not invalidate the old ones: emotional and intellectual appreciation go hand in hand, each enhancing the other.

In order to attain these ends, this book has been organized in a certain way. After the first two chapters, which are devoted to the establishment of some important basic concepts and terminology, each of the succeeding chapters treats in chronological order the periods of music history from the Renaissance to the present, exploring the important components of the style of each as exemplified in the works of that period's great composers. This exploration is contained in the same five sections of each chapter, the first of which provides an historical and biographical background, the second a discussion of the musical style, the third an exposition of formal and generative principles, the fourth a series of analyses of representative works, together with musical examples, and the fifth a comparison of the abstract style of the music with the visual arts of the time, wherever these run parallel. There is no attempt made to integrate the arts, but rather to assist comprehension of the music by showing similarities in line, rhythm, color and emotional content with paintings, sculpture and architecture. Also included in this final section is a list of important terms which have been explained and used in the chapter and suggestions for additional listening. The whole study is cumulative in the use of terms as well as in the degree of listening and analytical skill required. For that reason, thorough familiarity with vocabulary and formal diagrams is of the utmost importance.

In order to learn to swim, one must get into the water. In order to increase one's perceptions of music, one must immerse himself in it via phonograph, radio, television and most important of all, concerts. Recorded music, while a great benefit, can never rival the vividness of a live concert where the interrelation of performer and audience charges the atmosphere with an electric stimulation. One leaves the concert hall with the feeling that he has experienced something ennobling and spiritually rewarding. In our complex civilization with its emphasis upon material values, the arts, and especially music by virtue of its abstract quality, symbolize a whole world of the spirit, organized, harmonious and humane. Let us not ignore them.

I am indebted to my colleagues Peter DeLone and Robert Miller for many useful suggestions concerning this book, and to Kemble Stout, chairman of the Music Department at Washington State University, for the opportunity to test the book in class before publication.

iv

## Preface

And not least, I feel that the many classes in music literature deserve my gratitude for being the unwitting "guinea pigs" during the book's development period.

*William E. Brandt*

# Contents

# Contents

Contents

# The Way of Music

# I Theory

# for the Listener

Probably the first element of music of which we are conscious is that of sound: music consists of sounds arranged in order — not just any sounds, but tones of definite highness or lowness. These tones are said to have high or low pitch. Now sound results from rapid vibration of an elastic substance. Anyone who has snapped a bow-string or a rubber band knows this. The string vibrates back and forth: this we see. What we do not see are the ranks of air molecules jostled together then pulled apart by the motion of the string. The waves formed in this way travel from the vibrating string to our ear drum, and by alternately pushing and pulling it at the same rate of speed as the bowstring, cause it to vibrate at the same pitch. This vibratory motion is then transmitted via the apparatus in the ear to the auditory nerve and thence to the brain where it is experienced as sound. When a string, a reed, or a piece of metal vibrates at a certain speed, it produces sound of a specific *pitch*. For example, middle C on the piano is produced by the piano wire vibrating at 261.6 vibrations per second. But a reed or a metal bar producing this pitch vibrates at exactly the same rate. Moreover, most of these sound producers also vibrate at multiples of their basic or fundamental rates, thus producing not a simple sound, but a complex of higher sounds as well. These are called harmonics or overtones, and we shall have more to say about them later when we discuss instruments. Now, the faster the vibration, the higher the pitch becomes. The C eight white key above middle C vibrates at exactly twice 261.6, or 523.2 vibrations per second, and each C above that vibrates at twice the rate of the immediately preceding C (Example 1). The distance in pitch between these notes is called an *octave*. Similarly, each of the octaves below middle C vibrates at one-half the number of vibrations of the next higher C.

Traditionally, occidental music has divided the distance of the octave into twelve different equidistant pitches. If we examine a piano keyboard, this becomes clear (Example 1). Starting, for example, on middle C, and counting all the keys, both white and black until we have reached the next C, we find a total of twelve. These are called *half steps,* and are the smallest pitch divisions used in our music: two of these *half steps* constitute a *whole step.* When a series of pitches

EXAMPLE 1.

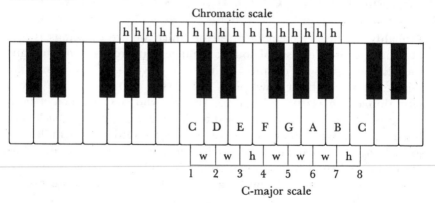

Chromatic scale

C-major scale

Middle C

130.8 v/sec.          261.6 v/sec.          523.2 v/sec.

w   indicates a whole step between adjacent scale tones.

h   indicates a half step between adjacent scale tones.

Pattern of whole and half steps in the major scale:
Tone:          1  2  3  4  5  6  7  8
Distance:        w  w  h  w  w  w  h

4

ter which is divided into duple or triple
*ly recurring stressed pulsations.* These
*ic rhythm.*

of assigning one pitch per pulsation, or
for more than one beat, or assign two or
This procedure results in the phenome-
d, briefly, by assigning *varying durations*
them to flow irregularly in time over
metric pulsation, and arousing interest

. Sing the pitches of the first part of
e River" with equal duration to each
rhythm (Example 4a). Uninteresting,

*ng of words.*

n      the      Swa - nee      ri - ver

Stephen Foster wrote it, assigning the
e, and tapping your foot in metric
the varied sequence of long and short

*ting of words.*

-on the Swa - nee      ri-ver

ong notes are not of the same length,
ll use the term *rhythm,* then, to iden-
d short durations which do not neces-
the metric pulsation.
rhythm may vary in *quality* as the
enteenth century music we may find
accented rhythms, while in the eight-
e to only lightly accented, smoothly
tion, in addition to indicating pitches,
s of these sounds, thus giving the

is arranged in an ascending pattern according to some prearranged
plan of half steps and whole steps, a structure called a *scale* is formed.
The one which we have constructed entirely of half steps is called the
*chromatic scale* (Example 1). Notice that when played it has no
tendency to stop on any particular note, but may continue on and on,
the choice of the final pitch being at the option of the player. When
the white keys from C up an octave to the next C are played, we have
an arrangement called the *major scale* (Example 1). Notice how this
scale contains half and whole steps in a definite pattern: if this pattern
is reproduced using any other pitch as the starting point, regardless
of whether that note is a black or white key on the piano, we still
have as the result a major scale (Example 2). Another important
quality of the major scale is its tendency to want to use that starting

EXAMPLE 2.

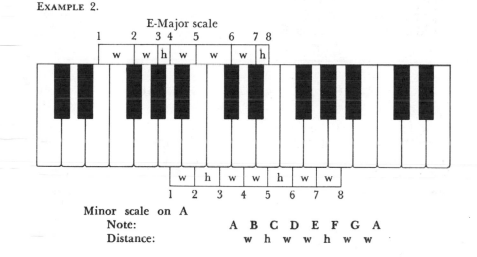

Minor scale on A

| Note: | A | B | C | D | E | F | G | A |
|---|---|---|---|---|---|---|---|---|
| Distance: | w | h | w | w | h | w | w | |

note as its final tone. This tone, then, is the ruler of the other tones.
There are two other notes upon which we may come to rest, but they
do not sound final. Always the basic note of the scale draws the
others to it. This *stable* pitch is said to be the *keynote* or *tonic note*
of the scale. The temporary resting places may be said to be *conditionally stable,* while others, particularly the second, fourth and seventh
notes of the major scale, are *unstable,* and wish to move to either the
*conditionally stable* pitches or the *stable keynote* of the scale.

If we begin a scale on the sixth note of the C-major scale, and continue it upwards one octave, the result is an arrangement of half and whole steps different from that of the major, and called the *minor scale* (Example 2). This scale, like the major, has a keynote; but while this tone represents the main point of stability in the scale, its attraction is far weaker than that of its major counterpart. The total sound of the minor scale is quite different from that of the major as a result of the different arrangement of the sequence of whole and half steps. Because the distance between the seventh tone and the tonic is a whole step, the tendency of this seventh tone, or "leading tone" to rise to the tonic is not strong. To improve this situation, the seventh tone in minor is often raised one half step ("sharped"), thus making it only a half step from the tonic, analogous to the relationship of these two notes in the major scale.

The notes of these scales, when arranged in a chosen order by a composer, furnish the pitches for a melody. But another basic element of music must be considered and applied before this series of pitches can come to life as a melody.

## METER AND RHYTHM

As we have applied a measuring scale to pitches, so now we use the yardstick on that important but elusive dimension of music, time. First of all, we realize that the flow of time may be broken up into small divisions, either noted on a watch dial, or experienced as sound in the regular dripping of a leaky faucet, the ticking of a clock, or the tapping of our foot. The time distances between successive sounds must be equal to be useful, and may be closely or more widely spaced, resulting in either a rapid stream of pulsations or a slower series. This speed of pulsation is called *tempo* in music, and requires a qualifying adjective to render it meaningful: thus, we speak of a fast, moderate or slow tempo. The Italian words printed at the beginning of compositions are the traditional way to indicate to the performer the approximate tempo of the music (a list of the most common of these appears in Appendix I).

The human mind tends to try to impose order on regularly recurring events in order to reduce them to a system; the endless, even flow of pulsations described above is no exception. Perhaps you have noticed that, when listening to that leaking faucet, you tend to feel

occur on the pulsations of me
sections by means of *regular*
songs are said to employ *met*

But suppose that instead
beat, we decide to hold some
more pitches to a single beat.
non called *rhythm*. It is forme
to the pitches chosen, causing
the constant and equidistant
because of this irregularity.

Let us try an experimen
"Way Down Upon the Swane
note; in other words, in metri

EXAMPLE 4A. *Metric syllabic setti*

Meter    *     *     *
     'Way    down    up - 

isn't it? Now sing the song as
correct durations to each no
rhythm (Example 4b). Notice

EXAMPLE 4B. *Rhythmic syllabic se*

Meter    *    *    *
Rhythm   _____
     'Way      down up

notes. Notice also that all the l
nor are the short notes. We sha
tify patterns of various long an
sarily coincide throughout with

Both metric and non-metri
emphasis changes. Thus, in sev
well-marked, sometimes heavily
eenth century these often chang
flowing pulsations. Musical nota
also shows the varied duration

performer a fairly accurate graph or set of directions for both melodic contour and rhythmic design.

When the rhythmic flow of a musical composition moves smoothly with the metric flow, coinciding with, or evenly subdividing the pulsations, it is said to be rhythmically stable. If, however, some interruption or displaced accent occurs, we have the condition of *instability*. Let us illustrate. Suppose that we have an even flow of beats in triple meter, with the normal stress or accent on the first beat of each group, thus: 1-2-3, 1-2-3, 1-2-3, etc. Try counting this aloud, tapping your foot on the count of *one*. This is stable metric rhythm. Now, insert into this stable flow, while still tapping the first beat with your foot, a misplaced accent on the second beat of two succeeding metric groups, thus: 1-2-3 1-2-3 1-2-3 1-**2**-3 1-**2**-3 1-2-3 1-2-3 1-**2**-3 1-**2**-3 1-**2**-3 1-2-3 1-**2**-3 1-2-3. Notice the surprise element afforded by this procedure, which is called *syncopation*. A similar result could be obtained by accenting the third beat of the group — a syncopation again. This is an unstable rhythmic condition which tends to return to stability. It may result from the rather simple procedure above, or may be much more complex, but the result is the same — rhythmic instability. Most compositions are fundamentally rhythmically stable, but often contain short sections of unstable rhythm to enhance the return to stability, emphasize a cadence or section, or merely to provide variety.

The metric units of two and three pulsations referred to above have received the name of *measures,* a term useful and less roundabout than *metric units.* So far we have discussed duple (two) and triple (three) meter. These are obviously the simplest kinds, but others of greater complexity may be derived by combining in various ways these basic units. A common combination of two duple units is quadruple meter. In this case, there is a relatively heavy stress on the first beat of the measure, a lighter stress on the third, and none at all on the second and fourth. When we combine a duple and a triple unit to form quintuple time, two varieties are possible, depending on whether we place the duple unit first (1-2-3-4-5), or second (1-2-3-4-5). In either case, the primary or heavy accent is on the first beat of the measure, and the secondary on the third or fourth, depending upon the arrangement.

When we combine two units of triple meter, two results are possible. First, at a moderately slow tempo we have 1-2-3-4-5-6, again with the primary accent on one, the secondary on four. But try repeating at a more rapid tempo several measures of this sextuple meter. You will notice that it tends to gather itself into a kind of duple meter in which the first half consists of beats 1-2-3 and the second of beats 4-5-6. This is called *duple compound* meter — *compound* being the designation which indicates that each of the large beats is regularly divided into three smaller pulses. This kind of transformation occurs whenever triple units are combined. For example, *triple compound* meter consists of three triple units, *quadruple compound* of four triple units, and so on.

Septuple meter and those with greater numbers of beats per measure are rather rare, and usually will be heard as combinations of duple and triple units with regularly recurring patterns. They are found almost entirely in the music of the twentieth century.

# MELODY AND ITS STRUCTURE

We have now all the necessities to form a perfectly satisfying kind of music, melodic and rhythmic. Indeed, the civilizations of the Far East use no other musical resources, nor, as far as we know, did the ancient Greeks and Romans. And European music up to about the 11th century was satisfied with only these basic musical resources.

Originally, all music was probably sung, using instruments only for accompaniment. This primitive music stays well within the range of notes available to the untrained voice, and, interestingly enough, the more primitive the music, the fewer notes are used, and the simpler the skips become. Such music, with a fairly limited range, and progressing by steps or simple skips, we shall call *vocal* in character. When instruments came into greater prominence during the Renaissance (1450-1600), composers took advantage of their capabilities and wrote passages with more extended range and wider skips than were possible to perform with the voice. Such melodic conduct we shall term *instrumental* in character. We must, however, take into account the fact that many melodic creations exist which are not wholly vocal or instrumental, but partake of both qualities to a greater or lesser degree: therefore, in describing a melody of this kind, we must indicate that it is, for example, *predominantly* vocal in character, or vice versa. The hymn "America" is an excellent example of a purely vocal melody, while the "Star-Spangled Banner" is more instrumental, and therefore harder to sing.

As we noted above, the human mind tries to impose order upon phenomena which might otherwise be regarded as random happenings; and, practically, the number of notes sung or spoken in one breath has a limit. So man developed a system whereby the melodic language of music paralleled the sentence structure of speech — if indeed it was not originally derived from that everyday commodity. If we examine almost any folk song we notice that when the *words* have completed a phrase there occurs a similar sense of completion in the *melody*. First of all, the pause is a rhythmic punctuation, sometimes assigning a long duration to the pitch of the last syllable, or inserting a measured silence after that last note. Either of these may have the sense of a comma, if the phrase is not complete, or of a period if it is finished. Secondly, in terms of pitch, the melody may come to rest on either a *conditionally stable* note, or a *fully stable* note — the latter being tonic note of the particular scale from which the melody has been created. Again, these are the pitch equivalents of the comma or the period. Sing "Way Down Upon the Swanee River," noting the stability of the tones upon which the melody pauses.

EXAMPLE 5.

Motive indicated by short brackets.
C designates caesura.

Upon listening to several melodies and analyzing their phrases, we may arrive at a general formula for these melodic stopping places, which are called *cadences*. First of all, they may be either *final* or *non-final* in effect. If no further phrase is required to finish the sense of the first phrase, they may be termed *final*. If a second phrase seems necessary, the cadence was *non-final*. An excellent example for analysis of this kind is the second movement (Largo) of Antonin Dvořák's Symphony No. 5 ("From the New World") (Example 5). This is the melody which has been made into a sort of popular song with the title "Rollin' Home." It is in slow quadruple meter, and the first phrase, consisting of two measures, ends on a conditionally stable note, hence a non-final cadence. The next phrase, also two measures in length, ends with a stable note, a final cadence. The next two phrases, of two measures each, are entirely unstable, suspended at some distance above a stable position. Then the first phrase returns exactly as heard before, followed by an altered version of the second phrase which now ascends to a climactic high note, and reaches a final cadence on the stable pitch one octave above the basic tonic note heard at the end of the second phrase. Since this higher pitch, while final in effect, still retains a newness and an unfamiliarity, the composer feels the need to emphasize it by repeating the last short section of the melody to render the cadence satisfyingly final. Other examples for analysis which you will hear may be derived from these compositions:

Mozart: Symphony No. 39-III; 40-I, II; 41-I, II.
Haydn: Symphony No. 94-II.
Rimsky-Korsakoff: *Scheherezade,* II.
Grieg: *Peer Gynt Suite* — "Ase's Death," "Anitra's Dance."

If we examine the Dvořák melody more closely, we will notice a number of less obvious traits, which, however, are important to the character of the melody. Sing the first phrase of the melody. Notice the slight pause felt after the first three notes? Then after the second three? The melody then continues without pause for five more notes and comes to the non-final cadence of the first phrase. These slight pauses are termed *caesuras,* and are important in that they often divide a phrase into smaller components or *motives*.

Notice the rhythm of the first three notes of the first phrase: it is repeated in the next three notes of the phrase, and many more times during the course of the complete melody. This short, rhythmic figure, then, is an important structural unit of the phrase. Such a figure used in this way is called a *motive*. Generally speaking, a motive may be either *rhythmic*, as this one was, or *melodic* if it repeats a pattern of pitches several times, as in the opening notes of the "Volga Boatman's Song." Very often both aspects are combined in a *rhythmic-melodic motive*. Normally, the repetition of the rhythmic pattern of the motive is the most noticeable factor in a composition. Clear examples are the first movements of the Fifth Symphony of Beethoven (Example 6) and the Thirty-fifth and Fortieth Symphonies of Mozart.

# The Composition of Music Using Melodies

Most musical works rely largely upon melody for their appeal and interest. We find an infinite variety of melodies written in all of the historic periods of man's culture, some designed to inspire religious meditation, others dance-like, still others war-like and exciting.

But how does a composer go about constructing a piece of music out of a melody? Obviously he must first state it, in effect saying, "This is what I'm going to work with." Now a good melody usually has a rather complete sound, and when it has run its course, our composer may be dismayed to find he has written only a few measures. (See the first two phrases of the Dvořák example, Example 5.) He then has two obvious choices: he may *repeat* what he has written, or he may write something new, introducing the element of *contrast*. Depending upon the character of his beginning phrases, either or both of these courses may be possible. Dvořák chose contrasting phrases to follow his basic melody, taking care, however, to include in them the rhythmic motive of the first phrases so that the degree of contrast would not be too great, and so that this middle section would be thus clearly related to the earlier part. But now what? Again, contrast or repetition is available. If contrast is chosen, new phrases are added, which, if continued too long, result in a composition resembling a meandering sentence which arrives nowhere. If, however, the total length of the work is not too great, this "through-composed" piece of music may be very effective, especially when it is a song whose words imply this ongoing quality. But if a composer wishes to write a more self-contained piece of music, he is apt to do just what Dvořák did: repeat the earlier portion of the music. Dvořák, however, introduced the principle of *variation* into his repetition, thus insuring it against loss of interest. When we examine the whole movement of the symphony later in this chapter, we shall find that it is made up of relatively small sections put together using the principles of repetition, contrast and variation on a somewhat larger scale than we have encountered them here, but with similar results. In all of the historical epochs of music, melodic ideas of greater or shorter duration have employed these natural means of extension, sometimes to fit a text, sometimes as purely musical forms.

The religious chanting of the early Christian church (600-900 A.D.) affords a treasury of vocal melody whose subtle melodic curves show various ways in which a musical line can be given inner unity by repetition and variation, and still retain its forward motion. During the Baroque era (1600-1750), a vocabulary of melodic patterns was developed, each of which carried a specific emotional meaning. In much of the music of that time, a small number of patterns having similar significance were varied and repeated to form an entire large section of music before contrasting material appeared. Still later, in the Classic period, a new method of composition was employed, one which seized upon rhythmic motives as its basis. The Romantic period (1827-1900), however, turned to song-like melody: the example by Dvořák is characteristic of this time. During the twentieth century, composers have exploited all of these means, usually using less vocal types of melody than before. An outstanding example of the use of pure melodic repetition — combined, to be sure, with harmonic and instrumental variation — is the famous *Bolero* of Maurice Ravel. This composition repeats the sinuous Moorish melody over and over without essential alteration to produce an almost hypnotic spell. The studied monotony of the repetition is relieved by fascinating use of various orchestral instruments.

A SPECIAL TYPE OF MELODY: THE THEME

A melody, such as the example by Dvořák, is the complete statement of a musical thought. The important word here is *complete*: such a melodic idea does not easily lend itself to the more continuous process of expansion often desired in lengthy orchestral music. A composition based upon a self-sufficient melodic idea is apt to proceed by stop-and-go sections, a process suited to some, but not all types of music. In order to produce a work which seems to evolve organically, the composer must discover musical material of considerable simplicity out of which more complex combinations may develop. Such basic subject matter is called a *theme*. Perhaps the best illustrations of simplicity of theme and complexity of development are to be found in the Beethoven symphonies, particularly the third and fifth. While it is difficult to give a concise list of the properties of a good theme, since variability is the essence of art, it may be safely assumed that a theme suitable for elaboration will have some of the following general characteristics. (1) It will contain or even consist of clear-cut rhythmic motives, less often of memorable melodic motives, but sometimes of both; such primary materials easily admit of repetition and variation. (2) It is apt to be more instrumental than vocal in melodic design, although this is not a stringent condition. An instrumental theme is usually more motivic than a vocal theme, or by virtue of more jagged contours may stay fixed in the musical memory more easily. (3) A good theme sounds rather unfinished: it *demands* continuation. Therefore, it often ends with some variety of non-final cadence, or indeed, sometimes is not complete at all. (4) Above all, it needs to be direct and simple, almost commonplace in some instances, so that organic growth can proceed with musical and, usually, emotional logic. As we go through our examination of the literature of music, we shall find some eras in which the emphasis is on the more intellectual use of rhythmic motives, and others in which the emotion-filled, highly melodic theme is most important. These differences represent varying points of view regarding the function of music in that time, and pose different problems for the composers.

### THEMATIC DEVELOPMENT

Let us examine some great symphonic themes, and see how, in their structure, they require expansion and musical explanation.

One of the simplest, yet most striking, themes used for development is that announced at the beginning of the Fifth Symphony of Beethoven (Example 6). As we shall see, this is really a rhythmic motive appearing as thematic material, and therefore is susceptible to certain procedures. The first and most important of these is *repetition*. Notice that after the initial two pronouncements of the

EXAMPLE 6.

INTRODUCTION

SECTION I
FIRST PHRASE, STATIC I

HARMONY. STABLE

SECOND PHRASE, STATIC V.

SECOND PERIOD, (PHRASES 3,4)

INTRO. MOTIVE

SECTION 2

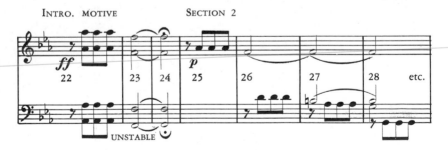

NOTE: 1. Clearness of introduction of important motive.
     2. Way in which motive is used to construct phrase.
     3. Variety of phrase length and construction.
     4. Contrast between static and progressing harmony.
     5. Classically balanced construction of the two large sections, first ascending, then descending.

motive a series of ascending phrases is formed by repetition of the rhythmic element upon various pitches, finally resulting in a heavy cadence upon a conditionally stable note. The next phrases are constructed in the same way, but descend. Further listening to the movement will demonstrate the important part that repetition plays in this kind of development. A selection from an earlier era, the Baroque, exhibits a similar procedure. The first movement of the third *Brandenburg Concerto* by J. S. Bach uses a rhythmic motive as an integral part of its structure (Example 7).

EXAMPLE 7.

Sometimes a composer selects a more melodic, less rhythmic element from which to create a larger structure. Listen to the first movement of the Symphony No. 8 ("Unfinished") by Schubert (Example 8). The beginning phrase, and particularly the first three notes of it,

EXAMPLE 8.

is a vital melodic element to be used in the middle section of the piece, an area devoted to thematic development. While not as concentrated as the work by Beethoven, it is an excellent example of the development of a more melodic — as compared to rhythmic — motive.

Another kind of development which we may call *combinative* uses the element of repetition in a different way. In the middle of the first movement of the Symphony No. 3 ("Eroica") of Beethoven, we find the main theme serving as a basis for other melodic lines above it: here these melodies are combined with the main idea, showing it in new lights, different surroundings.

A third kind of development might be called *evolutionary*, since the material grows, changes, and by musically logical processes gives rise to new-sounding material. Brahms is a great master of this kind of thematic sleight-of-hand. Notice how, in the first movement of his Fourth Symphony, he again and again takes the last few notes of a phrase or cadence figure, repeats them, expands them, makes them change before our eyes into something whose existence was unsuspected. This kind of development may involve rhythm, harmony, melodic pattern, or all three. A relative to this musical evolution is the process called "theme transformation." Here the rhythmic element of the primary material is often disregarded, and only the series of pitches has significance. These are given various rhythmic shapes, turned upside down or backwards, filled in with other pitches so that they serve only as the skeleton for a longer theme, used as the beginning notes of other melodies, and in as many other ways as the composer may imagine. The well-worn tone poem of Liszt, *Les Préludes* shows this process very clearly, as does *Till Eulenspiegel,* by Richard Strauss.

The above are some general ways in which material may be developed and expanded, much as an essayist or poet might unfold the ramifications of an idea. In the masterworks we shall examine, never will they be "cut and dried," but always infused with the insight of imagination, yielding meaningful and moving passages of music. Many times different ways of development are combined in only a few measures. Elsewhere a single, simple procedure may yield the best results. We shall have more to say about specific procedures as we examine the great compositions in their historical contexts.

## TEXTURE

Music may be compared to the weaving of threads together in needlework or tapestry. The simplest example might consist of a single-colored thread outlining a design on a neutral background. This corresponds to melody alone, and is called *monophonic* texture. But in music as well as tapestry this seldom happens. More often we have a series of threads of different colors combined in pictorial or abstract designs. Such is sometimes the case in music. Separate yet compatible melodic lines are woven upon the background of time, regulated by the metric warp and woof of the organization. Such music is said to be *polyphonic* in texture. Examples may easily be found. Almost everyone has sung a *round* such as "Row, Row, Row Your Boat," "*Frère Jacques,*" or "Three Blind Mice." Musically, this procedure is called a *canon*, which means a law. The law of such rounds is that

EXAMPLE 9A. *Canon:* "Frère Jacques."

everyone shall sing the same melody, but not simultaneously; rather the entrance of each group occurs after a certain number of measures of the preceding group have been sung, giving a staggered series of beginnings (Example 9a). This very old musical device is often used by composers to lend intensity, development, or interest

EXAMPLE 9B. *Fugal imitation: Handel's* Messiah, *Part II, "Behold the Lamb of God."*

to a composition. Sometimes only the first phrase is presented by an instrument or voices; when it has been played or sung, that particular instrument continues freely, using melodic phrases which combine with the other parts. Because they all begin alike, these parts are said to enter in *imitation* (Example 9b). These parts may also be said to exist in a *contrapuntal* relationship to each other. *Counterpoint* is the process which creates *polyphony*.

Suppose, however, the composer wishes to use a simpler procedure than polyphony, so that his melody may stand out more clearly. He may resort to what is called *homophonic* texture, or, more simply, melody with accompaniment. Let us see how this is accomplished.

If we examine the major scale again at the piano, sounding pairs of notes together (*harmonically*, rather than *melodically*, or one after the other), we shall find certain combinations which result in a smooth, agreeable concord, others which sound hollow and empty, and still others which clash and contain more or less tension (Example 10). This process may be repeated, using any note of the scale as the basis, with the same result. The first and second kinds of sound enumerated above are called *consonances*, and are the bases of most of the polyphony as well as the homophony to be found in our music. The *dissonances* (the last group) have an important function, however, which we shall examine more closely later. Now let us repeat the above process, except that this time we shall begin with one of the two-note consonances, for example that of the first and third notes of the scale. We shall find that only two other notes of the scale beside the octave create consonances with this combination, *i.e.*, the fifth and sixth notes, and that the combination with the fifth note is the more stable. Since we began on the tonic note of the scale, this group of tones will be called the *tonic triad*, or *tonic chord* (Example 10). In a way similar to the influence of the tonic note alone, this chord, in a sense, "rules" all other harmonic combinations, drawing them to itself like the force of magnetism or gravity. This tendency is called *tonality*, and regulates all harmonic flow within its domain, much as gravitation regulates events on our planet. The tonic chord is the most stable grouping in either of these scales. We might repeat the process with each of the other two-note consonances we discovered, and arrive at the conclusion that three note chords built on alternate notes of the scale afford greater stability than other possible formations. These, then, are the simple chords which, when used to accompany a

EXAMPLE 10. *Derivation of intervals and chords from the scale.*

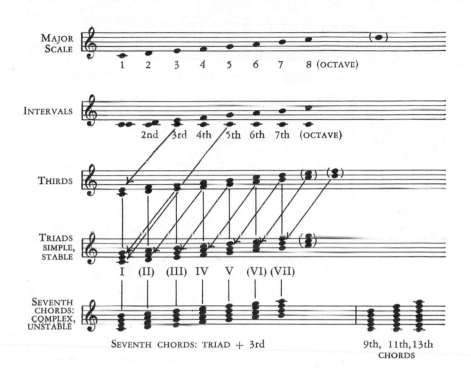

melody, create homophony, or homophonic texture. They may appear in "blocks" below the melody, as in a hymn, or they may be sounded note by note in some rhythmic pattern, a process called *harmonic diffusion,* which spreads the chord smoothly and equally over a longer period of time (Example 11).

We have noted above the importance of the tonic chord, sometimes called the I chord, since it is constructed upon the first note of the scale — the tonic note. Second in importance among the remaining chords are those built on the fourth and fifth degrees of the scale, the IV and V chords (Example 10). Many melodies may be satisfactorily accompanied using only these three basic chords, either in the major or minor scales. For example, "Way Down Upon the

EXAMPLE 11. *Harmonic accompaniments.*

Swanee River" uses this succession in the first phrase: I IV I V. A series of chords such as this is called a *chord progression,* since a definite feeling of movement from chord to chord is present when the progression is well devised.

Rather infrequently met is the phenomenon of static harmony. In its simplest form, this motionless quality may result merely from retaining a single stable chord. Wagner uses this device to keep us suspended, as it were, in the depths of the Rhine River in the opening scene of his music-drama *Das Rheingold*. At other times it may come about through the composer's using chord structures all of which possess the same degree of instability. In his prelude for piano, *Voiles*, Debussy uses a scale consisting only of whole tones: chords derived from this scale all have equal tension and are all constructed upon the same pattern. The piece eloquently describes becalmed sails upon a glassy sea.

## HARMONIC CADENCES

The harmonic support for a melody must enhance the rise and fall of the melodic line, and, most important of all, must verify the kind of cadence at the end of each phrase of the melody. We have, then, not only *melodic* cadences, but also *harmonic* cadences. These may also be divided into two classes: *final* and *non-final*. The final cadence represents arrival at complete stability, with no need to move further. (Sing the first line of "America": this concludes with a final cadence.) The non-final cadence implies that there is more to come, and represents an arrival at a plane of conditional stability (first phrase of the "Star-Spangled Banner"). In either case, the general formula for a cadence is: unstable chord → to → more stable chord. Everything we have discovered about the importance and function of the melodic cadence is emphasized when harmony is added.

The most important final cadences may be represented by the chord progressions of V-I and IV-I. The former is the cadence at the end of the first line of "America" ("—of thee I sing"). The second is the familiar "Amen" cadence used after hymns. An especially strong final cadence may be created by combining these two into IV-V-I, or V-I-IV-I.

The non-final cadences are numerous, but two deserve to be mentioned. One is the arrival at conditional stability. Musically it occurs when the melody or harmony comes to rest upon the V chord. This is called a *half-cadence*. It is the kind of cadence used at the end of the first phrase of "The Star-Spangled Banner" ("— by the dawn's early light"). The other is the *deceptive* cadence, or the substitution of another chord for the tonic chord in what appears to be a final cadence progression. In such a situation the melody usually finishes upon the expected note, but the harmonic support, while reasonably consonant with it, is not the chord expected. It is often used to give notice that the selection is about to end — but not just yet!

### UNSTABLE AND COMPLEX HARMONY

We have noted in our chord building thus far, that most of the simple triads derived from our major scale are relatively stable in that they contain little or no tension, and that they are mildly unstable in context due to the attraction of the tonic chord. Progressions of such chords will be characerized as "tonally unstable" in order to emphasize their movement toward stability in the final cadence. Individually, however, each of these chords is consonant and stable except for the one built upon the seventh degree of the major scale. Because of the pattern of whole and half steps in the scale, this triad is one half step smaller between its outer notes than are the others, creating an interval of considerable tension which tends strongly toward resolution in the following chord. This "tritone" interval (three whole steps) may be added to the V triad by extending that chord another third upward (Example 10, seventh chords) with the result that the dissonant V$^7$ ("five-seven") chord thus created tends even more strongly toward the tonic than before, enhancing the finality of any cadence in which it is used. The tritone interval is very characteristic of late Romantic harmony, although it appears in a more restrained way in several other musical styles.

Just as we made the V triad dissonant and unstable by the addition of a note above the original top note of the triad, so can we make the other ordinary stable triads unstable by this method. However, these more complex chords are unstable by virtue of the dissonance created between the new tone and one of the original notes, rather than because of the tritone, which is not available to them in the scale.

To these four-note chords a fifth note dissonant to two of the original notes may be added, and so on to even greater complexity (Example 10). Finally, the resources of the chromatic scale may be included to result in exceedingly unstable, complex chord formations.

24

When this happens, we enter a realm foreign to the familiar major and minor, a realm in which stability is only relative to the amount of tension in each chord due to its dissonance saturation. In this chancy area of music new methods of organization must be discovered and applied with care, otherwise anarchy results. This is the realm of contemporary music. We shall explore later the historic precedents of our modern version of the art.

## S O N O R I T Y

Music has another attribute which is called *sonority*. This term describes the total quality of sound at any moment in a piece of music, and requires a qualifying adjective. The sonority of a single piccolo playing alone might be described as "thin," possibly "weak"; that of a flute in the low register as "dull"; that of a trumpet in a high register as "brilliant," or "piercing." Similarly, a combination of low-pitched instruments sounding together in their bottom registers could be called "dark" or even "muddy." Such a judgment is obviously a subjective one: nevertheless, there seems to be sufficient agreement among listeners to render it meaningful. Several factors contribute to the kind of sonority produced. The number of separate parts, their pitch spacing, and the region where most of the tones are concentrated are important aspects of the problem. Moreover, many kinds of sonorities are found within a composition, although the composer may limit certain sections to a single type in order to express his thought more clearly.

## M U S I C A L   F O R M

Goethe said that "architecture was frozen music." Another writer stated that music was sounding form. Both had the same aspect of the art in mind: to be coherent, logical and meaningful, music must have a shape in time, consisting of a series of significant interrelated events, parts of which reappear with some frequency so as to give a feeling of unity to the whole composition. What is unity? This is the impression on the mind of the listener that all parts of the work

25

are about the same thing, and are thus interrelated. A musical work gains unity in the same way as a literary work: by means of flash-backs, reappearances of a main idea, symbol, or character, or by reflecting throughout the varied facets of one moral idea. If one theme is used throughout a composition to the exclusion of others, we have a very tight kind of unity. But such monothematic composi-tions are apt to be short, and frequently development of the theme takes the place of other themes. But what of *polythematic* works. How does one unify them? There are several ways in which this may be accomplished, but let us focus on the most important way first. A monothematic work develops unity by means of repetition: therefore, if we repeat an important theme several times during the course of a polythematic work, we shall develop more unity than the piece would have otherwise. Repetition: here is the crux of the matter. But unless it is skillfully done, boredom will set in, and this is the unforgiveable sin of the composer. If the themes of a polythematic work are carefully chosen with a suitable degree of contrast, then variety and unity can occur within the same framework. This is more often the case than in the monothematic work. Repetition and contrast, then, but what kind of repetition? Let us list some varieties: (1) simple, literal repeti-tion, as in many songs with several verses to the same music; (2) varied repetition, in which unessential changes occur. The *Bolero* of Ravel is an example of this. The melody is bodily transposed up or down in pitch register, while being played by different instruments. In both cases the theme is essentially the same throughout the repetitions. (3) More variation may occur, however, giving rise to a form of music called "Theme and Variations," examples of which we shall study later. Here the theme may be merely surrounded with new parts, remaining unchanged, as in the second movement of Haydn's Sym-phony No. 94; or it may undergo greater changes, as in the final move-ment of Beethoven's third symphony, or the *Variations on a Theme by Haydn* of Brahms. In the latter two, the basic thematic elements are developed, evolving new-sounding musical ideas behind which lurk only the shadows of the original material.

First, of course, if the composer is playing fair, we must hear the unadorned, simple themes or melodies with as little distracting accom-paniment or surrounding material as possible. Sometimes repetition is resorted to at once, in order to fix more firmly in our memories — and *form* for the listener is a function of his musical memory — the basic shapes, rhythms, and harmonies with which the composer is going to deal during the remainder of the work. Normally, after the simple statement of the beginning themes, we hear some different material — *contrast*. This may be effected in various ways also; sometimes a number of ways are combined in order to create a great deal of contrast, while other times the procedure may be quite simple. Here are some of the important single ways of gaining contrast:

1. By change of key — that is, by shifting from one basic scale and its material to another. This process, called *modulation*, creates a whole plane of conditional stability upon which the new, contrasting section rests. There should be felt the tendency to return to the first plane — and this usually happens later in the composition.
2. By change of meter, or rhythm, or tempo. This is one of the most obvious basic ways to show that a new and contrasting section of the composition has begun.
3. By changing to new themes. The new theme usually is of a different character from the one previously heard. If the first was instrumental in type, the second might be more lyric. We find exciting themes versus calm themes, sharply rhythmic themes versus flowing themes, and many other contrasts too subtle to describe in mere words.
4. By changing texture. This is a very effective means, and is often used in a middle section of a composition.
5. By changing the general dynamic level to some intensity of the opposite kind, for example, loud to soft.
6. By changing the kinds or combinations of instruments used, and therefore the tone color, which we shall discuss in Chapter II.
7. By changing the sonority: for example, from low, thick chords in the brass to thin, widely-spaced chords in the woodwinds or strings.
8. By changing the harmonic stability: For example, from simple, stable chords to unstable, more dissonant, and complex harmonics.
9. By changing from the relatively simple statement of themes or melodies to more complex, developmental procedures, sometimes involving one or more of the foregoing changes.

Let us now return to the music in order to discover how these form-building procedures operate. Listen first to the second movement (Largo) of the Dvořák Symphony No. 5 (Example 12) — the same movement whose main melodic material we analyzed in the section dealing with phrases. This is a predominantly homophonic piece of music whose unity is enhanced by the use of repetition and contrast not only of melodic and harmonic material, but also of rhythmic motives, and the all-important interval of the 3rd, out of which most of the melodic figures are fashioned. Sometimes this interval occurs as a skip, either upward or down (measures 7 and 11), while at other times, the skip is "filled in" with a central note (measures

EXAMPLE 12.

Cl. & Fg.        Str.        Cor.

*Un poco piu mosso*

Fl. & Ob.

Cl., Ob. & Str. Acc.

Fl. & Ob.        Cl.

Fl. & Ob.

Vl. & Cl. Acc.

Fl. & Ob.

Str.

46 and 54). We shall call this the "basic interval" upon which this piece of music is founded, and note that such a procedure gives a very strong, yet subtle feeling of unity to the composition. With these factors in mind, let us proceed with our listening analysis.

I. *First Section*

Introduction (measures 1-4): chords progressing from stability to instability, then back, forming by repetition of these progressions an impressive final cadence.

A. Short chord-diffusion patterns by the strings (measures 5 and 6) followed by the familiar lyric material stated by the English horn (measures 7-18). We may symbolize the phrases by lower-case letters as follows:

a a' (measures 7-8, 9-10): two similar phrases, but with a slight change in the second to bring it to a final cadence.

b b (measures 11-14): two exactly similar phrases, poised upon a tonally unstable chord progression. Note the use of the basic rhythmic motive and interval.

a a" (measures 15-16, 17-18): repetition of first two phrases, but with the second phrase changed to cadence an octave higher than before.

There follows a brief ending section (codetta, measures 19-21) which stabilizes this higher cadence by repetition of the last measure of the main theme, first identically, then in note values twice as long. The introduction returns (measures 22-26), now in the brighter color of the high woodwinds.

B. Now a short, slightly contrasting section appears (measures 26-35) which develops the rhythmic motive and the interval of the main theme, and flows via tonally unstable chord progressions into

A. A return of the first section (measures 36-39), only slightly changed, followed by its codetta (measures 40-41), after which the horns echo the first half of phrase a, pause on an unstable note (measure 45), pivot upon it, so to speak, and thus usher in the Second Section.

II. *Second Section*

New key, tone color (oboe), tempo, themes and rhythms are introduced without previous preparation so as to emphasize the contrast. Here the melodic material is organized into phrases, flows into a slight development which builds up to a small climax and subsides (measures 46-89). After the contrast of some animated patterns in the upper woodwinds and strings (measures 90-95), we hear in the heavy brass motives and rhythms which derive from the first movement of the symphony as well as from the rhythmic motive of this movement (measures 96-100); this "flashback" is designed to create a feeling of unity between the two movements.

## I'. *Return of the First Section, Varied*

The key, tempo, and themes return as before with new instrumentation — varied repetition. We hear phrases a a', b — but where a simple repetition of b is expected, Dvořák does a surprising thing: he pauses both before and after the last note, giving it in this way a kind of thoughtful emphasis it did not have before. The phrase continues, after which another pause intervenes. Then the intimacy is heightened by a change in orchestration to solo stringed instruments (measures 110-111) followed by a" in the combined strings of the orchestra. The codetta follows (measures 114-115), after which a larger ending section (measures 116-127) brings the entire movement to a stable close on the repeated tonic chord. The introductory material, which returns here, emphasizes the stability and finality of the cadence.

Note how Dvořák has created a rather long piece of music by means of contrast and repetition. Aside from the introductory material (which is also repeated from time to time), we have the over-all sectional repetition of I-II-I'. Within each of these sections the thematic material is repeated and contrasted in varying ways. For example, in Section I, the organization as shown in the foregoing analysis is A-B-A. If we should examine Section II more closely for the interplay of its two main themes, we should find c c', d d', c developed, d d", c; a more simple alteration of thematic contrasts than in the previous section. The animated woodwind figures (measures 90 *et seq.*) serve to create a rhythmic and dynamic climax which by contrast emphasizes the quiet lyricism of Section I' when it appears. Rather than prolong this section needlessly and risk loss of interest, Dvořák chose to state only the main melody, varied imaginatively, and to close the movement with a reminiscence of the opening chords, creating a feeling of completeness and unity.

Now let us examine a composition of the opposite texture — a polyphonic form called a *fugue,* which we shall encounter later in the Baroque period. This one is the C-minor fugue from the *Well-Tempered Clavier* by J. S. Bach (Example 13). This kind of composition uses only one phrase, stated first monophonically, for its thematic

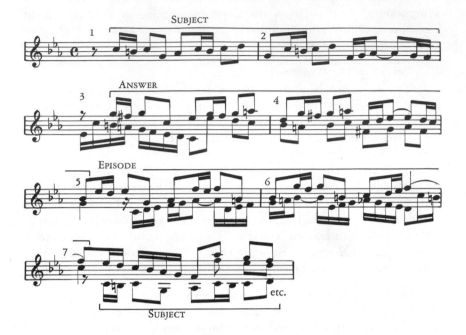

material. As soon as that phrase is finished, another part enters, imitating the same phrase at a higher pitch level while the first part continues, thus creating polyphony with the new part. Usually, when the second part has completed the theme there are a few measures in which the theme does not appear. Then (in this work) the basic phrase returns at a lower pitch level than ever before. Notice as the composition progresses how lightly the cadences are touched; the music flows right through them with continuous motion. Notice also how the theme appears from time to time on new pitch levels and in new keys, always entwined in counterpoint. Between these reappearances we hear material constructed out of motives from the main theme, moving, always moving, toward the next statement of the fugue subject. This particular fugue reaches a climax with the subject in the lowest part, then finishes with a coda based on the main theme. The attributes pointed out are quite characteristic of polyphony, which relies upon flow and unity (monothematic composition) rather than upon emphatic cadence points and contrasting themes.

For our third example, we have chosen a composition which unites

EXAMPLE 14.

FIRST THEME:
MOTIVE

CONTRASTING SECTION

LYRIC SECTION

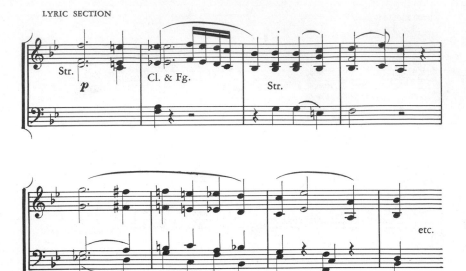

to some degree ,both textures, and many separate and combined procedures: the first movement of the Symphony No. 40 in G-minor of Mozart (Example 14). The piece begins its statement of themes without preamble. Note the motivic character of the first theme, how these motives are repeated on different pitch levels to construct phrases, and how the phrases reach emphatic cadences. Notice the bold instrumental outlines of the next section (contrast), and the grand flourish with which it reaches its cadence. After this point a change takes place: the agitated motion and instrumental gestures are replaced by lyric, wistful phrases, repeated, reaching cadences, and moving to another agitated section and echo of the first theme (repetition) which moves to a repeated and emphatic cadence of its own, followed by a pause for further emphasis. Then a new section begins with a sudden shift away from the key suggested by the cadence, and a return of the main theme, first rather simply, then in polyphonic combination with the bass instruments, later imitated in other instruments, and finally flowing into a repetition of the entire first section, agitated themes, lyric themes, instrumental gestures, cadences, and all.

The thematic analyses above and in the succeeding chapters are in no way intended to afford more than an approach to intelligent listening and intellectual enjoyment of music. They are, so to speak, some of the "rules of the game." The essence of the composer's expression depends, however, upon these and other related procedures: the material used, and its character; the degree of flow or contrast between sections, and the emphasis or elision of cadence "punctuation"; the psychological element suggested by the juxtaposition of similar or contrasting sections, and all of the other variable and intuitive selections possible in the realms of harmony, rhythm, tempo, tone color, and sonority. But to what end are these resources marshalled? Why should the composer spend his time and energy in this pursuit?

# SOME COMMENTS ON THE ESTHETICS OF MUSIC

In no other art is the axiom that the "total is equal to more than the sum of the parts" more true than in music. A great composer takes themes made out of simple notes arranged in rather simple rhythms, causes them to undergo whatever permutations and combinations his creative imagination may suggest, and there results a composition which may move us to tears, or excite us beyond rational control. Clearly, the sounds and rhythms by themselves do not accomplish this almost magical result. The particular individuality and temper of the composer, his musical intuition — in sum, what he has to "say" seems to provide the intangible "priceless ingredient" which welds the mechanical elements into an artistic whole. It is this unique way of combining the materials, then, which shapes the musical meaning, if such there is intended to be.

One of the most wonderful aspects of music is that it means all things to all men. Seldom does one find a piece of music that evokes the same responses, verbal or otherwise, in several people. Music is at once inexact in its information and precise in its definition of emotional and psychic states. It is most effective where we have no words which adequately convey descriptions of these states. Berlioz stated in his comments on his *Roméo et Juliette* (written for vocal soloists, chorus and orchestra) that where the emotion becomes inarticulate in words, the proper realm of the music has been reached. And Mendelssohn, when asked what a certain composition of his meant (always a foolish thing to ask a composer!), declared that if he could have set it down in words there would have been no reason to write the music.

What *does* music intend to convey? "Nothing," say some composers. "Everything," say their opponents. And here we have the matter in a nutshell. One view, of which Igor Stravinsky is an outstanding advocate, holds that music is purely an abstract design of sound in time, and has no intrinsic meaning in itself. Only the past experiences of the listener seem to make it meaningful. One feels sure that Beethoven would quarrel with this, for the German master felt that music had an ennobling lesson to impart, and that any composition which did not make its hearer a better person was not a good piece of music. This attitude passed into the notion that the sole function of music is to move the emotions. What we have here is the age-old dispute between classicism and romanticism, and further than that, between so-called "abstract" and "descriptive" music. Let us try to clarify the issues.

Classicism implies an objective attitude, the use of symmetry and balance, and a fully satisfactory combination of material with form. Not that this attitude is ever completely achieved! The works of Mozart are probably as close to the ideal as any, yet what a wealth of expression, even at times a carefully controlled romanticism they contain. How abstract can a piece of music be? Regardless of the composer's attitude, is it not impossible to hear music without feeling *some* emotion?

Romanticism, on the other hand, aims at the fullest possible emotional expression; form, balance, symmetry — often these are cast to the winds, or at most regarded as the irritating restraints of petrified tradition. In the white heat of this emotional state, any touch of classicism is apt to sound dry and lifeless. Yet most romantic masterpieces retain some aspect of the old forms which serve to give them coherence; better yet, they may create new and logical musical architecture out of the musical ideas.

Which attitude is right, the classic or the romantic? Here again it is impossible to say. Both have value, that of one balancing that of the other. But preferences vary — as they should. The beginning music lover usually dotes upon a diet of emotionalism, as represented often by the music of Tchaikovsky. As he listens more, his critical faculties are sharpened, and soon he arrives at Beethoven. Later stages may be represented by Brahms, Mozart, Bach, and finally, and usually last, contemporary music. Notice that the direction is toward abstract, more classical music, although romantic elements appear in somewhat varying degrees along the way. Best of all, the attentive listener retains his appreciation for the music of the previous stages, not abandoning it, but carrying it along with him as part of his valuable musical experience.

Romanticism and classicism form the balance pans of the scale of art, and the music of the centuries weighs heavier now in one, now the other. Never in a stylistic era does the balance shift wholly to one side. The opposite element is always present. In our listening we shall try to determine the predominant element in each era, as well as in the music of individual composers of that era, so as to be able to enjoy and understand them more intelligently.

## RELATIONSHIPS BETWEEN MUSIC AND THE OTHER ARTS

While it is dangerous to make comparisons on a one-to-one basis between the various arts of a period, certain aspects of one of them may assist in the comprehension of another. In the case of music, parallels drawn from the other arts are open to disagreement, if for no other reason than the fact that they are spatial and relatively enduring in nature, while music is evanescent and exists only in time or recollection. Nevertheless, the insights obtained by this comparison seem valuable enough to attempt such a venture.

In the largest aspect, certain resemblances of formal treatment might be pointed out. In each, music and painting as well as architecture and sculpture, sections are apt to be repeated, either literally or with variations, separated by some differing material. The original section may comprise, in painting, a color area of a certain intensity which may be repeated elsewhere with a different intensity, or even with a different color if the intensities are comparable. Or it may be made up of a certain pattern of lines, the general character of which may recur elsewhere, thus resembling the melodic and thematic elements of a piece of music. In the case of sculpture, the correspondences are more difficult to point out since this involves the comparison between a one-dimensional art — music, which exists only in time — with a three, or actually four-dimensional art. Certain parallels will be noticed, however, depending upon how obviously the sculptor has used his formal elements. In architecture, the balancing and symmetrical parts of buildings, the proportions, heights, ornaments and other features often make comparison quite obvious and easy, but one must always take into account that exactness of correspondence is neither to be looked for nor expected.

Because of the spatial nature of painting, artists have long employed a formal device which became a conscious factor in musical composition only near the end of the seventeenth century. This is the use of structural elements to "lead the eye" to the most important object or area of the painting — the "subject" really, of the whole effort. A correspondence may be seen in literature also, consisting of the sections in a play or novel — argument, complication, denouément. Opera, since it is dependent upon dramatic literature often is built upon such a principle. In music, compound forms, such as the cantata, the symphony, the sonata and the string quartet, offer valid comparisons. The cantatas of Bach, as well as other works by this master, show definite, well-worked out conceptions of centralization of important moments or movements in the structure, as do the later quartets of Beethoven and Béla Bartók, and many other works between. Even the asymmetric placement of the "subject" on the canvas is paralleled by the off center location of the climactic spot in a movement of music or in a series of movements. Certain characteristics of music, literature and the drama may warrant calling them the "time arts." The most important of these is that of emotional progression, in which the observer is carried along toward the climactic moment upon a tide of time. The progression of the Beethoven Fifth Symphony, or the Prelude to *Tristan und Isolde* are excellent examples of this. In the other arts, the painter and sculptor are obliged to accomplish this by a series of separate pieces showing developments of an action or drama, although this is rather crude compared with the time-arts, and precisely so because of the natural limitations of the medium. But examples of this do exist, particularly in art of the Middle Ages, where the painter often places multiple views of his subject under different circumstances within one frame (see Chapter III, Plate VII).

When we descend from the larger realm of form to more elemental components of the arts, we find again that certain congruences occur. Melodic line, for example, is quite comparable to line, or often outline, in painting and sculpture, sometimes in architecture. All may contain either "lyric" lines which are smoothly curved, or more or less angular lines which stride about with a feeling of boldness or tension. Or, in painting and architecture, the lines may be diffused by minute irregularities, the use of shading or the application of profuse ornamentation. Similarly in music, the skeletal structure of the line may be obscured and the line itself diffused by ornamentation —turns, trills, grace notes of various kinds— or by rapid stepwise movement around the skeletal structure, sometimes scalewise, sometimes with the use of a recurrent melodic or rhythmic pattern.

Harmony in music has often been compared to the phenomenon of perspective in painting as a means of adding depth. It must be added that the degree of intensity is in both art forms another potent factor in this illusion of depth. Any beginning painter knows how hard it is to make objects recede in his painting, for not only must the laws of diminishing perspective be used, but also those of diminishing intensity. A similar situation occurs to a conductor when he "balances" an orchestra by cautioning the oboe not to play too loudly — that is, to stay in the background — while another less sonorous instrument plays a "foreground" solo. Very often in an analogous way, harmony is used to provide the background to a foreground solo, especially in homophonic texture. The tones of the background blend in such a way as to provide a "canvas" upon which the nearer and brighter solo color may trace its line. If the background contains too many dissonances, and is too unstable or active, it will call attention to itself and not fulfill its primary function. These non-blending dissonances are like bright flashes of too intense color in a painting, intended to be background, but not receding because of their intensity.

Rhythm, too, has a complex but somewhat comparable role in both painting and music. Unfortunately, the use of the word in the graphic arts is not entirely the same as it is in music. Painters tend to use it in terms of repetition or "eye motion" of some element in the painting, whereas in music, it more often designates an onward-moving factor which, together with the subtle qualities of tension variation inherent in harmonic progressions, seems to cause the music to travel down the time dimension in an almost physical way. But in the larger aspect, rhythm has a similar function in both arts: it creates or relaxes tension by means of the degree of activity it possesses. A musical composition may be agitated due to the great profusion of rhythmic motives and their continuous motion, just as the lines and color factors of a painting may give a swirling or chaotic effect by allowing no quiet area to appear upon which the eye may rest. Rhythmic activity of line is one of the more important aspects of comparison between these art forms.

The factor of repetition is an interesting and somewhat ambiguous element in both arts. When used discreetly, it tends to create form. When overused, it tends to deaden the senses by sheer cumulative power resulting in, at worst, monotony, or at best, an effect of massive grandeur. In some medieval structures, for example, the endless repetition of undifferentiated statues or other figures, such as rows of small, Roman-arched windows, lends a certain immobility, sometimes impressiveness, to the structure, just as the long-drawn repetitions of only a few chords over a held bass note make Notre Dame organum of the Perotin variety static, massive, and eventually by cumulative effect, almost overpowering.

In art, the word "tone," when used to describe the general effect of a painting, may find a counterpart in the term "sonority" in music. We may say that the tone of a painting is bright, just as the opening of the Bach *Magnificat* is bright. And, by extension, works in both media may be monochromatic — using shades of the same color, or tone color — or polychromatic, sharply defined or blended, brilliant or dull. But we must realize that these are only generalizations, and therefore dangerous and inaccurate when extended too far. Proceed cautiously and, as always in this area, at your own risk.

To this observer, the various media employed in music and painting have a certain correspondence. The transparent quality of a chamber ensemble, consisting of from two to a dozen players, is comparable to paintings done in watercolor, or other transparent media, which, we must not forget, like chamber music may have strong contrasts and emotional quality. In the same way, the larger musical groups tend toward thickness and opacity — here also a function of how the instruments are used — so do oils, gouache, and other basically opaque forms of paint, add thickness to the picture. Drama, too, is more inherent in these heavier materials, it would seem.

A final consideration of the formal structure suggests itself — whether the music or picture is closed and classical in nature, or open and romantic. Many pictures are completely closed in that they presuppose nothing relevant outside of what is shown. The eye is led inward and around, never to the edges and thence outside the frame. Musical form in the Classic period has this same quality of completeness, whereas in the Renaissance, the motet-style forms are each inconclusive and, by the avoidance of repetition, are open in nature: any composer, working in the style, could add other sections on to those already in existence without doing damage to the work. Of course, these are text-based forms, and this single fact makes a great difference.

In the final section of each of the chapters devoted to the great historical epochs of music, we shall suggest comparisons between certain art works of that period and the music which we have examined. It is hoped that these interrelations will have the effect of offering visual interpretations not only of the cultural ideals of a period, but also of more specific parallel techniques of composition. The fleeting and abstract flow of music often profits by such comparison, and it is in this spirit that these sections are included.

# II The Instruments

To produce sound of various pitches accurately and controllably we must have mechanisms which set the air to vibrating in certain ways. These mechanisms — the musical instruments — achieve this in only a few simple ways. They are blown with the breath, struck with hammers or beaters, or rubbed. The orchestra is divided into three main groups by these differences: the wind instruments, the percussion instruments, and the stringed instruments. Let us discuss them in that order.

## THE WIND INSTRUMENTS

Immediately this class of instruments may be divided into two subdivisions according to the material from which the instrument is made: the *wood*winds, and the *brass* winds.

### THE WOODWINDS

There are four basic woodwinds in the orchestra: the flute, oboe, clarinet and bassoon (Plate I). Each of these consists essentially of

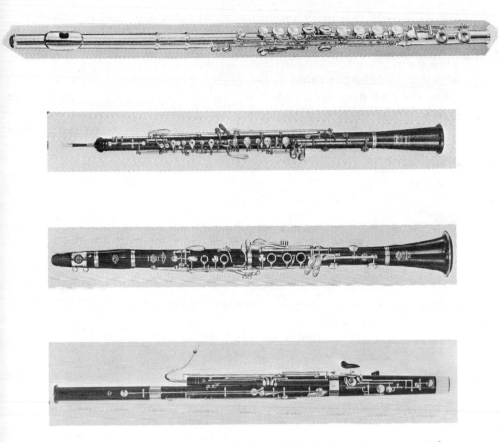

PLATE I. *Woodwind choir: flute, oboe, clarinet, bassoon. (Courtesy of Selmer Instrument Co.)*

a tube and a device to cause the air in that tube to vibrate. There are three of these devices.

Everyone has blown across the top of a soft-drink bottle to produce a whistle-like hoot. The flute operates upon the same principle. This instrument, a woodwind originally but now made out of metal, consists of a tube stopped at one end, near which a hole is cut into the side of the tube. The player blows across this hole, or embouchure. The jet of air strikes one side of the hole, splits, and sets up eddies both inside and outside of the tube. The turbulence within the tube causes the air column to vibrate, producing the sound (Example 15a). To make this tube capable of producing many tones, arranged in scale-like formation, holes are bored along the tube at certain locations, then stopped by the fingers or by key mechanisms. You have noticed that when the pop bottle was nearly full and the air space small, the tone produced was high, and that as you drank the pop, enlarging the air space, the tone deepened. This is exactly what happens in the flute, or any wind instrument. The holes control the sounding length of the tube. When all the holes are closed, the tube sounds its lowest note:

EXAMPLE 15A,B.

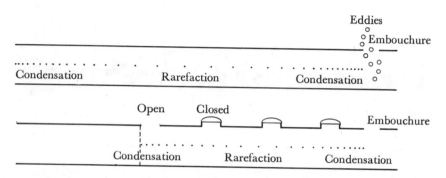

if we open the hole farthest from the embouchure the pitch becomes higher, and so on up toward the mouthpiece (Example 15b). This lowest tone is called the fundamental pitch of the tube. Now let us take our pop bottle again. First blow gently to produce the low fundamental. Now blow harder — a higher pitch results. If you have blown just hard enough, you will produce the octave of the fundamental pitch. Even harder blowing will bring out still higher notes. All of these notes of higher pitch than the fundamental are called harmonic tones, or overtones, and are produced by forcing the air column to vibrate in parts rather than throughout its whole length. For example, the second harmonic results when the air column vibrates lengthwise in halves, the third when the column vibrates in thirds, and so on (Example 16a). Many of these overtones are present in some degree of intensity when the fundamental tone is sounded on a good instrument. And each kind of instrument has a different pattern of overtones with a different degree of loudness for each (Example 16b). Thus, each kind of instrument produces a different quality of sound due to the presence and intensity of the overtone pattern —

EXAMPLE 16A. *Overtone series.*

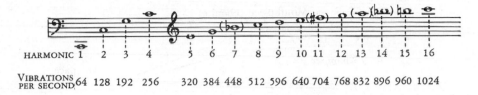

| HARMONIC | 1 | 2 | 3 | 4 | 5 | 6 | 7 | 8 | 9 | 10 | 11 | 12 | 13 | 14 | 15 | 16 |
|---|---|---|---|---|---|---|---|---|---|---|---|---|---|---|---|---|
| VIBRATIONS PER SECOND | 64 | 128 | 192 | 256 | 320 | 384 | 448 | 512 | 596 | 640 | 704 | 768 | 832 | 896 | 960 | 1024 |

EXAMPLE 16B. *Harmonic patterns of flute and clarinet.*

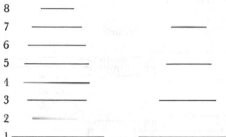

Fundamental or 1

Width of line indicates intensity

a quality characteristic enough to make us recognize it. The overtones are useful in another way: they are used to extend the range of the instrument. Suppose we have a flute with six holes bored in it at the right places to produce a major scale. However, we have no hole which produces the octave! So we close all the holes and blow harder, producing the first overtone of the fundamental — the desired octave. We then repeat the process with each of the holes, extending the range of our simple flute up another octave. Higher overtones might be evoked to extend the range still farther, but practical considerations tend to limit the usefulness of this practice. In the modern flute, extra holes and combinations of holes make the production of these higher notes easier and more accurate in pitch.

What we have discovered above about pitch and overtones applies generally to all of the other wind instruments. They differ from the flute only in the way in which the air in the tube is set in vibration. The clarinet and oboe use flexible reeds of cane fastened in mouthpieces to accomplish this. The clarinet employs a single, flat piece of cane, thinner at the vibrating end, bound to a whistle-like mouthpiece (Example 17). When the player blows into the mouth-

EXAMPLE 17A. *Clarinet mouthpiece with reed.*

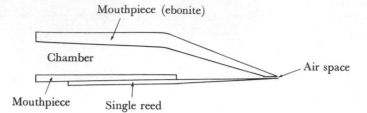

EXAMPLE 17B. *Oboe reed.*

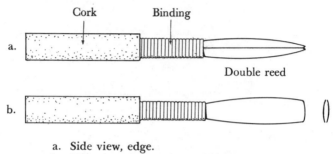

a. Side view, edge.
b. Side view, flat, and end view of reeds.

piece, the cane vibrates back and forth, deflecting puffs of air alternately into and out of the tube of the instrument, thus setting up sound vibrations. The key system and the production of overtones is like that of the flute. However, the overtone pattern of the clarinet is much different from that of the flute, and results in the typical liquid, expressive quality that makes this single-reed instrument so easily recognizable.

The oboe uses a *double* reed, which accomplishes the same result, however, as the single reed (Example 17). Two transversely curved pieces of cane are tightly bound face to face, producing a slightly flattened tube (). One end of this tube is inserted into the tube of the instrument. The other, which is sanded and scraped to make each of the canes thin and flexible, is inserted into the player's mouth. When he blows, the tips of the canes alternately open and close, sending *condensations* (areas in which the air molecules are crowded together) and *rarefactions* (places where the air molecules are fewer) down the tube. This double reed acts in the same way as a dandelion stem when blown into. Because of the double reed, as well as certain characteristics of the instrument tube, the overtone pattern for the oboe is much different from those of the other two instruments above. Its nasal, or oriental, quality is very characteristic.

Each of the above instruments is made in larger or smaller sizes, which therefore possess deeper or higher pitches. The little flute — about half the size of the ordinary instrument — is called the *piccolo,* and sounds an octave higher than the flute. The oboe family is more extensive, having three larger members, the English horn, the bassoon, and the contrabassoon. All operate upon the same principle as the oboe. The clarinet has both larger and smaller relatives. The E♭ clarinet is smaller and higher in pitch than the ordinary B♭ instrument. (The E♭ and B♭ refer to the fundamental pitches of these instruments. This nomenclature is also used for the trumpets and horns.) Larger members of the clarinet family are, in order of descending pitch, the alto, bass, the contrabass clarinets. All are single-reed instruments, and have the characteristic clarinet quality, although in the case of the deeper-pitched instruments this is not so obvious.

The total range of each of the woodwind instruments may be divided into three sections of contrasting quality. In general, the upper third of the range is bright in color, most noticeable in the case of the soprano and alto members of each family. The middle third of the range is neutral in character, usually more representative of what is felt to be the typical sound of the instrument. The lower third is usually hollow, nasal, or reedy, depending upon the kind of instrument. The variations in tone-quality afford the orchestrator with many choices of color within a given range of notes. For example, should the melodic line lie within the five notes from middle C up to G, there are available, among others, all of the four "standard" woodwinds: flute, oboe, clarinet and bassoon. In this register, the flute sounds "breathy," dull and thick, while the oboe has an almost disagreeable nasal quality, bringing to mind oriental bazaars and snake-charmers. The clarinet sounds rather neutral and not too strong on these notes since they form a transition area between its middle and deep registers. The bassoon is here playing in its upper register and the sound is somewhat thin and dry, almost complaining in quality. Depending upon the effect desired, the orchestrator will choose the instrument whose tone-color in this region is most appropriate.

49

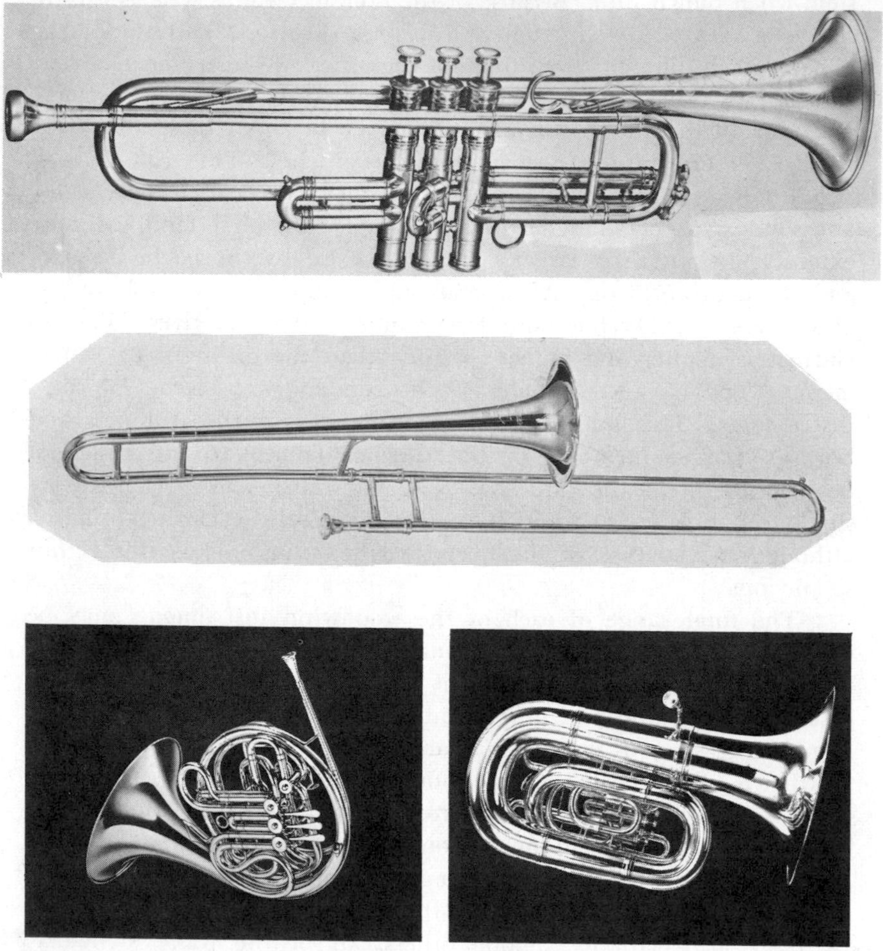

PLATE II. *Brass choir: horn, trumpet, trombone, tuba. (Trumpet and trombone courtesy of Selmer Instrument Co.; French horn and tuba courtesy of Conn Corporation.)*

## THE BRASS WINDS

This family comprises the trumpets and cornets, the French horns and tubas and the trombones as well as less orchestrally valuable relatives such as the various bugles, post-horns and others (Plate II).

These noble instruments all consist of a length of brass tubing,

50

sometimes cylindrical, sometimes slightly conical throughout part of all of its length, one open end of which is flared to form a "bell." In all cases, the vibrating medium, replacing the woodwind reed, is the player's lips. By relaxing or tightening his lips across a funnel or cup-shaped mouthpiece, the player may select any desired overtone. Since there are no finger holes in the brass tube, these would seem to be rather inflexible instruments, as indeed they were during the early part of their history. The bugle is the last remnant of these so-called "natural" brass instruments. It can produce only the overtones of its fundamental. To render the brass instruments more versatile, provision was made to "plug in" extra lengths of tubing to the basic instrument, thus lengthening the total tube, and giving a new fundamental and set of overtones. Every horn player was then obliged to carry about with him a set of these "crooks," as they were called, in order to hold any kind of orchestral job. Finally, three lengths of tubing were built into the instrument and a valve provided for each, so that they could be used singly, or in any combination of added lengths. This is the system used today on the trumpet, French horn, and tuba. The first valve lowers the fundamental (*and* its overtone series!) a whole step; the second lowers it one half step; and the third a whole step plus a half step. Used in combination, the first and third give a fundamental two and one-half steps lower than the original; the second and third give two steps lower; and all three result in a fundamental three whole steps lower than the original of the basic tube. The mechanisms for achieving this flexibility are different on the trumpet and the horn, but the principles are the same.

The trombone eliminates all of this trouble by using a sliding length of tubing which increases or decreases the total length of the basic tube by any amount the player wishes. The fundamental tone and the production of any selected note of the overtone series, like the trumpet and horn, supplies the player with different pitches.

The trumpets and cornets are the sopranos of the brass family, while the French horns might be said to represent a combination of alto and tenor qualities. The so-called "tenor" trombones also descend into the bass register and pass their particular quality on to the bass trombone. The tuba and his outdoor relatives, the Sousaphone and double B♭ basses inhabit the lower regions of the orchestra and band, providing a firm, if somewhat bulky, bass to the entire aggregation.

As with the woodwinds, the total range of each of the brasses is subdivided into three registers, acute (or brilliant), middle and low.

The trumpet and cornet are most usable in their middle registers, although solo passages in the upper range are extremely effective. The lower register tends to be rather weak and flabby. The French horns (often simply called "horns") are usable throughout most of their range. The upper register has the peculiarity of sounding higher than it actually is, the middle register provides warm tones which blend well with most other instruments, or may provide unobtrusive accompaniment, while the dark, rich notes of the low register, not as strong as those of the trombones or tubas, can adequately support a group of woodwinds or strings. The literature of the Romantic era is especially rich in beautiful solos and combinations for this instrument. The brazen voices of the trombones are most noteworthy when sounding triumph or doom, and are of such power that they cut through the full sound of the rest of the orchestra. But when played softly, they can provide backgrounds of organ-like richness. The trombone is seldom used as a solo instrument in symphonic literature before the twentieth century, and infrequently then. Composers seem to prefer the combined sound of the usual three or four instruments as an harmonic group. The tuba provides bass support for these and other groups, and, similarly, is seldom used in a solo capacity. The tone is full and round, never really brilliant, even in the highest register.

## The Percussion Instruments

Generally speaking, anything which emits a sound when struck is a percussion instrument! In the orchestra, however, certain members of this family have become traditional because of the particular quality of sound they emit. The most important of these are the drums (Plate III).

Ordinarily we have three kinds of drums in the orchestra: the kettledrums (or timpani), the snare drum, and the bass drum. The name kettledrum is completely descriptive. These instruments consist of large, hemispherical, copper kettles over the open end of which calf-skin has been stretched. They are capable of being tuned to definite pitches — the only members of the drum family where this is feasible. Many modern improvements in the tuning mechanism have been made, until now we have timpani whose tuning can be preset

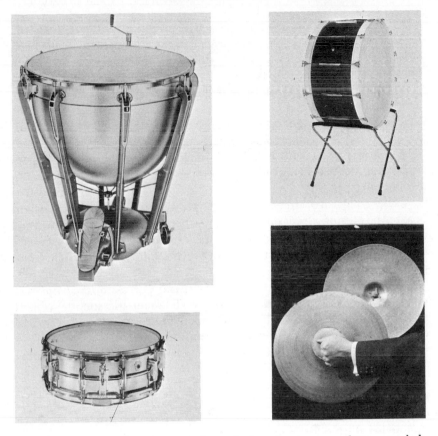

PLATE III. *Percussion group: timpani, bass-drum, snare-drum, cymbals. (Courtesy of Ludwig Drum Co.; cymbals courtesy of Avedis Zildjian Co.)*

before a concert, and changed during the performance by foot pressure on a pedal. These drums are played with sticks with padded ends of various materials, thus modifying the quality of the sound produced.

The snare drum is the small drum we see in dance bands, and sometimes in parades. It consists of a wooden or metal tube about six inches in length and twelve in diameter, over both openings of which are stretched calfskin "heads." The thicker, more resilient head is played upon with wooden sticks, while across the other are stretched cords or fine metal springs which rattle when the other head is struck. For pure exciting noise, this drum is hard to surpass.

The bass drum is a much larger version of the snare drum, without, however, the cords across one head. It is played with a heavily padded stick, and gives great emphasis to the sound of the full orchestra with its solemn boom.

Next in importance, at least from the listener's standpoint, are the cymbals and gongs. The former are dished metal plates of various sizes which have a bright metallic, "sizzling" sound. Two such cymbals may be clashed together at climactic moments, or one may be suspended and played with a pair of timpani or snare-drum sticks. In either case, these instruments rapidly raise the orchestral temperature to the boiling point!

The gongs are large, circular plates of metal, usually brass or bronze, possessing deep solemn tones when struck. They sometimes sound oriental, other times sinister and foreboding. As with cymbals and other percussion instruments, the level of loudness is highly important.

There are many other kinds of orchestral percussion instruments, most of them easily recognizable by the characteristic sound, such as bells, or wood blocks. The xylophone, marimba, vibraphone and celesta deserve more descriptive mention, however. In each of these instruments the sound-producing element is a small, tuned, rectangular bar of either wood or metal — wood in the xylophone and marimba, metal in the vibraphone and celesta. In the case of the first three, these bars are laid horizontally on a cushioned frame in a pattern like the arrangement of white and black keys on the piano; they are then struck with mallets of varying hardness. The marimba and vibraphone have tubes below each bar tuned to the pitch of the note produced by it. These reinforce and prolong the sound. In addition, the vibraphone has small, circular metal plates which fit inside the tubes, and revolve upon a rod turned by a small electric motor. This action causes the intensity of the sound to fluctuate, a more expressive effect possible than on the other instruments. In the case of the celesta, the metal bars are struck by hammers activated by a player at a piano keyboard. The tones are high pitched and silvery — rather sugary and sweet, hence Tchaikovsky's choice of this instrument to depict the Sugar-Plum Fairy in his famous *Nutcracker Suite*.

While the piano and harp are not, strictly speaking, classed as percussion instruments, they fit into no easy category, and so will be discussed briefly here. The piano is the closer of the two to the percussion group, however, since the player at the keyboard causes padded hammers to strike tuned strings. The tone quality and flexibility of this useful and expressive instrument are too well known to spend time upon them here. The piano has only recently become a member in good standing of the regular orchestra. Formerly it was used only as a solo instrument apart from the orchestra, and participated in few purely orchestral effects. Since the beginning of the twentieth century, however, its particular percussive quality, as well as the resonance of its bass notes, has gained it a place in the palette of orchestral sound employed by modern composers. Many interesting effects are possible.

If we should remove the keyboard and case from a grand piano, and stand what is left on its edge, we should have a kind of harp. To make it "pluckable" by human hands, however, the metal strings would have to be replaced by softer gut or nylon strings. This beautiful instrument adds depth and richness to orchestral sound, as well as being expressive and brilliant in its own right. One of the most noteworthy effects possible on it is the so-called *glissando* or "slide'" across all of the strings, making a splash of colorful sound impossible to any other orchestral instrument. Frequently harps are used in pairs to supplement each other in difficult passages, or to increase the volume of sound.

# THE STRINGED INSTRUMENTS

In the orchestra we have two sections of violins, one group larger than the other; a group of violas, one of violoncellos, and one of double-bass viols (Plate IV). In all of these instruments, the methods of tone production are basically the same. The strings, tuned by means of pegs to definite pitches five or four notes apart, may be plucked, like the harp. This effect is called *pizzicato* and is familiar to listeners of popular as well as serious music. Otherwise — and more frequently in the orchestra — a bow of wood strung with a band of horsehair is drawn across the strings, setting them in vibration and producing a tone which is amplified by the soundbox of the instrument. This bow is held in the right hand of the player, while his left lightly grasps a rather rounded, wide piece of wood fastened to and projecting parallel from the top surface of the soundbox. This is the fingerboard. The player presses the selected string tightly down on

PLATE IV. *String choir: viola, violin, double-bass viol, cello. (Courtesy of Scherl & Roth, Inc.)*

the fingerboard, thus shortening its vibrating length a certain amount which he knows will produce the pitch he desires. In the case of the violin, viola, and cello (short for violoncello), the strings are so tuned that starting with the open (not shortened) string, the player may span in scale steps the gap to the next string by using his four fingers to shorten successively the vibrating length of the starting string. This process may be repeated in turn on the other strings, which are arranged in increasingly higher pitches, to give a scale of over two octaves, with very little movement of the hand. The left hand may then move along the fingerboard closer to the sound box, thus affording an extension of the scale by means of the process described above. While determining the pitches to be sounded with the left hand, various kinds of bow strokes may be employed by the right hand to give long, short, bright, dull, loud, soft, yes — and even scratchy quality to the sound being produced! Or a small comb of wood may be fitted over the bridge which holds the strings off the soundbox. This *mute* damps out many of the brilliant overtones of the instrument as well as reducing the volume.

The overtones may be useful as sounds of particular tone quality and can be produced by touching the string lightly at the proper place while bowing, causing it to subdivide its vibrating length into segments. Thus, if the string is lightly touched at the half-way point, the octave of the fundamental tone is produced. Several of the harmonics are employed in the orchestra, and all have a silvery, ethereal sound quite different from the ordinary string sound in that register.

If the bow is moved rapidly back and forth lengthwise through a short distance while in contact with the string, a wavering, intense sound is produced. This is called the *tremolo*. It has been greatly over-used for emotional effects, but still remains a potent way to produce more sound from the string section. In addition to using only one string at a time, the violinist may play two at once, choosing the pitches to create harmony. This "double-stopping" may be further altered in sound by varying the kind of bow-stroke, or by using *tremolo* or *pizzicato*. Sustained harmony in triple and quadruple stopping is impossible since the strings do not lie in the same plane due to the curvature of the bridge and thus cannot be simultaneously stroked by the hair of the bow. But the effect of three or four part harmony can be suggested by sounding the lower notes quickly while the bow is en route to the two upper strings. This procedure gives brilliant, almost percussive chords in the orchestra. With the limiting condition of decreasing agility with increasing size, the techniques are the same for all members of the string family.

Each of the individual strings of these instruments has a characteristic tone-quality due to its thickness, density, tension and the degree of reinforcement by the soundbox. The lowest string is usually dark, almost rough in sound, and is often used for passages of great emotional or dynamic intensity. The two middle strings are smoother and sweeter, not of such marked character. The highest string is, naturally, the most brilliant, and is often used for solo passages. It is most successful on the violin: the top strings of the viola and cello tend to have a strained sound which, though intense, is not always pleasant. However, this is an asset rather than a fault and provides the composer with another tone-quality. In the various stringed instruments, then, we have an almost unlimited variety of tone qualities possible. For this reason they were long regarded as the basic instrumental group of the orchestra.

The string bass, or double-bass viol, to give it its correct name, belongs to an older family than do the above violin-like instruments. The tone is comparatively weaker, more nasal in character, and, because of its size and depth of its notes, the instrument is less agile and flexible than its neighbors in the string group. *Pizzicato* upon this instrument is very powerful, however, and is often used to relieve the orchestral texture of the heaviness of bowed notes.

## THE ORCHESTRA AS A MUSICAL INSTRUMENT

Music composed for the orchestra tries to exploit the various qualities of the solo instruments, as well as those of instruments in combination. The woodwinds, rather small and refined in sound, are intimate voices, each of which possesses a clearly defined personality, or tone color. Similarly in the brass, the trumpets are clearly different characters from the French horns or trombones. The same applies to the various strings. Orchestral compositions are said to be colorful when these individual personalities are exploited and contrasted with one another over a reasonably short period of time, resulting in what we shall term "color orchestration." This procedure might be compared to type-casting in the movies or in plays; actors with definite physical or vocal equipment are chosen for striking parts. The opposite may also be true, both in the use of the orchestra as well as in choosing actors. Possibly in a universal kind of play, such as *Everyman* or some of the Greek dramas in which the tragic action is more important than any one character — the people are merely vehicles through which the action takes place — this might be called functional casting, and so we shall term this use of the orchestra "functional orchestration."

We shall discover that functional orchestration is used largely by composers who are interested in the purely musical design of their works, while color orchestration is most used by writers who seek to describe less abstract things in their music, or rely upon highly emotional effects. One is classic, reserved, traditional; the other is romantic, emotional, radical.

The number of instruments in the orchestra may vary, not necessarily to change the volume of sound, but also to increase or limit the color possibilities. Normally we find the woodwinds in pairs, with one of each pair possibly playing an alternate member of the same family if required in the musical score. In the brass section, three trumpets, four French horns, three trombones and tuba are the normal complement. Because the sound of each of the individual stringed instruments is rather weak, we find greater numbers of these in the ordinary orchestra. Twelve to sixteen first violins, ten to fourteen second violins, six to ten violas, four to eight cellos, and four to six double-basses would be an adequate string section to balance the above winds. The percussion section is variable as needed.

This group of instruments forms a large, sounding body upon which the conductor plays in much the same way that a pianist controls and exploits the expressive possibilities of his instrument. The main function of the conductor is not to beat time. True, this is a rather important duty, but more significant is the fact that he must choose and maintain the tempo which feels most right to him. If his personality is such that he likes to bring out the songfulness of the music, his tempos will be slower, with more small variations in them to emphasize cadences, climaxes, and lyric elements. Should he be a dramatic, fiery type of person, however, his tempos will be faster, his climaxes will be louder, and he will drive with straightforward energy to the goals he feels in the music. In addition to these expressive functions, the conductor must balance the sound of the orchestra, making sure that the brasses do not drown out important string or woodwind solos, and adjust the sound of smaller groups to achieve blend or distinction. All of these things contribute to and derive from his conception of what the music is written to express. He has a great responsibility to the composer and to the audience. He must be a sincere and communicative musical artist as well as a commanding personality on the podium.

In addition to the large medium of the orchestra, composers also write for various smaller combinations. Works of this kind are called "chamber music," a title dating from the seventeenth and eighteenth centuries when the nobility employed composers and musicians to compose and perform music in their salons and dining rooms. A small orchestra consisting of single woodwinds, usually a pair of French horns, and sufficient strings to balance these wind instruments is called a chamber orchestra. Probably the most aristocratic of the standard small combinations is the string quartet, consisting of two violins, viola, and cello. Some of the greatest masterpieces of intimate and profound music have been written for these slim resources. Here music and musical thinking are of the utmost importance. No great variation in tone color or overpowering effect of intensity is possible. Other traditional groups are: the trio, composed of violin, cello, and piano; the duo, consisting of a solo instrument and piano; combinations of wood-winds such as the woodwind quintet which is made up of flute, oboe, clarinet, bassoon, and French horn. Until the beginning of the twentieth century the heavier brass were not included in chamber music. In modern music, however, the traditional patterns have sometimes given way to combinations especially selected to serve a prearranged style. For example, Stravinsky's stage work *L'Histoire du Soldat* employs an orchestra of violin, double-bass, clarinet, bassoon, cornet, trombone, and percussion. Nowadays anything is possible!

Before we leave chamber music, let us make one thing clear: only in the least artistic works do the lower instruments merely accompany, that is to say, play distinctly subordinate parts, throughout the composition. A good string quartet — and this applies to all chamber music — has been compared to a conversation between four friends, a conversation based upon equal give-and-take. Where this problem most frequently raises its head is in the sonata for solo instrument and piano. Both instruments share equally, each according to his particular capabilities, in the working out of the composer's musical ideas. Therefore, each will at some time have a leading part, the other a subordinate part: sometimes both may have material to play which is vital and important, resulting in a polyphonic combination.

An interesting medium halfway between the somewhat impersonal orchestra and the intimate chamber group is the combination of a solo instrument with orchestra. This kind of composition is called a *concerto*. It affords the soloist the advantage of communicating directly with his listeners as well as having a rich, flexible, and sonorous accompaniment.

ADDITIONAL LISTENING

The following list contains compositions in which the indicated instrument plays either a solo part, or is outstanding in the orchestral ensemble.

*Flute:*
Griffes: Poem for Flute and Orchestra
Tchaikovsky: *Nutcracker Suite,* "Dance of the Reed Flutes"

*Oboe:*
Handel: Sonata in B♭ for Oboe and Flute
Barlow: *The Winter's Past,* for oboe and string orchestra

*English Horn:*
Sibelius: *Swan of Tuonela*
Dvořák: Symphony No. 5, II, Largo (opening solo)

*Clarinet:*
Mozart: Concerto for Clarinet and Orchestra, K. 662
Copland: *Clarinet Concerto*

*Bassoon:*
Dukas: *The Sorcerer's Apprentice* (with double-bassoon)
Mozart: Concerto for Bassoon and Orchestra, K. 191

All of the woodwinds may be heard in incidental solos in such works as Rimsky-Korsakoff's *Scheherezade,* or the *Capriccio Espagnol.*

*Horn:*
Mendelssohn: *Midsummer Night's Dream; Nocturne*
Strauss: *Der Rosenkavalier,* Introduction

*Trumpet:*
Copland: *The Quiet City* (for trumpet, English horn, and string orchestra)
Vivaldi: Concerto in C for Two Trumpets and Orchestra.

*Trombone:*
Hindemith: Sonata for Trombone and Piano
Berlioz: *Roméo et Juliette,* Dramatic Symphony: I, beginning recitative

*Tuba:*
Strauss: *Don Quixote* (cello represents the Don, while the tuba portrays his companion, Sancho Panza)

The music of Wagner and Strauss abound in fine examples of writing for solo and combined brass. The Stravinsky Symphonies of Wind Instruments provide examples of more modern scoring.

*Harp:*
Ravel: Introduction and Allegro for Harp and Strings
Debussy: *Danses Sacrée et Profane*

*Violin:*
Bach: Partita No. 2 for Unaccompanied Violin
Beethoven: Concerto in D Major for Violin and Orchestra

*Viola:*
Walton: Concerto for Viola and Orchestra
Bloch: Suite, for Viola and Piano

*Cello:*
Haydn: Concerto for Cello and Orchestra
Bloch: *Schelomo*

*Double-Bass Viol:*
Beethoven: Symphony No. 5, III, Trio
Beethoven: Symphony No. 9, IV, opening recitatives, doubled an octave higher for clarity

*Special effects in the strings:*
  *Pizzicato:* Tchaikovsky, Symphony No. 4, III
  Double and triple stopping: Bach, Chaconne from Partita No. 2 in D
    minor for unaccompanied violin
  Harmonics: Ravel, *Ma Mère l'Oye,* "*The Fairy Garden*"
  Mutes: Tchaikovsky, *Nutcracker Suite,* "Arabian Dance"
  *Glissando* "slides" and *ponticello:* Bartók, Quartet No. 5, II (also muted)
  *Col legno* (with the wood of the bow): Berlioz, *Symphonie Fantastique,*
    IV, "Witches' Sabbath"

Several informative albums of phonograph records are available for the purpose of illustrating the sounds of the various instruments. One of the best is *The Complete Orchestra* by Wheeler-Beckett, issued by The Music Education Record Corporation, Box 445, Englewood, New Jersey. In addition, such compositions as Saint-Saens *Carnival of Animals,* Britten's *Young Persons' Guide to the Orchestra,* Prokofiev's *Peter and the Wolf,* and even Tchaikovsky's *Nutcracker Suite* may be used to show instruments and combinations within the orchestra. Rimsky-Korsakoff's *Scheherezade* and *Capriccio Espagnol* are also useful in this respect.

# III The Medieval Period, 600-1450

## Part I: The Romanesque Era, 600-1100

### HISTORICAL PERSPECTIVE

The history of Western music begins with the medieval period — the Middle Ages, between antiquity and what we are pleased to call modern civilization, usually regarded as beginning with the Renaissance (c. 1450) to the present. For all practical purposes, we may regard the centuries from 600 to 1450 as the medieval period, although it is obvious that no specific date is really accurate when large cultural changes, involving decades or even centuries, are being considered. Furthermore, this long epoch may be conveniently subdivided into two periods of contrasting culture: the Romanesque, (600-1100) and the Gothic (1100-1450). The first embraces the period of slow recovery from the barbarian invasions and the resultant disruption of both the *Pax Romana* and the laws by which it was maintained. This culture, almost completely dominated by the ascetic Christian church, is marked by a religious mysticism exemplified by the low, horizontal lines and dark interiors of the Romanesque churches (Plate V), and by the subdued and meditative plainchant, as impersonal and otherworldly as the sculptures and paintings which

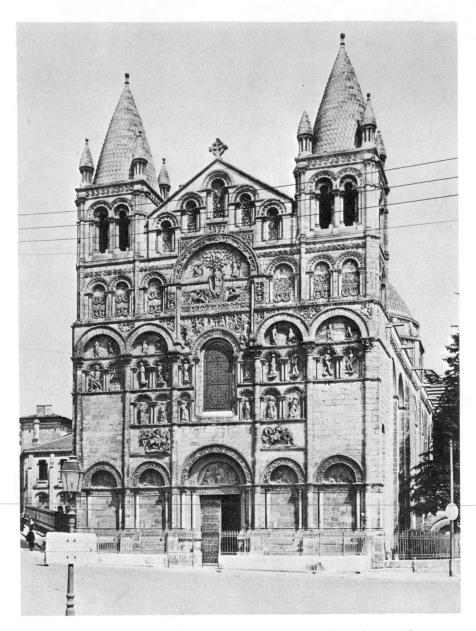

PLATE V.  *Romanesque Church of St. Peter at Angoulême, France. (Courtesy of French Government Tourist Office.)*

adorn the churches. To the men of these times, the earthly life was an interlude to be endured until death opened the doors to eternal bliss in heaven. The church was the sole power which held this world together, for civil power could not rule without the sacred sanction.

In the artistic realm, all forms of representational and musical art were marshalled by the church to teach its laws to the illiterate populace. To accomplish this, stylization, resulting in the submergence of the individuality of the artist, prevailed in order that the images and pictures by the uniformity of their symbols, would always be intelligible to the unlettered beholder. For example, St. Paul was always depicted as a bald man with a long beard. When such a figure appears in a painting, stained glass window, or as a statue, we can be sure who it is, just as could the man of the Romanesque era. Thus, by bowing to these rules, individuality was lost in the interest of intelligibility, and the artist of the period is largely anonymous. It would almost seem that man had no individual will of his own at this time, for he dared not invent or discover something without the sanction of some kind of authority, usually religious. The authorities for the musical science of the time were Boethius and Cassiodorus, through whose books the knowledge of the Greeks was passed on to the monastic musicians of these early days. It was a philosophical and scientific examination of the phenomenon of sound rather than an "art" in the modern sense of the term, one of the "quadrivium" of arithmetic, geometry, music and astronomy deemed necessary for any student before he studied the ultimate subject, theology. Let us take a moment to review in general the achievements of the ancient Greeks in music.

Only a few musical examples have come down to us from antiquity, and these are Greek. In contrast to them, the writings about music by the philosophers and scientists of this great civilization are numerous and illuminating. Pythagoras discovered the laws governing the vibration of stretched strings some 600 years before Christ, and his followers raised upon his work a mystic and speculative philosophy which often clouded the really valuable part of the investigation. By means of these laws, however, as transmitted by Boethius, the medieval investigator could construct a "gamut" or scale of whole and half steps like that which we use today. In Greek times, the scales thus constructed were called "modes," and the medieval musician took over this term as well as the more specific names for each of the four modes he used. These were originally the names of the various Greek tribes, but now indicate what are usually called the "medieval modes," or the "church modes." Let us examine them.

Suppose we have series of tones arranged in whole and half steps exactly like the white keys of the piano (Example 1, Chapter I). The half steps will occur between E and F, B and C. We may begin upon any tone of this series, F, for example, and by including the seven tones from this note up to its octave (F-G-A-B-C-D-E-) create a modal scale, in this case, the Lydian mode. Those modes beginning on C and A are our familiar major and minor modes. The others sound less familiar, since the arrangement of whole and half steps differs from major or minor, although they bear a certain resemblance in quality to these. The scale on B was never included in the medieval modes because of its instability, but the other four provided the material for the melodic, and later, harmonic constructions of music from the early Middle Ages up to the end of the Renaissance. The following tabulation shows the name of the scale and its fundamental note which was called the "final," from its cadential function at the close of a composition. (See Example 18.)

EXAMPLE 18. *The modal scales.*

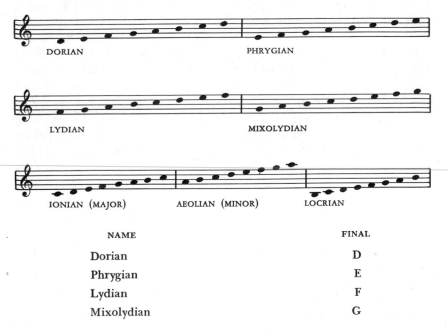

| NAME | FINAL |
|---|---|
| Dorian | D |
| Phrygian | E |
| Lydian | F |
| Mixolydian | G |

# The Musical Style of the Romanesque Period

Surprising as it may seem, harmony was not used in the music of this time. But for that matter, it had not been used by the Greeks or other ancient people either, as far as we can tell. And until the westernization of the Asiatic countries in our own time, harmony and polyphony were not used in the Far or Near East. The development in these countries had been devoted toward the refinement of melody and scalar melodic materials rather than harmony.

This monophonic music of the Middle Ages is exemplified on the sacred side by plainchant (Example 19), sometimes called plainsong or Gregorian chant, and on the secular side by the lusty or courtly songs of the minstrels, trouvères and troubadours (Example 20). Both

EXAMPLE 19.  *Plainchant.*

a.  SYLLABIC

b.  NEUMATIC

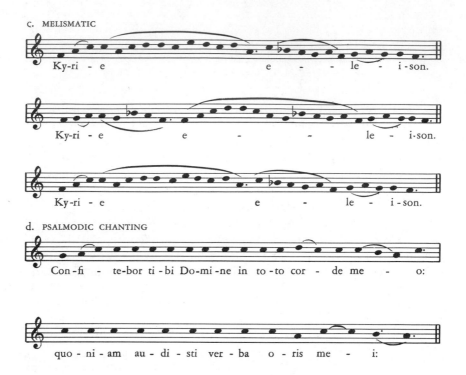

c. MELISMATIC

Ky-ri - e          e - - le - i -son.

Ky-ri - e          e - - le - i-son.

Ky-ri - e          e - le - i -son.

d. PSALMODIC CHANTING

Con-fi - te-bor ti - bi Do-mi -ne in to -to cor - de me - o:

quo - ni - am au - di - sti ver - ba o - ris me - i:

kinds employ modal scale material, both are monophonic, although it seems likely that some sort of simple accompaniment was used with the secular music, and both have strong points of resemblance in their melodic construction. Let us first examine plainchant.

This music is devotional and rather impersonal in nature, devised to carry all-important words, and therefore generally subservient to them. But it is highly artistic in the way it subtly heightens the meaning of the words — an artistry similar to that of folk song, and like folksong, of uncertain authorship. Melodically, it is exceedingly vocal in character, with no wide leaps, and usually moves within a rather restricted range, seldom greater than an octave in span. The text is set to it in four general ways, although in practice, mixtures of these sometimes occur. When each syllable of text bears one note, the setting is said to be syllabic (Example 19a). It is called neumatic when two or three-note patterns are set to each syllable (Example 19b), and melismatic when more occur (Example 19c). The fourth variety consists of a text set syllabically to repeated notes on a single pitch, usually combined with a beginning formula of rising notes and an ending one of descending tones. This is called "psalmodic" chanting, and was used for long and repetitive texts such as psalms and litanies (Example 19d). All of these varieties of chant are still in use in the rituals of the Catholic Church.

It will be noted that there is no recurrent metric pulse in this music, but that it flows in the rhythms of prose, a fluctuation among single, double and triple-note groups ("neumes") arranged in such a way as to lend movement, flow and grace to the vocalization of the text (Example 19b).

# FORMAL AND GENERATIVE PRINCIPLES

The forms used in plainchant are dependent upon the church ritual in which they appear, and upon the text to which the music is set. We shall concern ourselves with two of the main forms.

The most important single form is that of the chanting of a psalm. As an introduction and also a close (or coda) to the psalm itself, a short Biblical verse is sung to a melodically designed chant called an antiphon. The psalm is chanted as explained above, sometimes with alternating choirs. The whole form is rather like a three-part structure, A-B-A (antiphon, psalm, antiphon).

The most significant compound form in which plainchant is used is that of the Mass, or celebration of the Last Supper, sometimes called Holy Communion. This ritual may be divided into two main parts, the Ordinary and the Proper. The texts of the Ordinary, set to various chants, form part of every celebration of the Mass, while those of the Proper change according to the seasons of the church calendar. For example, a Christmas and an Easter Mass will have the same Ordinary, but different Propers. Because of this invariability of the Ordinary, composers from the fourteenth century to the present time have set these texts to more or less elaborate music. There are five main sections to the Ordinary named by the first few words of the Latin text:

1. Kyrie eleison ("Lord have mercy")
2. Gloria in excelsis Deo ("Glory to God in the highest")

3. Credo in unum deum ("I believe in one God," the Nicene creed)
4. Sanctus (Holy, holy holy ); Benedictus ("Blessed is he who cometh in the name of the Lord")
5. Agnus Dei ("Lamb of God, that taketh away the sins of the world")

There also occur hymns, in which the verses of a text are chanted to repetitions of the same music, and various other small forms which need not detain us here. What is important to remember about these forms is that they are all dictated by the ritual and by the text.

Secular compositions are often related to dance songs, and show verse-refrain divisions. As usually transcribed from the all too obscure

EXAMPLE 20. *Trouvère song.*

RICHARD COEUR-de-LION (1157-1199)

*
BALLADE: *"Ja nuns bons pris"*

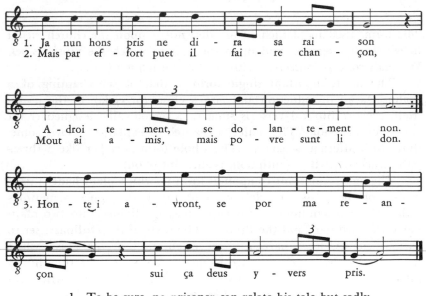

1. To be sure, no prisoner can relate his tale but sadly.
2. But with effort, he can make a song.
   Many friends have I, but poor are their gifts.
3. They will be shamed if, for my ransom,
   I am imprisoned here two winters.

Attributed to Richard the Lionhearted during his imprisonment by Leopold of Austria following Richard's return from the Third Crusade. Eventually his subjects ransomed him for a huge sum.

*Historical Anthology, Harvard University Press, 1949

notation of the period, they are modal, predominantly in triple or some variety of compound time, have clear, rather short phrases, are vocal in character and employ syllabic text settings. The words are typical of popular songs through the centuries, devoted to praise of a beloved, lamentation at the loss, estrangement or failure to win the smile of a sweetheart, drinking songs, martial airs (this is the time of the Crusades; see Example 20), and religious texts, often directed toward the Virgin Mary as the epitome of earthly and heavenly adoration. These pieces continue in much the same style well into the Gothic period, and exist side by side with the advancing polyphonic art of the church music as well as with somewhat more sophisticated court music.

## MUSICAL EXAMPLES

Many of the characteristics pointed out above will be noticed in any of the performances of plainchant and secular music which are plentifully available recorded on single records or in anthologies. In some cases, the recordings are accompanied by the written music, providing a design for the eye as well as for the ear. The most easily available book of chant, the *Liber Usualis,* may also be used. It may be obtained either in modern or Roman (square-note) notation. Of special interest is the secular play with music, *Robin et Marion* by Adam de la Halle. This work has been called the first opera, and while hardly that, it does present a typically stylized pastoral play adorned with charming folklike music.

### SACRED MUSIC: PLAINCHANT

1. History of Music in Sound (RCA), hereafter abbreviated HMS, Vol. II. Various kinds of plainchant, including some varieties which preceded the Gregorian reform. Includes many parts of both the Ordinary and Proper of the Mass.
2. Deutsche Grammaphon Archive Production (Decca Records) ARC 3001. Easter Mass; ARC 3031, Requiem Mass; ARC 3088/3090, Easter Liturgy; ARC 3050, Solemn Intercessions for Good Friday.
3. Masterpieces of Music before 1750 (Hadyn Society), abbreviated MM., Vol. I.
4. Gregorian Chants (MA-LP-1), released by the Gregorian Institute of America. A warmer, more romantic performance of various forms including hymns, parts of the Mass and litanies.

SECULAR MUSIC

1. HMS Vol. II. Latin, French, Provençal, English, German, Italian and Spanish medieval songs.
2. Music of the 12th and 13th Centuries, MS 201. Vocal and instrumental performances by the Pro Musica Antiqua of Brussels.
3. MM Vol. I. A trouvère and a Minnesinger song.
4. Deutsche Grammaphon Archive Production. ARC 3002, Adam de la Halle. Contains *Le Jeu de Robin et Marion,* 13 rondeaux, and 17 dances of the 13th century. De la Halle is known as "the last of the troubadors," hence the late date.

## Part II: The Gothic Period, 1100-1450

By the time of the Gothic period, Europe had largely recovered from the anarchy which followed the decline of the strong rule of Rome. She was now ready to resume more actively the cultural and social development which culminates in the brilliance of the Renaissance.

Of the many political, chivalric, literary and artistic achievements of this time, we may mention a few. These were the years of the Crusades, those fruitless but rewarding attempts to wrest the Holy Land from the Moslems — fruitless because no real gains were made, and much blood and money were wasted, but rewarding because the ventures into the Near East brought the travelling warriors into contact with two highly developed cultures, the Byzantine and Islamic civilizations, which had not suffered the fate of Rome at the hands of barbarians. In addition to bringing back the exotic trade goods, such as spices, silks and skilfully worked metal, they also returned with outlandish foreign customs such as regular bathing and the use of the fork in eating instead of the hands, as well as such aids to philosophy and science as the decimal system, arabic numerals and many translations of the Greek philosophers which were non-existent even in the best European libraries of the time. It will be noted that the search for the goods of these countries initiated many of the explorations of the fifteenth and sixteenth centuries, and that the books of the pagan Greeks, Aristotle particularly, led to the development of scholastic philosophy and thence to the founding of the universities.

The great cathedrals were built in these centuries (Plate VI). Few were the decades that passed without the cornerstone of some great church being set in place — Durham Cathedral in 1093; in 1133 the rebuilding of the Abbey of St. Denis; 1154, York Minster; 1163, Notre Dame de Paris; 1175, Canterbury Cathedral; 1185, Bamberg Cathedral; 1195, Bourges Cathedral; 1201, Cathedral of Rouen; 1211, Rheims Cathedral; 1220, Amiens and Salisbury Cathedrals, and so on for yet another century.

There were also the years of great kings — William the Conqueror, Frederick Barbarossa, Richard the Lion-Hearted, Saladin, St. Louis of France, John of England; of notable philosophers — Abelard, St. Thomas Aquinas, Roger Bacon, Duns Scotus; of men of

letters — Hartman von Aue, Gottfried of Strasbourg who wrote one
of the Tristan stories later used by Wagner, Joinville the historian,
Dante; of missionaries and travelers — Giovanni Carpini in Mongolia,
and Marco Polo in Asia; of important human documents — the Domes-
day Book, the Magna Carta; of the great universities of Paris, Mont-
pellier, Cambridge, Naples and Salamanca; and of meaningful stories
and legends for future times — the *Chanson de Roland,* the *Nibelun-
genlied,* the *Roman de la Rose, Aucassin et Nicolette* and *El Cid.* These
are but a few of the noteworthy items in the rich catalog of the
"Age of Faith."

# Early Gothic Style: 1100-1300

Because of the multiplicity of styles in this long period, we shall
content ourselves with a chronological narrative, mentioning along
the way the outstanding features of each style and indicating the line
of development throughout the period.

With the rise of polyphonic composition in the eleventh and
twelfth centuries, the center of musical investigation moved northward
to France. Little by little, music began to free itself from the bonds
of ecclesiastical authority and to enter the secular world. But at
first, the music itself was dependent upon the "authority" of plainchant, for the early polyphony consists of a section of chant with
which is combined a composed part. The two progress in parallel
motion at the interval of a fifth or fourth apart (Example 21a), and

Example 21a.

PARALLEL                                    Musica enchiriadis (ca.850)

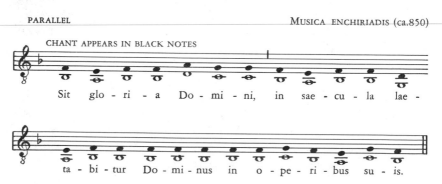

because of the continuous use of the same interval, have an unmoving quality resembling the static harmony studied earlier. Soon, however, the composed voice freed itself from this rather unimaginative combination and began to use contrary and oblique motion in relation to the fixed plainchant or *cantus firmus* part (Example 21b). These were all varieties of what was called *organum*, a term which has

EXAMPLE 21B.

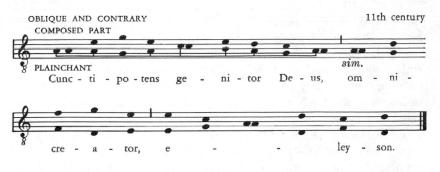

OBLIQUE AND CONTRARY
COMPOSED PART

11th century

PLAINCHANT

Cunc - ti - po - tens  ge - ni - tor  De - us,  om - ni -

cre - a - tor,  e - - ley - son.

were all varieties of what was called *organum,* a term which has nothing to do with the instrument, organ.

Melodically, the newly composed part was often very much like plainchant in its use of steps and skips, although in some cases the line became rather angular with comparatively large skips in order to satisfy the rules concerning the basic consonances which appeared at important points in the texture. These foundation intervals were the so-called "perfect consonances" of the fourth, fifth and octave (Example 10, Chapter I). The thirds, sixths, seconds and sevenths were not yet admitted to the hierarchy of important intervals, and sufficed as means to progress from one consonance to another. Often such a progression, when it occurs in two or three voices simultaneously, results in a clash of considerable proportions which relieves the "openness" of the harmonic structure. In addition, the dissonances between the parts above the cantus firmus were not regulated in relation to each other, but only in regard to the cantus.

Both the sacred and secular music of the late Romanesque was written in a notation which indicated pitch but not meter or rhythm — that is, proportional durations among the notes. This simple notation began as a means of remembering long chant melodies, and consisted of ascending, descending or other types of curved lines which indicated the motion of the music. Later, square symbols, less graphic in nature were developed and a four line staff was used so that pitch indication became precise. The record of the various other early experiments in the development of notation is a fascinating study in ingenuity, but too long for our present account.

The rise of polyphonic music in which the proportional durations between the parts were different precipitated the need for metric, or "mensural" notation. Basing their work upon the medieval recognition of "authority," the theorists adopted the quantitative meters of Latin poetry as the source of this first venture into mensural notation. In this system, accents were interpreted as long syllables worth two of the short, unaccented syllables. Evaluated thus, the common iambic, dactylic and trochaic poetic feet gave rhythmic patterns of triple or some variety of compound meter. This system of rhythmic classification was known as the "rhythmic modes," and held sway over sacred and, presumably, secular music from the eleventh to the middle of the thirteenth century. It was particularly used at the church of Notre Dame (not the present one) in Paris, where two choirmaster-composers, Leonin (latter twelfth century) and Perotin (ca. 1183-1238) set many chants in what was known as "discant style," using modal rhythm. In the case of Leonin, the sections employing modal rhythm are prefaced and followed by sections of a species of polyphony which developed at St. Martial Monastery, near Limoges (Example 21c). The plainchant cantus firmus progresses in very long, sustained notes in this style, while the upper part weaves arabesques in more rapid notes, often vocalizations on a vowel syllable of a text. The modal rhythms of the chant part — the "tenor," from Latin "tenere" (to hold) — in Leonin organum move rather slowly, but in the style

EXAMPLE 21c.

St. Martial and Compostela (c.1175)

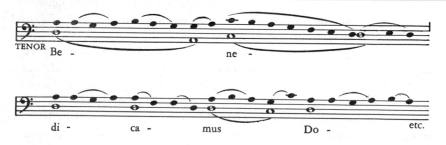

76

of his successor, Perotin, they are cast into short, rather rapid rhythmic patterns, yielding a dance-like quality to the music (Example 21d).

EXAMPLE 21D.

PEROTIN ORGANUM (ca. 1200)  Hec dies

TENOR

Hec

etc.

*Historical Anthology, Harvard University Press, 1949

While the harmonic structure of this music is theoretically based upon the perfect consonances, the use of other intervals, particularly thirds and sixths, tends to create major and minor triads in considerable quantity, especially in the rather few examples by Perotin in four parts. The harmony is not functional as yet, and cadences, if such they can be called, are merely arrivals at more "open" consonances than those occurring during the course of the music: there is no hint of V-I or IV-I, although these sound complexes do occur as a result of the polphonic combinations of voices.

## MUSICAL EXAMPLES

PLAINCHANT, GREGORIAN CHANT

1. MM Vol. I.
2. HMS, Vol. 1.
3. Gregorian Chant, Gregorian Institute of America, MA-LP-1

EARLY POLYPHONY

1. MM Vol. I.
2. HMS Vol. II.
3. Music of the Twelfth and Thirteenth Centuries, EMS 201 (Eleanor Music Shop).
4. Notre Dame Organa: Leoninus and Perotinus magister, EA-0021 (Expériences Anonymes).
5. Deutsche Grammaphon Archive Production, ARC 3051. Contains chansons and motets of the 13th century, organa of the Notre Dame School.

# MIDDLE GOTHIC STYLE: 1300-1400

As might be expected, music began to cast off its restraining bonds — the modal rhythmic system and the use of plainchant as a compositional basis — and to develop forms and techniques exploiting the new freedom. The triply-divided rhythmic modes were replaced by a new system which admitted duple subdivision of note duration — the *Ars nova,* or new art of music, as compared with the *Ars Antiqua* of the Notre Dame school. At first, it abounded in bewildering rhythmic complexities still difficult for musicologists to unravel and agree upon, but after this exuberant experimentation mensural notation settled down to substantially the system in use today.

In secular music, which far outweighed in importance the sacred music of the time, the use of a pre-existing melody as cantus firmus was largely abandoned, and all parts became original with the composer. In the small amount of church music written, however, this conservative and traditional method was still employed, but with a certain difference. We have mentioned above the fact that Perotin used short repeated patterns in modal rhythms for the part carrying the plainchant cantus. Now, in the procedure called "isorhythm," not only a series of tones — a plainchant section — is chosen, but also a rhythmic phrase some measures in length is set up as a standard pattern to be repeated throughout the composition. The rhythmic phrase is usually not extensive enough to arrive at its completion when the cantus does. When this point is reached, the rhythmic phrase repeats, using up the remaining notes of the cantus which then, in turn, begins its repetition, now in a different rhythmic guise from its former appearance. The process is repeated until the composer chooses to terminate it, or until the composition, as determined by the text, is finished (Example 22). The whole process is undetectable by the listener, and may be regarded as in the same class as the many mystifications and scholastic hidden meanings which delighted the medieval mind.

Most of the forms of this time are word-based. That is, they depend upon a text for their length, not upon purely musical procedures: even those compositions intended for instruments were often written with a text, although, of course, this was not sung. To be sure, the composer could expand the musical setting of the text by writing more than one note to each syllable, sometimes expanding a vowel sound into a lengthy melismatic passage. But the text was still the determining factor. This remained so for some time in musical Europe, but across the Channel, the English, along with some other unusual practices, produced the first written canon, "Sumer is icumen in, lhude sing cuccu." This is no simple piece, such as "Three Blind Mice," or *"Frère Jacques,"* but a four part canon accompanied by a two part canon! The date of this surprising work is a source of some argument, but dates from 1240 to 1310 have been advanced. It would seem, from the complexity of this music, that the English had probably been practicing this technique for some time previous. It has been transcribed in both duple and triple meter, but in either one retains its folksong quality and dance-like charm.

The French music of the fourteenth century is largely courtly and elegant in nature, and finds its most famous exponent in Guillaume de Machaut (ca. 1300-1377), who, however, is also responsible

for writing the first setting of the Ordinary of the Mass completely
composed by one person. The music of the Mass is isorhythmic in
structure, unified in style as well as by a short melodic fragment
which recurs frequently in all parts of every movement of the work

EXAMPLE 22.

"KYRIE," NOTRE DAME MASS                    GUILLAUME de MACHAUT

(Example 22). The polyphony of this composition, like that of the secular ballades and chansons, is very transparent, almost ascetic sounding to modern ears, and employs a peculiar melodic-harmonic cadence formula named after Machaut's Italian contemporary, Francesco Landini (1325-1397). The Landini cadence was not yet an example of functional harmony, but soon evolved into a rudimentary V-I progression, usually with the third of each chord missing, thus giving the "open" sound of the perfect consonances of the fifth and octave.

While Landini used little or no isorhythm, preferring a more direct emotional musical language, Machaut enjoyed working out somewhat mathematical puzzles in some of his works. Such a composition is the rondeau, *"Ma fin est mon commencement"* ("My end is my beginning"), a complicated triple canon in which one part is the exact reverse of the other. The key to the solution of this canon lies in the text — a kind of double unification as well as mystification.

It has by now probably become apparent to the thoughtful reader that the rise of polyphony and mensural notation in the early and middle Gothic period in a sense parallel the architectural developments of that time, especially the Gothic cathedral. In contrast to the dark and earth-hugging aspect of the Romanesque churches (Plate V), largely due to the round Roman arch and the emphasis on weight and horizontal lines, the Gothic structure is a vertical, upward-thrusting manifestation of the growing realization of the beauty of the earth and man, and the exaltation of the spirit in its yearning for the infinite (Plate VI). The balanced complexity of these webs of stone, in which the removal of one pier of an arch would cause the entire building to collapse, is paralleled by the webs of polyphonic sound so composed that each tone bears its share of the structure and is

PLATE VI. *A Gothic church: the Cathedral at Amiens, France. (Courtesy of the French Government Tourist Office.)*

similarly indispensable. The conduct of the melodic lines, no longer smooth and rounded in contour, but containing upward and downward leaps, resembles the points of the Gothic arches and towers; and the polyphony, too, with open spaces between the constituent voices (transparency), brings to mind the sense of "openness" of the Gothic cathedral, where windows form the greater part of the walls. Even the growing emphasis upon secular music is reflected by these "poems in stone," for such churches exhibited not only the religious feeling of the people, but also their pride, their realization of worldly knowledge and skill necessary to raise such structures, and a competitive spirit in trying to create a more beautiful work than other cities. Civilization had emerged from the dark mysticism of the Romanesque into the more worldly light of the Gothic, well on the way to the Renaissance.

That this period saw the first signs of the Renaissance is evidenced by the decay of scholastic philosophy and the rise of humanism, by the weakening power of the Church in many of the affairs of men (especially of the power of Rome over the heads of states resulting from the fragmentation of the Holy Roman Empire), and by the development of literature in the common tongue and painting in an uncommon manner. These are the times of Petrarch and Boccaccio, Giotto and Orcagna, the Black Death, Chaucer, the Hundred Years War, the growing interest in classical antiquity and the rise of the ruling families of Italy which were to play such an important part upon the glittering stage of the Renaissance.

### MUSICAL EXAMPLES

1. HMS Vol. II. Contains, among a few examples of fourteenth century polyphony, the canon "Sumer is icumen in."
2. HMS Vol. III. Contains secular French, Italian and English polyphony of the Ars Nova, as well as two selections by Machaut comprising the Benedictus from the Mass, and the interesting canonic rondeau, "Ma fin est mon commencement."
3. MM Vol. I. Contains the Agnus dei from Machaut's Mass and a ballata (ballade, dance derived) by Landino.
4. Deutsche Grammaphon Archive Production, ARC 3023. Contains Machaut's Mass complete plus ten secular works by this composer.

# THE LATE GOTHIC PERIOD: 1400-1450

The third step toward the typical style of the Renaissance is largely a harmonic one — the recognition of the intervals of the third and sixth as usable consonances, not merely as passing or "non-harmonic" sounds. As we have seen, the English had long shown a liking for this interval, but it seems not to have been shared by their colleagues on the continent until the English composer John Dunstable (c. 1385-1453) accompanied the Duke of Bedford, Regent of France who fought against Jeanne d'Arc, to that country in 1422. It would appear that Dunstable and other visiting English composers did much to change the French, or to be more exact, the Burgundian style during these years, for not long after, at the court of the Duke of Burgundy, there appeared one of the foremost composers of the time, Guillaume Dufay (c. 1400-1474).

The graceful and courtly secular works of this master composer depend less upon canonic and imitative devices than do the works of the preceding period, or those which follow. The lines are smooth and vocal, expressive with a warm, rather romantic sentiment which often reflects the meaning of the text. The sound ideal of the Burgundian group of composers, of which Dufay was a part, seems to have been a transparent, rather high-pitched sonority, ideal for the presentation of beautifully written polyphonic lines. Much of the church music, particularly that of the early part of the period, is composed in the same manner as the secular chansons, but a more reserved sacred style begins to develop in the late works of Dufay and others, a manner which is the forerunner of the polyphonic sacred style of the Renaissance. While Dufay wrote both sacred and secular music, his most famous contemporary, Gilles Binchois (1400-1460) largely confined himself to the secular and sensuous chanson. These miniatures are in keeping with the manuscript illuminations of the time, depicting with almost photographic clarity, if not fidelity, scenes of lovers, courtly dances and peasant frolics.

The next generation of composers carried on the development of a church style, each in his own individual fashion, to be sure, but tending toward a unified style which we shall call "Netherlands style" in the next chapter. Among these composers, Ockeghem (c. 1425-1495) and Obrecht (1430-1505), wrote much music that is all too seldom heard today. They were given to exploiting the possibilities of complex canonic and imitative writing, a trait which did not endear them to many historians, particularly those of the nineteenth century, who characterized these works as dry, complicated exercises in ingenuity rather than music. The modern listener, more accustomed to today's complex procedures is apt to find them beautiful, moving compositions, despite — or perhaps because of — the complexities of mirror canons, retrograde imitations and the like. In the music of Josquin des Près, however, a complete mastery of material and form is achieved, and we have arrived at the first great composer of the Renaissance, one who, in Martin Luther's words, was "master of the notes." In Josquin's music, artifice becomes art in the modern sense of the word. Imitation and canon disappear in the musical flow, whether it be a lament over empty pockets (*"Faulte d'Argent"*), or a moving piece of sacred music such as the *"Veni Creator Spiritus."* Most of the advance in style achieved by these three composers depends upon the treatment of dissonance. Whereas, in earlier compositions, each part agreed with the bass but not necessarily with each other, now all dissonant intervals are controlled, deriving from motion of the parts or from the use of stylized figures which resolve the dissonance to a consonance on the next metric pulsation. The general quality is one of consonance, for with this treatment the dissonance tends to be absorbed, and functions largely as a sonority which supports the rhythmic pulse. We shall try to define the style more clearly in its several aspects in the next section, where such a discussion is more appropriate.

To sum up then: we are indebted musically to the Middle Ages for the modal scales, notation, polyphony, concepts and treatment of consonance and dissonance and for a rich treasure of beautiful music, as enjoyable today as it was centuries ago, albeit from a somewhat different aspect. We should not regard this literature with disdain merely because it was written before the development of the melodic, harmonic or rhythmic features of music to which we are accustomed. The centuries from 600 to 1450 contain great and moving musical works if we will but take the time to understand them on their own terms and in their own times.

MUSICAL EXAMPLES

1. Deutsche Grammaphon Archive Production, ARC 3052. Motets of Dunstable, chansons by Ockeghem.
2. HMS Vol. III. Music by Dunstable, Dufay, Binchois, Ockeghem, Obrecht, de la Rue, Josquin des Près, as well as English and instrumental music from this period.
3. Pre-Baroque Sacred Music, FLP 70-202. Contains a Magnificat by Dufay, *"Veni Creator Spiritus"* by des Près, and other music of the early and late Renaissance.
4. Guillaume Dufay, Secular Works, EMS 206. An interesting selection of vocal and instrumental music by this master.
5. Josquin, Secular Works, EMS 213. Similar to the preceding. Contains Josquin's lament on the death of his master, Ockeghem.
6. MM Vol. I. Selections by Dufay, Binchois, Ockeghem, Obrecht and des Près.

# COMPARISON OF MEDIEVAL MUSIC WITH THE OTHER ARTS

When we examine the European architecture, sculpture and painting of the centuries between 600 and 1450, we are confronted with such a dazzling wealth of material that choices of individual works for examination are difficult. It becomes obvious from an examination of this art that masterpieces may occur at any time, and that art from 1450 to the present become not necessarily any better, but only different.

A few generalizations may be made about these centuries, however. We have noted the preponderance of church music; a similar situation exists in all of the other arts, for the Church employed them to present important religious teachings clearly and symbolically to the generally illiterate populace. Thus we have the hundreds of depictions in paint, stone or glass of the Annunciation, the Crucifixion, the Resurrection and the Ascension, as well as scenes from the lives of the Apostles and saints which adorn the altars, walls, windows and doorways of churches throughout these two periods. At first, the figures are impersonal — the portrait does not exist — but later, there is a change from the stiff ceremonial figures to characterizations consistent with the historical personality of the saint or sinner represented. Perspective, almost

PLATE VII. *St. Francis of Assisi by Berlinghieri from the Church of San Francesco, Pescia, Italy. Note the Byzantine impersonality of the figure in which all irregularities are omitted, thus creating a symbol rather than a portrait. (Photo Alinari, Florence.)*

entirely absent in the Romanesque, develops as we move toward the Renaissance, until, with Leonardo da Vinci, Michelangelo and others, it forms a highly important part of the painter's technique. Much of the art of both periods is dominated by architecture, and we find the subjects enclosed in arches or alcoves which are essentially part of the picture, not the frame. Little by little these give way to encircling bands of angels or cherubs whose structural function is similar. Both the arches and the angels do much to enhance the symmetry of these pictures, a quality which had the mystical significance in the Middle Ages of demonstrating the order of the universe and the harmony of all things therein.

Romanesque art is a development of the Byzantine mosaic, a medium in which small pieces of highly colored glass or pottery were set in cement to form designs and pictures. These mosaic representations of religious figures were highly stylized and impersonal, symbolic in the strongest sense of the word. When painters of the Romanesque illustrated Biblical stories, they copied these symbols, making them hardly less austere and impersonal. The outlines of the figures were clear, the faces were shown either in profile — a favorite pose — or full face, and perspective was nonexistent (Plate VII). In these respects, this art resembles the coexistent plainchant, for it is music in profile, with no harmonic perspective, impersonal, meditative and otherworldly. The earthbound church architecture of the time, dark because of the small windows which did not weaken the strength of the massive walls required to uphold the heavy horizontal roof, was full of dim corners where man could be alone with his meditations and his God. The dark color of male voices singing in the narrow and limited range of tone allowed to plainchant, itself meditative and prayerful, is the natural sound-parallel to the architectural style (Plate V).

In the Gothic era, the spirit of man began to expand in both earthly and heavenly directions (Plate VI). The sloping cathedral roof, shaped like an inverted V, was upheld by flying buttresses and supported upon a series of pointed Gothic arches pierced with large windows, so that the entire structure had a lightness and airiness both inside and out. No longer resting heavily upon the earth like the Romanesque church, it seemed ready to ascend to heaven like the prayers of the worshippers inside. We find a parallel in the music of the times, ranging from the massiveness of Perotin's quadruple organa to the transparency of Machaut's isorhythmically supported polyphony.

The Perotin polyphony, consisting of the rhythmic progression of

PLATE VIII. "Maria im Rosenhag" ("Mary in the Rosegarden") by Leonard Lochner (d. 1450). Note the late Gothic profusion of decoration similar to that used in illuminating manuscripts. In the original the predominating colors are rose, blue and gold. (Archive-German Information Center.)

quite individual voice lines above an equally rhythmic plainchant cantus firmus, strongly resembles the concentric bands of the tympanum above the doorway to a church or the long rows of statues such as those found in Chartres. In each, the individuality of the figure, whether it is rhythmic or statuesque, is lost in the endless sequence of similar figures. And the lines of the later Ars Nova style quite clearly call to mind the pointed and decorated Gothic arch not only in shape, but also in firmness of structure: like the apparently too slender piers of the arches which support the building, so does each note of the fragile polyphony exert its strength to uphold the structure built on the firm, but invisible, isorhythm.

By the end of the Gothic age, architecture, art and music have become exceedingly elegant and decorated. Indeed, the period is called "flamboyant" in most histories of architecture. Here we have the suave music of Dufay and the winding traceries of Ockeghem and Obrecht.

The sweetness of the third has entered music, and a similar sweetness, albeit somewhat artificial at times, permeates some of the painting, along with a trend toward a certain degree of naturalness. Like the art, music gained a warmth and humanity which was missing in the Romanesque and early Gothic periods. In the painting by Lochner (Plate VIII), we see a charming Madonna, ensconced in a Gothic rose garden surrounded by small musical angels, holding the infant Jesus who is no longer represented as a miniature man, as He was in earlier times, but now as a real baby. The colors are clear and transparent, the lines are sharp, the composition is closed and the counterpoint of straight, parallel, horizontal and vertical lines versus the enclosing curves and the curved lines of the figure are all closely comparable to the music of the Burgundians, with Dufay as the chief example.

## LIST OF TERMS

| | |
|---|---|
| Romanesque | Ars Nova |
| Gothic | canon |
| modal scales | imitation |
| final | cantus firmus |
| Plainchant, Gregorian chant | isorhythm |
| monophonic texture | perfect consonances |
| syllabic chant | |
| neumatic chant | Pythagoras |
| melismatic chant | Pope Gregory |
| psalmodic chant | Adam de la Halle |
| Mass | Leonin |
| Ordinary, Proper | Perotin |
| minstrels | Guillaume Machaut |
| troubadours, trouvères | Francesco Landini |
| mensural notation | John Dunstable |
| rhythmic modes | Guillaume Dufay |
| neumes | Gilles Binchois |
| organum | Ockeghem |
| polyphony | Obrecht |
| Ars Antiqua | Josquin des Près |

# IV The Renaissance Period, 1450-1600

## HISTORICAL PERSPECTIVE

The year 1450 is often accepted as a date marking the "rebirth" of learning, art and music. As we have seen, the change in music had been moving in this direction for some time, and the date 1450 has a certain arbitrariness about it. Nevertheless, it is a time when interest in humanity, both past and present, and the world as the setting for humanity, not merely a step to salvation, increased to the point where it overpowered the old Gothic attitudes. The rediscovery of classical antiquity was a revelation to philosophers, artists, architects, sculptors and scientists. Workers in the plastic arts and architects by the scores emulated the serene style of the ancients, and most men with any pretensions to culture studied and often spoke Greek and Latin in their "Academies." Science made advances in the investigation and discovery of important natural laws in physics, astronomy and medicine, often risking the terrors of the Inquisition for the sake of scientific truth. Great individuals arose who strove to make their marks upon the time — Lorenzo de Medici, Cesare Borgia, Francis I of France, Henry VIII and Elizabeth I of England, Machiavelli, Erasmus, Savonarola, Galileo, Copernicus, Paracelsus, Luther, Calvin, Knox, Raphael, Leonardo da Vinci, Michelangelo, Dürer, Titian, Gutenburg, Caxton, Palestrina, Lassus, Monteverdi; the list seems endless. This was the time of the last great struggle between church and state, of the Reformation and Counter-Reformation and the Inquisition. Exploration of the New World, followed by exploitation and colonization went on apace. It was, by our standards, an uncivilized and immoral age in many ways, individually, religiously and politically, yet it produced men whose examples and works have had a civilizing influence of incomparable power upon later times.

The literature of music from this period is one of the richest treasures of the past. There is no break with the preceding development of music, however, as there is in some other branches of culture, but only the eternal alternation between the repose of classic style and the agitation of romanticism. After the growing and inventive exuberance of the Gothic style, which really ended when Dunstable introduced and Dufay accepted the third as a consonance, a reversion to more classic ideals permeated the first years of the Renaissance until about 1530. The Netherlands polyphonic style became established, and the early frottole and madrigals appeared, along with the sacred music of Josquin, the first paintings of Raphael and the literature of Bramante. But the tenor of the times changed around 1530, and strong individuals arose who swam with the romantic tide, and probably had some effect in creating it. Among their works were the statues of Michelangelo, whose muscles seem to strain against the confines of their rigid substance, the jolly and vulgar peasants of Breughel, the lusty wit of Rabelais, and the daring, albeit hidden chromaticisms and modulations of Netherlands church music composers. In the latter instance, the music appears perfectly straightforward upon the page, with no excessive shapes or flats. But the combinations of certain harmonic or melodic intervals indicated to the trained singer that "corrections" in the form of raising or lowering one of the intervals were to be applied. This led to further corrections to adjust the succeeding parts to those first altered, and the whole process resulted in highly colored and emotionally-charged harmonic progressions. These, in true romantic fashion, often appeared as musical illustrations of some facet of the text.

However, in 1567, the tide turned toward serenity of expression in the mystic and refined music of Palestrina, Victoria and Morales, the Roman style of the architect Palladio and the idealizations on canvas of Bronzino. Paradoxically, however, certain countercurrents existed simultaneously with these ideals, eventually mixing with them to form a richer baroque style, especially in music. In art, Veronese and, in music, Giovanni Gabrieli (both significantly Venetians) handled the problems of brilliant color and mass with the greatest boldness. And Don Carlo Gesualdo, Prince of Venosa, created vignettes of tortured emotionalism out of the hitherto stylized and musically discreet madrigal. Yet certain indications of symmetry and balance occur in these and also in works of the romantic middle period of the Renaissance, showing that the elements of classical composition and structure were still exerting influence. Despite the wealth of music from this time, the major popular interest lay in painting, sculpture and architecture, especially during the early part of the period. An increasing emphasis upon and mastery of tonal materials developed as the culminating date 1600 was approached.

Nevertheless, music was an important adornment to life in those days. Princes vied with each other to secure noted and skillful composers for their courts, and paid and lodged them handsomely during their tenure. Consistent with the ideal of the Renaissance man, versed in all branches of learning and action, music was an important part of almost every gentleman's education. One was expected to be able to sing a part in the after-dinner performances of madrigals, or to play passably upon the lute, viol, recorder or keyboard instruments. The spinet and virginal — small household versions of the larger and more expensive harpsichord — were quite common, and provided delicate and sensitive music for gatherings of intimate friends. Many outstanding men of the time were proud of their musical accomplishments — Henry VIII of England, for example — and to raise the musical level of the common folk, popular instruction books were written, usually in dialogue form between a master and student, explaining in detail the mysteries of the art, and even how to compose a madrigal. Such a book is Thomas Morely's *A Plaine and Easie Introduction to Practicall Musicke* (1597), a charming discourse which sums up the theory and practice of Renaissance popular music in England.

The new art of printing contributed much to the dissemination of music. Previous to this, all music was copied by hand, often with artistic and beautiful results, but at considerable expense and sometimes with inaccuracy. Now many copies could be struck off a single set of plates, thus distributing the cost and lowering the price of each single volume. It was the custom to print only the part-books at this time. So few compositions exist in score, showing the complete combinations

PLATE IX. *"A Concert" by Costa. The center figure plays a lute, while in the foreground are a fiddle and bow, a straight cornet and a book of music. (Reproduced by courtesy of the Trustees, The National Gallery of Art, London.)*

94

of the parts, that it has been surmised that the composers actually wrote many works in part books. Considering the complexity of some of the compositions, this was no small achievement.

Italy was one of the major sources of music during the Renaissance, but she achieved this distinction through the efforts of musicians imported from the Netherlands by her nobility. Josquin himself, as well as scores of his fellow-countrymen were hired by the churches and aristocratic houses to furnish music for ritual or enjoyment, often to sing or play, or to direct others in these activities. The scarcity of music by genuine Italian composers until the middle of the sixteenth century is quite amazing. The Netherlanders brought their polyphonic style with them and grafted it upon the tree of Italian culture so firmly that it remained a part of Italy's tradition for several centuries, particularly in church music. In the same way, they influenced Italian secular music with their chansons, which also helped to shape Italian instrumental music. And when we consider that the English received the models of their renaissance style from the Italians, we begin to see the far-reaching influence of the men from the Low Countries. Germany was slow in entering the cultural trends of the times, but she too profited by having these men in important musical posts in the courts, cathedrals and towns.

For the purposes of our study, we shall divide the music of the Renaissance into three important categories: sacred music, secular music and instrumental music. The sacred music consisted, as heretofore, of the Masses, motets and psalm settings, plus the chorales of the new Protestant churches which were destined to be of greater importance in the seventeenth and early eighteenth centuries. The secular music of Italy and England produced as its most typical form the madrigal, matched in many ways by the chanson in France. Originally, vocal music provided literature for instruments, and was transferred to them with no change. Toward the end of the Renaissance, however, these vocal works became only models for compositions written to fit more closely the style, tone or idiom of certain instruments, and thus began an important branch of the art which in later centuries tended to overshadow in significance music for the voice. Lurking behind each of these divisions, more visible in some than others, is the unifying technique of the Netherlands polyphonic style. It becomes slightly modified in the works of composers with strong personalities, such as Josquin, Victoria and Lassus, and is heard in probably its most refined form in the works of Palestrina.

# THE MUSICAL STYLE OF THE RENAISSANCE

## MELODY

Melody as such is probably of less importance in this style than in many others for the simple reason that it becomes submerged in the polyphonic flow. Often dramatic melodic ideas are not desired, especially in the sacred music. Many times the composers seem to have been more interested in the total texture than in any individual part. For these reasons, the melodic ideas are not usually memorable. They are eminently singable, however, with rather close restrictions upon the size and direction of skips, the requirement that the line shall turn back when it has made one of these skips, and similar tendencies which unite to produce a refined vocal line. This line often reaches its highest point near its beginning and descends gently in a succession of short arcs to its final note.

## HARMONY

The harmonic combinations in this style are all triads — major, minor, rarely the more unstable diminished or the chromatically derived augmented triad — and they are obtained from the various modal scales, often including the Ionian mode, or major, and the Aeolian mode, or minor (Example 23). The triads are used in their most stable positions, with either the root or the third of the chord in the bass, hence the music is predominantly consonant and stable. The harmony is not functional; that is, we feel little sense of movement toward a cadential goal in this music, not only because the triads built upon the modal finals do not exert the strong pull characteristic of our major and minor tonal scales, but also because the chord succession seems absolutely free, unmotivated, and, to modern ears, wandering. The only point at which the harmony tends to take on functional motion is at final cadence points where the V, IV, and I chords are often made major, if they are otherwise minor, in order to create a strong authentic or plagal cadence. The interior cadences are usually left in their purely modal state, and weakened by the overlapping of sections, thus creating a continuous flow of music. Often these interior cadences seem entirely incidental and unimportant to the total composition.

Dissonance is very strictly controlled in the Netherlands style, and is one of the least obvious features of the music, although it is present to a considerable degree, at least when the written music is examined. In performance, it seems to be absorbed into the general consonance, and creates little instability. It is derived from the motion of the voice parts through the formula *consonance-dissonance-consonance,* and may appear only as a result of certain standard usages which, in part, help to create the style.

### RHYTHM

The rhythm of this music is individual with each voice line. The note durations follow the syllabic accentuation according to a general rule which specifies a long note for each accented syllable, thus creating accents of duration rather than dynamic stress. In polyphonic texture, these "agogic" accents create a subtle and interestingly random interplay among the voices.

Otherwise, the music moves to a steady unaccented pulse in simple

EXAMPLE 23.

Excerpt from PARODY MASS:
VENI SPONSA CHRISTI                                    PALESTRINA
SECTION TAKEN FROM THE "Agnus Dei"

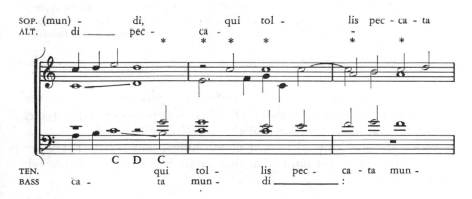

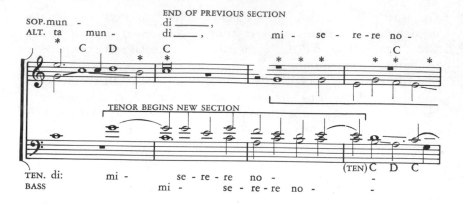

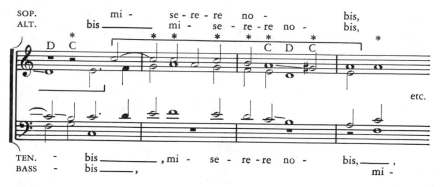

LEGEND

a. First motet section ends at beginning of measure 5 of this example; new section actually begins on third count of measure 4 by tenor announcement of the subject, which is then imitated in all parts (see bracketed notes).

b. C-D-C refers to suspension figure in which note is first consonant, then dissonant due to the movement of the other voices, then moves downward a step ("resolves") to create a consonant triad.

c. * indicates full triad constructions.

duple or triple meter, the former preferred in polyphonic sections, the other in homophonic portions. The rhythm is preponderantly stable, like the harmony, and pervades the gentle flow of metric pulsations which move at about the speed of the human heartbeat. There are no indications in the music that this tempo is ever intended to accelerate or retard.

### TEXTURE

Polyphony is the preferred texture for church music, relieved by rather short sections of homophony, usually in triple meter. Most polyphonic compositions begin imitatively and frequently employ this device rather consistently throughout. Often two parts are written in canon with polyphonic accompaniment by the others. Writing in four parts (soprano, alto, tenor, bass) had become quite standard, but for purposes of greater sonority, five and six parts were often employed, usually resulting from the addition of one or two new parts for the soprano (thus, soprano I and II), alto or tenor, rarely the bass. For interesting three-dimensional effects, polychoral writing was sometimes used; that is, compositions were planned for two or more spatially separated choruses which answered each other, or from time to time combined their forces. We shall find this technique to be a traditional one at the Cathedral of St. Mark in Venice, a technique which foreshadowed and led to the style of the Baroque in the seventeenth century.

### SONORITY

The Renaissance sound ideal is one of light-colored, transparent music of medium dynamic level, with few dramatic contrasts. The tone colors were secured by the ranges of the voices employed and by the spacing and quality of the harmony. Both sonority and harmony tended toward expressive extremes as the period drew to a close, but were balanced, mild and classical for the greater part of the era.

## FORMAL AND GENERATIVE PRINCIPLES

All of the forms of renaissance music are what might be termed "text-based" in that the lengths of musical sections are dependent upon the phrases, clauses or sentences of the text. These texts, in sacred music, consisted of the words of the Mass (especially the Ordinary), psalms and other biblical selections used in the rituals. Settings of this kind, exclusive of the Mass texts, were called "motets."

In secular music, any poem, however light or serious its subject matter, was material for the composer of madrigals. However, this poetry became very stylized during the first century of the Renaissance in order to make it more suitable to the elegant manners and music of the mid-century culture.

The motet-style of composition, as it is called, generally consists of overlapping imitative sections, each with its own melodic subject which bears the beginning words of a new phrase of the text (Example 23). Usually these melodic subjects are not repeated later in the work, but suffice to provide beginnings for only their section. In addition, there is generally no thematic development of these subjects, in the sense that motives are reworked and varied, although in some of the compositions of Josquin both repetition and a small amount of thematic development occur. The smaller sections of a composition are welded together by the introduction of the subject of the next section in one voice while the others are closing the previous one with a modal, and therefore usually somewhat indecisive, cadence. This procedure may be used throughout an entire composition, with the only strong cadence appearing at the end.

In order to unify this "run-on" series of sections in some degree, many devices were developed. One of these was to use canonic writing in each of the several movements of a Mass — a large structure which needed more than the consistency of melodic and harmonic style to hold it together musically. Such a technique recalls Machaut's use of isorhythm for the same purpose. And another device of that composer was also adopted, that of using a melodic or rhythmic fragment repeatedly in fairly prominent parts of each of the movements. The old cantus firmus technique was a frequent means of unification, although now the composers did not always use plainchant for the cantus, but often adopted popular songs for this purpose. Some of these, we might add, originally had texts which were extremely secular! Usually, however, the song melody is so buried in the texture that only the singers performing it might recognize it. And if it were recognized, it perhaps provided a moment of enjoyable recognition to the layman in the congregation. In any case, it is not until the late Renaissance that we read of the clergy complaining about the inroads of secular song into the sacred music of the Church. These cantus firmus masses are often named after the text upon which they are erected, as in the many settings from the fifteenth to the early seventeenth century based upon the song *"L'Homme Armé."* Perhaps the most complicated, most "modern" technique aimed at unification of the movements of the mass was one in which the entire musical structure — melody, harmonic successions and rhythms — of a pre-existent motet or secular composition was varied and extended to form each of the movements of the Ordinary. Such a "parody mass," as it is called, is also named after the source of the material used in it. (Example 23). Both the cantus firmus masses and the parody masses are examples of "cyclic" structure, so called because of the return of the basic material in each of the movements. We shall hear this term again when we study the symphonies of the Romantic period.

The methods and techniques of performance had a considerable effect upon the construction of the music also. The composers wrote for an ideal chorus of unaccompanied voices — the so-called *a cappella* style. Thus, the combined voice parts had to make complete and euphonious musical sense without relying upon a "fill-in" accompaniment. In practice, however, it seems quite certain that instruments were often employed to render the parts more secure in pitch or to reinforce the sound. In addition, it also seems quite certain that the singers took what we feel to be unwarranted liberties with the music, adding flourishes and freehand ornaments to the long-drawn, serene lines of the polyphony. This aroused ecclesiastical wrath, but seems to have left the composers unmoved! We must understand that written music in this period and for the following two centuries was regarded by performers as the skeleton upon which they were licensed to hang any amount of decoration their fancies and tastes suggested. One of the first objectors to this practice was the great baroque composer, Handel, who threatened to throw one of his leading sopranos out of the window if she did not sing his music exactly as he had written it. But it would seem that the Renaissance composer was more liberal in this respect. At any rate, we now perform the music exactly as written — even more strictly, without accompanying instruments — than did the people of the Renaissance.


# S A C R E D   M U S I C

*"Ave Maria"* by Josquin des Près (MM Vol. I, band 19).

This motet is freely based upon a plainchant and draws motives from it which are used throughout in a discontinuous manner: in a sense, this is a choral variation of the chant. To be noticed first, are the imitations of the opening subject announced by the tenors, imitated after the first three notes by the sopranos, then altos, and finally basses, who sing only four full measures before the first section, devoted to the words *"Ave Maria, gratia plena,"* comes to a cadence. The sopranos and tenors finish the cadential measure, and as they conclude, a new figure begins in the alto to the words *"Dominus tecum,"* consisting of a long note followed by short notes in a descending scale pattern. The motion is fairly continuous from section to section, and the modality sometimes makes it difficult for modern listeners to determine when a cadence actually does occur. Many of them use chromatically altered notes and dissonance to heighten the conclusive feeling, but the movement of other voices through the cadence, bent upon melodic movement of their own, makes the effect anything but final. Josquin often treats the voices in pairs, in this way giving symmetry to the form and lightness and variety to the texture. There is a very final-sounding cadence about two-thirds of the way through, and after a pause, the music resumes, now in triple meter, and more or less homophonic in texture, although the way that Josquin deploys the voices in groups of two or three nevertheless gives the music a slight feeling of polyphony. There is a short concluding section in quadruple meter which brings back the scale figure mentioned above, and the motet concludes with a plagal cadence (IV-I). Note the flowing quality of the motion and the smoothness of the vocal writing.[1]

*"Tristis est anima mea,"* by Orlando Lassus (MM Vol. II, band 1).

This motet, representative of sacred music of the High Renaissance, exhibits many of the stylistic features of the preceding one. However, it is written for five voices rather than four, and has a sonority of greater richness. There is no insistence upon clearly defined imitations, and, except for a few places in the second half, the imitations employ only two notes: the sound is rather homophonic for this reason. Lassus uses text-painting to some degree in this motet, although this technique is more frequent in secular than sacred music. An outstanding example is the musical pun on the word *"fugum,"* which, in the text, means "to flee." The musical meaning implies imitation — eventually crystallizing in the form known as *fugue* — and Lassus treats it so repeatedly, using a descending scale figure of five notes imitated every other beat for a total of eleven imitations! Evidently he does not want us to miss it! The whole piece is written in the Ionian (major) mode.

*"Agnus Dei"* (1) from the Mass *Veni sponsa Christi* by Palestrina (MM Vol. II, band 2; Example 23 in part).

The mass from which this movement is drawn is a parody mass based upon Palestrina's own motet, *"Veni sponsa Christi,"* which in turn is written on the plainchant melody of this antiphon. Palestrina usually begins a movement, as here, with two voices in canon for a longer period of time than did either Josquin or Lassus. The imitation is then taken up by the other voices, here bass and tenor, while the other parts sing free (non-imitative) counterpoint above them. The overlapping section technique is plainly in evidence here. Now and then a voice drops out of the texture, but not with the regularity with which Josquin does it: in this work we expect the re-entry of the missing voice, whereas in the music of Josquin, it is obvious that there is to be a short section for only two (or three) voices.

*"Ego sum panis vivus,"* by William Byrd (MM Vol. II, band 3).

This music, by perhaps the greatest English composer of church music during the Renaissance, exhibits his personality within the narrow range in which this is possible in the style. Particularly noticeable after the smoothly flowing rhythms of Lassus and Palestrina is the more broken quality of Byrd's treatment, enlivening the texture with cross rhythms and elongating the phrases until the even duple pulsation is lost or changed into sextuple. Notice the text-painting on the words *"descendit"* (came down), *"vivus"* (living — in faster note values) and *"coelo"* (heaven — on a high note). The concluding "Alleluia" uses repeated note-patterns beginning on scalewise ascending or descending steps (sequence), a device which is rather rare at this time.

The four examples discussed above should illustrate the style; they only hint at the multitude of works of the Catholic church composers of this period. Other works by these composers should be explored, and many are available on recordings. Josquin's *Missa Pange Lingua*, the *Missa Brevis* and the *Missa Papae Marcelli* of Palestrina, the *Lamentations of Jeremiah* by Lassus, the masses and motets of De Monte, Byrd, Tallis, Gibbons, and the emotional fervor of the works of the Spaniards Victoria and Morales — all these are available in their full richness of devotional expression.

The Protestant churches which arose during the Reformation turned away from the elaborateness of the Catholic service music in one degree or another, and often sought for church music which would be closer to the people. The most important kind of this music to survive to modern times is the Lutheran chorale which was derived from many sources. Luther remarked that "the devil should not have all the best tunes," and thus popular and folk songs were rearranged and given Reformation texts, as were some plainchants familiar to the congregation. Luther himself, it is said, composed some of the tunes, most noteworthy of which is *"Ein feste Burg"* ("A Mighty Fortress") with which we shall have to do later. These chorale melodies were used as the basis of many instrumental preludes and postludes to be played in church services, and were also harmonized homophonically for congregational singing by many Protestant composers up to J. S. Bach. We sing them today in church: at Christmas, "Lo How a Rose E'er Blooming," "From Heaven High," "How Brightly Shines the Morning Star," and at Easter, the Passion chorale "O Sacred Head," "Christ Lay in Death's Dark Prison," "Christ Is Arisen" and many others. The real development of these chorales, however, belongs to the succeeding era, the Baroque.

The Huguenots felt quite differently about music and replaced the elaborate Catholic liturgy with one in which music played a fairly small part. The hymns sung by the congregation were in the simplest homophonic style and were based on a hymn-tune placed in the tenor part like a cantus firmus. We still sing some of these in church, most notably the Doxology "Praise God from Whom all blessings flow." Oddly enough, elaborate, motet-like arrangements were made for family devotional use. But it may be safely said that in general, the French Protestants distrusted what seemed to them to be the pagan and Romish power of ritual music, thus retarding the progress of this branch of the art for many years in Switzerland, Scotland and some of the American colonies.

## SECULAR MUSIC

When we think of popular music in this period, the term *madrigal* comes first to mind, as well it should, for it was assiduously cultivated, first in the land of its birth and later in England. The contemporane-

EXAMPLE 24.

"QUANDRO RITROVA"                                   COSTANZO FESTA

Quan - do ri - tro - va la mi - a pas - to - rel - la

Al      pra - to con      le pe - cor' in pas - tu - ra,

etc.

lo mi gli a - cos - t'e pres - to la sa - lu - ta

> When I discover my little shepherdess
> In the meadow with the sheep at pasture,
> I go to her and quickly greet her.

*Historical Anthology, Harvard University Press, 1949

ous French chanson, similar in many respects to the madrigal, is the other important form of the time (Plate IX).

The Italian madrigal began as the *frottola*, a short, homophonic choral work for four voices, with dance-like rhythms and a simple text, often pastoral in nature. Example 24 shows the typical appearance of this kind of composition. Note the chordal style, the absence of imitation or other polyphonic devices, the dance rhythm and the pastoral text. This piece, although called a madrigal, is very close to the original frottola. Costanzo Festa, the composer, was one of the few native Italians to compete with the Netherland invasion which brought such men as Philippe Verdelot (1480-1540), Jacob Arcadelt (1505-1560) and Adrian Willaert (1505-1560) to the sunny peninsula. The works of these men are usually somewhat more polyphonic than our first example and establish the style of the madrigal for the remainder of the period.

The main features of this somewhat more advanced style are these: (1) the use of modal scales, although a tendency toward major is evident; (2) the parts are easily sung; (3) the usually amorous text is carefully set so that the accents of the words become musical accents of height, duration or metrical accents; (4) there is somewhat more emphasis upon metrical or "bar-line" rhythm, and dance-like rhythmic patterns often appear, especially in homophonic sections; (5) the text is treated in the manner of a motet, one line per section, sometimes with slightly varied repetition in order to expand the section; (6) there is frequent use of overlapping parts at cadence points in order to weaken the finality of the cadence and promote the flowing movement of the music; (7) there is a free alternation between polyphonic and homophonic texture, depending upon the expression of the words or the desire of the composer to emphasize the text; and finally, (8) the music interprets the symbolism or description of each line or phrase by means of text-painting. Example 25, by Jacob Arcadelt, illustrates a number of these points. Here the piece begins with an imitation of the rising skip of the tenor part, followed by a scale line which descends in the bass and tenor, but pulls away from them in the soprano and alto, illustrating by this contrary motion the concept of "going heavenward." There is a cadence on the first beat of measure 4, but the next phrase begins immediately in the bass, followed by a change to homophonic texture in measures 5 and 6. Again the overlapping and imitation begin the new phrase "Co'l vostro chiaro lum'e," turning to homophonic texture for a measure before establishing a more important cadence on the first beat of measure 12. Since this is the final phrase of the line, followed by a period and requiring an important structural cadence, Arcadelt repeats the phrase "Co'l vostro chiaro" . . . ("With your bright light and my songs"), and reaches the end of the first section at measure 16. The intervals used in the

Example 25.

"VOI VE N ANDAT' AL CIELO"                                    JACOB ARCADELT

†Ye     go heaven-ward                                        eyes

blessed     and     holy,     with     your

bright     light     and     my songs,                    with . . .

. . . songs          etc.

*Historical Anthology, Harvard Univ. Press. 1949
†Translation not intended for singing.

107

parts are "natural" skips of thirds, fourths and fifths, plus much stepwise motion. The vocal lines are graceful and flowing, and the modal harmony exhibits several pleasant spots, even though the piece is centered about the F-major scale.

The middle period, so-called "classical madrigal," shows little change from the foregoing, except possibly more polish and expressive writing, and somewhat more emphasis upon text-painting. Generally, there is a more liberal use of sharped and flatted notes to widen the harmonic range (*i.e.,* a chord naturally minor in the mode may now be made major, and vice-versa), as well as to increase the finality of structural cadences. The composers of this period are still predominantly Netherlanders — Cipriano de Rore (1516-1565), Philippe de Monte (1521-1603) and the peripatetic Orlando Lassus (1532-1594).

Balanced between the classicism of the middle period and the expressionism of the third, is Luca Marenzio (1553-1599), called the "sweetest swan of Italy" by one of his contemporaries. His wedding madrigal, *"Scendo dal paradiso"* (Descend from paradise) forms the excerpt of Example 26. Here are the same general devices as before, but noteworthy is the way Marenzio increases upward the range used by the upper voices. Observe the falling scale line which depicts the descent of Venus from paradise and the E♭ in measure 12 on the word "guida" (literally guide), a tone which strongly "guides" the chord toward the resolution on the next chord. This is the first such chromaticism to appear in this madrigal, a fact which lends it special significance in conjunction with the text, for these composers write for the eyes of their singers as well as for their voices! Later, the Graces are given properly graceful lines, and the laughter is dealt with quite realistically. Note the change to homophony for the portrayal of serenity near the end of the printed excerpt. In this madrigal, there is much more text-painting than in the previous one, and the text is richer in illustrative words: just such texts were sought for madrigals by the composers of this period. They deal with approximately the same subjects as popular music does today, except that there are frequent allusions to mythological gods and goddesses, places and happenings, and the style of the poetry is apt to sound rather artificial and stilted to us. Nevertheless, the emotional Italian temperament treated many of these verses, especially if they dealt with some aspect — any aspect — of love, with the utmost intensity of expression current in the musical vocabulary.

Indeed, the final period of the madrigal is one of romantic

EXAMPLE 26.

(Original note-values halved)

*etc.*
(Sung a semitone higher)

TRANSLATION

Descend from Paradise, O Venus, and bring with you your little Cupids. May the Graces and laughter be gayer than is their wont, and beneath a tranquil sky may the Tiber bear to the Tyrrhenian Sea his horn adorned with pearls instead of water.

---

expressionism, for the composers turned away from the representation of the most obvious nouns and verbs of their texts, and lavished their imaginative and technical resources upon the delineation of emotional states. Now, while "ascending," "laughter" and even "serenity" have obvious musical interpretations, how shall such terms as "death," "life" and "unhappiness" be translated into tones? Not by musical patterns or figures, but by that unique dimension of music which moves the emotions quickly — harmony. But this is only a part, although important, of the whole picture, for effective harmony must be combined with exactly the right melodic, rhythmic and textural components to achieve the desired effect. The two outstanding madrigal composers of the late Renaissance, Carlo Gesualdo (1560-1613) and Claudio Monteverdi (1567-1643), possessed the genius to do this. These romantic compositions which hint at the imminent end of an era, are really miniature music-dramas whose intensity is all the greater for being compressed into a few measures. Melodic and harmonic chromaticism, strangely twisted chord progressions, difficult vocal writing, obsession with the interpretation of a single key word and morbid texts: these are all components of the madrigal of the passing Renaissance. One of the most famous is *"Moro lasso"* ("Let me die") by Gesualdo (Example 27), which has hardly been surpassed as a tonal portrait of despair since its publication in 1611. Gesualdo goes beyond mere text-painting here, for what he is seeking to depict are the psychological states suggested by important words of the text. The means are largely harmonic, and consist of progressions of unrelated chords such as that which opens the piece. Here the composer goes beyond not only the modal system of his time, but also beyond the tonal system of the next three hundred years to achieve a startlingly modern effect. Listen to the melodic and harmonic chromaticism which appears on the words "morta" and "moro" (death, die). More conventional text-painting is reserved for "vita" (life), consisting of rapidly moving notes. Note the striking despair of the unprepared chromaticism on "Ahi" (alas) each time it occurs, and the clash of the soprano part of the word "darmia" in the phrase "e non vuol darmia vita." After this point, the whole verse is repeated with minor changes in text but with considerable alteration and expansion in the musical treatment, which is still, however, roughly parallel with the music of the previous verse. The concluding two lines, beginning "O dolorosa sorte" ("O unhappy fate") provide an ending which abounds in dissonance (the soprano "Ahi" on the high F), unexpected resolutions, and chromatic voice-leading. To modern ears, the final chord sounds almost a little too tame, coming as it does after such emotional intensity, but upon recollection, one finds that most of the chords in the piece are just such major triads!

Not all of the madrigals of this composer are so intense in feeling, for he wrote many of the more conventional kind, but those by which we remember him best are the advanced ones like *"Io pur respiro"* ("I still breathe in such deep sorrow"), *"Io tacero"* ("I shall keep

EXAMPLE 27.

Alas,  he kills me    and does not

Ahi  che m'an-ci —— de e non vuol

Ahi

dar - mi vi - ta,  e non vuol dar - mi vi - ta.

want to give me life;  and does not want to give me life.

dar - mi vi - ta,  e non vuol dar - mi - vi - ta

dar - mi vi - ta,  e non vuol dar - mi vi - ta.

I die ex-hausted in my  sorrow, And he who can

Mo - ro las - so al mio duol - o, e chi mi

keep me alive, And he who can keep me alive———

può dar vi - ta E chi mi

And he who can keep me alive———

può dar vi - ta

Alas, he kills me and does not

Ahi che m'an-ci - de, e non vuol

want    to    help   me    And  does  not    want    to  help

dar   mi  i - ta    e  non vuol  dar   mi -

me,    O     unhappy  fate,        O

i - ta    O   do - lo - ro - sa   for - te,    O

unhappy   fate,       He who can   give me  life

do - lo -ro - sa    for - te,    Chi dar vi - ta mi può

silent"), or *"Mercei grido piangendo"* ("Mercy! tearfully I plead"). The personal, "inside" expressionistic view of life and suffering is obvious from these first lines, and the music matches it.

The madrigals of Monteverdi, the great transition composer who stands with one foot in the Renaissance and the other in the Baroque, reveal a similar mastery of depicting emotional and dramatic situations. But the attitude of Monteverdi is healthier, more given to outward dramatic gestures rather than the almost psychopathic expressionism of Gesualdo. He uses less conspicuous chromaticism, and then only where it will be most effective. His chord progressions seem less arbitrary, and, while he often sets poetry similar to that which Gesualdo used, his music is less morbid. Often, in Monteverdi's later works, dramatic effects are achieved by the rapid declamation of the text upon repeated notes of the same pitch, called by him the "stile concitato," or excited style. This device passes into the baroque lexicon of affects with hardly a change. A good example of Monteverdi's madrigal style may be heard in one from Book Four (1603) entitled *"A un giro sol"* (To but one turning of the beautiful shining eyes), which consists of two stanzas. The first is conventional in its harmonic and melodic qualities, and is mostly devoted to text-painting with such words as "laugh," the "sea" and "winds." But the second section begins on a foreign note, and the first sentence, "I alone have eyes weeping and sorrowful," is set to a drooping, exhausted line: while it is being finished, the tenor declaims rapidly in "stile concitato," "Yes! When you were born so cruel and guilty, my death was born!" This outburst is imitated in the other voices, and the piece ends with a feeling of helpless rage, excited and defiant.[2]

The English madrigal has many representatives, but by common consent, the masters of this form are John Wilbye (1574-1638) and Thomas Weelkes (1575-1623), with Thomas Morley (1558-1603) coming close behind with a handful of madrigals and a goodly number of dance songs with fa-la refrains called "balletts" after the Italian *balletti*. The English were introduced to the madrigal in 1588 by a printed edition of the classical Italian works in this form called *Musica Transalpina* and adopted the genre wholeheartedly. During the Elizabethan period, there were literally hundreds of these compositions produced and printed. Much of the poetry was created expressly for the music, and often by the composer himself. The musical settings follow the middle-period Italian examples with which the Elizabethans were familiar in that they interpret the text phrase by phrase. There is a certain difference from the Italian style in sonority, however, even in compositions which are rather parallel otherwise. The English seem to favor a lighter, less emotional setting and harmonic style, although feeling is often present, especially in melancholy examples. Much of the poetry is highly artificial, with references to the stock figures of Grecian mythology, especially nymphs and shepherds with names like Phyllis, Cloris, Flora, Daphnis and Amaryllis. The underlying ideas, too, are often what Shakespeare called "pretty conceits," and as such are treated with a light hand by the composers. Many of the printed editions indicated that the music was "apt for voyces or viols," and was undoubtedly often performed wholly or partially by instruments.

The English madrigal is easily understood on these terms, and one need only observe the text-painting, the light touch in the setting of the text, the tripping counterpoint and its fascinating cross-rhythms and the general elegance of the whole proceeding to derive considerable enjoyment from this music (see MM, Vol. II for example).

The French chanson is roughly the equivalent of the English and Italian madrigals, although simpler and always entrusted to four voices. The most striking difference lies in the frequently strophic treatment of the text in the chanson, where several verses (strophes) may be sung to the same music, a repetition which seldom happens in a true madrigal. These songs frequently begin with a characteristic rhythm (long-short-short) which found its way into the instrumental transcriptions so important at the time, and thereby became a trademark of the later, purely instrumental *canzona*. One of these chansons, the Christmas piece *"Allons gay bergeres"* (Hasten, shepherds) by Guillaume Costeley (1531-1606) is rather frequently performed. Other composers of this music are Clement Janequin (1485-1560), Claudin de Sermisy (d. 1562), Claude le Jeune (1528-1600) and Jacques Mauduit (1557-1627). (See MM, Vol. II; HSM, Vol. IV for examples.)

# Instrumental Music

While the Renaissance is often regarded as the period in which the composition of *a cappella* choral music flourished, we must not lose sight of the fact that both the sacred and secular vocal music was often accompanied by instruments in order to render the ensemble more powerful or more secure in pitch. At times, especially in the soloistic music of the madrigal, when a performer was missing, it was often necessary and quite permissible to play that part on a suitable instrument. In fact, during the late Renaissance, pieces entitled madrigals were written for a solo voice with instrumental accompaniment.[3] And in addition, we must also remember that this was an age of social dancing, requiring much music. There were three sources for instrumental music at the beginning of the Renaissance: vocal pieces performed instrumentally just as written; transcriptions of vocal music for instruments, in which certain procedures more native to the voice were changed so as to be more effective when played; and unharmonized dance tunes or basses upon which a group of players could improvise or have a "jam session." As the sixteenth century passed, more music for instruments was written and printed, although improvisation was still important, and music constructed upon vocal models such as the chanson or the motet, drew away from servile imitations of these forms and was eventually conceived in the composer's mind especially for instruments and their peculiarities.

The instruments themselves were, of course, the ancestors of those we have today: the oboe, flute, bassoon, trumpet, horn and trombone. In the case of the woodwinds, the sound produced by these imperfect instruments was coarse and inaccurate in pitch due to larger reeds than we use nowadays and the lack of adequate key-systems. On the other hand, the brasses were weaker in sound than their modern counterparts, and thus were often used to double the voices of choruses. The horn and trumpet were without valves and were narrow in bore. The trombone was also a narrow-bore instrument and was built in several more sizes than we now use.

The stringed instruments were quite different, for they belonged to the viol and lute families, rather than to the modern violin and guitars. The viols had the shape of the modern bass-viol: round shoulders and flat backs. In addition, there were metal frets on the fingerboard like the ukelele or guitar, thus making the pitch secure for the player. They were played with a bow, and produced a pleasant nasal sound, much less loud and brilliant than our modern strings. It was customary to build these instruments in families, sometimes storing such a group in a cupboard especially made for this purpose. This was known as a "chest of viols," a term found frequently in the literature of the day. Similarly, there were chests of recorders. The plucked stringed instruments belonged to the lute family, and were characterized by a pear-shaped body with a long fingerboard bent back at right angles at the peg end (Plate IX). These were plucked by the fingers, later with a pick for special effects, and sound much like the modern "classic guitar."

The keyboard instruments were the organ, clavichord and harpsichord. Often they were made in small sizes whose correspondingly quiet sound was suitable for solo chamber music, such as the "Bible Regal," a small organ built in the shape of a large book, and the virginal, a small harpsichord popular in Elizabethan England. The larger organs were located in churches as they are today, and followed the same principles of sound production, but without the romantic richness we associate with the modern instrument. In addition, most renaissance organs had no pedal keyboard, except for some in Germany and the Netherlands, and therefore the music is simpler, being limited to two hands on the manual keyboards.

Of the stringed keyboard instruments, there were two main types, constructed in various sizes to suit the need and pocketbook of the player. The first, the clavichord, produced a weak, but sweet tone by striking a metal string with a brass blade or "tangent." This tangent not only produced the sound, but, by its position on the string, determined the pitch of the sound. The harpsichord, on the other hand, utilized a device which plucked the string when the key was depressed, and produced a comparatively louder and more brilliant sound. While the clavichord could produce a small variation in loudness dependent upon the force with which the tangent struck the string, the harpsichord was more limited, and depended upon a series of stops which changed the stiffness of the plucking device in order to vary the intensity of sound.

Much accurate information has come down to us concerning these instruments in books which sought to include pictures and descriptions of all the known kinds, as well as some highly imaginative devices for making music. Such works are Sebastian Virdung's *Musica getutscht und ausgezogen (Music taught and explained)*, and Michael Praetorius' *Syntagma Musicum (Treatise on Music)*, 1618.

Many of the instrumental compositions show little divergence in type of writing and style from the vocal models, the chanson and motet. In the transference from voice to instrument, however, the names become somewhat different: the gayer chanson became *canzona*, the

Italian equivalent, and was characterized by a light sectional style, with a textural balance between polyphony and homophony. Such works frequently began with a rhythmic motto of a long note followed by two short ones

and thus have a certain dance quality. The more serious motet adopted the name of *fantasie,* or in the Elizabethan tongue, *fancy.* The English composers were especially attracted to the fancy, and we possess a large number of these pieces both for the viol ensembles ("consorts") as well as for the virginal.[4] Another term used for this same type of composition was *ricercare,* the style of which is usually more strictly contrapuntal than that of the fantasie, and the chief examples of which were written for viols. As the period advanced, the differences between the vocal models and their instrumental equivalents become greater, largely through the adoption of a more idiomatic style for the instruments, which features trills, rapid scales and revolving clusters of notes, all difficult for the voice, but suited to the bowed string or the keyboard. The transference of polyphony to the lute caused some difficulties, for this is not a really polyphonic instrument. To get around the problem, the lines coalesce into homophony after the imitations. The procedure tends to fool the ear and is thus reasonably successful.

One other form, this time with quite ancient antecedents, was popular, particularly with composers for the keyboard instruments. This was the *variation,* especially the type in which a given tune was used as the bass, or cantus firmus of the composition. In England, this bass was called a "ground," and so we find in the literature frequent references to "variations on a ground," or "divisions on a ground." Very often such music was improvised, with one performer playing the ground while the other indulged in more or less free flights of fancy — the jam-session again! Of course, there were other variations which used the given theme in other ways, perhaps more imaginatively, now decorating it with ornaments, now concealing it in an inner part, or often making it the basis for "points of imitation." In addition to the English, who were enthusiastic writers of variations, the Spanish, especially Antonio de Cabezon (1510-1566), and the Germans, who were by now employing chorale tunes for this purpose, provide most of the variation literature of the period.[5]

At this time, the suite had not yet assumed a definite form, but was merely a collection of dances, usually paired in a slow-fast tempo arrangement. There is considerable variety in the kinds of dances, such as the passamezzo, gagliarda, saltarello and the padovan, some of which bore thematic relationships to each other, either because of the bass or because they were variations of the same melodic idea appearing in different meters and tempos.

We have so far seen the progress of separate classifications of music and the styles which grew from them: now let us look at the fusion of vocal and instrumental music in the work of the Venetian composers, particularly those appointed to the influential position of choirmaster at that city's great Cathedral of St. Mark. From the early years of the Netherlander, Willaert, until the end of the Renaissance and beginning of the Baroque, the musical performances of this church had emphasized the pomp and splendor characteristic of the strong, proud and cosmopolitan city. Noteworthy in the succession of choirmasters after Willaert were the two Gabrielis, Andrea and Giovanni, uncle and nephew. Andrea had studied with Willaert, and Giovanni was Andrea's pupil. During the years of writing music to be performed in the great cathedral, the composers had drawn farther away from the classic Netherland style of the Romans as exemplified by Palestrina, and had created a brilliant, massive, largely homophonic style which employed not only voices, often divided into two or more choirs, but also brass and woodwind instruments and organ. The opulence and color of these compositions is characteristic of what has been called the "Venetian style," and this style heralds the baroque love of massive effects, the interplay of different qualities of sound, the exuberant ornamentation and the strongly emotional appeal of the music. In listening to Giovanni Gabrieli's impressive motet *"In Ecclesiis,"* which sounds to modern ears much like what we have come to call a cantata or oratorio, one can close the eyes and picture the colorful processions around the Square of St. Mark, with the Byzantine domes of that great structure in the background (Plate X). We hear the choirs echoing each other from opposite sides of the church, and the blaze of glory as the brass instruments sound is like the musical reflection of the gorgeous trappings at the altar.

Together with Monteverdi, the universal genius of the transition period, Giovanni Gabrieli shares the credit for assigning certain instruments to each of the musical parts of a composition. Formerly, the instrumental forces used in concerted music were not prescribed,

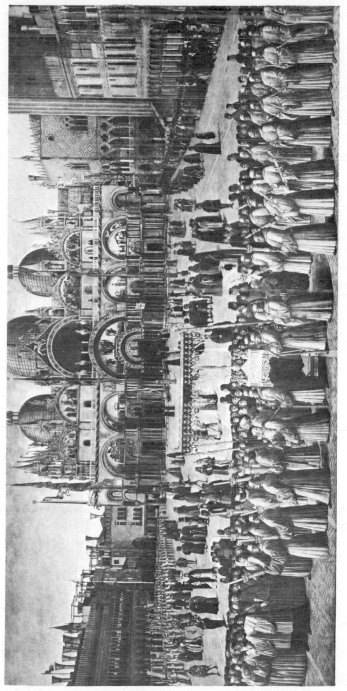

PLATE X. *Procession in the Piazza San Marco, Venice by Gentile Bellini* (1430-1516). *(Photo Alinari, Florence.)*

but the orchestra was a somewhat fortuitous gathering. As the score of *"In Ecclesiis"* shows, Gabrieli definitely wrote parts for the three cornetti (wooden or ivory horns with fingerholes, blown with a cup-shaped mouthpiece), the violino (usually now played on the viola), and the two trombones; in addition, of course, to those for the two choirs, one of soloists, and one of the normal grouping. He was also one of the first composers to indicate in his scores the degree of intensity he desired. His *"Sonata pian'e forte"* (c. 1600) carry these indications, although there is evidence that the idea was not original with him.

We have discussed and heard, then, examples of the pervasive Netherlands style in sacred music, the counterpart to this in the secular music of the various countries, the independent way taken by instrumental music and finally the combination of instrumental and choral music in one grand synthesis. This has led us to the beginning of the Baroque.

## COMPARISON OF RENAISSANCE MUSIC WITH THE OTHER ARTS

Almost all Renaissance art sings a paean of praise to the earth and its creatures: adoration to God and the panoply of heaven is inevitably cast in artistic parables formed out of human experience. Only in the exalted music of the Roman style and in the ecstatic medieval longing for God portrayed in the Byzantine paintings of El Greco does one sense that humanity and the earth have become subordinate. For now the artists have cast off the asceticism of the Middle Ages and the inhuman stylizations which it produced, and begun to look around them at the colors and shapes of the physical world.

The warmth and sensuous beauty of all of the arts increases in the Renaissance. Matching the rounded contours and curved lines of Da Vinci, Bellini and Botticelli are the arcs of the polyphony, whether they be the short ones found in the madrigal or the longer, more flowing lines typical of the Netherlands polyphony. In secular music, especially, there is a tendency toward greater activity of the parts, comparable in painting to the inclusion of many figures and details in the depiction of such scenes as the Last Judgement. There is an increasing secularization of religious subjects in painting, and we need only recall the structure of the parody mass for a musical counterpart. At the same time there is the classicism of Holbein, and the clear and clean draughtsmanship of the Dutch and Flemish painters. Here one might discern a parallel to the simplicity of the homophonic French chanson and the Italian frottola, especially since the texts of these compositions, like the subjects of the pictures, dealt with experiences of the middle and lower classes, not necessarily the nobility.

It must be admitted, however, that there was a good deal more of romantic feeling in the painting of the period than in most of the music which has come down to us — at least until the High Renais-

PLATE XI. "Madonna del Graduca" *by Raphael. Note the purity of line, the balance of the composition and the general classical serenity of this painting. Compare with Plate XII. (Photo Alinari, Florence.)*

PLATE XII. *"St. Jerome" by El Greco. Note the elongation of the extended arm and leg, the mystery of the dark background and the sense of strain as the saint turns his face upward to the light of heaven to receive divine guidance in his translation of the Bible into Latin. Mark the contrast with the repose of Lochner's Mary and Raphael's Madonna. (National Gallery of Art, Washington, D.C., Chester Dale Collection, gift.)*

sance, where we encounter Gesualdo, Monteverdi and Gabrieli. But, side by side with these daring spirits is found the sober classicism — almost mysticism — of the Roman school of sacred music, dominated by Palestrina, and including Victoria and Morales. Perhaps the translation of their classicism onto canvas may be found in the works of an earlier painter, Raphael (Plate XI), or closer to them in time, Bronzino or Botticelli. But their mysticism has a parallel in the works of El Greco, a spirituality embodied in upward straining lines, unearthly colors and distortion of figures (Plate XII). The last element —

distortion — if found in less spiritual surroundings, might well be chosen to represent the harmonic and melodic strangeness found in Gesualdo. And in pioneering spirit and sheer audacity, we might easily find comparisons between Michelangelo and Monteverdi, with the realization, however, that Monteverdi did not have at his disposal a medium as massive as did the great sculptor.

In point of color and mass, perhaps the Venetians stand out most significantly. Gabrieli, in his ceremonial music for organ, brass and double choir, handles these colorful media in broad and magnificent strokes. His fellow Venetians, Titian, Tintoretto and Veronese reflect similar attitudes in their love of color, solid composition and the dynamic balance of line and mass to be found in many of their works. Few changes in these are needed to enter the world of Rubens and Caravaggio, the Baroque. In fact, with these Venetians, we have already crossed the threshhold.

### LIST OF TERMS

Renaissance
Mass
Motet
Netherlands style
chromaticism
a cappella
cantus firmus
parody mass
cyclic structure
sequence
chorale
madrigal
frottola
text-painting
balletts, *balletti*
chanson
idiomatic (instrumental) writing
transcription
viol
lute
clavichord
harpsichord
Renaissance organ
recorder
"chest of viols"
canzona
fantasie, fancy

ricercare
consort
ground; variations on a ground
Venetian style
Roman style
*Musica Transalpina*
Thomas Morely
Petrucci
Attaignant

Josquin des Pres
Orlando Lassus
   (or Orlando de Lasso)
Palestrina
William Byrd
Martin Luther
Costanzo Festa
Jacob Arcadelt
Luca Marenzio
Carlo Gesualdo
John Wilbye
Thomas Weelkes
Guillaume Costeley
Clement Janequin
Sebastian Virdung
Michael Praetorius
Antonio Cabezon
Giovanni Gabrieli

[1] Scores for this and the other works discussed in this section may be found in the anthology *Masterpieces of Music before 1750* by Parrish and Ohl, W. W. Norton and Co., N. Y., 1951.

[2] Recording WL 5171.

[3] MM, Vol. I.

[4] Examples of both kinds may be found in HMS, Vol. IV. In addition, this recording includes English and Italian dances of the time.

[5] Vol. II of MM contains examples of the keyboard canzona and variations, as does HMS, Vol. IV, which includes Italian and German compositions.

# V  The Baroque Period, 1600-1750

We have seen the two opposed streams of artistic thought, especially in music, which ran concurrently in the late sixteenth century: a restrained classic outlook as represented by the Palestrina style, and an exuberant emotionalism which permeated the late madrigal. Added to these was the grandiosity of the Venetian polychoral style, with its instrumental magnificence. These mingled elements were to be characteristic of the Baroque era also, a time when the heart and the head were at extremes. The tensions which were created by this warfare often reached release in exaggerations on either side: the classic trend led to dry imitation and academicism, especially in France, and the romantic emotionalism created some of the most fantastic art the world has ever seen. Yet permeating both trends was a degree of rationalism which was perhaps best exhibited in the scientific achievements of the time. A list of the great scientific figures easily brings to mind these accomplishments: Newton, Descartes, Harvey, Bacon, Leibnitz, Galileo, Kepler and a galaxy of others — men upon whose attainments the world has built to the present time.

Religious and social tensions were also a characteristic of the time.

The movement toward the New World in search of religious and political freedom was in full swing, and men like Descartes, Spinoza, Pascal and Locke endeavored to make rational sense out of man's relation to man and to God.

Music, too, responded to the pull of these tensions. While the Venetians were busy with the creation of increasingly impressive church music and the Roman polyphonists were spinning their mystic webs of sound, a group of musical amateurs and writers was theorizing in the house of Count Bardi in Florence. This group, named the Camerata, was drawn together by a common admiration for the culture of classic antiquity, a passion quite normal to Renaissance man. But in comparing those golden days with their view of the decaying present, they were dissatisfied on many counts. One of the most important of these was music, an art which they, like the Greeks, held in high esteem. But music seemed to have lost its power since those golden days, and the men of the Camerata wondered where it had gone. They concluded, finally, that polyphony was at fault, that it diluted the power of music to move the emotions, and therefore they set out to create a musical style which would reproduce in tones the passions of men and evoke in the listener a vibration sympathetic and persuasive. The musical practice which they invented was called *monody,* the early form of what we shall later term *recitative.* It consisted of a text set to a melodic line which imitated the rise and fall of the speaking voice in musical pitches, but with the difference that the effect of the various emotions was emphasized in the height or depth, angularity or smoothness of the line. This was supported by slowly moving sustained bass tones, played by some instrument such as the cello. The distance between these two parts was somewhat filled by chords on a keyboard instrument or the lute, but these were sounded only when the bass note changed. Here, in miniature, we find a summation of baroque compositional technique: the importance of the upper and lower surfaces of the music — the voice part and the bass — the imitation of the passions by the melodic line, and the foundation, rendered harmonic by the chords played by the keyboard instrument upon the bass tone, against which the voice part moved to create consonance or dissonance as the emotional situation demanded.

The first masterly use of this procedure resulted in the opera *Orfeo* by Monteverdi in 1609, and as the period progressed, the use of monody changed until it differed radically from the theories of the purists of the Camerata. For one thing, polyphony had arrived to stay,

PLATE XIII. *"St. Theresa in Ecstasy," by Bernini. This dramatic sculpture is the altarpiece of the Coronaro Chapel in the Church of Santa Maria della Vittoria, Rome. Here the baroque sense of drama and motion is expressed in stone and metal. The emotional element is heightened by the activity implied by the folds of the dress, the clouds and the tense, expectant poses. (Photo Alinari, Florence.)*

and little by little invaded not only the opera, but also monody itself, replacing the single upper part with two, three or more lines which often intertwined in contrapuntal texture. The bass was speeded up, and with it the chordal motion of the keyboard instrument, but the importance of the top and bottom of the music remained unchanged.

Meanwhile, the dramatic contrasts of the Venetian choral and instrumental style attracted many imitators, some of whom showed how this device could be used structurally, thus creating the concerto style. The element of contrast — voice against instrument, chorus against orchestra, soloist versus group — was assimilated into the general style which gathered shape and character during the first fifty years of the seventeenth century.

Another important theoretical development also occurred about this time. The modal scales, sufficient for the music from the early Middle Ages to the latter part of the sixteenth century, at last broke under the strain of chromaticism and yielded to the tonal, or major-minor scale system. We have already noted the weak attraction of the final, or modal tonic note, for the other notes in the scale. This was replaced by the strong gravitational pull exerted by the tonic note and chord of the major or minor scales, a pull which became of structural importance for this period and the one to follow. Purely musical form, independent of words and their literary rule, now evolved according to the formula:

Statement of key :: departure from key :: return to key — this all-embracing basic concept of form interpenetrated the smallest musical structure and gave it coherence and meaning. Music, now free of words, could evolve under its own power, a fact attested by the phenomenal increase in amount and importance of instrumental music during this time.

But vocal and choral music was still of great importance, especially in the church and the opera. Both of these became increasingly dramatic, and enlisted all of the devices of text-painting to make the message of the words more vivid. Soon a body of stock patterns and turns of phrase grew up around certain expressions such as "death," "rage," "fear" and "sorrow," and procedures illustrated and suggested by them were incorporated into a system known rather grandiosely as the "Doctrine of the Affections." It was based upon a static theory of human feeling which held that each emotion was unmixed with any other during the period of time it occupied the soul. For the clearest depiction of any passion, or "affection," the composer should choose, therefore, an affective motive representative of the predominant soul-state and erect a composition of sufficient length upon it to convince the listener. Thus, in any section of a baroque composition, we hear a consistent presentation by the voice or accompaniment or both, of the affective motive. When the emotion changes, a new section with its own descriptive motive must be started. This theory provided the composer with ready-made musical patterns: he merely had to be a good enough craftsman to create a work by spinning them out to a conclusion.

These affective motives, originally vocal in idiom, were gradually adopted by the instrumental music, thus making the same compositional process possible, and, to the understanding listener, resulting in the same emotional appeal. But there was also an interchange in the opposite direction: instrumental idioms, especially those of the new and brilliant violin, were seized upon by composers for the voice, and unvocal but marvelously effective compositions were the offspring of this strange marriage. Music for the keyboard instruments shared the interchange also, giving up their idioms to the voice or violin, and sharing in return the figures natural to those instruments.

Possibly the Italians participated least in this exchange, for their music was based upon the voice, and this view colored all they wrote. Handel and Corelli epitomize this national style, while the music of Lully and Rameau in France projects the image of the resplendent court life under Louis XIV with grand, noble, and it must be admitted, rather-pompous music, or its opposite, intimate, refined and miniature, as represented by the writers for the harpsichord. The German style tried to combine these elements — the singing quality of the Italians and the nobility and spirit of the French — with the sentiment and depth of expressive power their more developed sense of harmony afforded them. Bach is the summation of this synthesis.

The instruments with which they produced this music were not new, with the exception of the violin, which had recently come into favor because of its strong and brilliant sound. But the viols were still used, as well as the recorders, clavichord and harpsichord, and organ, larger than in the Renaissance but still not as large as ours. What was different was the way in which the composers used them, emphasizing the contrast of sonority and intensity. Indeed, the concept called "terrace dynamics," while a natural result of the inability of the harpsichord and organ to gradually increase or decrease the intensity of their sound, was adopted by the infant orchestra as a clarifying device. The orchestra was basically a group of stringed instruments at this time, sometimes with more violas than violins, to which was added, in accordance with the changing mood of the music, oboes, recorders, flutes, bassoons, or members of the brass family, still without valves. The most fascinating of these was the trumpet in D, the so-called "Bach" trumpet. This was a small trumpet whose fundamental tone was high enough to place the usable scale notes of its harmonic series in the second and third octaves above middle C. It has a very bright, gay quality, and enormous agility at these dizzying heights. It was added to the orchestra for festive occasions, and was often associated with tympani.

While the entire century and a half of the period abounds with important composers, we shall limit our investigation to the works of Handel and Bach, with a sidelong glance at Corelli and Vivaldi. The reason for choosing these two composers above all the others lies in the fact that they sum up their age, Handel in the Italian style, and Bach in the German, with more genius and in more works of various kinds than do any others of the time. True, they are different from the experimental early composers who were groping toward the goals achieved by these two, and whose music is of considerable interest. But their works are seldom heard on modern concert programs, whereas those of Bach and Handel are frequently performed. In addition, the works of these two men have a vigor, clarity and decisiveness which make them attractive to us in the twentieth century.

### JOHANN SEBASTIAN BACH, 1685-1750

The external life of this devout Lutheran was uneventful. He served as organist and music director, first at the court of the Duke of Weimar (1708-1717), later at Cöthen (1717-1723), and finally spent the remaining years of his life as cantor of the St. Thomas Church in Leipzig. He was famous in Protestant Germany as an organist and learned contrapuntist, but not for his compositions. His first positions were under the patronage system, whereby he was obliged to compose music and perform at the courts mentioned. In his latter capacity at the St. Thomas Church, his duties included composition, performance, and instruction of choir and orchestra personnel attached to the church. We are amazed at the large number of compositions he created, but we must realize that this was part of his job and expected of him.

PLATE XIV. *Johann Sebastian Bach. Painting by Elias Gottlob Haussmann (1746), (Museum Geschichte der Stadt Leipzig.)*

Bach is important because he sums up all of the polyphonic lore of the preceding two centuries and firmly integrates it into baroque performance style. Moreover, he surpasses all the previous composers on their own ground! Excellent biographies of Bach were written by Charles Sanford Terry and Albert Schweitzer. The latter one, in two volumes, may prove too formidable for the non technical reader. The book entitled *The Bach Reader,* by David and Mendel presents documents, essays and criticisms dealing with Bach's life and work. An excellent short biography for the student is the paperback volume *Johann Sebastian Bach* by Russel M. Miles (Prentice-Hall, 1962).

### GEORGE FREDERICK HANDEL, 1685-1759

This internationally famous composer, German by birth, wrote in the Italian style, and spent the most productive part of his life in

PLATE XV.  *George Frederick Handel. Painting by Thomas Hudson. (The Metropolitan Museum of Art, gift of Francis Neilson, 1946.)*

England.  He was an accomplished performer on the organ and harpsichord, renowned in all Europe for his skill in improvising upon these instruments.  He spent four formative years in Italy absorbing the national style, and composing and performing his works.  After visiting Germany, although he had an appointment in Hanover, he traveled to England where he settled down to a prosperous life.  In London he wrote and presented Italian operas, which were much in vogue.  They remained so until 1741, at which time both of the opera companies in London were bankrupt.  Handel then decided to capitalize on the English tradition of choral singing, and turned to the composition of oratorios using English texts.  In all he composed some 26 works of this kind, almost all very successful.  These had a prevailing influence in British musical life for nearly one hundred years.  The oratorio corresponds to opera presented without scenery or costumes, and need not be religious in content.  The most famous of these oratorios, *Messiah,* deviates from this definition in that it reviews the Christian idea of redemption from its origin in prophecies of the Old Testament to the final triumph of Christ in the New Testament, not as a dramatic story so much as a musical sermon on religious concepts. Handel was a prolific composer from necessity. Often he staged his own works, and wrote to supply his needs. He seems to have been a fairly astute business man, frequently withdrawing an unsuccessful work quickly and substituting another better composition in its place.

(Three fine biographies of Handel are available in English: one by R. A. Streatfeild, the second by Newman Flower, and the third by Herbert Weinstock. A less complete, but equally interesting, one is the short account by E. J. Dent.)

# The Musical Style of the Baroque

## MELODY

The two prevailing styles of the late Baroque are the Italian vocal and the German instrumental types, although it must be understood that these classifications are generalizations.

The Italian vocal style favors phrases of moderate length, as regulated by the breath of a singer, with clear terminal cadences (Example 28a). It does not matter to us now that these serenely moving, long-breathed melodies were ornamented almost past recognition by baroque singers; now they are always performed exactly as written.

The German style, usually more instrumental in character, is also more continuous in its motion, employing caesuras upon unstable tones or weakened cadences through which the melodic line moves with little or no hesitation (Example 28b). The line itself, often plainly constructed upon the notes of triads, is often ornamented by the application of a profusion of small affective motives, sometimes borrowed from violin or keyboard technique, and analogous to the vitalized architectural ornament of the time. Portions of a melodic line are often repeated upon successively ascending or descending scale steps, in this way giving organization, direction, and harmonic

EXAMPLE 28.

VOCAL MELODY                                                          HANDEL

INSTRUMENTAL MELODY                                                   BACH

RISING SEQUENCE

PATTERN

FALLING SEQUENCE

PATTERN

etc.

TEXT-PAINTING, ACCOMPANIMENT                                          HANDEL

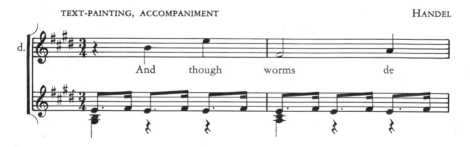

And      though      worms      de

significance to the motion of the melody. This device is called "sequence" (Example 28c).

In both styles, and in the French manner, dance music usually has fairly short phrases with clear concluding cadences corresponding to the "figures" of the particular dance. But even here, Bach, whose penchant for continuity amounts to a passion, often bridges these cadences by using a moving melodic part or by motion in the basso continuo.

When supplied with words many of both types of melody tend to illustrate in their melodic action the meanings of the words. This practice is called "text-painting." For example, a vivid figure of this kind occurs in the central portion of the aria "I know that my Redeemer liveth," from Handel's *Messiah* (Example 28d). The text is, in part: "Though worms destroy this body . . ." The accompaniment naively represents these wriggling creatures by a wriggling melodic figure. And the aria "Why do the nations so furiously rage together?" is largely devoted to an affective motive for rage (Example 28e).

## HARMONY

Baroque harmony is functional in that by the movement from tonally stable through tonally unstable chords and back it defines the key. Therefore, the departure from the tonic chord and the return to it have structural significance. Cadences are meaningful, and can be effective as final or non-final. The old modal harmony was not functional, except possibly at cadence points, which were often altered to the equivalent of a major V-I cadence, thus moving out of the mode, paradoxically, in order to clearly define the final by means of a tonal cadence!

Baroque practice favors the clear, unequivocal statement of the main key and central plane of stability of a composition immediately at the beginning. This is accomplished harmonically by the repetition of the most important functional chords, I and V (occasionally IV or its substitute, II). Melodically, the notes of these triads often serve as the scaffolding for ornamentation which gives them an affective character, or otherwise obscures the plainness of the figure.

When the texture is homophonic, the cadences are usually clearly defined and strong. As polyphony begins to develop, the tendency is to drive through the cadences, not stopping on them even though they are "final" in nature, thus weakening the cadential effect in favor of continuity and forward motion. Strong structural cadences which halt the flow at important points in the form are evident, however, and serve as functional harmonies to clarify the key at that moment.

The basso continuo combination of sustaining bass instrument and chordal instrument, often the harpsichord or organ, has the function of stating the harmonic background through and against which the melodic and polyphonic elements move. It is precisely in this relation to the chord that baroque polyphony differs from that of the Renaissance, where the chord is a byproduct rather than an element of equal importance, at least structurally, with the polyphony. In combinations of a solo instrument with harpsichord, the bass sustaining instrument is usually omitted from the ensemble and the harpsichord assumes that role as well as its own.

There were national styles in harmony as well as in melody. At opposite poles are the Italian and German styles, with the French somewhere between. The type of chord structure favored by the Italian composers was of either the pure triad or the dominant seventh chord variety. The triads moved in patterns of typical tonal progressions, while the seventh chords acted as intensifying agents in the movement from chord to chord or key to key. The German style used both of these plus chords of greater instability due to the chromatic alteration of various tones within the seventh chord structure. This added richness to the sonority, color to the harmonic progressions, and the means for profound emotional expression.

## RHYTHM

The most noticeable aspect of the rhythmic quality of music in this time is the continuity of flow, the repetition of rhythmic patterns, and the emphasis placed upon the metric pulse in many rapid movements, such as the first movements of concertos. The flow, in part dependent upon the other two qualities, is constant throughout a main section, and when a new tempo indicates a change of mood, the tempo changes immediately, in a way reminiscent of terrace dynamics. We have already noticed the importance of rhythmic-melodic affective motives. The accented metric pulsation of the rapid concerto movements, machine-like in its emphasis and repetition, we shall call "motoric rhythm."

## TEXTURE

The prevalent texture, aside from pure homophony, is a species of polyphony which is dependent upon the chord progression expressed in the basso continuo. The music is conceived as the simultaneous interaction of the melodic and harmonic flow: here the polyphony and the harmony exist in agreeable balance. For this reason, as well as to indicate the continuo procedures, we shall call this hybrid "continuo-polyphony."

As in melody and harmony, so in texture are the two opposite tendencies representative of the preferences of composers of Italy and Germany. The Italian style tends toward the homophonic texture with only short sections in continuo-polyphony unless, of course, the fugal concept is the basis of the composition. But even in polyphonic movements, the texture is apt to break down into a sort of chord-diffusion homophony. The Italian style lays great stress upon the understandability of the words, a factor favored by homophony and all but destroyed by polyphony with its overlapping parts. The German style is rather uncompromisingly polyphonic, in which case the text often becomes merely a vehicle for the music and supplies the vowel sounds upon which the singers vocalize the long, decorative, baroque garlands of affective melody.

In the orchestra or in chamber ensembles, instruments of contrasting tone-quality were often chosen by the composers of this time for the performance of the individual lines of the polyphony in order to separate these to some degree in the total sound. Thus we find Bach using flute, oboe and violin in the fugal second movement of the *Brandenburg Concerto* No. 2 for this reason.

### SONORITY

The Baroque composer worked with sonorities in the same way as his brother artist, the painter, worked with colors. In the productions of both there is a leaning toward rich effects, strong contrasts of bright and dark, and formal organization by the use of both devices. The concerto principle, as we shall see, juxtaposes large and small sound-masses and sonorities. Bright sounds resulting from the tones of woodwinds or the high trumpet are contrasted with rich, homogeneous string sound of less brilliance. And there is a definite effort to include all of the notes of a chord despite the somewhat angular part-writing this may entail: gone — for a while, at least — are the days of the typical renaissance final chord made up of an octave enclosing a fifth, a bare sound-remnant from the Middle Ages.

# FORMAL AND GENERATIVE PRINCIPLES

### MONOTHEMATICISM

As might be expected from the application of the Doctrine of the Affections, most baroque compositions use only one main thematic idea throughout, although there are often accompanying motives of distinctly subordinate importance. In the instances in which two or more principal themes appear within the same formal section, these are apt to be quite similar in affective significance in order to preserve the mood of the music at that time. Thematic contrast is generally foreign to this music, which is created out of thematic motives by a process of constant variation and repetition.

### IMITATION

This procedure was discussed in Chapter I, and little needs to be added here except to remark upon the great frequency of its use during this period. Close imitation, called *stretto,* is often employed as a tension device. It consists of introducing the imitation before the leading voice has finished the theme, and when four parts are involved represents a climactic "piling up" of the material.

### THE CONCERTO PRINCIPLE

This simple but important formal principle means merely the alternation of the sonority produced by a large group of instruments with that created by a small group, or a soloist, or a vocal combination.

The first thematic statement of a composition employing such a design is frequently by the large group, called the *ripieno,* and is usually homophonic in texture. Often this section returns entire or in part, again played by the ripieno; such a musical passage is often referred to by another Italian term, *ritornello,* meaning a *short return* of the passage. Hence forms employing the concerto principle are sometimes called "ritornello forms." After the opening ritornello, the small group enters its own musical material or proceeds to develop the themes of the ritornello. The small group is called the *concertino*.


## VARIATION

Most music of the Baroque, since it is predominantly mono-thematic, consists almost entirely of variation of one kind or another. There are a number of definite species, however, which we shall identify.

### The Chaconne

Here we have a hymn-like chord progression of usually four phrases complete with cadences, over which a melody unfolds. This chord progression, not the melody, is the theme of the chaconne, and remains substantially unchanged throughout the piece except for occasionally being transposed bodily to other keys. The variation element consists either in treating these chords in different rhythms, or deriving melodies, sometimes polyphonically combined, from them. A modern practice which is exactly similar in technique, is the "blues," where a series of chords supplies the 12-measure chordal theme upon which the members of the band create melodic patterns. Like the old chaconne, the "blues" repeats over and over to make an extended piece of music.

### The Ground and the Passacaglia

A ground is a relatively short pattern of notes in the bass register, usually concluding in a stable manner. It is repeated many times while over it polyphonic or semi-homophonic parts are added. The passacaglia merely lengthens the bass pattern of the ground to eight measures, thus creating a melodic unit which provides a longer format for each variation. Sometimes, however, the upper parts do not cadence when the theme does, resulting in a more continuous flow and more unified variations. The great Passacaglia and Fugue in C-minor by Bach is an outstanding example of this form, but we also find it used in the "Crucifixus" movement of his B-minor Mass, and in the moving "Lament" from Henry Purcell's opera *Dido and Aeneas*. Our modern counterpart, while not exactly the same as the passacaglia, is the "boogie-woogie."

## The Chorale-Variation

The hymn melodies of the Lutheran churches of Bach's time were called chorales. We are familiar with many of them today, and most people, like those of his congregation, know the melodies if not the words to "A Mighty Fortress," "Sleepers Wake" and "O Sacred Head," among others. The church organists of that time often used these melodies as the basis for improvisatory preludes and incidental music for the church services, and later these improvisations were written out and given the name "chorale prelude." Bach wrote a great many of them for organ — actually variations on the chorale — which used the familiar hymn-tune in many ways. Often it served in a capacity much like that of the passacaglia bass, that is, as a cantus firmus, just as the old plainchant had done in the Renaissance. Sometimes the tune was dismembered and varied, imitatively or otherwise, phrase by phrase. In addition to the purely instrumental use of the chorale, Bach also employed it with highly effective — and affective — results in choral music, sometimes as a cantus firmus, but not necessarily in the bass. Often, as in the opening chorus of the great *St. Matthew Passion*, the chorale floats above the other interweaving voices with an unearthly beauty. That it is so easily recognizable by the listener, whether he be of Bach's time or our own, is psychologically important: in this way Bach brings home the import of the Crucifixion drama to everyone. Many cantatas, especially those of the master's last years, were based in some way upon the chorales. Perhaps the best known of these is the Easter Cantata, *"Christ Lag in Todesbanden"* ("Christ Lay in the Bonds of Death"), which is actually a set of choral variations on the hymn melody of that name. Handel found no use for these chorales in his sacred music, which, after all, is more closely connected with the Italian style and not that of Germany.

## The Polyphonic Variation

Finally we have the kind of variation which provides polyphonic development. Here there is no repetition of large-scale elements, but rather the use of rhythmic motives derived from the thematic substance. These motives are tossed back and forth among the instruments, or given brilliant idiomatic treatment by a single solo instrument, such as the violin. They form the substance of the music in the episodes of a concerto or a fugue, for example. Many compositions called variations use this kind of treatment rather than the others mentioned above. Listen to the first movement of the third *Brandenburg Con-*

*certo* by Bach, or the same composer's *Goldberg Variations.* In the latter work, the separate movements of the variations take on the forms and styles of baroque dances, overtures, toccatas, and canons, thus combining two individual elements in a brilliant synthesis.

### RECITATIVE, ARIOSO AND ARIA

Music for the solo voice fell into three commonly used categories during this period. The type of setting chosen depended upon the function of the text at that particular point within the larger framework of cantata, oratorio or opera. When the function was that of narration, as often happened in oratorio, or conversation, as in opera, the words were set in a manner quite close to the old Florentine monody. The voice declaimed the text in free rhythm, now hastening, now slowing as the meaning of the words seemed to require, over the slow-moving chord changes of the basso continuo (Example 29a).

As the recitative becomes more dramatic, it may break into a style called *arioso.* The voice line is no longer rhythmically free in this kind of setting, but moves in measured motion above the supporting harmony of a more sonorous accompaniment than that of the recitative. This accompaniment is also in metric motion, not static, and the union of the voice with it emphasizes the meaning and emotional appeal of the text in a more purely musical way than the song-speech of the former (Example 29b).

EXAMPLE 29. St. Matthew Passion, *J. S. Bach*

a. NARRATOR:

And when they had sung an hymn,

a. CONTINUO

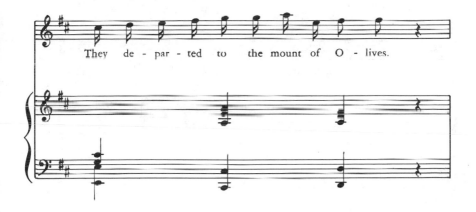

They de - par - ted to the mount of O - lives.

JESUS:

Then said Je - sus to them: Ye all shall be of - fen - ded this

b. Vivace

night be - cause of me, for it is writ - ten, I will

b. Vivace

smite, I will smite the shep - herd, and the

sheep of the flock shall be scat - tered a -

a. Moderato

broad. But af - ter

a. Moderato

I am ri - sen a - gain, I will go be - fore you in - to Ga - li - lee.

In the recitative (a) of this work the words of Jesus are always accompanied by the strings as a characterization of His divinity. The narrator, on the other hand, has only occasional chords and figures by the continuo from which to derive his pitch. Although a meter is indicated, this is more for the convenience of the conductor than anything else: only when the tempo changes to the arioso (b) is it necessary for both singer and orchestra to keep strict time. After this, much of the latter part, at *moderato,* becomes relatively more free. Notice the affective intervals on the words "offended," and the text-painting in the voice at "they departed," "but after I am risen again" and in the orchestra at "the sheep of the flock shall be scattered." Also typical is the modulatory quality of the whole example, beginning in D-major and ending in F-major, after having passed through several other keys.

In the third category, the aria, or song, the musical treatment becomes master of the words, and the dramatic action stops for this lyrical moment. Here the voice is set against a full-fledged accompaniment, often with a decorative part assigned to a solo instrument (an *obbligato*). Often two or three solo voices are used, in which case the name *aria* is replaced by *duet,* or *trio.* The style is melodic, as has been described under melody earlier in the chapter. There are three main forms of aria in use during this period. The simplest is the strophic aria, in which several verses are sung to the same music. The next is the binary aria which consists, as the name would imply, of two sections. The first of these states the melodic material, then modulates and cadences in the dominant key. The second section returns to the tonic key and usually re-presents the thematic material. The third form is a three-part structure in which the first section is repeated after a contrasting middle portion, thus A-B-A. It is called the *da capo* aria because these Italian words signifying a return to the beginning of the movement appear at the end of the B section, thus eliminating the necessity of reprinting the A section. Often an aria is preceded by a recitative which explains the dramatic situation and in this way prepares for the contemplative or emotional song.

## IMPROVISATION

One of the essential qualities of a baroque keyboard performer was the ability to improvise, or "make up" music as he played. Not only did it make his *continuo* playing more interesting, but it was an absolute necessity for the church organist who was often obliged to fill in pauses in the service with music. Many baroque forms use written-out music in the style of an improvisation to create either the whole form, or contrasting sections of a composition otherwise not improvisational in nature. We find the pieces called *toccatas* (literally "touch pieces") to be of this nature, also exhibiting the keyboard dexterity of the performer, by the way. Many compositions entitled *Prelude, Capriccio,* and *Fantasia* use sections which sound as though they are being composed at the keyboard on the spur of the moment. Of course our modern equivalent is the whole realm of jazz, especially the more improvisatory "Dixieland."

EXAMPLE 30. *Generalized diagram of a typical fugue.*

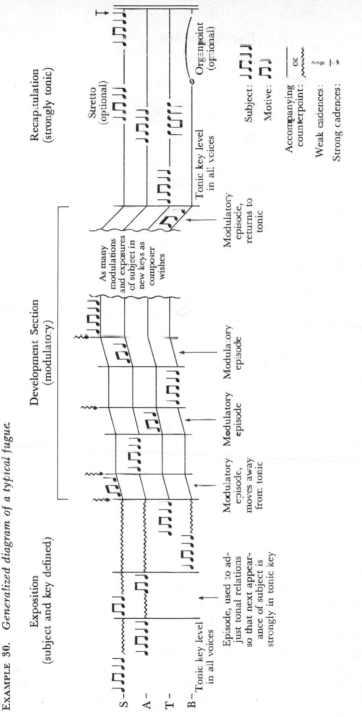

# IMPORTANT FORMS AND EXAMPLES

### THE FUGUE

For our first example we shall choose the second prelude and fugue in Bach's *Well-Tempered Clavier* (Example 30). The music appears on page 153 with the important sections and thematic elements identified. It is not necessary to be able to read music to follow the progress of the form. The note patterns may be interpreted like a graph — which is what they are. Do not worry about the time elements: listen to them without necessarily trying to find their counterpart on the page.

We hear first the prelude, a kind of warm-up improvisatory composition, in which one basic melodic pattern is repeated many times. Pay particular attention to its harmonic significance. It consists of a long chord progression enlivened by the melodic motive. When the composer felt that a climax had been accumulated, there occurs an improvisational passage of broken chords after which we hear an *organpoint,* or held note in the bass, over which two parts move in canon for two phrases. This intensifies the excitement which climaxes in the *adagio* (slow) recitative-like measure, after which broken chords over a tonic organpoint bring the piece to a close.

The fugue which follows is a typical one—at least in the regularity of its structure (Example 31). Bach seldom wrote two fugues exactly alike, since he regarded the fugue as a procedure rather than an invariable form. All of his fugal compositions have points in common, but differ widely in mood and methods of exploiting the material. Before we go further, let us examine the materials used and exposed here. First of all, notice that the subject consists of a rhythmic motive — two short notes followed by three notes twice the duration of the short ones — a rhythmic motive which is easily recognizable. Next look at the scale line of rapid notes which occurs in the first voice at the point where the answer enters. Here we have the precedent for many of the scales to be used later in the fugue. Now let us examine the fugue more closely:

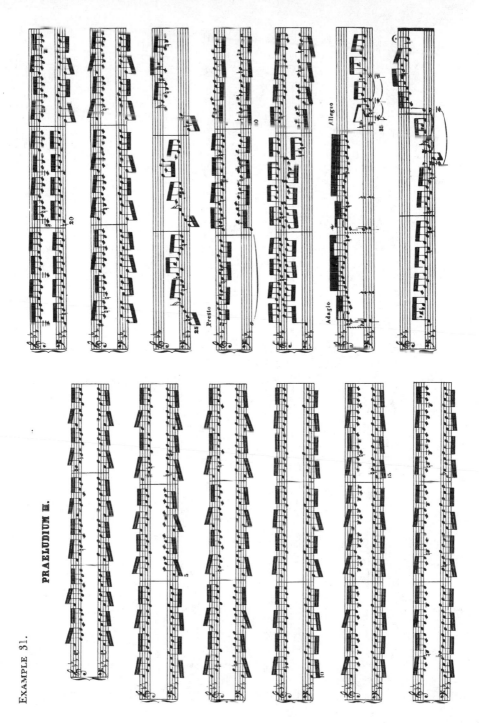

Example 31.

PRAELUDIUM E.

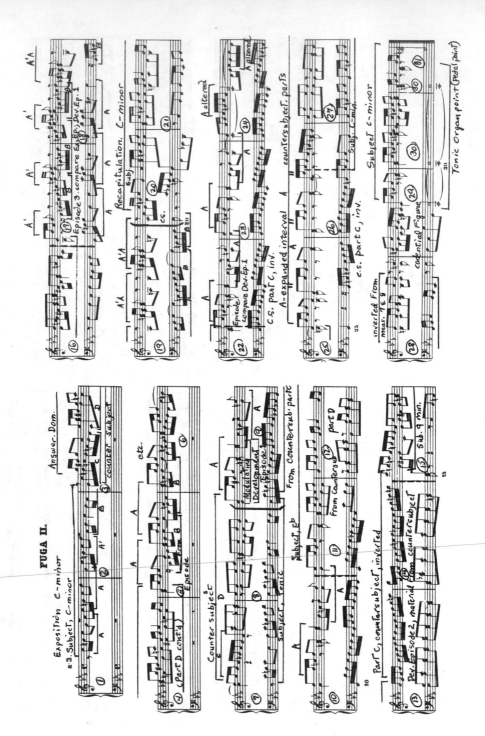

154

EXPOSITION

Measure    1, 2    Announcement of the subject in the tonic.

3, 4    Answer by soprano.

5, 6    Episode based on motive A.

7, 8    Announcement of subject by the tenor.

DEVELOPMENT

Measure    9, 10    Episode, modulating to new key, uses motive and scale.

11, 12    Subject in new key, soprano, accompanied by D.

13, 14    Episode, modulating, uses C and D.

15, 16    Subject in new key, alto, accompanied by C, later by D.

17, 18, 19    Episode, modulating back to tonic key; composed of two sections, the second of which interchanges the tenor and alto parts of the first.

RECAPITULATION

Measure 20, 21    Subject in soprano accompanied by D, tonic key.

22, 23, 24    Episode, non-modulatory, extending material of measures 9, 10.

25, 26    Subject in soprano with expanded intervals, accompanied by C.

26, 27, 28    Subject in tenor, low register, leading to climactic pause.

29    Firm cadence figure leading to held note in tenor (organpoint).

29, 30, 31    Coda, subject in soprano, leading to strong final cadence.

An equally interesting prelude and fugue is the one which opens the first volume of the *Well-Tempered Clavier* (Example 32). Here the prelude consists entirely of chord diffusion patterns in an improvisatory manner such as a continuo player might use in an orchestral piece. It is entirely homophonic, with cunningly devised chord progressions which lead to climactic sections just as might happen in melodic compositions. In the fugue the emphasis is on the stretto process, with non-thematic material at a minimum, and no consistent use of the same accompaniment ideas.

Let us now turn to one of Bach's monumental fugues in the

EXAMPLE 32.

Prelude

Fugue

B-minor Mass, that of the second Kyrie (Example 33). This fugue is rather unusual in that it stays very close to the tonic key throughout. The chromatic subject is exposed as in the C-minor fugue analyzed above, and lends itself to two strettos later in the movement. The central section is devoted largely to the development of episodic material. The subject enters from time to time, but the really note-

EXAMPLE 33.

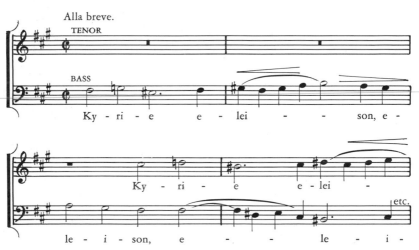

worthy effects appear in the cascading imitations of episode material. This movement also illustrates Bach's technique for grandeur through accumulation, rather than always through dramatic procedures. It is like a long argument in its effect.

THE CONCERTO

Let us now hear the concerto principle in action. A concerto grosso employs two groups of instruments: a fairly large string orchestra with *continuo,* called the *tutti* (all), or *ripieno* (remainder). The massive sound of this group is contrasted with the more transparent and soloistic sound of a small group, the *concertino* (little concertizing group), whose constitution is variable. The middle-Baroque Italian composers, such as Corelli, used only stringed instruments for this group, and Handel, Italianate to the core, copies them in this. Later Italian and German composers, such as Vivaldi and Bach, used woodwinds, horn, and "Bach" trumpet as well as strings for the concertino. Notice that here the element of contrast is greatly emphasized, which is not so much the case when both groups are made up entirely of strings.

*Corelli: Concerto Grosso No. 8* ("Christmas" Concerto)

This concerto is typical of the middle baroque style of Corelli (1653-1713) in its seriousness and the richness of the idiomatic string writing. Corelli was the first composer to define the elements of the Italian concerto grosso, using string orchestra in contrast with a concertino of two violins, cello and harpsichord. This is the format adopted by Handel, but used more dramatically.

The "Christmas" Concerto, especially the final movement, is said to be a musical rendering of Botticelli's painting, "The Nativity." The movements consist of sections of contrasting tempos and textures, and might be outlined thus:

I. *Vivace* (very fast) : a short introduction of 7 measure by the whole ensemble (tutti).
   *Grave* (very slowly): an imitative section for the tutti.
   *Allegro* (fast) : a binary movement using the concerto principle.
II. *Adagio* (very slowly) : a ritornello form in which the ripieno doubles the concertino from time to time.

    *Allegro:* a curious movement for the tutti, consisting wholly of chord-diffusion of the harmonic progressions.

    *Adagio:* return of the former material, with a new coda.

III. *Vivace:* a short, fast dancelike movement in binary form. Some contrast between the ripieno and concertino as well as the use of the orchestra as an accompanying medium.

    *Allegro:* an imitative ritornello form, binary in structure, which makes some use of the echo effect. It flows directly into the next movement.

    *Largo pastorale* (slowly, suggesting a graceful rustic dance): a slow dance movement in quadruple compound meter, of the type called the Siciliano. Binary in form with ritornellos, and uses the echo effect. Unlike the preceding movements which have been in minor or related "flat" keys, this one is in G-major, and provides a luminous contrast in the string sound and a pleasant conclusion to the work.

*Vivaldi: Concerto Grosso, Op. 3, No. 8 in A-minor.*

"*Il prete rosso,*" or the "red priest," as Antonio Vivaldi (c. 1678-1741) was known to his fellow Venetians because of the color of his hair, was the prolific composer of 49 operas, 540 instrumental works and many large vocal and choral compositions. He wrote much of this music in the concerto style and cultivated especially the solo concerto, featuring in most of these the violin, although there are works in which other instruments, especially winds, are important. He was a composer of an original and experimental turn of mind, and explored the possibilities of musical description in some of his concertos. His cycle *The Seasons* and the individual concertos entitled variously *The Tempest on the Sea, The Hunt* and *The Night* feature original and interesting effects, mostly achieved through the use of idiomatic figuration for the ripieno as well as the solo violin.

The concerto grosso we have selected is typical of this composer's general attitude toward the form, whether solo or grosso, and the materials. There are three movements, marked *Allegro, Larghetto* and *Allegro* (fast, rather slowly and fast). These are clearly ritornello forms in which the string concertino does little to develop the orchestral themes, but rather indulges in brilliant idiomatic violin figures. The rapid movements have the motoric rhythm characteristic of the concerto, and the slow movement uses a striding orchestral theme much like some of Handel's. The first movement opens with a clear statement of the tonic key by means of what has been called "hammer-strokes" — full, decisive block chords on I-V-I (Example 34). The

EXAMPLE 34.

CONCERTO GROSSO, OP. 3, NO. 8                                       VIVALDI

texture is mostly homophonic, even when the concertino is playing, although there is a little imitative work between the solo violins in the slow movement.

Perhaps the most important aspect of this and the Corelli concerto is the idiomatic character of the string writing, both for the ripieno as well as the concertino. Indeed, in addition to bringing the instrument itself to a high degree of perfection, the Italians developed most of the string figures used during the following centuries and laid the foundation for subsequent string technique in these and similar works.

*Handel: Concerto Grosso No. 3, in E-minor* (Example 35)

In this work we find a concertino composed of two violins, accompanied by harpsichord and cello continuo. This is the usual group which, when not in concerto grosso format, is called the *trio sonata.* As usual, the ripieno consists of string orchestra. The work opens with a form much used in French opera, called the *French overture,* consisting of a slow, rather homophonic section (Example 35a) followed by a rapid, fugal movement (Example 35b) which returns for a few measures at its conclusion to the tempo of the beginning section. In the slow section the ripieno and the concertino alternate, while in the faster fugue, the concertino is always combined with

EXAMPLE 35.

the orchestra, resulting in a purely orchestral movement. The striking fugal subject has an important accompaniment — so important that this might be called a double fugue — that is, one with two subjects. The last slow section is very short, comprising only the final cadence formula. The next movement (No. II, since the two main sections of a French overture comprise a single movement) is a fast, typical concerto movement, with alternating sections of *ripieno* and *concertino*. In this movement, the following alternations of ripieno and concertino take place:

TUTTI (ripieno plus concertino): introduces vigorous main subject. Passes to variation of main subject out of which a short descending scale passage is evolved. Modulation.

CONCERTINO: first violin spins out the evolved figure in idiomatic fashion for four measures.

RIPIENO: long ritornello based upon repetitions and imitations of main subject.

CONCERTINO: more violinistic figuration accompanied at first by only part of the ripieno, which then gradually increases in number of instruments.

RIPIENO: ritornello of main subject. .
CONCERTINO: figuration.
RIPIENO: figuration over thematic fragments in the lower instruments.
TUTTI: prepared by soft section, "terracing" to the final statement of the
subject at high dynamic level.

It is noteworthy in this movement that the solo instruments are occupied with idiomatic string figures, never directly with the main theme
of the tutti. The third movement is a polonaise, not to be confused
with Chopin's concert pieces of the same name. Only a small share
of the work falls to the concertino in this movement. The whole
concerto ends with a graceful, moderately rapid movement, introduced
by the concertino, which makes extensive use of the echo effect.

In this concerto, Handel approaches the conformation of the
baroque suite, which consists of an overture (usually of the French
type), followed by dance movements. This work also resembles the
so-called "church sonatas" favored by Corelli in his concerti grossi.
We have found no strict or extensive fugal procedures, but the employment of the orchestra for rich harmonic effect has been masterly.

### Bach: Brandenburg Concerto No. 2, in F

The six examples of concerto grosso which Bach composed in 1721
sum up, in their diversity and perfection, the various aspects of that
form in its most brilliant era. They were written for the Margrave of
Brandenburg and presented to that nobleman with a fulsomely com-
plimentary letter by Bach. We have no record of their ever having
been performed, and the manuscripts, still tied in the original package,
were sold after the Margrave's death for a ridiculously low sum. Fortunately, a Bach scholar and admirer, J. Kirnberger, purchased them
and thus preserved them for posterity.

The one which we have selected for examination is typical
(Example 36). First, it has three movements arranged in the order
fast, slow, fast. The ripieno is, as usual, composed of stringed instruments, but the concertino represents an experimental departure from
the norm, perhaps inspired by the work of Antonio Vivaldi. The solo
instruments are trumpet ("Bach"), flute, oboe, and violin. Note the
diversity of color possible here, as well as the combination of the
brilliant trumpet with softer instruments. Clearly Bach has in mind
the elements of contrast and clarity so dear to the baroque imagination.

The opening section states the extremely stable melodic material in the combined colors of the ripieno and concertino. There follow alternating sections of concertino and ripieno in which the solo instruments are introduced one by one, each later solo being accompanied by the instrument introduced in the previous concertino section plus the basso continuo. In this order, then, we hear violin, oboe, flute and trumpet. The whole section is summed up by a longer ritornello which

EXAMPLE 86.

THEME AND BASSO CONTINUO

Str. & Concertino

etc.

modulates to a new key. After only a few measures of the concertino alone, the orchestra enters, but not as a ritornello. Rather the function is one of accompaniment, which uses thematic material, however. Eventually the concertino appears alone for a short imitative section, now followed by a real ritornello in a new key. During the course of the ritornello, however, the process again becomes one of orchestral accompaniment, and the repetitive development of thematic motives continues. The recapitulation section may be divided into three parts: ritornello - concertino - ritornello. And the final cadence, in true Bach fashion, is constructed from the thematic material.

The slow movement is a most expressive piece of chamber music. Here Bach omits the trumpet and the string orchestra, retaining only the concertino flute, oboe, and violin, accompanied by the basso continuo. The movement relies heavily upon imitation, without really becoming a fugue, however. Its mood is one of sensitive melancholy, very much like that to be exploited in the Rococo era by one of Bach's sons, Carl Philip Emmanuel. Note the "sighing" cadential passages of three descending notes, the quiet yet inexorable march of the basso continuo, and the transparent texture which allows each instrument to be clearly heard.

The final movement is a lively fugue. In its rollicking motion, highlighted by the bright notes of the trumpet, even the clumsy basso continuo is persuaded to take part. In this interesting combination of the fugue and concerto, the concertino introduces and states the subject, while the ripieno is used for the episodes and accompaniment. One marvels at the agility of the trumpeter for whom Bach first penned this brilliant part. The other instruments are hardly less noteworthy in point of technical difficulty. One is left almost breathless as the movement runs its rapid course, and finishes — again Bach, the economical genius — with a quotation of the fugue subject in the high trumpet.

### THE SUITE

Bach wrote a number of compositions of this type for the keyboard, as well as four of them for orchestra. They all consist of some kind of introductory movement followed by a series of stylized dances of the period. In the case of the suites for orchestra, the overture — always of the French type — was the most important movement. To illustrate this importance, composers often entitled such a work "Overture — and so forth." The overture to the first suite, in C-major, is most interesting. This work is scored for two oboes, string orchestra and continuo which includes bassoon. The monumental slow introduction is followed by a brilliant fugal-concerto movement in which concertino-like sections for the three wind instruments appear. There is an impressive slow ending of some length modeled after the opening section. The dances which follow are the courante (a rather rapid, "running" dance) ; two gavottes arranged in ternary form (A - B - A) ; a Venetian dance called the Forlane; two minuets, again arranged A-B-A; a pair of bourées in ternary sequence; and two passepieds, also ternary in arrangement. In the next historical era, this ternary scheme will be included in the symphony as Minuet and Trio. Bach often varies the instrumentation used in these dances. For example, the second bourée is scored for the woodwind trio, while other movements add or omit this group for contrast.

The third suite, in D-major, shows Bach's handling of the so-called "festival" orchestra. Here we have two oboes, three trumpets, timpani, and a rather large group of strings. Again a French overture is used, followed by an "air" (aria) and three dances, gavotte, bourée, and gigue ("jig," imported from Ireland to the continent, and made less hilarious!) . The air is justly famous, having been arranged to be played on only one string of the violin, the G, by a nineteenth-century violin virtuoso. The steady progression of the bass by alternate wide leap and step is typical of Bach, and may be found elsewhere in his compositions. Equally typical is the long-phrased lyric melody, so expressive in its formal gestures.

The second suite is scored for flute and strings, and forms a kind of concerto for this instrument, while the fourth suite, like the third, employs the festival orchestra.

### THE VARIATION

As we have already remarked, baroque variations often are formed over a repeated bass pattern, or chord progression. We shall examine two masterpieces by Bach to illustrate this procedure.

The first is the monumental Passacaglia and Fugue in C-minor for organ. The theme over whose repetitions the variations will be constructed, is stated in the bass in the first eight measures (Example 37a). There follow some 20 variations of increasing complexity, during the course of which the theme is removed from the bass to upper voices for variety. The work concludes with a monumental double fugue, one of whose subjects is derived from the passacaglia subject (Example 37b).

The second is the agonized "Crucifixus" ("Crucified") movement of the B-minor Mass. To gain the greatest dramatic effect, however, this movement must be heard preceded by the "et incarnatus" ("and was made man") and followed by the "et resurrexit" ("and rose again"). The first of these three opens with a short introduction by the orchestra, subdued, grieving, with a drooping affective motive whose meaning is immediately clear. The five-part chorus enters in imitation with a skipwise descending figure, which perhaps symbolizes the descent of the Holy Ghost as the words unfold — "et incarnatus est de Spiritu Sancto ex Maria Virgine" (" and was incarnate by the Holy Spirit of Mary the Virgin"). There is a short ritornello by the orchestra alone after the chorus has sung this, then the text is repeated to the same melodic designs. Again the ritornello, and in hushed tones of wonder, while the orchestra foreshadows the tragic eventual death, the chorus intones "et homo factus est" ("and was made man").

The "crucifixus" movement (Example 38) consists of polyphonic variations on a ground of four measures repeated 12 times. The orchestral accompaniment consists only of the expansion of the continuo chords appearing on the main beats of the measure. The single word

EXAMPLE 37A.

"crucifixus" and its drooping melodic motive are repeated imitatively
twice in each of the four voice parts before the sentence "etiam pro
nobis sub Pontio Pilatus" ("and was crucified for us under Pontius
Pilate") enters, also in imitation. A cadence is reached at the end
of the phrase "passus et sepultus est" ("died and was buried"). The
next section repeats the text of the first part, but with a chromatic
version of the first motive used in order to create tension, and to
picture the anguish of the Christian soul in contemplating these words.

EXAMPLE 37B.

There follows one of the most staggering dramatic blows, not only of all baroque music, but also of all music since Bach. The exultant shout of the five-part chorus, together with the festival orchestra, trumpets, woodwinds, timpani and strings, proclaims the resurrection in a fugal-concerto movement of rapid tempo and brilliant figuration. The text and sequence of parts are as follows: "Et resurrexit/And rose again (repeated many times) tertia die secundam scripturae/on the third day according to the second Scripture"; ritornello: "et ascendit in coelum, sedet ad dexteram Dei Patris/and ascended into heaven where He sits at the right hand of God the Father"; ritornello: "Et iterum venturus est cum gloria judicare vivos et mortuos; cujus regni non erit finis/and will return again in glory to judge the quick and the dead; whose reign shall have no end"; short ritornello: repeat of the preceding words; final ritornello. This movement exhibits considerable text-painting. Notice the rising vocal melodies at the words "et resurrexit," and the ecstatic vocalization of some of the syllables of those words. The same kind of vocal line is used for "et ascendit." The bass solo offers a nice touch of variety in an otherwise choral movement. The last bit of musical illustration occurs at the second time the words "cujus regnit non erit finis." Here the long vocalization on the first syllable of "regnit" symbolizes the eternity of that kingdom, emphasized near the end of the choral section by slowly moving—almost static—harmony over repeated bass notes. The whole movement is not only a spiritual affirmation but also a musical victory by the cantor of the St. Thomas Church.

EXAMPLE 38.

The chorale variations, previously discussed, will be illustrated in the next section, devoted to the cantata. Of the remaining variations, the most important is that masterly work for harpsichord, the

*Aria with Thirty Variations,* the so-called *Goldberg Variations* written by Bach for a virtuoso pupil of that name to please his patron, Baron Kaiserling. The general procedure is that of the chaconne, with the harmony and variation length the same throughout. However, each variation is of a different type. The list includes canons at various intervals, fugues, inventions, overtures, pastorales, toccata-like movements, and a quodlibet, or mixture of popular songs of the day with the aria chosen for the theme. The work requires consummate skill and artistry to play — just as it required these qualities to compose.

## THE CANTATA

The word cantata signifies a piece to be sung, in contrast to the word sonata, which means a piece to be played upon instruments. Simple cantatas, both secular and sacred, existed in profusion before Bach came upon the scene. They consisted largely of sets of recitative-and-aria, sometimes with chorus and orchestra, other times for one or two voices with only continuo accompaniment. Throughout Bach's life his various positions in the Lutheran churches obliged him to compose cantatas for many occasions. These are often of the simple solo or duet type. But for particular occasions such as Easter, Christmas, and Ascension Sunday he wrote more elaborate works for larger forces. Often he would use a hymn tune (chorale) as the thematic foundation of these works, hence they are called *chorale cantatas.* In a manner of speaking, since the text of the cantata was that of the chorale, and since the melody was present in most of the movements, these chorale cantatas represent a kind of large variation form. The work which we have chosen to discuss is not simply a set of variations, but will illustrate several procedures and forms common to baroque operatic and church music. It is the Cantata No. 80 based in part on Luther's magnificent hymn-tune. *"Ein Feste Burg ist Unser Gott"* ("A Mighty Fortress is Our God"), which has been called by the poet Heine "the Marseillaise of the Reformation" (Example 39). Bach wrote the cantata for the bicentennial celebration of the Augsburg Confession, and therefore used festival orchestra, soloists, and chorus. Movements 1, 2, 5, and 8 are variations on the chorale,

EXAMPLE 39.

1. A strong-hold sure our God is He, A trust - y shield and weap - on; Our help He'll be, and set us free, From ev - 'ry ill can hap - pen. That old ma - li - cious foe, Means us_ dead-ly woe: Arm'd with_ might from Hell, And deep-est

2. And were the world with dev-ils fill'd, All ea - ger to de - vour_ us, Our souls to fear should lit - tle yield, They can - not o - ver - pow'r_ us. Their dread-ed Prince no more, Harms us_ as of yore; Look grim_ as he may, Doom'd is his

3. Still shall they leave that Word His might, And yet no thanks shall mer - it; Still is He with us in the fight, By His good gifts and Spir - it. E'en should they take our life, Wealth, name, child, or wife Though all_ these be gone, Yet noth-ing

craft as__ well, On earth is __ not his fel - low.
an - cient sway, A word can o - ver - throw him.
have they won, God's king-dom ours__ a - bid - eth.

while the others are recitative and aria combinations. Let us examine the cantata movement by movement, noting the musical procedures and the text, which, in such a work, is of profound importance and suggests to the composer the mode of treatment in accordance with the Doctrine of the Affections.

### FIRST MOVEMENT.

Text:   A stronghold sure is God our Lord whose strength will never fail us; He keeps us free from all the horde of troubles that assail us. Our evil foe would fain to work us woe; with might and deep guile he plans his projects vile; on earth is not one like Him.

This movement, which starts full force without introduction, takes in turn each phrase of the chorale melody in embellished form and subjects it to a choral fugal exposition, nine of these in all. At the conclusion of each exposition the high trumpet sounds the chorale phrase on high, answered canonically one measure later by the bass instruments and organ. The total musical effect is indeed one of a "mighty fortress."

### SECOND MOVEMENT. Aria for Bass and Soprano Choir.

Text:   Soprano Choir: (second verse of the hymn)
        Standing alone we are undone, the Fiend would soon enslave us; but for us fights a mighty One whom God has sent to save us. Ask ye who this be? Christ Jesus is He, Lord God

of Sabaoth, there is no other God; He can and will uphold us.

Bass solo (free text, not from chorale) :
Every soul by God created, has by Christ been liberated.
They whose Jesus' standard bear, to His service dedicated,
all will in His victory share.

In the orchestral accompaniment of this movement, according to
Schweitzer, we hear the tumult of battle and the sound of horses'
hooves. Over it the sopranos sing in concerto-fashion the second
verse of the chorale. The bass "interpreter" of the soprano text asserts
his message of hope against the background of these two elements,
much as decorative elements are superposed in baroque architectural
ornament.

THIRD MOVEMENT. Bass Recitative and Arioso (not chorale text).
Text: Thou child of God, consider what complete devotion the
Saviour showed for you in His supreme atonement, whereby
He rose triumphant over Satan's horde, and human sin and
error and all things base. Let not, then in your being, the
Evil One have a place. Let not your sins convert the
heaven there within you into a desert! Repent now of your
guilt in tears (here arioso begins) that Christ the Lord to
you be fast united.

This is recitative typical of Bach in its melodiousness and expressiveness, following lyrically the voice inflections of speech. When the
text becomes too emotional for this mode of expression, the arioso,
more melodic and with an underlying metric pulse, begins.

FOURTH MOVEMENT. Soprano Aria.
Text: (not from chorale)
Come dwell within my heart; Lord Jesus I adore Thee.
Bid evil all depart and let Thine image ever shine before
me. Away sin, how base thou art!

This lovely aria is accompanied simply by the basso continuo,
and is of the *da capo* type of construction. The poetry of the text belongs to the pietistic movement current in the Lutheran church of
Bach's time. We do not know the author of the free texts Bach has used
in this work.

FIFTH MOVEMENT. Chorus: Chorale text and melody.
Text: Though fiends appear on every hand all eager to devour us,

we need not fear; we can withstand and baffle all their power. The Arch-Fiend of all shall not us appal, his might is laid low, he cannot strike a blow; one Word from God will fell him.

In this exciting movement in concerto style, the symbolism of the pilgrim band withstanding the power of Evil is vividly pictured by the massing of the chorus in unison on the chorale melody while the orchestra seethes around them.

SIXTH MOVEMENT. Tenor Recitative and Arioso (free text).

Text: So take thy stand with Jesus' blood bespattered banner, O soul of mine; and trust thee ever in His power divine! Yea, He will lend His might to gain for thee thy crown of glory. Go joyous forth to fight! If thou but hear God's word and do as He command thee, no foe, however mighty, can withstand thee, (arioso begins) salvation now is sure, thy refuge is secure.

This movement matches the Bass recitative, III, both in the fact that it is recitative, and that it concludes in arioso style.

SEVENTH MOVEMENT. Duet for Alto and Tenor (not chorale text).

Text: Blessed he who praises God, whose Words will sanctify him; more blessed still is he who bears Him in his heart. With him will grace abound nor can the foe come nigh him; at last will he be crowned when death shall set him free.

This is a so-called Italian chamber duet, with oboe *obbligato* (or decorative part) really creating a trio. Note the imitative passages, and the occasional parallel movement between the voices, giving a sweetness and grace to the texture. The predominantly tranquil mood is broken momentarily near the end of the movement, where the words "and death shall set him free" *(wenn es den Tod erlegt)* are set to a rather grotesque chromatic figure.

EIGHTH MOVEMENT. Chorale.

Text: The Word of God will firm abide against our foes assailing, for He will battle on our side, an ally never failing. Though they take from me here all that I hold dear, I will not complain, their vantage will be vain. God's might is all prevailing.

The final movement consists of a harmonized version of the original chorale by the orchestra and chorus.

# THE BAROQUE SPIRIT IN THE
# OTHER ARTS

Now that we have examined some of the characteristics of the music of this time, let us now compare them in general terms with some of the other arts in order to reach a clearer understanding of the baroque spirit. Two prevailing tendencies are apparent, and these exist in varying degrees in almost all of the creative work to come out of this century and a half. One, from which the era first received its name, was earlier taken to be the chief quality of the time — an unbridled and fantastic exuberance of decoration, motion and emotion. We know now that this is not entirely true, and furthermore, that specimens of this tendency in the pure state are few and do not represent the period as a whole. For parallel to the riotous imagination was a vein of rationalism which controlled, channeled and technically enhanced the initial enthusiasm, without, however, rendering it cold and classic in the worst sense of that overworked word. These qualities may be seen in our illustrations: Rembrandt, "The Night Watch" (Plate XVI); Bernini, "St. Theresa in Ecstasy" (Plate XIII); and Borromini, façade of the Church of San Carlo alla Fontana in Rome (Plate XVII).

First in importance, and most obvious to the eye, is the passion for large and noble subjects, whether these be long musical epics like the *St. Matthew Passion* of Bach, or Handel's *Messiah,* the great canvases of Rembrandt, Rubens and Tiepolo, or the large buildings of Borromini. In the opera of the time, only demigods, princes and kings were allowed to be the heroes, and in the same way Rembrandt dignified the honest burghers of Amsterdam with apparent nobility in his painting. The subjects and situations are generally larger than life and more intense.

The force of the exuberant imagination may be found in many details and techniques of these art-works. Dramatic contrast is one of them. The love of contrasting tone colors and sharp changes in intensity so frequent in the music has parallels in painting. Here the masses of bright and dark colors provide comparison to the terrace dynamics of the orchestra, and to the tone colors of the winds, especially the trumpet, against the monochromatic string background. In architecture, a play of light and shadow is created by the projecting

PLATE XVI. *"The Night Watch" by Rembrandt. Note the dramatic use of dark and light, the impression of space extending far down the street and the various motivic repetitions of parallel lines. The sense of activity and motion is typically baroque. (Courtesy of the Netherlands Information Service.)*

and receding portions of the building. The love of continuity and motion has already been remarked upon in the music: now examine the garments of St. Theresa, the activity of the figures of "The Night Watch" and the movement implicit in the buildings. In the latter motion is created by the inward or outward bulging of façades and stairways, the twisting of columns, the profusion of decoration and the curved moldings and carvings which lead the eye from one part to another.

Along with nobility of subject, richness of effect was desired by these artists. This was often created by the colors used — many times shades of the same color — the amount of detail, and the depth of perspective, or in music, the richness of harmony, which bears a close resemblance to pictorial perspective. St. Theresa seems suspended in limitless space, for example, and the many folds of her robe add to

PLATE XVII. *Façade of the Church of San Carlo alla Fontana, Rome, by Borromini. Here is baroque activity transferred to architecture. Note the play of shadow caused by the outward-bulging structure and the ornamentation. (Photo Alinari, Florence.)*

177

the impressive effect. The multitude of figures in "The Night Watch" creates the same effect of richness, and the avenue behind the soldiers stretches away to the limits of the imagination. The detail of the architecture has already been mentioned, and it is hardly necessary to point out the immense importance of perspective in this art. Now listen again to the first movement of the cantata *"Ein' Feste Burg"* with these qualities in mind!

And the sum of all these techniques is the communication of emotion. Of course, this is less so in the case of architecture, for such communication is not its prime function. But like the musical episodes whose feeling is ruled by the Doctrine of the Affections, both Rembrandt and Bernini have caught in their works an intense moment of drama which is emphasized by every detail of the composition, just as it is in music. Rational enthusiasm and exuberance then, an all-encompassing imagination, and the deployment of every artistic technique in order to impart emotion to the beholder are the ideals and methods, so often successful, of baroque art.

## LIST OF TERMS

| | |
|---|---|
| aria | *stretto* |
| basso continuo | fugue |
| "Doctrine of Affections" | ritornello |
| recitative | tutti |
| harpsichord | concertino |
| terrace dynamics | *obbligato* |
| baroque organ | ground-bass |
| text painting | passacaglia |
| motoric rhythm | chaconne |
| concerto style | French overture |
| imitation | toccata |
| improvisation | organpoint, pedalpoint |
| clavier | episode |
| suite | festival orchestra |
| mass | cantata |
| sonata | chorale |
| chorale cantata | arioso |
| echo effect | ripieno |

## ADDITIONAL LISTENING

*Handel:*

Concerti Grossi, 1 through 12
*Water Music*

*Fireworks Music*
*Harmonious Blacksmith,* Variations
*Messiah*

*Bach:*

D-minor Mass
*St. Matthew Passion*
Cantata No. 4 *("Christ lag in Todesbanden")*
Concerto for Two Violins and Orchestra, in D-minor
*Brandenburg Concertos* Nos. 1 through 6
Suites for Orchestra 1 through 4
Flute and Harpsichord Sonatas
*Goldberg Variations* (Harpsichord)
*Italian Concerto* (Harpsichord)
*Well-tempered Clavier* (Harpsichord)
G-minor Fugue, the "Little" (Organ)
Toccata in D-minor (Organ, Orchestra)
Chorale Preludes for Organ: "Jesu, Joy of Man's Desiring,"
    "By the Waters of Babylon," "A Mighty Fortress"

*Vivaldi:*

Concerto for Trumpet and Strings
Various solo violin concertos

*Corelli:*

Various Concerti Grossi

*Purcell:*

*Dido and Aeneas* (opera)
Various odes and anthems

*Buxtehude:*

*Magnificat,* cantatas, organ music

# VI The Classic
# Period, 1750-1827

*Part I: Haydn and Mozart*

The eighteenth century is the last act in the political and humanistic drama whose tensions began in the Renaissance and whose accumulated power exploded in the American and French revolutions. This century must be viewed as a continuation of the growth of humanistic and scientific thought which began in the sixteenth century, and one which enriched the parade of man's intellectual and social progress with the achievements of Lavoisier and Priestley, Watt, Jenner, Kant, Voltaire, Rousseau, Lessing, Hume, Adam Smith and Goethe. Enthusiastically bearing the banner of reason, men of this time ever more confidently stormed the barriers of religion, superstition and ignorance, attempting a rationalistic interpretation of the universe and man, an undertaking impossible of failure in their eyes. They realized with increasing clearness the tyrannical, frivolous and vicious aspects of their political and social organization and criticized them in plays, novels, pamphlets and essays which ranged in tone from vitriol to ironic wit. They believed that intelligence could set men free of the old bonds, mentally as well as physically, and they strove mightily to attain this freedom.

As is usually the case, many of these bonds were forged during the period immediately preceding, but they were not restraints at that time. Rather they were acceptable ways of behaving, of governing, of writing, of painting and of composing. Those in the vanguard of Enlightenment, however, felt that these customs had become petrified, outworn and useless, and they sought to be free of them in order to set up more vital styles and modes of behaviour. Nowhere in Europe is this more evident than in the changes which took place in France in the eighteenth century. Under the absolute monarchy of Louis XIV, the style of the grand baroque held sway, formal, regal, pompous and, to a degree, noble. During the Regency period, before Louis XV ascended to the throne, as a result of social rebellion against the repression of absolutism, an astounding change took place. Only state ceremonies retained the last vestiges of the pomp of the previous monarch: we now find a frivolous, amoral, sensuous and artistic court, bent only on pleasure and amusement. Manners were refined and elegant, and the greatest social error was to betray strong emotion. The art was pretty and playful, made for elegant salons and boudoirs, decorative, void of the passion and depth of Rubens, Rembrandt and El Greco. This was the Rococo, the period of the *style galant*.

A more restrained classic manner appeared after the middle of the century, partly as a result of a new emphasis on Greek and Roman culture and partly from the realization of the terrible state of the political and economic situation. The consequences of aristocratic extravagance became increasingly apparent and provided fuel for the fires of moralists, philosophers and social critics, fires which became general in the holocaust of 1789.

Nor was this succession of social modes of only local importance to France; as always, the French court was regarded as the last word, and smaller versions of Versailles were to be found, scattered about Europe from Potsdam to St. Petersburg. To be sure, the rococo *style galant* suffered certain changes at the borders of the various countries; in Germany where the courts were under the control of "enlightened despots" such as Frederick the Great, the French style lost some of its lightness and wit and became more sentimental. Italy changed least, perhaps, because of the differing nature of its scattered political system, and possibly because of its head start, having never had a grand baroque of the rigid French style. Austria, centered at the crossroads of Europe, absorbed all of the national elements and synthesized them under the benevolent, if somewhat inept, rule of Maria Theresa, thus providing fertile soil for the musical styles of the great Viennese Classics — Mozart, Haydn and Beethoven.

Let us now take a closer look at the musical scene of 1715, the date usually accepted as the beginning of the Rococo sub-period. J. S. Bach was at the court of the Duke of Weimar and had not yet written his greatest music. Handel was in London composing and presenting Italian operas with great success to the English subjects of Hanoverian George III. The *opera seria,* based upon the heroes and gods of classical Greece and Rome was the theatrical attraction of the day. At its best such an opera was a fusion of drama and music, each supporting and intensifying the other. At its worst it became a "concert in costume" attended by those who wanted to hear only the marvelous vocal art of the singers. Little by little this style of opera went out of fashion, superseded by more native works such as the ballad operas in England — John Gay's *Beggar's Opera* — and by the Italian *opera buffa,* or comic opera in Europe. To be sure, the old *opera seria* was overhauled during the middle of the century by Gluck, but this rather hastened than postponed its demise. In the preface to his "reform opera" *Alceste* (1767), Gluck writes that the music must be subservient to the demands of the text and the dramatic action, neither obscuring the one nor halting the other. To attain this end, Gluck replaced the ornate music of the opera seria with arias and recitatives written in a truly classic style, lyric, simple and straightforward. The old mythological plots are retained, but are strengthened and made dramatically persuasive. One of the clearest examples of this reform style is Gluck's *Orfeo ed Eurydice* (1762) from which the recitative and aria *"Che farò senza Eurydice"* is often drawn for concert performances. In this music we feel the great grief of Orpheus at the loss of his wife even more poignantly because of the restraint with which it is presented. These operas used a large orchestra which included woodwinds (piccolo, flute, oboe, clarinet and bassoon) in pairs, pairs of trumpets and horns, and three trombones in addition to timpani and strings. As we shall see, many good things came from the opera in addition to the modern orchestra.

The rococo style, or *style galant,* may be described as light, elegant, spirited and aristocratic, the counterpart of the paintings of Watteau (Plate XXII), Boucher and Fragonard. Paradoxically, at the same time there appeared a style diametrically opposed to the rococo, the so-called "bourgeois" style, filled with sentiment, simple and democratic. We find it in the paintings of Chardin (Plate XXIII) and Greuze and in the music of Haydn, Beethoven and Schubert as well as some of the early romantic composers. Let us examine each of these two related styles in turn.

The *style galant* is homophonic, using simple harmony, short phrases resulting in frequent cadences, and many ornaments in the forms of trills, turns, grace notes and "sighing" appogiaturas. In addition, the phrases are often composed of melodic and harmonic clichés — stock patterns — which change in mood from measure to measure, resulting in continual variety. It was an art of the miniature, designed for salons and intimate friends. Its spirit was French and its foremost composer was Couperin *"le Grand"* (1668-1733).

The problems of transition from the architectural baroque forms which resulted from the expansion of a single affective motive by means of tonal changes and motoric rhythm were in a large part solved on the keyboard. It is due to the nature of the French harpsichord and its idiomatic treatment that the rococo style is ornamental and miniature. This instrument, the clavecin, had a small tone which did not sustain for more than a moment; therefore, in order to prolong the sound certain ways of repeatedly plucking the string had to be invented, of which the trill was the simplest solution — a more or less rapid alternation of the principal tone with an adjoining one. Other ornaments were engendered in similar ways, some for purely esthetic reasons, others, like the trill, deriving from the mechanism of the instrument. The keyboard instruments also solved the problem of transition from the fixed number of polyphonic parts of a baroque composition to the freely homophonic style of the rococo by merely disregarding the strictness of baroque writing and employing few or many parts as the sonority demanded and the fingers of the player could manage! Such music was merely transferred to instrumental ensembles and formed the basis of the homophony of the later eighteenth century.

Perhaps the greatest difficulty which the Rococo composer faced was that of formal coherence. Baroque form resulted, as stated above, from the expansion of an affective motive. When the material had been exhausted, the movement came to an end. But the new style avoided such intensive motivic work and disliked the motoric rhythm which propelled the motive through its adventures. Repetition and sequence of a number of motives now replaced baroque monothematic variation, and these were woven into the simple dance forms of the suite. Little by little developed the idea of thematic dualism — the use of two contrasting themes in the evolving sonata-allegro form to make more memorable the tonal areas to which the music progressed. And finally, the three-movement form of the Italian operatic overture was detached from the stage work and served as the basis of the first symphonies. This is a far cry from the elegant tinkling of the clavecin in a white-and-gold, candle-lighted salon in Paris. But these early orchestral works expressed equally clearly in their medium the society which had produced them, a frivolous dream-world where pleasure and novelty were the highest ideals. Their counterpart may be seen in the paintings of Boucher, Fragonard and Watteau, and in the interiors of the palaces and theaters at Potsdam, Dresden, Vienna and Versailles.

In contrast, the coexistent bourgeois style replaced the elegant artificiality of the Rococo with a plainer view of reality, closer to the lives and sentiments of the middle class citizens, and more honest in its simplicity and sincerity. This naturalism is reflected in the paint ings of Chardin, Boilly and Greuze in France, and those of Graff and Chodowieki in Germany and Austria. Such a style, however, may come dangerously close to insipidity and sentimentality, especially when practiced by a people all too prone to sentimental effusions, like the Austrians and Germans. Indeed, even the witty Rococo suffered a turn in this direction when it was adopted as the *empfindsamer stil* in northern Germany.

But there was mutiny in the ranks of both the Rococo and rationalists! In 1756, Burke wrote in his "Essay on the Sublime and the Beautiful" that in art there is an element which transcends beauty: "Whatever is fitted in any sort to excite the ideas of pain and danger, whatever is in any sort terrible, or conversant about terrible objects, is the source of the Sublime." In short, authors and composers in search for emotional truth rebelled against the frivolity of the Rococo as well as the efforts of the rationalists to explain and tame nature, and sought inspiration in the free play of the imagination. This movement was called the *Sturm und Drang* (*Storm and Stress*), after a play by Friederich Maximilian von Klinger, and enrolled such progressive spirits in its ranks as Schiller, Goethe and, in his "back to nature" movement, Jean-Jacques Rousseau. In this style, which found its ultimate fulfillment in music, we find the explanation of those outbursts in the minor key, *fortissimo* passages and otherwise inexplic able dissonances which lend unexpected depths of expression to the symphonic movements of Haydn, Mozart, Beethoven and Schubert. And here, too, is the romantic spirit arising again from the intuitive imagination of these creators, preparing for the artistic developments of the nineteenth century.

There remains the style of the Italian *opera buffa,* or comic opera, important because of its strong influence upon the music of Mozart, whereas Haydn's derived largely from the Austrian version of the Rococo plus a strong folk music influence, and that of Beethoven is a fusion of the bourgeois and *Sturm und Drang* styles which owes little to either rococo or *opera buffa.* From the Italian comic opera come the piquant and lyric melodies which often appear as secondary themes in a symphonic movement, the swift orchestral motion, the spirit and verve, and the kaleidosocopic changes of mood, all translated from vocal to instrumental terms. The constructive German spirit welded these refractory, often rather formless and form-defying elements into a logical symphonic web that was to be unsurpassed by the composers of any other nation for a long time to come.

With the derision of the militant modernist, the baroque polyphonic style was named the "learned style," and was felt to be suited only for church music, conservative as always. But the art of Bach — and Palestrina as well — came to be valued highly by the great composers of this era. The middle and late periods in the creative lives of Haydn, Mozart and Beethoven were times when these men immersed themselves in the study of counterpoint, immeasurably enriching the works which followed with their interpretations of fugue and the devices produced by polyphonic writing.

So we see that the music which we so glibly term "classical" is compounded of many different, even opposing styles. The various composers use different proportions of each of these styles combined in a purely personal manner to achieve the particular synthesis which we recognize as typical of Haydn or Mozart, Beethoven or Schubert. But the *manner* of classicism is important too. Ideally, the Classic artist retains an objectivity toward his materials, carefully controlling the balance of form and content, while expressing his ideas clearly. He creates *absolute music,* for the most part, abstract designs in sound. He presents his material straightforwardly and affirmatively, raising no philosophical questionings. The degree to which such feelings appear indicates the amount of admixture with romanticism, an element which is never wholly absent. Generally, the Classic composer works well within a tradition, seeking no surprises or innovations for their own sakes. He may, by the constant practice of his art, broaden and gradually expand the tradition in which he began, bringing it to new heights hitherto unsuspected and unappreciated by his contemporaries. But this, we must remember, represents the evolution developed during a lifetime of music. The materials with which he chooses to work are usually simple and clear, the basic realities of his art, and he desires no more than that these qualities inform the result. This is the ideal situation, attainable most completely by an IBM machine. In practice it turns out that composers are flesh-and-blood beings who have sorrows, joys and the multitude of experiences common to all mankind. Overtly or not, these experiences color the composer's attitude toward the ultimate realities which he imparts in his music, making it meaningful through shared experience. No classic composition of any merit is free of these elements — indeed, the "impurities," like the strength-giving alloys of steel, give the works their unique value. In the music of Haydn and Mozart we sense the personalities of the composers, a restrained (by good taste) view of their attitudes toward life and its problems — the spirit of sensitive human beings.

### FRANZ JOSEPH HAYDN, 1732-1809

This man, the first outstanding composer of the classic style, was born in a poor peasant hut in the little village of Rohrau in Austria. His native musical talent was noticed at an early age, and after some local musical instruction he was sent to Vienna, where he received further training and sang in the choir of the Church of St. Stephen. He was an assiduous pupil, and, while learning all that the meager instruction at the church afforded, studied compositions by other composers as well as theoretical works on harmony and counterpoint. He was turned out of the choir to fend for himself when his voice changed, and he managed to earn a pittance by giving lessons, accompanying, and playing in cafes and theaters. After some years he was able to secure a position in a nobleman's establishment, where he composed and directed the small musical organization. One of the great patrons of music in Vienna, Prince Esterhazy, became favorably impressed with Haydn's efforts, and secured his services for the rather large musical establishment at the castle of Esterhaza, some eighty miles from

PLATE XVIII. *Franz Joseph Haydn. Portrait by Thomas Hardy, 1792. (A. C. K. Ware, Ltd., London.)*

Vienna. Here Haydn had an orchestra with which to experiment, and experiment he did for the next twenty-nine years. Not only did Haydn conduct the orchestra at the numerous balls and concerts, but also he composed most of the music played, repaired and tuned the instruments, supervised the clothing, food and shelter of the musicians, and, withal, kept an even temper and sunny disposition. Almost all of his compositions produced at this time were the property of Prince Esterhazy, but upon the death of that prince and the accession of one not so interested in music, Haydn, then fifty-eight years of age, decided to retire from his post and release his works for wider public performance. He was aided in this by the London impresario, Salomon, under whose auspices Haydn made two highly successful trips to England. For those voyages he wrote two sets of six symphonies each, now called the "London Symphonies," the last compositions in that form he was to create, numbering from Symphony No. 93 through

104. Haydn and Mozart were fast friends who admired each other's music greatly. While in England, Haydn was therefore shaken upon hearing of his friend's death at the early age of thirty-five. Haydn himself remained alive for two more decades during which he composed little, and that slowly. That little was pure gold, however, for to these declining years we owe the two great oratorios, *The Creation,* and *The Seasons.*

While not "the father of the string quartet and symphony," as he has often been called, Haydn did much to establish the distinctive styles and contents of these important forms. He developed the nucleus of the composite instrument which we call the orchestra, and established a manner of writing for it that exploited many of its capabilities. He employed the predominantly homophonic style of the eighteenth century but explored the possibilities of polyphonic development of thematic material, making this texture a potent device in the style of his later works. He gave an impetus to the concept of thematic development that would be of prime importance to Beethoven and all subsequent composers.

Many volumes have been written about Haydn. The book by Karl Geiringer entitled *Haydn, A Creative Life in Music,* and that by Rosemary Hughes, *Haydn,* are both excellent. The former is somewhat technical, however. The older biographies, such as that by Nohl, are also useful.

## WOLFGANG AMADEUS MOZART, 1756-1791

This man, one of the few really authentic geniuses of music, was born in the town of Salzburg, evinced exceptional performing and composing talent at an early age, and was taken on a concert tour of Europe by his father when he was six years old. During the next ten years other tours were made which served as a liberal education to Mozart in musical styles as well as in the ways of the world. With his phenomenal memory for music and extraordinary musical powers, he assimilated the diverse elements of the Italian, French and German styles, and blended them in his own personality to a perfection seldom realized in any age. Mozart's father was an excellent musician and parent, and trained his son to the best of his abilities in both roles. Clearly, such a talented and trained musician as Wolfgang, who knew the outstanding musical figures of all Europe, might well expect success to fall into his lap when he decided to venture forth on his own. This happened all too rarely during his short life. There are many reasons for Mozart's lack of worldly success, not the least of which was the general feeling that his music was too complicated. This opinion seems well-nigh incredible to us today, but it had the effect of limiting performances of his works. Secondly, he was unable, or disinclined to become a musical servant in the houses of the nobility, as Haydn had done. As a matter of fact, this system of patronage was beginning to totter, so that his luck with it might not have been too great. Then too, Mozart was somewhat impractical and considerably too generous in financial affairs, often depleting his own resources in order to help out a friend. So he was obliged to eke out a comparatively poverty-stricken existence in Vienna by teaching, giving concerts, composing and borrowing money. During the last ten years of his life, one jump ahead of his creditors, and physically exhausted, he wrote some of his greatest music.

PLATE XIX. *Wolfgang Amadeus Mozart. Unfinished portrait by Lange, 1782. (Courtesy of the Austrian Information Service.)*

Mozart composed some 600 complete works, including 22 operas, 52 symphonies, 25 piano concertos, 12 violin concertos, 14 concertos for other instruments, 24 string quartets, 60 solo works for piano, and 27 choral works. These were first numbered in chronological order by the Viennese botanist and Mozart enthusiast, Köchel, and later revised by the Mozart scholar, Alfred Einstein. Thus, from the "Köchel number" we may place a work's location in Mozart's creative life (*e.g.*, K. 400 was written about midway).

One of the important central aspects of Mozart's musical style is the use of idioms from the Italian opera of his day, whether the work be instrumental or vocal. The bustling, bubbling instrumental themes characterize musically the stock comic characters of the *opera buffa,* just as other lyric, sometimes chromatically languishing phrases indicate the entrance of the pathetic heroine. A work which illustrates this aspect of Mozart's style particularly well is the Symphony No. 34 in C-major, K. 388. Both the first and last movements are in *opera buffa* style, while the slow movement is a lyric scene with instruments instead of voices. Indeed, Mozart regarded himself as primarily an opera composer. In his letters to his father he is always longing to find a commission to write a stage work. The longing is perforce appeased in his instrumental music.

An informed appraisal of the work of Mozart must assign to him the culmination and perfection of eighteenth-century musical style. But he represents more than that. Now that the tide of nineteenth-century romanticism has receded considerably we are able to see the real values of his music. The Romantic critics and composers, while professing to admire, were always a little patronizing toward Mozart, engrossed as they were in compositions of huge size and overpowering expressiveness. But now that the temper of the times inclines us toward economically constructed, balanced, meaningful works of music, Mozart has come to mean more than he ever did, possibly at any previous time, including his own lifetime. Sainte-Beuve has phrased it thus: the music of Mozart "seems to dwell at the very source and center of all existence and to be able to move, as the occasion arises, in any direction." But we must have ears to hear, not disdaining the transparent, restrained orchestra, the comparatively short movements, and the aristocratically controlled emotion. Let us realize that here we have the joy too full for laughter, the pathos too deep for tears.

Many biographies of Mozart exist, some fictionalized, like Marcia Davenport's, others containing factual accounts, which, by the very nature of Mozart's life are almost romantic enough! To this class belong the excellent works by Turner and Burk. A more technical, but vastly rewarding volume is that by Alfred Einstein. The collected letters of Mozart and his family are also available in translation, from which a paper-backed edition of selections has been published.

# THE MUSICAL STYLE OF THE CLASSIC PERIOD

### MELODY

In contrast to the general baroque practice, music of the Classic period is usually polythematic and employs the contrast between vigorous melodies of instrumental cast and smooth lyric phrases to emphasize and characterize the structural elements of the most frequently used forms. Instrumental themes are apt to be triadic in construction, either using the chord plainly, note by note, in various inversions and rythmical designs, or by making the broken chord serve as the skeletal framework which is filled out by short, often stereotyped figures resembling the baroque affective motives. The lyric themes, usually more stepwise in construction, sometimes contain chromatic inflections which serve to emphasize the pathetic or graceful quality, feminine in expression, especially when contrasted with the more masculine and vigorous instrumental themes.

Again unlike the baroque, the phrases in classic style are apt to be short and composed of melodic formulas of a few notes which reach frequent caesuras and cadences. This epigrammatic construction, however, makes it possible for the composer to repeat a significant melodic or rhythmic motive within the phrase, thus impressing it upon the listener's memory so that developments of the motive will be recognized and rendered meaningful.

Departing from the baroque conception of melody and bass, the composers of this era directed their attention principally toward the melody. In the case of composers less sensitive and skilled than Haydn and Mozart, this preoccupation often led to static and uninteresting basses. Both of the above composers were acutely conscious of the lower surface of the music, and while not as melodic in its move-ments as in baroque style, the bass progresses logically and satisfyingly.

### HARMONY

This element is usually much simpler than in baroque style and is more obviously stable. The three main chords — I, IV, V — of the keys involved supply the harmony for most of the music. Certain more complex and unstable chords are often used to emphasize the motion toward a strong, usually structural, cadence. In minor keys especially, and in the works of Haydn, there are rather frequent abrupt shifts of tonality to remote keys for the purpose of expressing profound emo-tional states. This is a personal quality of Haydn's style probably arising out of his blending of the bourgeois and storm and stress styles. Such moments occur far less frequently in the music of Mozart, and, when they do, last for a much shorter time, often seeming to emphasize the home key by contrast rather than weakening it. Beethoven adopts Haydn's practice, but, as usual deepens the implications and emotional content.

Since the texture of this period is mostly homophonic, the har-monic elements need to be enlivened rhythmically. This is accom-plished by various devices of harmonic diffusion: repeated notes and chords, and stereotyped broken chord patterns such as that given the name "Alberti Bass."

Harmonic cadences, paralleling melodic procedures, are frequent. They consist of final cadences of both kinds (V-I, IV-I), and non-final cadences, mostly of the types which come to conditional stability on the V-chord of the key (half-cadences). There is an occasional use of the deceptive cadence, frequently near the end of a movement, where such a progression has the effect of slowing the harmonic motion, and forecasting the approaching conclusion of the music.

In addition to the light cadences at caesura points and phrase-endings, there are emphatic, sometimes repeated cadences at the close of major structural sections. For intelligent listening, the importance of these structural cadences can hardly be overemphasized. They cor-respond to the use of paragraphs within a chapter — main sections within a movement — and in a musical work these "paragraphs" are apt to be more important than in a literary composition. Significant cadences are often followed by a short pause, again stressing the effect of separation and punctuation. The cadences themselves are final or half-cadences. Infrequently, near the end of a movement, as indicated above, a deceptive cadence may receive some emphasis.

### RHYTHM

As in baroque style, the tempo of a classical movement seldom changes. But the rather mechanical reiteration of the metric pulse so common to many baroque compositions is varied in the classic style. For one thing, there are occasional pauses which interrupt the flow of the music, allowing rhythmic rest-points and cadences. Again, the metric pulse is often not emphatic, but lightly and quietly present, lending grace and elegance to the movement of the music. And the motivic thematic rhythms are always more plainly in the foreground than the simple metric pulse.

### TEXTURE

This quality of the classic style is basically homophonic. The use of simple imitative procedures from time to time does not invalidate this statement. Both Haydn and Mozart showed an interest in polyphonic texture, but it is not the thorough-going polyphony of Bach, but rather a simplified, clearly chord-based counterpoint, most often used as a developmental procedure. This developmental polyphony frequently employs thematic fragments in imitation, corresponding roughly to a fugal exposition. Such a section is called a *fugato*. More consistently polyphonic compositions — the "learned style" — appear in the conservative church music of both composers. In operatic ensembles, Mozart was able to write graceful and effective polyphony using *galant* and bourgeois elements fused with the Italian *opera buffa* style. Perhaps the outstanding monument to Mozart's use of polyphony occurs in the final movement of the Symphony No. 41 ("Jupiter"), where the sonata-allegro and the fugal styles are combined. Haydn and Mozart both wrote canonic and fugal movements for chamber music combinations during the mature periods of their creative lives.

### SONORITY

Any discussion of the prevailing sonorities of the classic style must take into consideration the classic orchestra. This graceful and flexible instrument developed from the basic string orchestra of the Baroque with the routine addition of a few woodwind instruments, first oboes and bassoons, then flutes, horns, trumpets and timpani for emphatic effects, and finally the clarinets and still later the trombones. The woodwind instruments were usually used in pairs, as were the horn and trumpet. These latter were the so called "natural" instruments without valves, and were therefore capable of playing only the notes of a particular harmonic series. By this time, the fashion, and quite possibly the technique, of the high "Bach" trumpet had disappeared, and the brass instruments were limited in function to playing held notes around which the harmony revolved, or simple bugle-call themes. One of the clichés of the period is the hunting-horn call, either for solo horn, or more often for a pair of horns in two-part harmony. The trumpet is seldom a solo instrument, but is used for dynamic weight. The trombones, soon to enter the orchestra as useful members, were employed by Haydn and Mozart only in church and operatic music.

The continuo had by now disappeared, except in church and opera. Its function was given to the "inner" instruments of the orchestra, those whose unobtrusive tone-quality blended well into the harmonic background. Important in this capacity were the horns, bassoons and violas. So-called "pedal harmonies" — sustained chords — in the woodwinds and horns are a remnant of continuo procedure.

The flexibility of this new classic orchestra was used in different ways by the composers, each according to his own "sound ideal." Haydn's sonorities are apt to be thinner and somewhat harsher than those of Mozart, more transparent, less rich and full-sounding. He relied more heavily upon the strings, whereas Mozart showed a typical Teutonic fondness for passages in which the woodwinds play without string support. The late "London" symphonies of Haydn, however, exhibit a somewhat different approach to the use of the winds, coming closer to the Mozartian sound than is usual in the earlier works.

## MISCELLANEOUS CONSIDERATIONS

The "Doctrine of the Affections" had now gone the way of the continuo, although the depiction of moods in music was still valid. No longer was there the insistence upon one emotional phase per movement but rather a kaleidoscopic style, veering quickly from one mood to another for purposes of contrast. Seldom do we find the consistency of mood demonstrated by the first movement of the Mozart Symphony No. 40. More typical are the corresponding movements of Symphonies Nos. 39 and 41.

Contrast, symmetry and formal balance are of great importance in the classic style. These may be noticed in the four measure phrase formations, in repetition of previously heard themes at symmetrical distances from intervening sections, and in the preference for forms which contain symmetrically arranged sections.

# FORMAL AND GENERATIVE PRINCIPLES

## THE COMPOUND FORMS OF THE CLASSIC PERIOD

### *The Sonata Type*

This highly important sequence of movements has a rather definite pattern which can be described in terms of possible individual forms and tempi as follows:

1. First Movement: *Allegro* (fast): sonata-allegro form, with or without introduction, coda.
2. Second Movement: *Andante* (somewhat slowly): broad sonata-allegro form; sonatina; theme and variations; three-part (ternary) form.
3. Third Movement: *Moderato* (moderate speed): minuet-and-trio, each part in binary form: *or* scherzo-and-trio, same form but more rapid tempo.
4. Fourth Movement: *Allegro* to *Presto* (fast to very fast): sonata-allegro form; sonata-rondo form; rondo; less often theme and variations.

When such a compound form is written for one instrument alone or two instruments in combination, such as violin and piano, the work is called a sonata. When written for three instruments, it is called a trio; for four, a quartet; for five a quintet and so on. When the dimensions of the performing group reach that of a small orchestra, the work is called a symphony. Thus, one might define a symphony as a sonata for orchestra.

To turn for a moment to the varieties of combinations used other than orchestra, we find the solo sonata limited largely to the piano. The duet combination exists mainly in the form of violin-piano sonatas, although combinations of piano and other instruments do occur. The trio may be made up of three stringed instruments (variably: two violins and cello; violin, viola and cello; or two violins and viola); three woodwind instruments; or, more usually, piano, violin and cello. The main form of the quartet in this period is that of the string quartet: first and second violins, viola and cello. However, much literature exists for the mixed quartet of one wind instrument plus violin, viola and cello; and Mozart wrote for this string trio combination plus piano. The latter works are called piano quartets. This does not signify music written for four pianos. When piano is combined with a string quartet, we have the piano quintet; combinations of the string quartet with other single instruments are named accordingly (e.g., clarinet quintet). The other kind of quintet most frequently encountered is the so-called woodwind quintet. This has a standard instrumentation of flute, oboe, clarinet, bassoon and French horn. The larger combinations, both of the string and wind varieties, have no standard plan, and approach the sonorities and possibilities of what is known as a small, or chamber, orchestra.

## The Concerto Types

For the most part, the concerto grosso construction, both as to instrumentation and form had disappeared by Classic times, although the principle of alternation of sonority and mass was still valid. The only rather rare exceptions are compositions usually called *Sinfonie Concertante* for two or more instruments and orchestra. In these works, however, we find the classical *sonata* format, *not* the baroque kind of construction. Mozart wrote three beautiful examples of this kind of multiple concerto: the *Concertone*, K. 190 for two solo violins, oboe and cello; the Sinfonia Concertante for violin, viola and orchestra, K. 364, and the one for four woodwinds and orchestra, K. 297B. The sonata-ideal had so penetrated the formal design of this era that we may expect to find it in the concerto, the compound form of which is as follows:

1. First Movement: *Allegro:* concerto-allegro (to be discussed later).

2. Second Movement: *Andante:* broad sonata-allegro; sonatina; theme and variations; ternary form.
3. Third (and last) Movement: *Allegro* to *Presto:* sonata-allegro: sonata-rondo; rondo; theme and variations.

Notice that the dance movement — the minuet and trio — is omitted.

### The Divertimento Types

This is a rather loose classification including, besides the divertimento, the serenade *(serenata)*, and the cassation. These works were usually written for small combinations of instruments, and were designed to be played out-of-doors (in which case wind instruments were usually used), or as salon "music for conversation." The style is light and pleasing, as a rule, although Mozart ventured some profound thoughts in certain of his compositions in this form.

The divertimento types consist of a variable number of movements, usually from five to seven. Those intended for outdoor performance often begin and end with a march-like movement, suggesting that the musicians may have marched in, played their music and marched out. In the case of those composed for strings, the outer movements correspond in style, though not in workmanship, to the first and fourth movements of a symphony. Between these boundaries occur slow movements and dance movements, usually minuets. The slow movements are often very lyric, in the case of the indoor variety approximating the slow movement of a violin concerto — it might be expected that there would be at least one superior player within the group! Some of the most charming and representative rococo music of the period was composed for these musical diversions.

## THE SINGLE FORMS OF THE CLASSIC PERIOD

### The Binary, or Two-Part Form

Structurally, the binary form is one of the simplest, yet, as we shall see, it has complex transformations. As in the Baroque period, tonality is the real basis for form. Simply stated, binary form results from the *statement* of a key, the *departure* from it, and finally the *return*. But this is basically the format for three-part form also. How do they differ? Let us examine a movement in binary form first, in order to be able to differentiate between them when the occasion arises.

EXAMPLE 40.

Menuetto
Allegretto
Section 1
Flauto
Clarinetti in B Sib
Fagotti
Corni in Es Mib
Trombe in Es Mib
Timpani in Es B Mib Sib
Phrase 1
2
Allegretto
Violino I
Violino II
Viola
Violoncello e Contrabasso
I
unstable
5
Fl.
Cl.
Fg.
Cor.
Tr.
Timp.
Vl. I
Vl. II
Vla.
Vlc. e Cb.
mfp
p
10
15
Half-cadence
V
Section 2
unstable
a 2
Vlc. e Cb.
20
Stable
Return of Section 1
thematic material
25
30

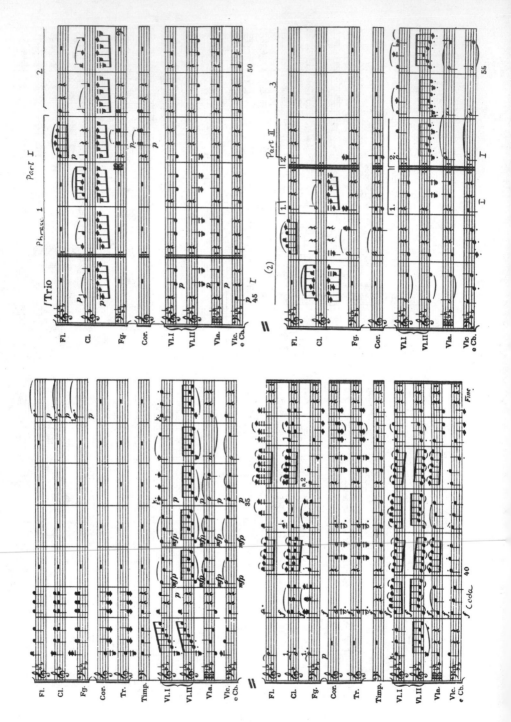

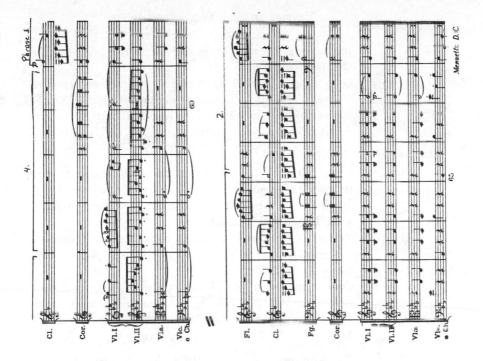

Where shall we find such a movement? Generally speaking, all dance forms are binary in a structure, hence the minuet movement of a classical symphony should provide material. If we were to look further, we should find that most themes of theme-and-variation movements are in binary form. But let us examine a typical minuet, that of Mozart's Symphony No. 39 in E♭, K. 543 (Example 40). Perhaps the easiest way to show the construction of this form is to examine this minuet measure by measure in order to see what happens. Here is the "roadmap":

SECTION I

> Meas. 1-4: Block chords, followed by the ascending broken-chord theme which concludes with a non-final cadence (on IV).
>
> 5-8: Similar thematic material, concluding with final cadence on I; the melodic cadence note suggests that more is to follow.
>
> 9-12: Lyric cadential figure, leading to caesura upon an unstable note which resolves weakly on the third beat

of measure 12, and serves to lead to the beginning of the next phrase.

13-16: Ornamented V triad leads to half-cadence on repeated V chord. Two beat silence after the last chord. Double bar with two dots before it signifies that the entire Section I is to be repeated.

**SECTION II**

Meas. 17-24: Return from V to I, called retransition: main quality is instability moving toward a strong cadence on I. In this case, the thematic material of measures 1-4 is used for this subsection.

25-40: Repeat of Section I with the measures corresponding to 13-16 changed so as to lead to the next phrase without a pause.

41-44: Concluding section, called "codetta," consisting of decorated V and I chords, each lasting one measure, and adding up to repeated and emphatic final cadences. Double-bar with dots: repeat Section II.

What then, is significant about this binary form? The statement, departure from, and restatement of the principal tonality. The small amount of thematic material used. The unstable nature of the retransition section, and the fact that it uses thematic material introduced previously. And finally, the return of the thematic material of the first half. Diagrammed, this *rounded* binary form appears in Example 41a.

There is another kind of binary form which is only slightly different from the above, which we shall call *simple* binary form; it is used by Mozart for the second minuet, called the trio, of this movement (Example 42). Originally, a smaller instrumentation — often that of the trio — was used for the second minuet in order to create contrast, much in the manner of a baroque concerto grosso.

EXAMPLE 41A. *Rounded binary form.*

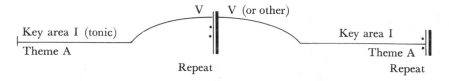

**TRIO: SECTION I**

Meas. 45-53: Two phrases whose melodic material is centered in the clarinets; echo in the flute connects the phrases; light string accompaniment. Section I *begins and ends in the tonic* key. Upon repetition, second ending is used, which leads directly into Section II.

**SECTION II**

Meas. 54-68: A six measure phrase in the strings indicates the re-transition: it ends on the dominant, and a stereotyped horn passage of two measures prolongs the section to the more standard eight measures after which Section I appears in its entirety. Section II is repeated, after which the directions at the end of the trio (Menuetto D (a) C (apo) — return to the beginning of the min-uet) lead us back to the first minuet which is now traditionally played straight through without its internal repeats (*i.e.*, Section I followed by Section II).

The diagram of this kind of binary form (simple) appears in Example 41b. The same conclusions drawn above for the rounded

EXAMPLE 41B. *Simple binary form.*

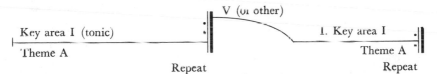

binary form are applicable. Especially important is the nature of the retransition — that of a bridge, structurally but not necessarily the-matically important. We shall hear other binary forms which are longer than these examples, possibly more complex thematically, but the conclusions drawn above will still be valid.

Upon the conclusion of the trio, the first minuet is always re-peated, but without its internal repetitions. If we denote the entire minuet by the letter "A," and the trio by "B," the total form can be represented by the formula "A-B-A," which is a three-part, or ternary form, which we shall discuss more fully in a later section. But let us first explore the more complex relatives of the rounded binary form.

## The Sonatina Form

Suppose we begin with a rounded binary form and expand the sections to a considerable degree. We should have first a fairly long section in the basic key, characterized by certain thematic material. Then there should follow a section, called the transition, which changes the tonal center and makes a cadence of conditional stability in the new key. This new key area might be expanded to some greater number of measures to prolong the departure from the principal key, and in doing so would establish itself as a new stable plane related to the former one in the way we have shown. This new key area might be made even more contrasting if different thematic material should be used. Schematically it would look like Example 42, Section I. A

EXAMPLE 42. *Sonatina form.*

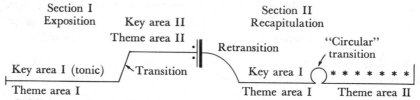

subsidiary section, called variously the coda, codetta or closing section was often placed at the end of Section II to round it off, and give the listener the impression that what he had heard was a large structural portion of the work, now given the name of Exposition. Normally, neither of the two large sections (I, II) of a sonatina is repeated, especially when the tempo is slow.

Suppose, again, that in Section II of this binary form, we retain the rather short retransition, but repeat the previous material of Section I in the same way. But it ends on a *conditionally* stable plane, whereas the logic of musical form demands a return to complete stability at the conclusion of a structure. In order to accomplish this we maneuver the direction of the modulatory chord progression of the transition between Key Areas I and II, so that instead of changing key it describes a "circular" path and returns to a cadence which states or strongly implies the tonic key. The previous Key Area II has now become tonic, and we hear the themes of Thematic Area II now in that key, with the final cadence of the section emphasizing the state of tonal stability. What we have arrived at by this expansion is the form called *sonatina form* (sonatina: a little sonata-allegro). In

EXAMPLE 43.

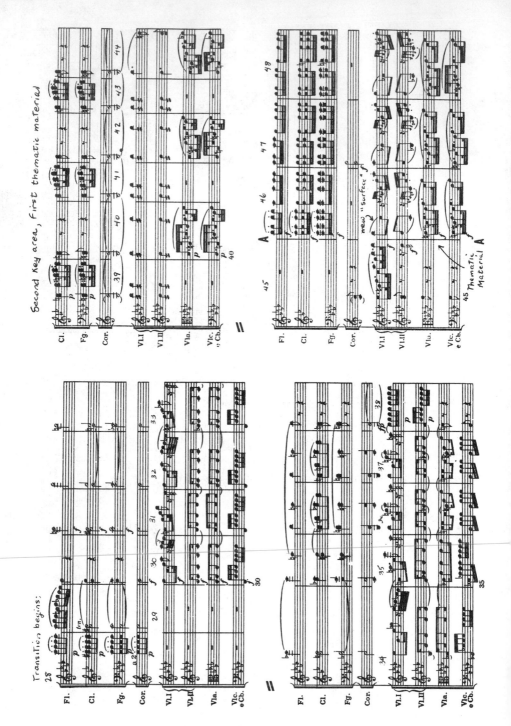

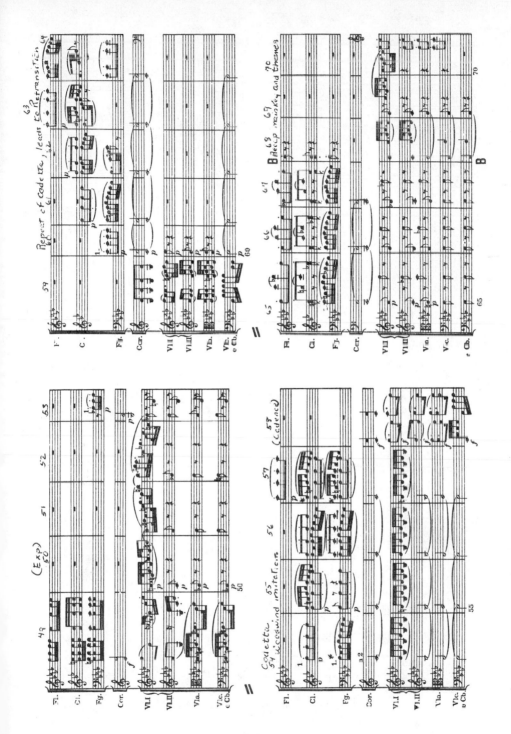

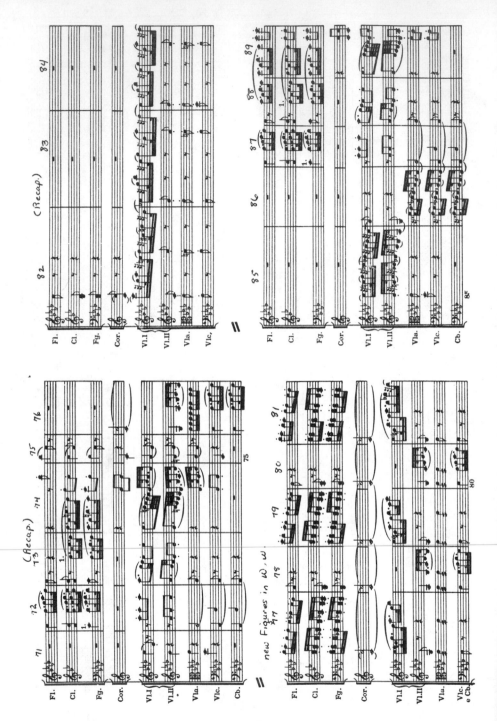

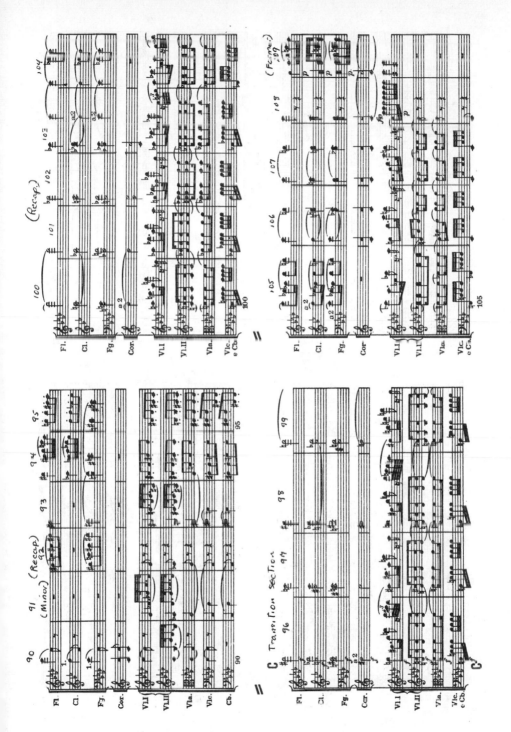

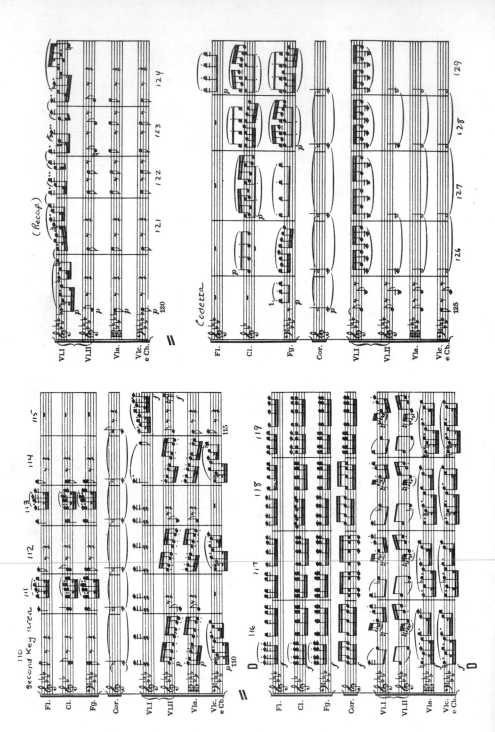

210

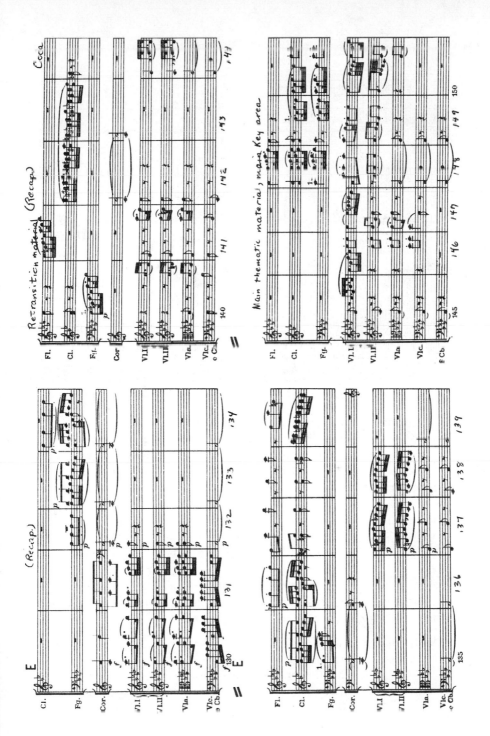

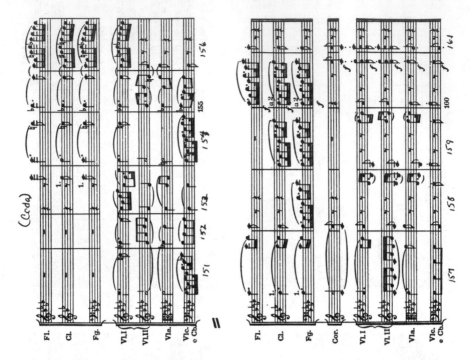

compositions of this form written in the Classic period, we usually find
new thematic material in the second key area, or sometimes the first
thematic material re-presented in such a way as to sound new. This
latter type of sonatina will be referred to as monothematic, although
it is not usually strictly so. Haydn seems to prefer the monothematic
forms more than does Mozart, probably as a result of his economy
and penchant for thematic development. For clearness of outline,
however, let us examine a movement in sonatina form by Mozart.
This example is also drawn from the Symphony No. 39, and is the
second movement — a monothematic sonatina form engineered to be
played at an andante tempo (Example 43). That a sonatina need
not be a miniature is demonstrated by this movement, one of the
longest in Mozart's symphonic compositions.

EXPOSITION (see Example 43)
    *Key Area I, Theme Area I*
        Meas. 1-27: Small rounded binary form: Section I, meas. 1-8; Sec-
                tion II, meas. 9-27. Note that this internal binary
                form is particular to this movement, not necessarily

to be found in other sonatina movements. Main thematic material in serious *galant* style. Thematic rhythmic motive.

### Transition

Meas. 28-37: "Storm and Stress" style; begins in minor using bold instrumental theme incorporating thematic rhythmic motive from exposition. Unstable, leading to non-final cadence in meas. 38.

### Key Area II (uses same thematic material as Key Area I)

Meas. 38-53: Return of thematic material of exposition in contrasting sonorities of winds versus low strings. Two short sections, the first comprising meas. 39-45, the second meas. 46-49. In the latter a new part in the violins is added to the thematic rhythm in the low strings while the winds play sustained continuo harmony. This leads to a passage for the first violins similar to that of meas. 14-19 in the first Key Area.

### Codettas (still in Key Area II)

Meas. 53-63: Imitative polyphony in the woodwinds terminated by an expressive sighing cadence figure in the strings. A repetition of this is begun, but modulation ensues, thus becoming the retransition.

### Retransition

Meas. 63-67: Unstable, leading to cadence on I, which begins the recapitulation.

#### RECAPITULATION

### Key Area I, Theme Area I

Meas. 68-95: Thematic material as before; binary form, but without internal repeats; newly orchestrated, now adding important contrast in sonority by use of woodwinds. Turns to minor at meas. 91 in order to make smooth connection with transition section.

### Transition

Meas. 96-108: Substantially the same structurally and thematically as before, but begins in new key so that the harmonic movement is toward the tonic key. In the generalized

213

formal diagram this will be called a "circular" transition to describe the movement away from and back to the tonic key, which replaces the tonality of the previous Key Area II.

*Key Area I* (replaces former Key Area II)

Meas.109-125: Return of measures corresponding to meas. 38-53 of exposition, but now in the tonic key. Slightly reorchestrated.

*Codettas*

Meas. 125-144: As before, now with repeat of codetta leading back to tonic via a passage in the clarinets to the coda (larger concluding section).

*Coda*

Meas. 144-161: Repeats the main thematic material. Repeated cadences to round off the movement satisfyingly.

Now let us compare this extended movement with the brief and uncomplicated rounded binary form (Example 41a). The differences are obvious, but it is the correspondence of certain procedures which is important. Both make an economical use of thematic material, repeating and developing themes already introduced rather than bringing in new ideas. Actually, the sonatina movement just examined uses only two really different groups of important motives — those of the principal theme and those of the transition. More economy we could not ask for!

The second important factor is that of structural motion. A musical composition may often be compared to a bridge. It spans a certain duration of time, and both ends are usually firmly placed in the principal key. Intermediate cadences or key sections are comparable to piers supporting central sections of the structure. Using this parallel, we find that both rounded binary and sonatina forms resemble a bridge of a single span, with no intermediate piers. Translated into musical terms, this means that a noticeable and almost essential element of these forms is the feeling of movement *from* the principal key at the beginning *toward* its return near the close of the movement. This is accomplished by creating a somewhat unstable interior of the form through modulation, conditional or non-final cadences and chord progression. In the music of the Classic period this "tonal bridge" is not as obvious to modern ears as it will become near the close of the Romantic era.

Notice the relative symmetry of the design we have revealed in this movement. A statement, whether of key or theme, at the commencement of the form is balanced by a restatement later in the work. Even the number of measures of each large section, exclusive of the coda, balance nearly exactly. The coda, with its repetition of the principal thematic material and its frequent cadences does not have the upsetting effect we might expect in such a delicately poised work, but serves largely as a steadying influence in regard to key.

Example 44 shows a diagram of sonatina form deduced from the particular form of the movement of the Mozart Symphony No. 39 we have just examined. We shall find sonatina movements both larger and smaller than this one in our journey through the literature of music. And we shall find that the name is sometimes loosely used by certain composers, not to designate a form so much as to signify a small sonata.

### The Sonata-Allegro Form

It will be noticed that the retransition was the only part of the binary form which was not greatly enlarged when the sonatina form was evolved. This final change creates, in effect, the sonata-allegro form. But how is it enlarged? By substituting for the simple passage-work the important technique of thematic development. This procedure reflects upon the choice of thematic material for the movement. A sonatina, as we have seen, can be a lyric movement, even melodic; but a sonata-allegro is usually less lyric, and almost certainly one of the themes, be it ever so unimportant, contains a rhythmic or melodic motive which will lend itself to some species of development. The *structural* function of the development is the same as that of the retransition — to modulate back to the principal key area — but its scope is far greater. The retransition returns by a rather direct route, since few measures are allotted to it; but the development traverses a more roundabout path, touching, perhaps, on several key areas during its return. To balance this longer journey, the development usually concludes with a more or less lengthy section which prepares for the return of the tonic key (I) by sustaining in some way the V chord, creating thus an elongated V-I cadence. This section is called the "dominant preparation" (dominant signifies the function of the V chord), and is the vestigial remnant of the retransition.

EXAMPLE 44. *Formal diagram of second movement, Symphony No. 39 by Mozart. This is the particular sonatina form of this movement.*

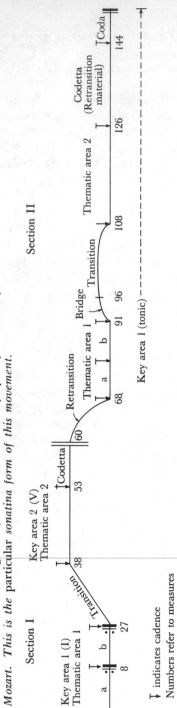

Section I

Key area 1 (I)
Thematic area 1

Key area 2 (V)
Thematic area 2

↑Codetta

Transition

Section II

Retransition
Thematic area 1

Bridge

Transition

Thematic area 2

Codetta
(Retransition
material)

Coda

Key area 1 (tonic)

a    b    a    b

8    27   38   53   60   68   91   96   108   126   144

↑ indicates cadence
Numbers refer to measures

EXAMPLE 45. *Generalized diagram of sonata-allegro form.*

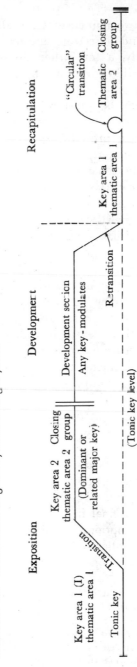

Exposition

Development

Recapitulation

Key area 1 (I)
thematic area 1

Tonic key

Transition

Key area 2
thematic area 2

(Dominant or
related major key)

Closing
group

Development section

Any key - modulates

R-transition

Key area 1
thematic area 1

(Tonic key level)

"Circular"
transition

Thematic
area 2

Closing
group

Essentially, these two refinements are all that are necessary: developmental themes and a section devoted to exploiting this trait (Example 45). Actually, a few other things may happen, for the sonata-allegro is a flexible form, as the fugue was, and the music exhibits endless variety.

First, the form may be substantially monothematic — which is Haydn's favorite type — or it may have sharply contrasting themes, which is Mozart's normal procedure. (Both species, however, occur in the works of either master.)

Secondly, it may have separate (and sometimes important) themes for the transition and codettas; or the transition may be constructed of instrumental figuration having no thematic significance — scales, running figures, and chords; or it may be formed from motives derived from the first thematic material, a more symphonic procedure. Haydn often employs the first method, while Mozart and later Beethoven use the second.

Thirdly, the codetta may be fashioned of new material, or on the other hand recall thematic elements from the previous sections, most frequently from the first thematic group. These materials, new or old, are handled in such a way as to cadence repeatedly, giving the whole section quite a secure feeling of conditional stability.

Fourthly, the development may begin with a repetition of the material from the closing group, or codetta, thus enhancing the continuity of material over the structural cadence separating the first section (the exposition), from the beginning part of the second section whose function is development of material (the development section).

Fifthly, the final coda is optional. If present, it may be of any length the composer deems suitable, and often repeats elements of the first thematic group, again, like the codetta, emphasizing cadences, this time fully stable and final in nature.

One other feature is optional. This is the use of slow introductory section before the sonata-allegro form actually begins. This introduction may have several functions:

1. It may serve to heighten by contrast the initial statement of the first thematic material.
2. It may serve to create a more commanding impression than the thematic material might, especially if that thematic material is lyric and unassuming in character.
3. It may clearly introduce the principal key of the movement, allowing

the composer to move sooner into the transition and second key area.

4. It may introduce themes or thematic motives in rhythmically elongated form (augmentation) which are to be used in the faster sections to follow.

When sonata-allegro form is used for fast movements, the first thematic group is apt to be bold, vigorous, or march-like in character, while the second thematic group usually is constructed of more lyric, feminine, and graceful phrases. This kind of choice highlights the contrast of themes, as well as the key contrast. These themes provide landmarks, as it were, for the easy recognition of the two important sections. We have called these sections "thematic groups," and this is often exactly what they are — not single themes, but groups of thematic fragments combined for a common purpose. The opening of Mozart's Symphony No. 41 illustrates this clearly.

We have mentioned the importance of cadences before. In this rather complicated form they are even more so. They usually provide clear indications of structural elements — punctuation.

Let us now turn to a full-fledged example of this form, this time the first movement from the Symphony No. 39 of Mozart (Example 46).

INTRODUCTION

*Key Area I, Theme Area I*

Meas. 1-25: The introduction begins with a full, rich chord in the principal key of the work, E♭, followed in slow tempo by rhythmic repetitions of the chord, thus constituting a rhythmic motive which will be repeated several times before the *allegro* section arrives. This rhythm and parts of it are combined with a scale figure of some length in the strings, first descending, then ascending. The tension, created by these two factors together with the harmonic motion, rises to a climax replete with dissonances, then subsides and harmonically prepares for the principal theme and key area of the *allegro*. What has been accomplished by this introduction? It introduces no themes or motives, but it does make an impressive, rather romantic, gesture which captures our attention and arouses our expectancy.

EXAMPLE 46.

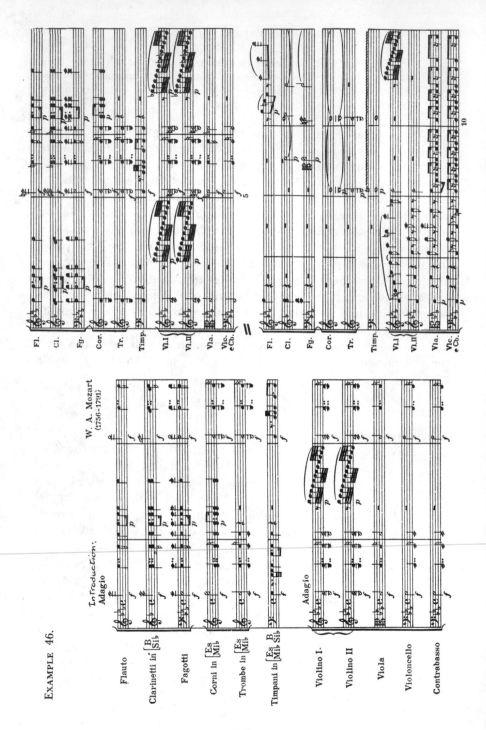

W. A. Mozart
(1756-1791)

220

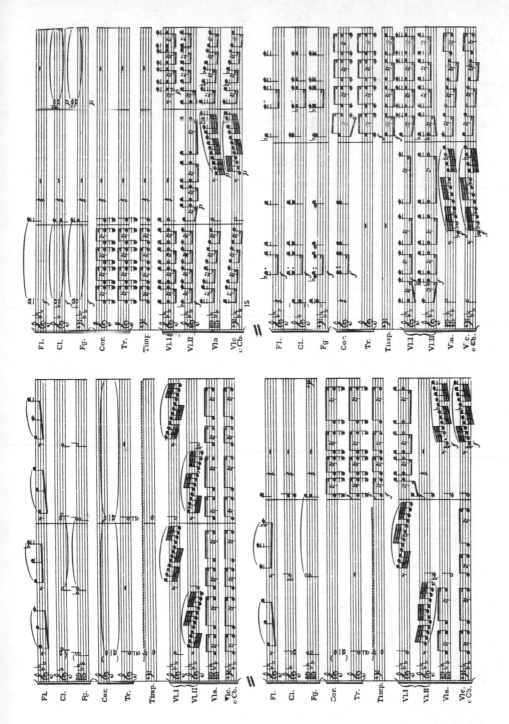

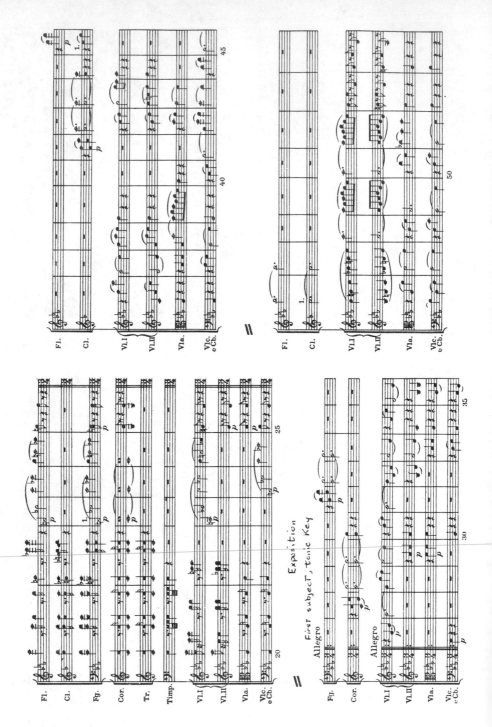

First subject, tonic Key

Exposition

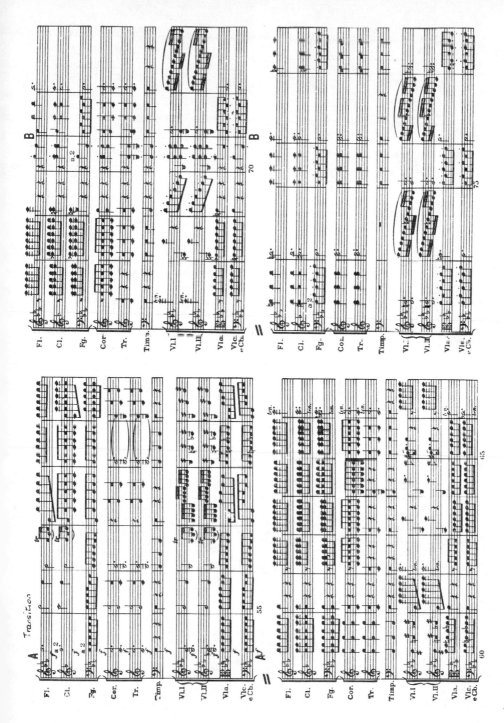

223

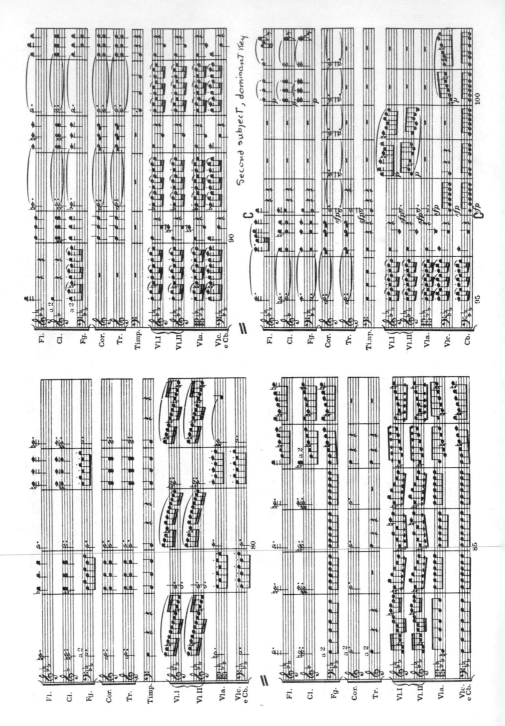

Second subject, dominant Key

224

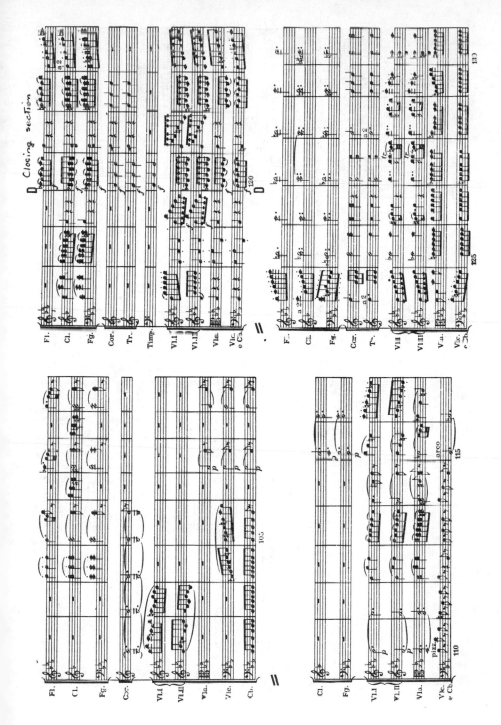

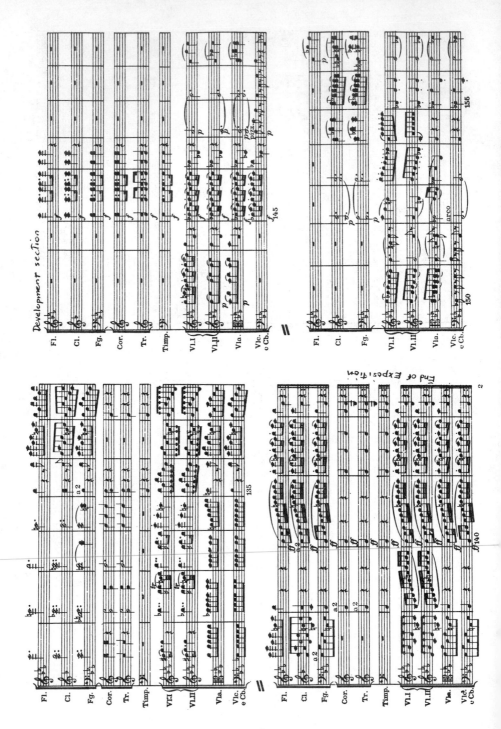

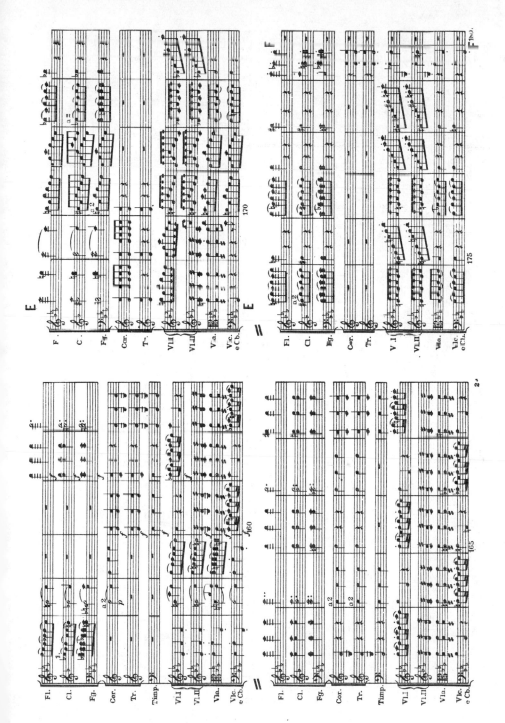

227

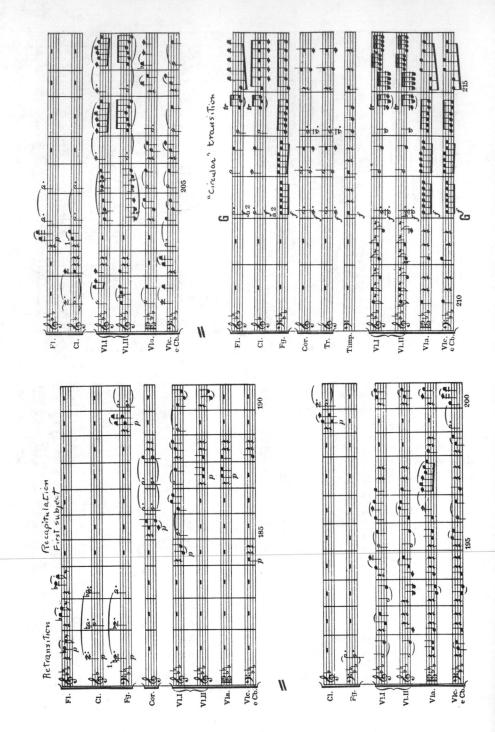

228

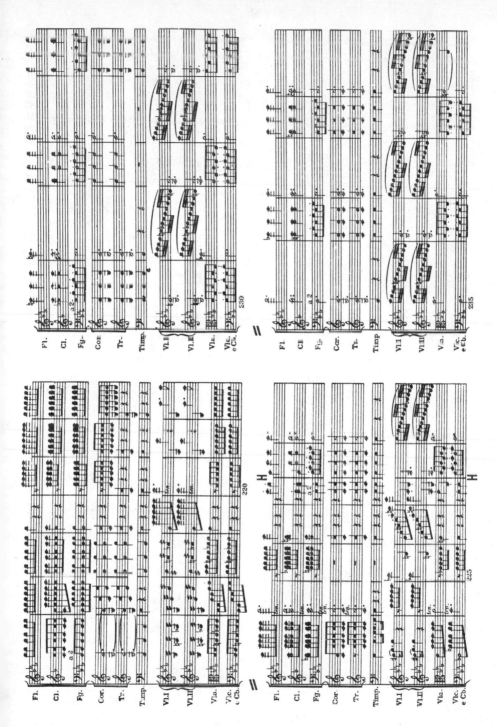

229

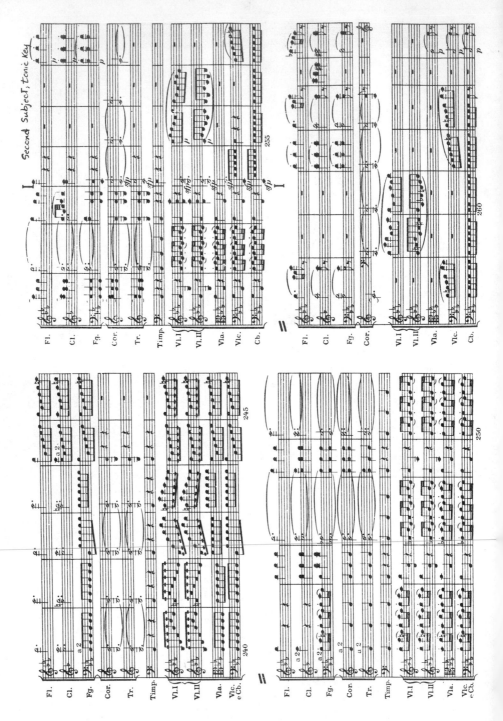

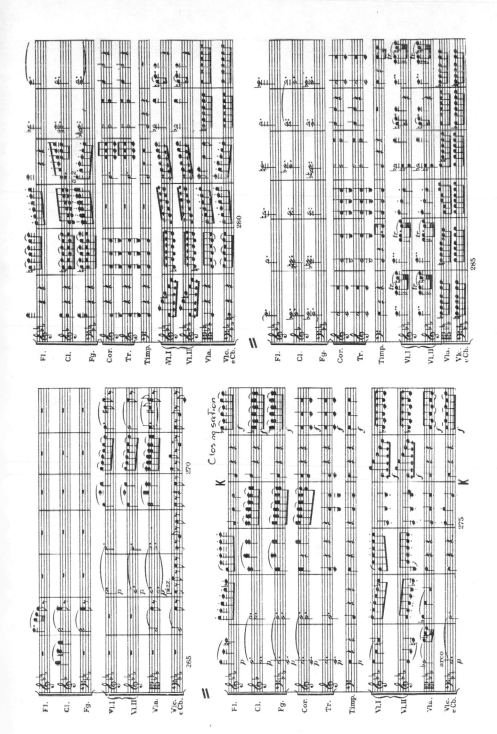

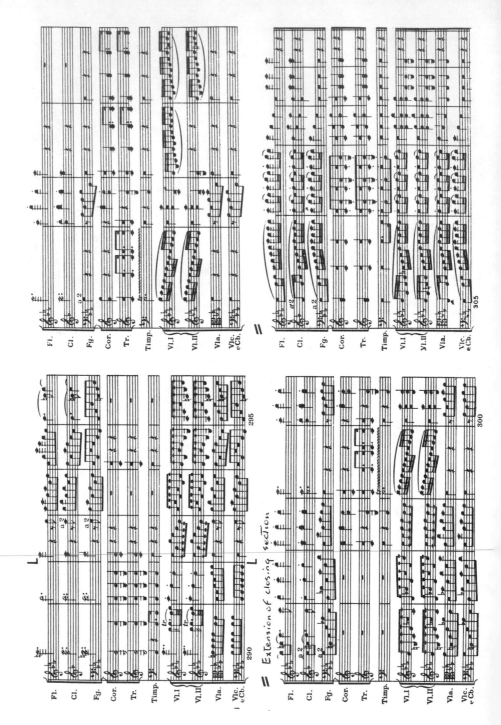

232

**EXPOSITION**

### Key Area I, Theme Area I

Meas. 26-53: The movement proper begins in *galant* style with an unassuming broken chord figure in the violins imitated by the bassoons an octave lower. After it has run its course it is repeated in an inverted arrangement: first the lower instruments, then the higher in imitation. Following this repetition, an outburst in the full orchestra using the key-defining chords and a motive from the first theme leads to an emphatic cadence which closes the first key and thematic area.

### Transition

Meas. 54-97: There follows an animated transition section, constructed from chords and scales recalling the introduction, which gradually changes key and makes several cadences which lead to a surprisingly quiet arrival at the second theme and key area.

### Key Area II, Theme Area II

Meas. 97-119: This section is well described as a group of themes. There are four distinct elements, together with several subsidiary cadential figures. The first is a winding phrase in the upper strings which is answered by a rising scale in the lower strings. This idea is immediately repeated. Then follows a two-measure cadence figure in the woodwinds, and after its repetition, a rather dance-like *five* measure phrase in the strings. The latter is not repeated, but evolves into a more elaborate version of the dance-like figure, this time more fully scored.

### Codetta

Meas. 120-142: The closing section (codetta) explodes immediately from the cadence chord of the last section, and, after a series of eight measures of scale and cadence figures, settles down to a more melodic, although impassioned, phrase in the upper strings which employs a deceptive cadence before repeating itself. Then more broken chord patterns ensue, concluding with the stereotyped little cadential figure we heard at the

end of the transition section and an emphatic cadence.

DEVELOPMENT

Meas. 143-183: The development opens with a repetition of the
last-mentioned figure, followed by an extended version of the dance-like element of the second group
of themes. When this is finished, the stereotyped
transition figure is treated in imitation in alternate
measures by the high and low strings. An equally
vigorous passage derived from the codetta comes
next, and after it a measure of silence and three of
quiet movement toward the principal key, at which
point the last (recapitulation) section begins.

RECAPITULATION AND CODA

Meas. 184-303, The recapitulation is essentially repetition of the
303-309: exposition with the key differences cunningly ad-
justed. Only the more acute will be able to hear
the changes. There is a short coda which builds
up energy and excitement for the final cadence
which is accomplished by the transition section's
little cliché.

The foregoing roadmap of form does very little to explain how
Mozart has created this beautiful piece of music. But we must realize
that the life of this work does not depend solely on the sensitive and
*galant* elements that it contains, but rather on how these elements are
employed, one played off against the other, or combined in some
subtle way. Musical composition does not wholly consist of being able
to create beautiful or meaningful themes, but, maybe more importantly, *how* these themes are used — in a word, the form.

The three last symphonies of Mozart, Nos. 39, 40, and 41, exhibit
widely different approaches to this form, as do those of the "London
Symphonies" of Haydn. The music of the latter composer is often
less formally clear than that of Mozart, but this is not to say that it
is confused! Far from that, for Haydn's structures are rather exploratory, and place an emphasis upon thematic development which
Mozart's works do not generally exhibit. Even the exposition and
recapitulation sections of Haydn's sonata-allegros are apt to be develop-

mental, and the music of this composer, while often not as elegant as that of his younger colleague, abounds in wit and surprise.

## The Concerto-Allegro Form

This variety of the sonata-allegro form was developed by Bach's son, Johann Christian Bach, and other composers of the time. It remained for Mozart to bring it to a point of classical perfection. Mozart had considerable need for concertos, and in those days of expensive printing and no copyright laws, the most reasonable course for a pianist or violinist to follow was that of composing the works for himself — if he were able. Mozart was indeed able!

If we recall the binary form, we remember that the first section is repeated, and that when the form is expanded to the sonata-allegro form, this repetition is still indicated by a sign in the music at the end of the exposition section, whether honored in actual performance or not. The concerto-allegro follows this procedure, but instead of merely writing the repeat indication at the end of the exposition, the composer *writes out in full two complete expositions* (Example 47). They are not exactly alike, however. The first exposition uses only the orchestra — not the soloist; and instead of employing two key areas, it remains in the principal tonality throughout, much like the recapitulation section of an ordinary sonata-allegro. When this first exposition has finished, a few measures usher us into the second, which is shared between the solo instrument and the orchestra, and is regular in its use of two keys and contrasting themes. The development is regular, and is shared as is the recapitulation. Near the end of the closing section (codetta), however, the second irregularity occurs. Shortly before the place where the final cadence would be expected, were there no coda, the orchestra drives dynamically and rhythmically to an emphatic non-final cadence, the last chord of which is held for a moment. This last chord usually occurs within a final cadence formula. The orchestra now pauses for the soloist to complete the cadence ornamentally, hence the Italian name used for this procedure, *cadenza,* or cadence. In effect, this is the opportunity for the soloist to exhibit his skill upon the instrument in a virtuoso passage which should be constructed from thematic material of the foregoing movement. In Mozart's time, these passages were improvised, presumably "on the spot." We are fortunate in having a few cadenzas which Mozart wrote out for the use of his students. The end of the cadenza is usually

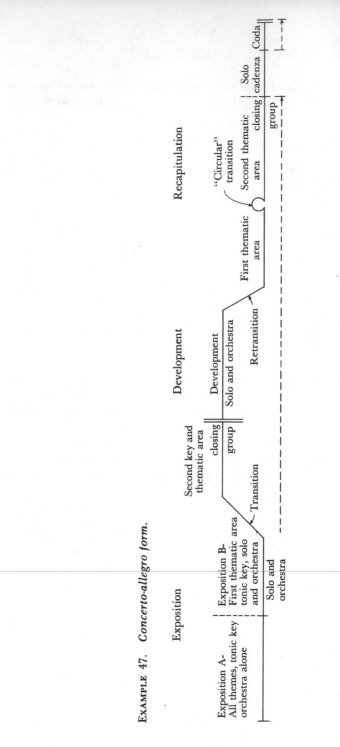

EXAMPLE 47.  *Concerto-allegro form.*

signaled to the conductor of the orchestra by a trill in the solo, after which the orchestra enters, and, alone or with the solo, completes the movement with a short coda. The other movements of a concerto may have cadenzas, but often do not. They consist of the regular symphonic forms shared by solo and orchestra and, resulting from this sharing, expanded in length. There are always three movements in a concerto, corresponding to the first, second and fourth movements of a symphony.

What we have described here is especially true of the piano concertos. In concertos for the violin or for wind instruments, Mozart allows himself more freedom in the use of the orchestral exposition, often abbreviating it or, more rarely, omitting it entirely. Many of these and other changes occur in early works at a time when the form had not been developed either in the composer's mind or in the common practice of the day. A late example, however, is the great clarinet concerto (K. 622) in which the cadenzas are entirely eliminated.

### The Sonata-Rondo Form

This hybrid, which is often mistakenly called *rondo,* results from a slight change in sonata-allegro form. The essential element in rondo form is that a particular theme and key must return again and again, alternating with episodes employing different themes and keys. The letter formula might read A-B-A-C-A, where A represents the fixed returning element, and B and C the episodic ones.

If after completing a normal exposition of a sonata-allegro form, a composer were to begin the development section as though he were going to repeat the exposition — that is, in the tonic key, with the first thematic elements — then veer off into the real development, we should have the change necessary to create the sonata-rondo (Example 48). As if to support the rondo element, the coda of such a movement is often devoted to a more or less complete return of the A section before the final codettas and cadences.

Close attention must be paid to the music to recognize this variant form; more than likely, the listener is apt to hear the rondo element rather than the sonata-allegro element. The final movement of the Symphony No. 35 ("Haffner") of Mozart is an excellent example of this form.

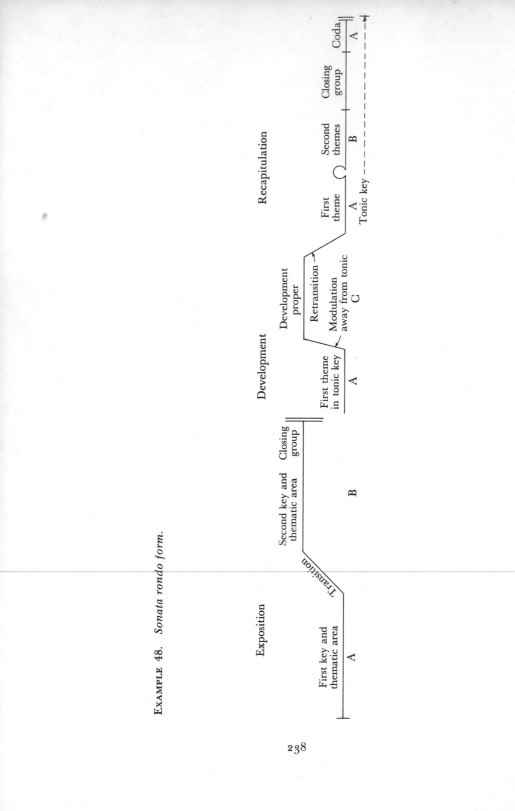

EXAMPLE 48. *Sonata rondo form.*

*Ternary or Three-Part Form: A-B-A*

We have already mentioned this formal arrangement as that of the minuet-trio-minuet. This is a simple case. More complex — and more artistic, usually — ternary forms are often used for the slow movements of symphonies and concertos.

Ternary form is a sectional form. The formula A-B-A implies contrast between A and B. This is achieved by the means already mentioned — by key and by theme. Tone color is usually a supporting factor, especially when the work is orchestral. Contrast of tempo, however, does not usually appear in ternary forms of this period.

Ternary form is clearly exhibited by the slow movement of Haydn's Symphony No. 92 ("Oxford"). The bourgeois style thematic group A is introduced and developed slightly within the tonic key. The B section is a storm and stress section in minor, and leads back to a developed version of the A section. There follows an expressive coda which makes good use of non final cadences of various kinds, together with meaningful pauses — often characteristic of the sensitive style of Haydn's slow compositions.

The delightful second movement of Haydn's Symphony No. 101 ("Clock") furnishes a good example of a somewhat more elaborate ternary form. In this movement, the first A section is in binary form, with both sections marked to be repeated. The B section is again stormy and in minor, but rather longer than the one in the "Oxford" Symphony. The final A section makes use of both developmental and variation techniques, and ends with a rather long coda.

*Rondo Form: A-B-A-B-A; A-B-A-C-A; A-B-A-C-A-B-A*

Like ternary form, this is a sectional form based upon the alternation of a main section with contrasting episodic sections. The returning section A must present the same themes in the same key, while the episodes must be in other keys and present other themes. Of course the B sections match, although it is permissible to vary the key. The theme usually remains constant.

While the rondo form is usually considered characteristic of the Classic era, good examples are hard to find. One suspects that too many sonata-rondos have been mistaken for the simpler form and so called. The ritornello forms of the Baroque are more rondo-like in structure than many classical examples (see Handel, Concerto Grosso

No. 9, II; Bach, Concerto for Violin and Orchestra in E Major, III).
It would also appear that some of the composers of so-called "rondos"
used the title loosely, for these compositions are often sonata-rondos
or even sonata-allegros!

One of the nearest approaches to the true rondo form is the Ro-
manza movement (II) of Mozart's charming serenade, *Eine Kleine
Nachtmusik* (*A Little Night-Music*). Here the form is A-B-A-C (in
the minor)-A: if all the indicated repetitions are played, the form
A-A-B-A-B-A-C-A results, still technically a rondo. Another good example of the symmetrical rondo is the final movement of Beethoven's
C-minor Quartet, Op. 18, No. 4. We shall find a few examples of this
form in the music of Beethoven, and still more in the works of composers of the Romantic era to whom form was all too often merely a
mold to be filled, and not the living shape of a vital musical organism.

*Theme and Variation Form: A, A', A", . . . etc.*

We have already touched upon the variation form in Chapters I
and V: there remains little new to be added. The theme is usually
a binary form with a well-defined melody and rather simple harmony.
The sectional repetitions may or may not be honored, according to
the composer's instructions. The ensuing variations are usually of
exactly the same length as the theme, and present an embellished and
decorative version of the melody supported by the original harmony
of the theme. In this latter aspect they resemble the baroque chaconne.
The prevailing texture is homophonic, allowing for slight excursions
into imitative polyphony, often in canonic form. There is usually at
least one variation in the opposite mode, that is, if the theme is major,
a variation in minor may be expected, and vice-versa. The keynote
is usually retained in such cases, only the third, sixth and seventh
degrees of the scale being changed to create the so-called *parallel* minor.
There is often some variation in meter and tempo, especially in these
minor variations, where the expressive qualities of the pathetic bourgeois style, or the romantic storm and stress are used. In addition, the
minor variation often requires some musical engineering to make a
smooth transition back to the major, and so these variations are
somewhat longer than the original theme as a rule.

One of the simplest yet most characteristic sets of variations constitutes the second movement of Haydn's Symphony No. 94, the "Surprise." This little tune, so artless in its simplicity, became a folk song

during Haydn's lifetime, and he thought enough of it to use it again for a rustic touch in his oratorio, *The Seasons*. The only comment necessary is to call attention to the interesting tonal changes in the minor variation, and to the bridge which leads to the next variation.

Another justly famous set of variations is that of Haydn's String Quartet Op. 76, No. 3. The theme of these variations is the Austrian national hymn which Haydn composed in 1797. He is reported to have said that this hymn pleased him more than any of his other works. The variation technique which Haydn employs here is somewhat more polyphonic than usual; the more rapidly moving parts are still decorative and treat the melody in the old cantus firmus manner, somewhat analogous to the passacaglia bass.

The symphonies of Mozart exhibit no variation movements: we must look for these in the slighter divertimenti and chamber music, in the many sets for piano solo, and in a few concertos of various kinds. One of the most moving and impressive of the latter kinds is the finale to the Piano Concerto in C-minor, No. 24, K. 491. This, unusually enough for Mozart, consists of variations on *two* themes, arranged in three-part form. Later, we shall find that Beethoven is fond of using two themes, but that master states them both at the beginning of the movement, rather than in a formal arrangement of this kind. The first theme of the Mozart concerto finale is a kind of grim march, in C-minor, stated first in full by the orchestra alone, then varied by the piano. After a few variations this theme is stated in major, slightly changed rhythmically, and serves to usher in the second theme, also in major, but not the *same* major scale. This second theme is an appealing little melody with a touch of the *galant* style, but a wistful *galant* rather than capricious or witty. The middle section lasts but a moment — it is little more than a statement of the binary form with repeats — and we are back to the grim little march. There is a place for a cadenza by the piano during this last section, just before that instrument states the chromatically varied theme in duple-compound time. Both kinds of treatment prevail to the end of the movement, and there is no softening of the anguished C-minor tonality, but rather its qualities are heightened by the increased use of chromaticism.

A different variety of this form constitutes the final movement of the Sinfonia Concertante for wind instruments and orchestra in E♭, K. 297b. Here we have ten variations and coda based upon a charming *galant* theme. What lends an especial attractiveness to these variations is the refrain, or ritornello, played by the orchestra at the close of each section. Each of the instruments has a chance to display its agility and tone color in its own variation, and Mozart's expert touch with woodwinds is amply demonstrated in several of the sections. The beginning of the coda is serious, almost tragic, for a moment, but the movement concludes merrily with a speeded-up final variation of the theme.

# WORKS OF HAYDN AND MOZART

Because of the rather complete analyses in the section immediately preceding, only outstanding features of important compositions will be mentioned here. It is also felt that a summary of the individual styles of each composer might be useful at this point.

## HAYDN

*Stylistic Traits*

1. Themes and melodies are less of the *opera buffa* variety of the *style galant* than are those of Mozart, retain a folklike quality, especially the minuets. Uses bourgeois style more.
2. Instrumental themes containing motives which can be developed are favored.
3. Monothematic sonata-allegro form is preferred. Formal procedures are apt to be experimental and not always "by the book." Considerable development usually occurs. Haydn is more interested in this procedure than Mozart, consequently he writes longer development sections.
4. Usually simple and clear harmonic texture. Sometimes, however, for profoundly expressive effects Haydn resorts to unexpected unrelated chords, achieving a wide swing away from the principal tonality; the return is usually highly expressive.

*Symphony No. 92* ("Oxford")

*First Movement: Adagio — Allegro spiritoso* (Example 49). This movement is a monothematic sonata allegro with a typical slow introduction. It is characteristic of Haydn that most of the important thematic material is introduced more or less casually in the first twelve measures of the *allegro* section.

Exposition Key Area I, Thematic Area I: The first four measures contain four ideas which will be thoroughly developed: (1) a descending scale figure, (2) the rhythm of this figure (— — —), (3) the decorative ascending figure of the next measure, and (4) the wide upward skip which finishes the theme. The "second act" of the exposition consists of loud relatively non-thematic passage work which provides contrast and leads to a repetition of the first six measures of the *allegro*.

Transition. This section begins as a continuation of the passage

EXAMPLE 49.

FIRST MOVEMENT: Adagio-Allegro spiritoso

INTRODUCTION Adagio

SECOND MOVEMENT: Adagio
FIRST SECTION: A

SECOND SECTION: B

MINUET

work heard before, but now modulates to the dominant and pauses on a half-cadence.

Key Area II, Thematic Area II. The four measures of the principal theme appear again in the strings, but a decorative scale figure in the oboes is added. There follows loud passage work based upon the rhythm of (2) above and broken chords in the strings, soon dissolving into scales and eventually arriving at a cadence. The closing section introduces a new thematic idea — an insignificant repeated-note figure with a twirl around one of the middle notes — after which the exposition concludes with a flourish of scales.

Development. There are four subsections. The development

begins with a repetition of the little closing theme. Motive (1) of the principal theme appears and develops into a diverging and converging figure given to the oboes and bassoons. The principal theme is now combined with itself in syncopation, simultaneously with which is also the closing theme, in imitation. The principal theme again comes to the fore and is used in imitation, expanding finally into a longer scale figure. Passage work like that of the exposition now ensues, comes to a pause, and Haydn is now ready for the recapitulation.

Recapitulation: This section is so irregular that we shall not divide it into subsections, but rather try to follow it through, theme by theme. It is characteristic of Haydn to treat the recapitulation in the broadest manner, regarding it less as a return of themes than as a reaffirmation of the tonic key. In view of this attitude, then, it does not matter whether the sequence of themes is exactly that of the exposition, nor that considerable development occurs. In fact, Haydn is apt to regard his themes somewhat as characters who emerge from the storm of the development section as changed individuals, just as characters in a novel are changed by their experiences.

At first the procedure is much like that of the exposition, except for the imitation of the principal theme an octave higher and one measure later in the flute. The passage-work ensues, also in imitation, and this is followed by not the transition which we heard before, but, of all things, the closing theme! Is Papa Haydn going to fool us, and bring the movement to an early conclusion? Not so, for upon the return of the principal theme, we find it changed to a more intense minor version of its former self. Now the wide skip with which this theme concludes is developed harmonically, the chords sliding away chromatically beneath it. It is transferred to the brass instruments, and leads back to the closing theme. This is developed slightly, and leads in turn to the principal theme, the wide-skipping final notes of which are echoed in the woodwinds, then the strings. The bassoons begin a duet version of the first measure of the principal theme which is imitated a measure later by the oboes and strings, and develops into the "accordion-motion" we have heard once before in the beginning of the development section. This then breaks up into the broken-chord and scale figures now so familiar, cadences by means of the wide upward skip motive, and the closing theme takes over to end the movement with emphatic final cadences. But no! Haydn is not yet ready to conclude. The coda approaches quietly, borne on the rhythm of the principal theme. This coda consists of three short sections. The first is devoted to the principal theme, extended by repetitions of its final skip. The second is the already familiar rhythmic-harmonic section, but now in a highly colored unrelated key. Haydn now proceeds to show how it may be related to the tonic key of the movement, arriving at the third section which restates the principal theme, moves quickly into an abbreviated version of the closing theme, and concludes with broken chords and cadence figures.

*Second Movement: Adagio.* This movement has been analyzed under the section dealing with ternary forms (p. 237).

*Third Movement:* Minuet and Trio. *Allegretto.* Both sections of this combination are in rounded binary form, somewhat extended. The minuet is a typical Haydn peasant minuet, with heavy accents as of boots — not the elegant salon minuets we hear in the Mozart symphonies. It has an unexpected and interesting pause near the beginning of its second section. The trio is longer than might be expected, and deals almost exclusively with syncopation. Here too, are pauses between interior sections. The minuet is normally played upon its return without the binary-form repeats.

*Fourth Movement: Presto.* This is a typical Haydn finale in its speedy tempo and verve. It is simpler in construction than the first movement, although it exhibits considerable development. The principal thematic section consists of two elements: the first (1a) is an eight measure melody repeated three times; the second (1b) is a kind of cadence-figure theme, two measures in length, which evolves into a transitional passage employing 1a in the bass about midway of its course. The transition concludes with an emphatic cadence, and there follows a new second theme (2), instrumental in character, not especially noteworthy as to shape or motivic construction, and sounding something like a blood relation of 1a. The closing section quotes 1a in the bass, followed by a scale derivative of 1a which concludes the exposition with an extremely non-final cadence.

The development begins amusingly with six of the eight measures of 1a in minor quoted by the woodwinds, followed by a long silence. More timidly, the first violins venture the first two measures of the same, now in a different minor key, again followed by a silence. This process is repeated once more, softer, and in a still different minor. Then the whole orchestra plunges into the fray, developing

1a by imitation and sequence, finally reaching a clear cadence. Statement and development of 2 follow, first imitatively, then more boldly in unison and octave, returning to the opening motive of 1a. The dominant preparation clearly stated by the strings, is echoed softly by the flute. As though to increase our suspense, Haydn inserts another measure of silence before the cadentially satisfying beginning of the recapitulation.

This section is much like the exposition, but is not so repetitive. Since the themes were so clearly stated, and so easily recognizable in the development section, there is no reason to repeat them tiresomely several times here.

The coda is almost a small development section in itself, adapting motives from 1a and 2a to cadential purposes. Near the end, the strings have an amusing extended version of the first theme. Here the caesuras are placed on unexpected and unstable notes. The usual emphatic cadences follow, ending not only the movement, but also the symphony.

In general the procedures and methods we have noted in this symphony will be found in the others, as well as in the chamber music and concertos. But Haydn revels in the unexpected — watch out! Each work is unique because Haydn approaches it with the freshness and curiosity of youth. His skill and subtlety are not inconsiderable, although in this day of rich harmony and large orchestras his compositions often tend to sound simple and rustic. But he is well worth listening to carefully.

We have mentioned the increased orchestral richness of Haydn's last works. No better example of this new sonority exists than the overture to his oratorio, *The Creation.* Haydn has here the staggering task of depicting, with the small classic orchestra, the state of chaos before the creation. "The earth was without form and void, and darkness was upon the face of the deep, and the spirit of God was moving over the face of the waters." That he succeeds so beautifully is no small tribute to both his skill and imagination. The sonority is new, the themes strikingly illustrative, and the harmonies bold, more than that, unheard-of in their day. The whole orchestral prelude moves surely toward the entrance of the chorus, and the beautiful effect at the words "And there was light." The whole oratorio is a masterpiece, all the more impressive when we realize that it was composed by a man in the evening of his life, when he might be expected to sit back and reap the rewards of fame for his lifetime of music.

### MOZART

*Stylistic Traits*

Mozart's themes are chiefly in the *galant* style of the Italian comic opera, more courtly than the folk-like phrases of Haydn.

The sonata-allegro uses groups of contrasting themes in the main expository sections. Those of the first group are apt to be vigorous and march-like, often very instrumental in character, usually containing broken chord figures. The second group of themes emphasizes lyricism, often with chromaticism to enhance the "pathetic" quality.

Except in the three last symphonies, Nos. 39, 40 and 41, the development sections in Mozart's sonata-allegros are rather short, and not as exhaustive in their treatment as those of Haydn. The craftsmanship is usually more elegant, especially at the retransition passage, and there is no attempt to use surprises or silences except as these grow logically out of the pure musical material.

Mozart's harmony is usually quite straightforward and simple. Toward the end of his life, however, a taste developed for chords derived by chromatic motion. We have already heard one instance of this in the finale of the piano concerto in C-minor. This chromaticism is often associated with minor tonalities. A touch of the parallel minor often occurs in otherwise major passages to darken the atmosphere for a moment.

There is less use of "busy work" in Mozart's music than in Haydn's. The latter often creates noisy transition passages from scale, chord and rhythm work which has little or nothing to do with the thematic material; whereas Mozart usually employs either previously heard thematic material, or presents a new theme with which to accomplish the modulation.

The sonority of Mozart's orchestra is smoother and fuller than that of Haydn. Mozart often prefers a full, harmonically diffused accompaniment, while Haydn, in the same circumstances might use a very sketchy, thin accompaniment of a few rhythmic chords. Mozart has a fondness for the clarinet, an instrument whose rich color adds to the orchestral sonority. Haydn often omits clarinets, and depends largely upon the oboes and bassoons.

*Symphony No. 39, E♭, K. 543*

The first, second, and third movements of this symphony have

EXAMPLE 50.

already been discussed in the section on forms. There remains the finale (Example 50). This movement is a straightforward, monothematic sonata-allegro of the *opera buffa* type. It opens with the principal theme, followed by a transition of clear chordal movement carried by the figures in the strings, and supported by harmony in the woodwind and brass. In its guise of second theme, the principal theme is somewhat altered, but not unrecognizably so, and the opening motive provides activity over the chordal motion which propels this section to the closing group. This brilliant conclusion is compounded out of a number of elements: a syncopated figure, brilliant scales in the strings, the opening motive of the principal theme and stereotyped cadence chords.

The development opens brusquely with the motive used so frequently in the exposition, but now changed to a more agitated and tense version. This motive supplies almost all of the material used for development, and is presented to us in imitation, unison, and sequence patterns, finally sliding, with the help of woodwind harmonies, back into the tonic key and recapitulation, which is substantially identical with the exposition. There is a short coda of three measures, giving us a last glimpse of the important motive upon which the movement is largely based.

The mood of this final movement is rather strange. Given the principal theme by itself, we might expect a gay, rather shallow, operatic finale. But this lightweight little melody reveals an inner agitation and anguish during the development section that raises the level of the work from mere "finale music" to a profound work of art, revealing, as it does, the composer's controlled effort to subdue his bitterness to a fatalistic resignation. It is also this quality that makes the music universal, for one of the universal experiences of mankind is to be caught, as Mozart was, in the inexorable march of events, unable to influence or change that march in any way.

*Symphony No. 40, G-minor, K. 550*

The mood of the last movement of the 39th symphony here becomes darker and more defiant. This is a more emotional work, and as such, was better liked by the critics of the Romantic era. But, somehow, one gets the feeling, after reading their criticisms, that they missed the point. Schumann, usually a penetrating commentator, remarks that this symphony "is a marvel of Grecian lightness and grace." This comment touches only the surface of the work.

*First Movement.* Exposition: The G-minor symphony (Example 51) is a very economical work in point of size and expression. This is especially true of the first movement. Here are no introductory flourishes, but an immediate statement of the uneasy principal theme over a dark string accompaniment. This theme reveals an important motive in its structure, and we might rightly expect to hear it again. Upon its restatement, the theme modulates, flows into a tense passage of broken chords and rising scale figures, and finally reaches a defiant cadence. The second theme is chromatic and descending, suggesting a meekness which contrasts strongly with the mood of the previous section. This compliant theme is handed about the orchestra, and via a development, reaches a cadence. The closing section brings back the principal theme, now in a major key, and the exposition closes on a conditionally stable chord.

Development: Whatever stable quality this chord may have suggested is rudely destroyed by the three desperate chords which follow

EXAMPLE 51.

FIRST MOVEMENT: Molto allegro

FIRST SUBJECT

IMPORTANT RHYTHM AND MOTIVE, SECOND PART OF TRANSITION

SECOND SUBJECT

CLOSING SECTION

SECOND MOVEMENT: Andante

FIRST SUBJECT

TRANSITION MOTIVES

(Derived from A rhythmically.)

(Note use throughout movement.)

SECOND SUBJECT

CLOSING MATERIAL

THIRD MOVEMENT: MENUETTO E TRIO

TRIO

FOURTH MOVEMENT: Allegro assai

FIRST SUBJECT "MANNHEIM SKYROCKET"

IMPORTANT MOTIVES

Transition is constructed wholly from material quoted above.

SECOND SUBJECT

Closing section is constructed from elements of the first subject, with scale-figures, rhythms and cadential figures added.

it. The main theme, now in a new key, begins a series of modulations; soon imitations in the brass join the action, and the development is under way. There are three parts to this development. The first uses polyphonic methods and is generally loud, climaxing in a repeated cadential section. The second section is soft, high and light in sonority, and works with the motive only, repeating it in the winds and strings. These repetitions build tension which explodes in a loud imitative section using the motive both in its original form and inverted. At the same time, an organpoint in the horns informs us that this is the retransition passage, preparing for the recapitulation. The woodwinds have the task of leading back to the final section, but before their wistful chromatic passage has reached its cadence, the strings impatiently begin the principal theme.

Recapitulation: The recapitulation somewhat expands the proceedings of the exposition, especially in the transition and latter part of the second theme. This second theme, by the way, is now in the tonic minor, a change which renders the chromaticism and harmony more poignant. The coda begins after a meaningful upward struggling scale passage in the strings, and consists mainly of reiterations of the motive and cadence chords.

*Second Movement.* This slow movement is a lyric sonata-allegro form. The theme unfolds in successive imitations, followed by a number of short, two-note cadences in the "sensitive" style culminating in a half cadence. The section is repeated, but now with the previous melodic ideas in the bass counterpointed by a slowly rising chromatic line in the upper strings. This develops into an important counterpoint of the theme, emphasizing its expressive qualities. Now there appears in the violins a quick two-note figure (A) repeated on the notes of a broken chord. This figure takes on increasing importance as the movement progresses. The succeeding measures employ it to modulate to the dominant key for the statement of the second group. It will be remembered that the first theme began with an upward leap: the second theme begins with a skip of the same size, but downward. The little skip (A) appears here too, but upon the repetition of this theme it gives way to an impressive chromatic chordal passage which moves toward the cadence. The closing section occupies only four measures, and merely decorates the cadence.

The development section is fairly dramatic, for all the lyricism of the exposition. Here we find figure A assuming importance, combined with chordal progressions. A new-sounding figure consisting of a short, rising, somewhat chromatic scale appears toward the end of the development, and is used from time to time as a counterpoint to some of the thematic motion. Figure A occupies a rather important part in the recapitulation, but this section is otherwise essentially the same as the exposition.

The whole movement has a rather resigned and pensive air, despite the summoning-up of energy in the development section.

*Third Movement.* The minuet, on the other hand, is a forceful, bold proclamation of defiance, with its vigorous chordal theme and striking syncopations and dissonances. No greater contrast could be imagined than that achieved by the delicate chamber music of the trio. Here the pastel colors of strings, woodwinds and horns are used most effectively. Particularly lovely are the short passages for the horns.

*Fourth Movement.* The finale continues the vigor of the minuet. Here we have an uncomplicated sonata-allegro form, with themes typical of Mozart: a bold ascending broken-chord first theme, and a lyric, chromatic second theme. The abruptness of the development section recalls the final movement of the 39th symphony; here too is the dramatic use of polyphony, and the defiant gesture. The recapitulation is regular, and the movement concludes punctually without a coda.

It is interesting to note that this symphony does not include trumpets in its scoring, whereas its two companions do. Why the omission? Could not Mozart have used them to good advantage in the more defiant sections of this work? Do we miss them? No, and no. This is a symphony of futile struggle and eventual resignation to the powers of fate. The bright, triumphant tone of the trumpets would have been out of place, whether in their modest continuo function, or in adding weight to the ensemble. No, this is still a classic work, and more than that, a work of the bitter last years of Mozart's life.

*Symphony No. 41, C-major, K. 551*

This olympian work (Example 52) turns away from the introspection of the G-minor, and reveals a spirit poised, serene, and confident. May we suspect that this is Mozart's musical vision of an ideal world?

EXAMPLE 52.

FIRST MOVEMENT: Allegro vivace
FIRST SUBJECT

SECOND SUBJECT

CLOSING SUBJECTS

SECOND MOVEMENT: Andante cantabile
FIRST SUBJECT

THIRD MOVEMENT: MINUETTO E TRIO

TRIO

FOURTH MOVEMENT: Allegro molto

FIRST SUBJECT

MOTIVES USED IN FIRST SUBJECT AND TRANSITION

SECOND SUBJECT

TRANSITION SUBJECT

SECOND SUBJECT

CLOSING SUBJECT

(Ia)

IMPORTANT SUBSIDIARY MOTIVE

*First Movement. Allegro vivace.* The movement opens with an
important-sounding — and thematically significant — march-like flourish (Ia), answered by a lyric questioning figure (Ib). The process
is repeated, and is followed by a longer march-like section based on
chords in rhythmic progression combined with a downward version
of (Ia). There follows a restatement of the first eight measures (Ia,
Ib), decorated by a counter-melody in the flute and oboes. Ib begins
to emerge as an important figure, and a quotation of (Ia), dashes
rhythmically into the transition, which concludes with a repeat of the
march-like section, now in the proper key for the second thematic
area. The first of these themes is lyric, as might be expected, and the
first phrase is answered canonically by the cellos and basses. This
theme consists of two motives that become important: (IIa) the beginning three notes, rising chromatically; and the little decorative rhythmic figure (IIb) which is repeated three times near the end of the
last phrase. The music arrives expectantly at a pause, followed by a
tutti section in minor leading to the first part of the closing theme.

Actually, this sounds like a transition, and is based upon motives (Ib and IIb) which resemble each other. After a pause like the one following the transition, we are treated to one of Mozart's purest *opera buffa* themes (IIIa) — one that he actually used previously in an opera. The exposition closes with the "refrain" of this theme, plus cadences using (Ia).

The development begins in a deceptively quiet manner with a woodwind phrase that picks itself up out of the previous key, and drops into a new and, for a moment, strange tonality. The closing theme provides the material, and soon there is imitative polyphony developing the last little scale line of that theme. This, worked over thoroughly, dies away over a sustained chord, and we have a quiet recapitulation of the beginning of the movement. But it is a false recapitulation, in the wrong key, and Mozart soon shows us what he has in mind: this has been merely a device to recall to our minds the motives (Ia) and (b) before he continues. The next part of the development deals with sharp chords linked together by (Ia), and flows into the retransition, which is fashioned out of the motive from the closing theme which was developed earlier, and thence into the recapitulation.

The recapitulation is identical with the exposition, except for a touch of minor at the beginning of the transition, and of course the necessary key adjustments as required by the form.

*Second Movement. Andante cantabile.* This rather neutral movement is introduced by the principal theme, *empfindsamer* style, which is soon transferred to the bass, and answered by an ornamental line (Ia) in the upper strings which will become very important. This section comes to a close, and the transition presents an agitated, "storm and stress" set of syncopated figures in the parallel minor key. The subordinate themes begin with a chorale-like pair of phrases, and are answered with two rather *galant* phrases. Another pair of phrases acts as a closing section and rounds off the exposition. The first violins continue, however, and provide a link to the devlopment.

This working-out section is largely devoted to the transition material, and flows into the recapitulation via a figure resembling Ia. This figure is now used extensively throughout the principal theme and transition. The second group and closing themes are uneventful, and Ia again returns in the short coda. This movement rather resembles a rondo, and if we let A stand for the first group, B for the transition, and C for the second group and closing section, the form may be expressed as *A-B-C B A-C-A*. The spacing here shows the division into sonata-allegro form.

*Third Movement*. Minuet and trio. Formally, these offer no surprises. The minuet is a rather regal movement employing a chromatic theme; the trio has an interesting touch at the beginning, since it repeats the cadence formula of the immediately preceding section of the minuet, thus charmingly providing continuity.

*Fourth Movement. Molto allegro*. Here we find a consummately realized fusion of the learned and *galant* styles. Most of the thematic material (Example 52, Fourth Movement) with the exception possibly of the first four long notes with which the movement opens (a), is derived from *galant* sources, (b), principally the Italian *opera buffa*. The movement opens as though nothing unusual were going to happen, but after the impressive and brilliant first statement of the principal thematic materials concludes with a resounding half-cadence, the restatement of the principal material begins with a well designed *fugato* which leads into the transition. Imitation is used consistently throughout this section. The *galant* second group (e) begins homophonically, but the opening theme of the section is answered by two figures from the previous sections, one embodying a rhythm and a scale (c), the other characterized by a trill (d). These soon predominate, and a polyphonic ensemble built on imitations and scales evolves. This flows through a cadence, and the closing group remains polyphonic in conception, with the addition of a new thematic element, becoming homophonic only near its final cadence, which is not accented.

The development consists largely of imitative sections using the long-note theme and the rhythmic motive followed by a scale. The recapitulation begins quietly, and the order of events is much like that of the exposition. The movement has a long coda which begins with the above rhythmic motive-scale figure now inverted and ascending followed by a short canonic section composed of the long-note theme inverted. Little by little the other motives enter, multiple imitation is resorted to, and the texture becomes thicker until five thematic ideas are projected simultaneously. After this has run its course, the texture becomes homophonic, cadence figures appear, (thematic, to be sure!), and the movement ends vigorously.

Despite the complexity of the counterpoint in this movement, the sonority remains transparent and brilliant, the flow has continuity and briskness, and the whole complex business sounds as though it were the easiest thing in the world to accomplish.

But now, having heard the preceding two symphonies, especially the 39th, let us notice the shift in balance and emphasis of the movements of the 41st. In the usual classical symphony, like the quip of a contemporary about the concerto grosso, the first movement "shows what the composer can do, the second shows how he can feel, and (skipping the minuet) the last movement shows how glad he is that the whole thing is over!" Departing from the usual gay but perfunctory finales, Mozart has here undertaken to balance the first and last movements more artistically, thus providing two substantial pillars upon which the whole four-movement form may rest. Beethoven inherits this formal view from Mozart, and it results in the magnificent finales of his third, fifth, seventh and ninth symphonies, finales which seem to sum up the preceding movements and draw them together into a closely unified musical utterance.

### LIST OF TERMS

rococo
*style galant,*
style bourgeois
   pathetic, storm and stress
*Empfindsamer* style
   sensitive or sensibility
learned style
classicism
Köchel Catalogue
*opera buffa*
chromaticism
caesura
broken-chord pattern
*fugato*
concerto
divertimento; cassation; serenade
transition, bridge
retransition
sonata-allegro
sonatina
binary form: simple, rounded
ternary form
rondo

principal theme, first group of
   themes
subsidiary theme, secondary
   theme, second group of themes
finale
polythematic
monothematic
dominant preparation
introduction
parallel minor
classic
classic orchestra
sonata form
symphony
trio, quartet, quintet
   (various kinds)
*Allegro, Andante, Moderato,*
   *Allegretto, Presto, Adagio*
development section
recapitulation
minuet and trio
codetta, closing section
coda

LIST OF TERMS (*Continued*)

concerto-allegro
sonata-rondo
theme and variations
exposition

instrumental figuration
modulation
cadenza
half-cadence

ADDITIONAL LISTENING

The literature of these composers is so full of treasures that choices are difficult. Those below are only a few possible ones.

HAYDN

*Symphonies*
No. 94 ("Surprise")
No. 98, E♭
No. 100 ("Military")
No. 101 ("Clock")
No. 102
No. 103
No. 104 ("London")

*Concertos*
Trumpet Concerto
Cello Concerto

*Chamber Music*
String Quartets:
Op. 33, Nos. 1-6
Op. 54, Nos. 1-3
Op. 64, Nos. 1-6
Op. 71, Nos. 1-3
Op. 74, Nos. 1-3
Op. 76, Nos. 1-6
Op. 77, Nos. 1, 2

*Choral Music*
*The Creation,* Oratorio
*Lord Nelson Mass*

MOZART

*Symphonies*
No. 29, A-major, K. 201
No. 34, C-major, K. 338
No. 35, D-major ("Haffner") K. 385
No. 36, C-major ("Linz"), K. 425
No. 38, in D-major ("Prague") K. 504

*Concertos*
Piano Concerto No. 9, E♭, K. 271
Piano Concerto No. 14, E♭, K. 449
Piano Concerto No. 20, D-minor, K. 466
Piano Concerto No. 21, C, K. 467
Piano Concerto No. 23, A, K. 488
Piano Concerto No. 24, C-minor, K. 491
Violin Concerto No. 4, D, K. 218
Violin Concerto No. 5, A, K. 219
Sinfonia Concertante for Violin and Viola, E♭, K. 364
Sinfonia Concertante for Winds, E♭ K. 297b
Concerto for Bassoon, B♭, K. 191
Concertos for Flute, K. 313, 314, 315
Concerto for French Horn, E♭, K. 495
Concerto for Clarinet, A, K. 622

*Chamber Music*
String Quartet No. 15, D-minor, K. 421
String Quartet No. 19, C, K. 465
String Quartet No. 20, D. K. 499
String Quintet G-minor, K. 516
Sonata for Two Pianos, D, K. 488
Sonata for Violin and Piano, B♭, K. 454

ADDITIONAL LISTENING *(Continued)*

### Chamber Music

Piano Quartet, G-minor, K. 478
Piano Quartet E♭, K. 493
Clarinet Quintet, A, K. 591
Serenade for Thirteen Wind Instruments, B♭, K. 361
Serenade in G, *Eine Kleine Nachtmusik,* K. 525

### Choral Music

Mass in C-minor, K. 42
Requiem Mass, D-minor, K. 626

### Operas

*The Marriage of Figaro,* K. 492
*Don Giovanni,* K. 527
*Cosi fan tutte,* K. 588
*Die Zauberflöte,* K. 620

## HISTORICAL AND
## BIOGRAPHICAL PERSPECTIVE

The world into which Ludwig van Beethoven was born was a world of political and cultural unrest. The forces which were to cause the two revolutions, one in America in 1776, the other in France in 1789, were in motion, fed by discontent and a desire for freedom. Discontent was spawned among the population not only by the artificial aristocratic society in France, but also by the rising tide of romanticism making itself felt especially in the decade of Beethoven's birth, the decade of "storm and stress" (*Sturm und Drang*). Seeds within the capsule of classicism had germinated, and were soon ready to burst forth. Musicians like Haydn and Mozart, whose roots were firmly planted in the Classic era, the age of reason and enlightenment, were little affected by these revolutions, although in those works dependent on literary meanings, the operas, we find a hint of the rebellious goings-on: Figaro, the servant, resolving that his master, the Count, shall "dance to his tune," and the nobleman Don Giovanni being punished for his amoral activities. But music was still social in its function, and compositions were written only on commission. The works of Haydn and Mozart still addressed themselves largely to the aristocratic intellect, not consciously striving for novelty or to move the emotions more than was considered proper, and maintaining a balance between the appeal to the heart and to the head. Beethoven received not only the heritage of the Classic period in his youth, but also the rising elements of romanticism, and these factors combined with an especially strong and individual personality to produce a musician who was of both the classic and romantic persuasions.

First, how is Beethoven classical? In several ways, but in none so plainly as in his conception of musical form which is the natural outcome of his musical logic, just as it is with Mozart and Haydn. But Beethoven has larger ideas than either of those composers, and the inherited ways of handling musical matter grew in his hands. It is not a simple process of expansion, for it is organic and created of necessity. But the final forms are recognizably those of the Classic period. This is so until the time arrives when these forms no longer suit the demands of Beethoven's musical ideas, at which point the ideas begin creating their own forms, but as developments of some aspect of the inherited ones. So Beethoven is classic to the end, in the matter of form and content.

Secondly, he is classic in his logic. Haydn labored long to bring the symphony into being, to discover the logic of symphonic development. Mozart joined in this, especially in his last three symphonies. Beethoven was a good student of the music of these men, and carried onward the synthetic approach so necessary in symphonic writing. But he was a dramatist too, on the purely musical plane. His actors were often more heroic than those of his predecessors, and he needed a bigger stage and more time to prepare his climaxes, points of repose and introductions. But he worked economically, with nothing more than the material presented in the exposition sections, and employed it in varied ways to create the heroic or intimate substance of his dramas. We shall find that often in the Romantic era, a composer resorted to endless repetition, treading water as it were, when his developmental logic failed. Never Beethoven. Every measure, every chord was precalculated with enormous precision and perception. Nothing is wasted, and nothing is present which is not needed. Classically symphonic? No one was ever more so.

Now what about the romantic elements? If Beethoven is so great an example of classicism, how can there be room for any romantic dreaming and poetry? This is a rather complicated situation which first of all must take into account Beethoven's peculiar character and life.

Ludwig van Beethoven was born into the family of a ne'er do well musician in Bonn, Germany. The father, a drunkard, saw that the boy had talent, and, with dreams of producing another *Wunderkind* like Mozart, drove the boy to music. How narrow an escape, in the light of modern child psychology, did the world of music have then; it would have seemed most logical that the boy would hate music, and resolve to learn a trade or profession as far from music as possible! But the genius that lay half-awake in young Ludwig seems to have reversed the usual process, and, by the time he was ten — no child prodigy — he was proficient enough on the piano, viola and organ to support his mother and brothers (and probably spare a coin or two for his father) certainly not in a lavish style, but one that was somewhat removed from poverty. Beethoven's schooling was quite inade-

266

PLATE XX. *Beethoven during his first Vienna years. Painting by W. J. Mohler, c. 1804. (The Bettmann Archive.)*

quate in academic subjects, and probably aroused in him his lifelong interest in self-education. Bonn offered many opportunities to hear good music and see operas and of these we may be sure Beethoven took advantage, often playing in the orchestras. In 1779 an experienced and well-trained musician, Neefe, was appointed court organist, and, under his influence, Beethoven exhibited such talent and progress as to cause Neefe to predict that his pupil would be Mozart's successor. Also during this period, through the friendship of Franz Wegeler, a young medical student, Beethoven made the acquaintance of the von Breuning family, in whose home he tasted the joys of appreciation and association with refinement.

In 1792 Beethoven set out to conquer musical and aristocratic Vienna. His piano playing and brilliant improvisations soon made him famous among the music lovers of the nobility, who soon took him under their protection, just as they had Haydn and, to a lesser extent, Mozart. But there was a great difference. The older composers had almost the status of servants, obliged, in the case of Haydn, to wear the uniform of the prince who employed them; Beethoven was accepted on an equal footing — indeed, he arrogantly insisted upon it, and through the force of his personality and musicianship succeeded. But his aristocratic friends, the Lichnowskys, Brunswicks, Lobkowitzes, and Lichtensteins soon perceived that the composer in Beethoven should be encouraged over the virtuoso, and made it possible for him to write and experiment with instrumental groups. The string quartet employed by Prince Lichnowsky was placed at his disposal, and Prince Lobkowitz even provided him with an orchestra from time to time!

Beethoven's genius, now free from monetary considerations, soared beyond the aristocratic circle which fostered it. His compositions were not "social music," but addressed to a larger audience, an audience of middle-class music lovers who immediately understood him, even if the critics did not. For these worthy gentlemen, expecting compositions which followed the strictly classical trend, were often outraged at the "novelty," sometimes "barbarism," of this powerful music.

Occasionally these qualities arose in Beethoven's social behavior, shocking and momentarily outraging his friends. But so often was Beethoven aware of man's shortcomings when compared with the ideal man he envisioned, that the disparity could not but enrage him, and cause him to utter a "hearty free word," as he put it. His, or his offender's apologies were usually tendered soon after the incident, and the break quickly mended.

Another factor tended to increase his irritability. During his late twenties he had been bothered by a buzzing in his ears, and by 1802 he realized that in spite of all the doctors could do, he was becoming deaf. The realization of this loss, so obviously fatal to his music, brought on a crisis which nearly ended in suicide. But the indomitable will-power which he had developed from his difficult childhood, and the equally unconquerable force of his genius conspired to keep him alive. Little by little he realized that his life was not ruined, but an inexorable change accompanied this truce with his affliction. A deaf musician, he felt, would seem ridiculous to most people, and this attitude his pride would not suffer. No longer could he meet humanity on the terms he had set up before; indeed, humanity — in the concrete — seemed now too prosaic and disappointing, and Beethoven withdrew to semi-seclusion, having converse with only a small circle of true friends. Meanwhile, during the years from 1802 to 1812 the music poured from his pen, undoubtedly a result of his gradually becoming aware of the indomitable creative force within him. In this decade he completed some sixty-odd compositions, including the series of symphonies from No. 2, Op. 36, through No. 8, Op. 93, as well as the fourth and fifth piano concertos, the three "Rasumowsky" quartets, and a number of the greatest of the piano sonatas. During this period he became familiar with a number of outstanding literary works, as well as some of their authors. The Greek classics, as well as the works of Goethe (whom he met personally), Schiller and Klopstock opened new horizons. Some of these works provided occasions for music, such as the incidental music to Goethe's play *Egmont,* and Kotzebue's *Ruins of Athens.*

As time went on, Beethoven withdrew more and more from the world. His increasing deafness and the realization that he could not marry, nor lead a normal life, were deciding factors. Then too, his preoccupation with the pure and spiritual realms of tonal expression, the translation of experiences too profound for the traditional syntax of music, effectively removed him from earthly worries and desire to mingle on equal footing with his fellow men. During this last period of fourteen years were produced compositions whose content can only be described as sublime, in the true sense of that over-used word. They include the great piano sonatas Opp. 101, 106, 109, 110 and 111; the *Missa Solemnis,* or Solemn Mass in D; the colossal Ninth Symphony; and the last series of string quartets in which the new language is most fully used, Opp. 127, 130, 131, 132 and 135. Then, in his fifty-seventh year, he succumbed to his final illness.

Now we must return to our previous question. What about the romantic elements in Beethoven's music? First, the individuality, the uniqueness, appeared at a time when it was not usually to a composer's advantage to be unique. Second, the forceful and expressive language of his music made its message quickly and completely understandable to a larger public. Beethoven did not clothe his musical utterances with the politely phrased, somewhat inhibited language that classicism felt proper. Beethoven's music, however, is always carefully controlled — his lifelong struggle, as we have already mentioned, was directed toward managing the products of his unruly imagination, and giving them shape in what we call the inherited forms of his time. Hence his classicism. But he felt that he had an important ethical message to impart in his music, and if the auditor did not depart a better person for hearing it, he, Beethoven, had failed. To make sure that he was understood, Beethoven seldom accepted a musical idea in the first form his imagination suggested, but revised it again and again until he was satisfied. The result impresses us with a kind of "inevitability" that is the product of this reshaping to the satisfaction of Beethoven's critical faculty. The tendency of many Romantic composers to write self-consciously "profound" works is often modelled after this natural consequence of Beethoven's universal thought.

A third presentiment of the Romantic era appears in his music, although it would be difficult to guess whether the romantics would have happened upon it if it had not occurred there first. This is the desire to unify the separate movements of a symphony, to bind them together by the use of quotation, or by forming them so that they deal with various facets of a single experience. With Beethoven this process begins at least with the "Pathetique" Sonata, Op. 13, and is used in many of his major works thereafter.

Fourthly, there is the enormous length of the symphonies, and the hardly less large sonatas, comparatively speaking. The elements of contrast and of continual movement which we found to be a part of the development section of the sonata-allegro are emphasized throughout the movements. And the change in harmonic quality foreshadows the interest of the Romantic period in colorful and varied homophony. The Romantic era might almost be called the period of harmonic exploration, and, while this was not started by Beethoven, he gave it added impetus.

A fifth characteristic, although minor, is the use of program, or descriptive music, a type of music in which compositions which pretended to transmute into explicit music the literary plots and actions upon which they were founded. Most composers of programmatic symphonies traced their musical lineage back to Beethoven, for did not that master write a pastoral symphony in which he describes certain scenes of country life? True, in the Symphony No. 6 Beethoven did use some naturalistically descriptive sounds, but often in a half humorous way, and the imitations are immediately turned into musical ideas, which are then manipulated *as themes,* with not too much regard for their descriptive connotations. And to direct our attention to the *real* "program" of the symphony, we are told by Beethoven's notes throughout the score that the work is "more an expression of *feeling* than painting," and that another movement describes "cheerful *impressions* received upon arrival in the country," and "happy and grateful *feelings* after the storm." The whole symphony is created with classic techniques and intents, and resembles only superficially many romantic works which seek to justify themselves by its example.

So we see elements in the works of Beethoven which are at the time of their composition, or which will later be, characteristic of the Romantic movement of the nineteenth century. And yet, we notice that these qualities are held in a typically classic balance by this master composer. We find Beethoven, then, standing *between* the classic and the romantic at the point where the streams join, belonging *wholly* to neither one, but in the main reflecting classic procedures. In his individuality and stature he is unique, one of the hero-figures of the history of music. And more than being merely of historical value, the music which he wrote is as meaningful and profound to us today as it was to his long-suffering, patient, invaluable aristocratic friends.

## ESSENTIALS OF BEETHOVEN'S STYLE

Most frequently this composer's creative life is divided into three rather well-defined periods: 1795-1802, those years before the serious onset of deafness; 1802-1813, the period of struggle and triumph over his affliction; and 1813-1827, the latter years when he withdrew from the world into himself. But throughout the entire creative life of this master there is a steady growth of stylistic traits, many of which are noticeable in the early works.

There are rather few compositions before Beethoven which demonstrate the dramatic power of the sonata-allegro form. This master deploys his themes like the characters of a novel or play, and allows them room to develop their individuality. Indeed, development, the heart of symphonic composition, is one of Beethoven's greatest achievements. Most of his themes are designed to be developed, and while he could write a beautiful melody when he felt it was required, malleable themes are his first interest. The second thematic area of the sonata-allegro, where lyric musical ideas are expected to flourish, is often composed of a single phrase, repeated at various pitch levels in the same key, in the movements by Beethoven. And the coda of the sonata-allegro, heretofore consisting of cadence figures designed to slow the flow of music, becomes a second development section in the hands of this master. This emphasis on development alters the time-scale of the movement, requiring larger sections to achieve stable formal balance, and we find that the Beethoven symphony or sonata is accordingly larger in scope and longer than those of previous composers.

To fill this longer formal span, Beethoven develops devices which become hallmarks of his style. We may summarize them under the heading of what are called *tension devices* — ways of creating anticipation in the musical consciousness of the listener — and note his inspired use of them. One of the most obvious of these is that of preparation, especially that of following a quiet section by a loud passage, thus throwing the second into high relief. Unstable harmony and/or rhythm often contribute to the success of such preparation. Sometimes either of these is used alone: the harmonic implications of the introductions to the first and last movements of the Symphony No. 1; and the reeling rhythmic instability of part of the first key area in the opening movement of Symphony No. 3 are examples of this. This flux of preparation-resolution, instability-stability, tends to create a more continuous flow of music, assisted by cadence-weakening devices. These consist of replacing the final cadence with some species of deceptive cadence, or by rhythmic displacement so that the final chord of the cadence falls upon a weak beat of the measure.

In addition to these syntactical tension devices, there are others of an unprepared variety. They often arise from Beethoven's desire to emphasize the dramatic quality of certain passages. Who would expect military trumpet-calls and drum-rolls in a movement of a Mass, especially in the *Agnus dei* (O Lamb of God, who takest away the sins of the world, have mercy upon us . . . give us Thy peace) ? Nevertheless, to Beethoven's mind, peace is associated with its opposite, war, which was especially a military matter in the Napoleonic era; hence this outburst, this "unprepared" inspiration which moves us so profoundly at the end of the *Missa Solemnis*. And many other examples might be cited.

272

Another means of achieving emotional effects which Beethoven used was the unprepared change of key — that is, the absence of any modulatory passages between two often distantly related tonalities. The first few measures of the coda of the first movement of Symphony No. 3 is a good example of this procedure. It extends also to the key relationships between movements of a compound form: Beethoven often chooses a key three scale steps up or down from the previous tonic, throwing the passage or movement (most often the slow movement) into a warm, dark tonal region which soothes us after the dynamic energy of the preceding section.

Add to these the *quality* of Beethoven's ideas — their universal appeal, their breadth and weight, their heroic or pathetic quality: in a word, their noble symbolism. To set forth these qualities as clearly as possible, Beethoven developed a characteristic way of scoring, not only for the orchestra but also for the piano and other instrumental combinations. This scoring is not necessarily more beautiful than that of Mozart, for example, but is more appropriate for what Beethoven has to say. The mass of sound is more full, often to the point of being thick and opaque, and there is greater exploration of the extreme ranges, both high and low, of the pitches possible to the instruments of the time. There is also the use of instruments unusual to the orchestra of that period — piccolo, trombones, contrabassoon — and often a new use of existing instruments, such as the revolutionary passages for the double-basses in the third movement of the Symphony No. 5.

Another element which we find in the music of Beethoven is humor, often robust and hearty, as in Haydn's works, at other times more subtle and of an essentially musical nature, such as the good natured fooling in the opening measures of the last movement of the First Symphony. The Eighth, Sixth and Fifth Symphonies also display humor and wit, as do many of the chamber works.

The devices mentioned above, by themselves are not sufficient to guarantee great or even good music: in the hands of lesser composers they become tricks which may catch our passing fancy. Beethoven's use of them raises them to new realms of symbolic significance.

SYMPHONY NO. 1, C-MAJOR, OPUS 26

*First Movement: Adagio molto — allegro con brio.* Introduction. Note the rather dissonant first chord, and the successive repetitions

EXAMPLE 53.

FIRST MOVEMENT:

INTRODUCTION: Adagio molto

FIRST SUBJECT

b. Allegro con brio

TRANSITION

d. cresc.

SECOND SUBJECT

274

SECOND MOVEMENT: Andante cantabile con moto

MAIN SUBJECT

THIRD MOVEMENT:

MENUETTO E TRIO

MENUETTO

275

TRIO

FINALE: Adagio; Allegro molto e vivace

INTRODUCTION

Allegro molto
e vivace

PRINCIPAL THEME
PART 1.

PRINCIPAL THEME
PART 2.

PRINCIPAL THEME
PART 3.

Str.

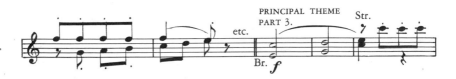

276

Br.

TRANSITION 1.

n.

*sf*   *sf*

TRANSITION 2.

n.

Low str. 8va lower   *sf*

SECOND SUBJECT

o.

Str. *p*

CLOSING GROUP

Ww.   Ww.

p.

*sf*   Str.   *sf*
*sf*

(Example 53a) all of which tend toward the tonic, thus arousing anticipation for that chord at the beginning of the *allegro*.

Exposition. The first thematic area is made up of the main
motivic element (Example 53b) and a cadential figure (Example 53c).
The transition is created from the first thematic figure (*cf.* Example
53b and d), after which the themes of the second thematic area appear
(Examples 53e, f). The first of these is a 1½ measure figure which is
handed around to various instruments rather than being melodically

completed. The second is a cadential figure which emphasizes syncopation. The closing theme (Example 53f) bears a resemblance to Examples 53c and e, and also employs syncopation.

Development. At the beginning of this section, Beethoven abruptly shifts the key a whole step upward, after which an economical development ensues. The retransition passage out of the development is much like the one entering it.

Recapitulation. The statement of the first theme is scored for the full orchestra, and the following two chords plus the short, rapid scale figure are developed, forming a new transition to the second themes. Woodwind doublings at the octave intensify and vary the sound of these. The rest of this section is much like the exposition, except, of course, for key. The non-developmental coda brings the movement to a brisk and satisfying close with some typical slashing chords.

*Second Movement.* The second movement has a passing resemblance to the opening of the corresponding movement in Mozart's G-minor symphony, but is more artless, less brooding, and less resigned. It is Haydnesque in several respects besides the simplicity — almost naivete — of its theme (Example 53g). It is a sonata-allegro which is closer to simple binary form than is usual. What inclines it in this direction is the resemblance of the secondary thematic material to the first, almost a development of it, in fact (Example 53l). The closing figuration in the first violins is so obviously subsidiary in importance that it does not weaken the almost monothematic quality of the first section (i). At the beginning of the development we have again a plunge into a remote key, but this is accomplished smoothly, since the function of a slow movement is to provide a rest point in the action. The development is properly transitional, and deals with the secondary theme, whose opening leap resembles and may be analyzed as an expansion of a similar smaller leap with which the principal theme begins. The recapitulation of the first thematic group is enriched by an *obbligato* scale figure in the cellos at first, then inverted and placed above the thematic material. The harmonization of this section is scored more fully than it was in the exposition. The coda develops the principal thematic material somewhat, and brings the movement to a peaceful close.

*Third Movement.* The third movement is labeled, as we might expect, menuetto, but the tempo indication is *allegro molto e vivace* (very fast and vivaciously). This is obviously no minuet to dance to! As a matter of fact, this is a *scherzo,* a designation first used by Haydn, and the first appearance — under an assumed name — of a type of movement which is to become most individual with this composer. The thematic motive here is a scale step, either whole or half (Example 53j). The first section presents this motive organized as a halting to emphasize the motive — ascending scale. It accomplishes its ascent in eight measures, and is repeated immediately. Classically enough, this scale now descends, but hesitatingly, rocking back and forth on its notes, and taking twice as long to come down as it did to go up (Example 53k). This process begins what seems to be a repetition, but now the bass rises, a half step at a time, arousing suspense which is dispelled by return of the opening rising scale, now full-orchestra. The section then uses a series of two half steps in a syncopated rhythmic figure to conclude the menuetto. The trio, scored for the most part more lightly, consists of a series of woodwind chords alternating with scale and half step figures in the strings (Example 53l). It becomes a little more emphatic toward the close of the second section.

*Fourth Movement.* No explanation is really needed of the humorous beginning of the final movement (Example 53m). This sets the mood, and no darker emotions disturb the gayety. The transition (Example 53n) turns the tantalizing scale figure of the introduction upside down so that it descends, and flows into a charming dance-like second theme (Example 53o). The concluding section makes use of syncopation and alternate woodwind and string figures in its cadences (Example 53p). The development uses the scale figure, the rhythm of the first part of the opening theme, and the syncopated figure from the closing section in some mild contrapuntal fooling, nothing very serious, and the recapitulation is ushered in by a mock-dramatic development of the upward-rushing scale figure. In the recapitulation, the transition is shortened — rendered almost nonexistent, in fact — thus making this section very brief. This leaves room for Beethoven to indulge in a little more wit in the coda, and he is quick to take advantage of the opportunity. The scale figure is used to build up a climax of considerable proportions which comes to rest on a dissonant chord, then on still another. There follow mice-like scurryings, using the scale figure, and the orchestra quickly gets back on the track with the principal theme, followed by stereotyped horn figures, scales and cadences all of which conclude the movement in a whirlwind of good feeling.

In this symphony there are a number of Beethoven's characteristic devices used; but more than the sum of all the parts, this work is definitely not similar to any composition by Haydn or Mozart, except in a superficial sense. The degree of power, assurance, clarity and directness of musical thought is more typical of Beethoven than of the other two masters. Let us now examine some works of the second period of composition, and see how these characteristics grow and combine with other new traits to produce the heroic composer with whom we are becoming familiar.

### SYMPHONY NO. 3, IN E♭ ("EROICA"), OP. 55

The Second Symphony of Beethoven was composed during the year of torment, 1802, after the "Pathetique" Sonata, Op. 13, the first two piano concertos, and the fifteen variations on a theme from his ballet, *Prometheus,* which was in the process of composition. This second venture into symphonic waters is an intensification of the qualities and forms used in the First Symphony, but the work still belongs recognizably to the Classic era in its manner and content. However, the subconscious hero in Beethoven had overcome, or at least come to terms with, Fate by the time the Third Symphony was ready to be written (1804) and the experience was transmuted into this heroic music, full of struggle, full of victory. The companion works of this period reflect the same viewpoint: two sonatas for piano, (Op. 53 ("Waldstein") and Op. 57 ("Appassionata"), which are so long and difficult to perform that they are like concertos without orchestral accompaniment. This kind of composition returns from time to time, as in the "Coriolanus Overture," Op. 62, three years later (1807), but the grouping above represents, possibly, the climax of Beethoven's musical expression of his struggle with destiny, until the Ninth Symphony presents the distillation of these experiences in the mystic art of the third period.

Beethoven here unifies a long compound form by giving it an emotional program, much as he did in the "Pathetique" Sonata, but much more intensely. J. W. N. Sullivan, in his excellent book, *Beethoven, His Spiritual Development,* has given us a possible interpretation of the composer's purposes. The first movement, he says, contains everything Beethoven knows about courage and the struggle

with malign fate. Symbolically enough, the main thematic unit of
this movement is an idealized bugle-call. The second movement, a
grim funeral march, represents a mood of black despair, punctuated
by fist-shaking motions of defiance which subside into the hopeless
stammering of the last measures. But in the next movement, the indomitable creative energy makes itself felt, first with distant tremors and
shakings, finally exploding into a heaven-storming fanfare by the
horns. The last movement is a set of variations on the theme Beethoven
had used earlier for both his *Prometheus* ballet, and the set of fifteen
variations for piano. Prometheus was the hero of Greek mythology who
first brought fire to men from heaven, and subsequently was punished
by the gods for his daring to lavish the divine gift upon mortals. Such
a hero now symbolized to Beethoven the triumphant creativity by
means of which he had weathered his personal tragedy and emerged
beyond it triumphant, if scarred. Now let us examine each movement
in a little more detail, and see how Beethoven communicates these
ideas.

EXAMPLE 54.

FIRST MOVEMENT: Allegro con brio

FIRST SUBJECT

SECOND SUBJECT

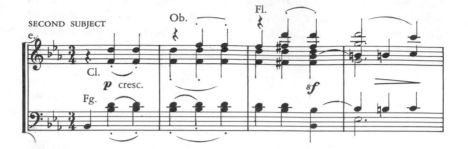

CLOSING MATERIAL

NEW THEME

SECOND MOVEMENT: Adagio assai
PRINCIPAL SUBJECT

TRIO

THIRD MOVEMENT: Allegro vivace
SCHERZO

TRIO

THEME, PART 1.

*First Movement: Allegro con brio.* The meaning of the first movement is summed up for us at its inception. The two crashing chords
proclaim anything but serenity, whether musical or personal, and the
harmonic instability which arrives so surprisingly during the first
statement of the bugle-call theme forecasts the struggle to come
(Example 54a). We have the usual statement and restatement of the
principal thematic idea, but now on a grander scale than ever before.
Notice particularly the simplicity of this theme, and how, because of

this simplicity it demands expansion and development. The rushing impetus is made even more stormy by the rhythmically unstable section which occurs between the statement and restatement. We are now presented with three separate transitional ideas, all basically motivic and suitable for development (Example 54b, c, d). The first is a repetitive three-note idea which starts on the second beat of the measure and is handed around among the woodwinds until an emphatic half-cadence is reached. The second transitional idea follows immediately, and consists merely of a rising scale figure which flows into the third theme, an active, motivic, instrumental idea which will contrast with the yearning second theme (Example 54e). It is significant that when we come to the development we find that it is concerned with only the principal and transitional themes, leaving the second theme untouched as a moment of lyric relief which now highlights the more active elements within the exposition. The closing section is introduced by a crescendo in dynamics and instrumentation, and is concerned thematically with various developed versions of the main theme (Example 54f). There is a stunning section of rhythmic shocks, setting up a grand instability that the cadence, with its dissonant dominant chord-tonic pedal combination, energetically brings to a close.

The development is so lengthy and varied that mere words become meaningless, but attention should be called to a number of occurrences within it. First, after the first transition theme has been developed, note the rising version of the principal theme in the bass which introduces the third transition theme. Later, a short *fughetta* (small *fugato*) develops this first transition theme polyphonically, building up to a climax of dissonances and unstable rhythms in which the whole orchestra participates in large block-chords. After this battle the orchestra seems to withdraw in defeat, only to be consoled by a *new theme* (Example 54g), another temporary rest point of touching lyricism like the second theme in function, a moment of surcease from the conflict. But the mighty first theme returns in strength, and the struggle resumes. The new theme returns soon, and again leads to an increasingly dramatic return of the first theme. In the retransition section, which is surprisingly subdued, although still unstable, there occurs one of Beethoven's dramatic strokes. At a point where the suspense has become almost unbearable, the horn enters softly with the first four notes of the principal theme in the tonic key, but dissonant to the quiet dominant harmony of the background. The rest of the orchestra seizes upon the last note of the horn-call and proceeds to create a big V-I cadence out of it upon the last chord of which the recapitulation begins.

The recapitulation is a reasonably exact counterpart of the exposition, but for changes in instrumentation, and a certain increased lyrical feeling.

The coda which follows dwarfs every other symphonic coda written up to this time in length and function, for it acts as a second development section balancing and opposing the first. Here is a classic symmetry where one would least expect to find it. This final section begins with a dramatic shift in key, first down a whole step from E♭ to D♭, then down a half step to C, where the developmental action begins with a decorative *obbligato* over the principal theme. The new theme used in the development section appears, after which, in an internal ABA form, the *"obbligato-*over-the-theme" procedure returns. The second act of the coda introduces another *obbligato* theme which resembles the third transitional idea, but which descends and is more lyrical. This is soon combined with the principal theme which rises to a great shout in the trumpets and horns, then a brief quotation from the second theme, as though summing up the drama, and, finally, a grandiose final cadence followed by two short and terse chords which seem to imply that there is more to come, that the drama is not finished. It will be noted in retrospect that the primary development section is active, full of dynamic crises and unstable sections — a conflict, in short — while the coda, the secondary development section, is lyrical, containing no upheavals, and of markedly stable harmonic and rhythmic construction. Here the drama inherent in the sonata-allegro form is expanded to include not just themes, as before, but whole large sections whose intent is dramatically different. The person who has weathered the storms of the middle part of the work, Beethoven seems to imply, is a different person when he arrives at the recapitulation and coda, and this must needs be shown in the music. He is, it would seem, a stronger, more confident, more serene person, if we read the implications aright.

*Second Movement.* The second movement is the famous "Funeral March," set in the key that seemed to have the blackest connotations for Beethoven — C-minor. Now, the fact that this is a march has certain formal implications to Beethoven, and, in general, he follows them. A march is a stylized dance; to create a longer composition than just the eight or sixteen measures that a dance form (binary structure) comprises, a trio is added, as with the minuet and a three-part form consisting of march-trio-march results. This is what Beethoven uses, but there is a difference.

The hushed, somber march theme with which he begins was arrived at after numerous versions were sketched and discarded, re-shaped and recomposed (Example 54h). The decorated triad, sup-ported by the deep notes of the double basses calls up in the imagina-tion all of the tragedy and solemnity that would attend the death of a hero. The oboe proclaims the second period of the theme, after which it cadences on its related major key. A more consoling theme in the strings enters (Example 54i), giving way, after two mild climaxes, to the return of the main theme. But only the beginning of it is quoted, and the major theme appears now in the winds sup-ported by the strings. A codetta follows, which contains as its high point an astringently dissonant chord in the winds, and the first march section ends.

The second section, the trio, is in the parallel major key, and exhibits a little more motion as a result of the chord-diffusion patterns in the string accompaniment (Example 54j). The high points are the two climaxes, quite war-like in nature, employing full orchestra with emphasis on the trumpets and timpani. After the second of these, a strong descending phrase brings the harmonic movement to a half-cadence, and we are now ready for the return of the march. The normal procedure would now be to recapitulate the first section with some changes in scoring, probably shortening the repeated sections, add a brief coda — the movement is already as long as most slow movements — and move on to the next movement, the scherzo. Let us see what Beethoven does.

The somber main theme begins just as we remember it, at least for the first phrase; but the second, that upward, questioning scale line which ends on a dissonant note, is repeated, and we make a cadence in a new key. Now *that,* in itself, is not too surprising — but on the cadence note a fugal passage of great tension and gripping dramatic power begins, to grow by imitative addition until the whole orchestra is involved. Finally, the fugue is spent, and the movement quiets down to what will surely be the last repetition of the main idea. But it has no sooner begun than it trails off on a high note. A forceful return of the "battle" passage of the trio ensues, here developed at length, and in the harsh minor tonality possibly reminding us with its crushing force that this was a hero. Subsequent to this, the "consoling" theme referred to above returns so we see now that the developmental section, full of drama and surprise (more than one would expect in a funeral march), was inserted between the main march theme and its major key follower. The remainder of the recapitulation of the march is regular, but is almost completely rescored, giving more important parts to the wind instruments, and fuller, more rhythmic accompaniment to the strings. Instead of the expected final cadence, a deceptive one is used, and this chord is immediately treated as the tonic of a new key with moving results. Beethoven reveals to us at this point his overwhelming humanity and sympathy. Only a few measures, but how poor this already meaningful work would be without them. In the final measures the music seems to be moving forward toward a cadence glimpsed in the distance. But Beethoven has still one thing to say. The main theme begins in the first violins, accompanied only by the *pizzicato* cellos and basses. But it is slightly changed, and then it breaks into fragments, gasping, trying to convey, for the last time, its unutterable grief.

This has been a long movement, but notice how Beethoven realizes *when, exactly* when, to jar us, to arouse our attention and interest by variation, polyphony, or orchestration. The "Funeral March" must be listened to with the realization that Beethoven is here saying immensely profound things about despair, tragedy and death. That is, it must be listened to seriously and intensely, with participation in each event.

*Third Movement.* The scherzo reaffirms the life impulse, and the upsurging creativity of a heroic spirit. "Oh, life is so beautiful — to live it a thousand times!" said Beethoven. This movement is one of the two most masterly scherzos in all of the nine symphonies, and it is significant that the other one occurs in a symphony which runs a rather parallel course in meaning and ethical idea to the "Eroica." This other symphony is the Ninth and has as its "program" the human search for the highest value in life.

The form is regular — scherzo-trio-scherzo with coda. The first measures, which of course are quoted repeatedly during the piece, consist of the rapid alternation of two chords, setting up a kind of duple "harmonic rhythm" (Example 54k). This is contained in a triple meter, and the conflict between the two creates a nervous tension. Beethoven emphasizes the tension by directing that these measures be played in a very soft and *staccato* manner. Such tension must eventually explode, and Beethoven allows it to do so, but not too soon — only when he has aroused our expectations to the breaking point. There is a forceful descending broken chord passage in syncopated rhythm which is worth taking note of, for upon its return Beethoven changes meter to duple for four measures in order to intensify the instability. Needless to remark, this procedure is very rare in the eighteenth and early nineteenth centuries, and demonstrates the manner in which Beethoven will break with tradition if such action heightens the expressiveness of his music. The trio is based upon an elaborate fanfare, first stated by the horns and repeated several times during the section (Example 54l). It is not just another fanfare, however, but puts the virtuosity of the players to a severe test. Beethoven takes the first horn up almost to the top of its range, while the low horn of the group has rapid notes to play in its lower register where such action is not only difficult but also precarious. But no matter! This is a heaven-storming passage, and, as Beethoven probably knew, when instrumentalists are confronted with difficult passages, they soon learn to perform them, and the erstwhile impossible enters the literature as not only possible, but even probable! So it is with these horn passages, although even with modern instruments they offer a challenge. One wonders how they sounded in Beethoven's day.

*Fourth Movement.* The last movement storms in with a rushing introduction, not in the expected E♭-major tonic of the symphony, but in a kind of G-minor. By the time the introduction is ended, however, the tonality has settled down to the expected key, and the introduction concludes with a half-cadence. The theme of the variations to follow is now ticked off by the *pizzicato* strings, punctuated by a few loud and assertive chords in the wind instruments (Example 54m). If you listen carefully you will hear that this theme is a small rounded binary form with both sections repeated. But whoever heard of understating a theme so completely? We shall find this skeleton underlying or within — sometimes even used as melody — all of the variations of this large movement. According to Sullivan, Beethoven here chooses the variation form to show the varieties of achievement possible to him after triumphing over his difficulties. But these are no mere "character" variations. While some of them stay rather close to the theme, or to the gay, dance-like melody that combines with the theme and reappears from time to time, the best description of the procedure is *developmental*. Indeed, this developmental variation technique is one of the achievements of Beethoven, not to be matched by Romantic composers until we reach Brahms, at the farther end of the century. Let us also keep in mind that Beethoven probably knew this theme quite well, after having used it in a ballet, and after having written fifteen piano variations on it!

A series of variations obviously has unity, but Beethoven has sought here not only to emphasize this quality, but also to provide variety of a kind not usually encountered in variations, by subjecting these to a larger formal plan. The movement, after the introduction and the statement of the theme, is organized as follows:

*Tonic Key:*

Var. 1: Theme in middle register, played by the strings, surrounded by simple two-part broken polyphony.

Var. 2: Theme in higher register, played by the strings, with running scale accompaniment, changing at times to repeated chords.

Var. 3: Theme in bass, higher upon repetition: dance-like melody (n) in upper parts, often running passagework in strings.

*Transition to Other Keys:*

Var. 4: Fugal development of first four notes of theme.

Var. 5: Dance-like melody, "flute" variation, beginning with few instruments, finishing with all strings and woodwinds. Cadence repetition.

Var. 6: March, using first four notes of theme as *ostinato* accompaniment. Codetta spins out cadence figure.

Var. 7: Transitional variation, first four notes of theme as *ostinato* accompaniment to dance-like melody which appears first in major, then minor, then developed, modulating simply to Var. 8.

*Tonic Key:*

Var. 8: Development of inverted version of first four notes of theme as double fugue: other subject is scale figure. Dance-like melody appears once above the polyphony. Much attention toward end to theme notes; long variation.

Var. 9: Slow variation of dance-like melody, new harmonization; instrumentation grows to Var. 10.

Var. 10: Twin of preceding, but on larger scale: winds have dance-like melody, now sounding more important because of emphasis (horns especially) and tempo; remainder of orchestra plays repeated chords or broken chord figuration.

*Coda.*

Tonic key: various lyric sections which make one suspect variation, but if so, very developed. Return of introduction, now in right key, followed by motives from dance-like melody: growing jubilation to the end.

Let us now attempt to summarize some of the innovations of this symphony. One of the most obvious characteristics is its bigness, not only in time duration, but in quality. The inherited forms have been expanded, but are still subject to the traditional analysis. What, then has caused the expansion? First of all, there is a sureness about the procedure — Beethoven knows where he is going, and foresees the end and how to move irresistably and logically to it over long distances. The vehicle for the journey is the theme, and Beethoven searches for just the right one, the simplest and most direct kind of theme to use. Once discovered, the theme *demands* development. A good example of this kind of theme is that of the "Eroica's" first movement. It means very little by itself, but when allowed to grow organically it becomes expressive. So the process of unfolding — development requires more space and time than traditionally allowed. Note the kind of theme usually chosen. It is frequently instrumental in style, and contains a clearly defined rhythmic or melodic motive. Lyric material is usually unsuited to developmental procedures, and Beethoven uses it mostly for contrast, posing intimacy against grandiose moods. This contrast is felt to be so necessary that new themes appear during developments or codas to create even stronger contrast. So the form has been expanded, and the contents intensified. This is especially true, of course, of the large works such as this symphony.

To hold these contrasting sections together, Beethoven creates an energetic rhythmic flow, employing rhythmic imbalance to create cadences in much the same way that harmonic imbalance does. The rhythmic flow is often thematic (*i.e.,* rhythmic motives derived from themes), but if it is not, scales, repeated chords, or chord-diffusion patterns are employed. Interior cadences are often weakened by either harmonic or rhythmic procedures or both. In this way, the "seams" are concealed, and the music flows in larger blocs than previously. From time to time polyphony of Beethoven's personal kind is used. This practice also forms long uncadenced sections, but the time for use is very carefully chosen, and the duration of such a section is precisely limited.

The movements of this symphony "belong together." They are

members of a family. This was not necessarily so of previous classic symphonies, although a work like Mozart's G-minor has a similar kind of unity because of its pervading mood. But the "Eroica" is the first symphony unified consciously by the composer. It presents several facets of a single experience so clearly stated that one movement without the others is well-nigh unthinkable.

SYMPHONY NO. 5, C-MINOR, OP. 67 (C. 1805)

In the "Eroica" Beethoven revealed himself to be an idealist and an optimist. Let us now examine a work based upon the same attitude, but quite different in the means used. For many people, the Fifth Symphony of Beethoven is *the* symphony. Their admiration is not misplaced, for this symphony meets all of the requirements.

*First Movement.* The first movement is one of the most concentrated musical creations in existence, based as it is upon the motto of four notes defiantly hammered out by the orchestra at the beginning (Example 55a). These are repeated a step lower. Then, quietly, the motive is linked together, chainlike, ascending in a pyramidal structure. This is repeated, and a forceful half-cadence is reached. The thematic motive is thundered out once more, the linking process takes place again, but this time descending, and the motivic flow builds to a considerable climax which concludes with two sharply accented non-final cadential chords. The bright notes of the horn sound out a short passage beginning with the motto, and we have arrived at the second theme. This theme consists of a lyric phrase transposed up or down and handed around to the various wind instruments (Example 55b). But the restless nature of the motto theme asserts itself in the accompaniment, comes to the fore, and dominates the music to the end of the exposition. It dominates the development also, the only other material appearing there being from the horn passage before the second theme. The recapitulation has two interesting changes over the exposition. At the half-cadence after the first ascending passage Beethoven has given the oboe a pathetic little cadenza which serves by its lyricism to emphasize the ruthless energy of the battle; and the horn-call before the second theme is now given to the bassoon, implying the change in meaning and character after being subjected to the conflict of the development section. The coda is developmental in nature, with a tearing *obbligato* passage in the strings over repetitions of the third, fourth, and fifth notes of the second theme, pronouncements of the motto theme at the beginning and the usual repeated cadences. The whole movement is quite short, concentrated in material, and almost monolithic outwardly. It has none of the expansiveness of the "Eroica" — everything is sacrificed to economy. For this reason, in performance the exposition is often repeated.

*Second Movement.* The second movement, *andante con moto* (somewhat slowly but with motion), is interesting structurally as well as beautiful musically. It might be classified as a set of variations on two themes, or as a set of variations on one theme which has two distinct and contrasting sections. For clarity these themes, or sections, will be called theme 1 and theme 2, after the order of their introduction. The key is Ab-major, a third away from the tonic of the first movement: note the restful feeling it imparts.

Theme 1 is a lyric, 8-measure phrase with no real interior cadences but caesuras on unstable tones, and is given to the violas and cellos in unison (Example 55c). This opening phrase is followed by a simple repetition of its closing cadence figure, then two extended versions of it, first in the woodwinds, then in the strings. The tiny four-note figure which concludes these expansions is in turn echoed by the winds and strings. The second half of theme 1 serves as a transition to theme 2 (Example 55d) and is fashioned out of a typical horn motif which rises to an unstable, questioning high note, followed by a decisive, full orchestra cadence in the new key. This key relationship is one which Beethoven is destined to exploit, and tends to replace the traditional tonic-dominant (I-V) change. In this case the change is

EXAMPLE 55.

FIRST MOVEMENT: Allegro con brio
PRINCIPAL SUBJECT

SECOND SUBJECT

SECOND MOVEMENT: Andante con moto

THEME 1.

TRANSITION

THEME 2.

THIRD MOVEMENT: Allegro
SCHERZO E TRIO

TRIO

Vla.                                                                    etc.

**FOURTH MOVEMENT:** Allegro

h.

*ff* Full orch.                                                          Str.

i.

etc. Str. *f*

j.

etc. Str. *8f*        *8f*            *8f*            *8f*       etc.

**TRANSITION**
k.

*f* Cor. & Ww.                                                           etc.

**SECOND SUBJECT**
l.

*ff* Str.         3                    *p*                          etc.

295

CLOSING THEME

m. Ww.

from A♭ to C, the distance of a third upward, and results in the bright triumphant sound needed for theme 2, which is a brass fanfare theme, beginning loudly and bravely, but dying away in questioning in much the same way as the transition. It is as though the nagging doubts which interrupted the continuation of the lyric section, even after the reassurance of the repeated cadences, return now to destroy the momentary triumph of the second theme. The questionings, already unstable harmonically, now move through a still more unstable region, finally arriving at a cadence in A♭, the key of theme 1, and we are now ready for the first variation.

The first variation matches the theme exactly in length and sequence of events, but only theme 1 is actually varied. Beethoven here fashions a smoothly flowing line with few skips from the rather disjunct theme, still keeping it in the tenor register of violas and cellos. The many small cadences pass in review, and the only change in the transitional and theme 2 sections consists of more rapid accompaniment in the strings. During the questioning phrases of this part we hear in the lower strings a rhythmic motive which is related to the motto of the first movement, surely a recollection of the conflict there.

The second variation begins as though it is to be simply a double of the first, that is, having note values which move twice as fast as those used previously, keeping the tempo the same. But after the first statement of theme 1 in the violas and cellos, the same thematic line is taken up into the first violins, still moving in rapid notes, and accompanied lightly by the other strings and staccato notes in the bassoons and clarinets. Then the theme returns to the lower regions, this time carried by the double-basses and cellos, while the full orchestra plays repeated block chords above the moving parts. This time, the end of theme 1 is marked by a loud half-cadence, marking the point at which the transition is to begin. Since theme 1 was developed in variation 2, we might expect the transition to expand, and this is exactly what happens. Beethoven develops a passage of woodwind music in which pairs of instruments are used in contrary motion. Theme 2 now appears in full orchestra, but this time is not followed by the questioning phrases, but is allowed to remain statically on its climactic note — which has the effect of almost negating the triumphal effect of that note. There follows a rather long transition, begun by the strings in broken chord patterns using increasingly rapid subdivisions of the metric pulse, and, when stability of this accompaniment has been reached, a minor variation of the first phrase of theme 1 appears in the form of a little march in the woodwinds. The last seven measures of this transitional variation are devoted to scales whose unstable quality arouses cadential expectation subsequently satisfied by a full orchestra version of theme 1, this time as a canon between the violins and the upper woodwinds. The multiple cadences follow, after which the coda begins with a bassoon solo, and in a slightly faster tempo. The material here is largely taken from the transition section and the cadences following theme 1, but now used to conclude the movement. Notice how few times theme 2 appears, and that it is never really developed in the same sense that theme 1 is. This might lead to some speculation concerning Beethoven's attitude toward premonitions of victory long before they are justified. Like a good novelist, he cannot afford to do more than hint at the outcome of the story.

*Third Movement.* The scherzo has been compared by some commentators to a depiction of a grotesque dream — and it must certainly have seemed so to the double-bass players of the orchestra which first performed the work. For this lumbering instrument is called upon to play rapid passages in which the agility of the smaller stringed instruments seems called for. Beethoven knew what he wanted, however, and since the music is so great, these difficult passages were mastered and are now part of the orchestral technique of any good bass player. The form is traditional: scherzo-trio-scherzo. But the treatment of the contents is Beethoven's own. The movement begins with a shadowy, rising broken chord figure in the cellos and basses, capped by an equally quiet cadence in the strings and woodwinds (Example 55e). This is repeated. Then, like some elemental force, the motto theme of the first movement is hurled forth by the horns (Example 55f), and soon joined by the rest of the orchestra, but minus the trumpets, which are being saved for a later use. There is

297

now a repetition of this whole first portion, altered and developed somewhat, followed by a second repetition which lands firmly upon a final cadence. The motto theme has been prominent throughout. Now the famous double-bass passages begin the trio, imitated by all the upper strings in turn (Example 55g). The second half of this binary structure commences with a series of false starts in the double-bass passages. Here Beethoven compounds difficulties with humor! The repeat is re-composed, and becomes almost lyric before the shadows begin to gather, and the trio disintegrates into a few *pizzicato* notes that lead us back to the scherzo. This section is completely rescored and abbreviated. What we now hear is a ghostly echo of the first part of the movement. The sinister notes of the bassoon, doubled with the *pizzicato* cellos, echo the rising chordal theme, and the motto, no longer defiant, is given to the chirping solo woodwinds or the dry *pizzicato* of the strings. The effect is to arouse a somewhat fearful expectancy which is by no means satisfied by the sudden drop into a quiet, dark deceptive cadence, punctuated by the throbbing of the timpani. The first violins begin an echo of the scherzo theme, repeating the last three notes in various distorted forms, but never growing louder until the suspense is almost unbearable. Then the remainder of the orchestra joins in a magnificent crescendo of power on the dominant seventh chord which resolves on the brilliant and victorious opening notes of the finale.

*Fourth Movement.* The last movement is a hymn of exultant power and triumph. In form it is a broad sonata-allegro constructed out of four distinct themes: the opening fanfare-like first theme with its retinue of smaller rhythmic motives (Example 55h, i, j); a chorale-like transition theme, again based on a horn-call idea, but stirring and majestic (Example 55k); the second theme which uses a rapid version of the motto theme, and is constructed of short, vigorous scale sections (Example 55l); and the closing theme, consisting of a four-note descending scale with the lowest note repeated, the whole used motivically (Example 55m). It is notable that Beethoven here chooses a motivic second theme, and devotes the entire development to working it out, rather than trying to make something of the more static first or transition themes, although the latter is capable of some expansion as we shall see. An awesome stroke of genius occurs at the end of the development after the dominant preparation of the retransition section. Instead of plunging into the opening fanfare of the recapitulation, Beethoven recalls a section from the shadowy repetition of the scherzo, like a backward glance at a region whose difficulties have been mastered, but still linger in the memory. This section grows dynamically and re-prepares for the recapitulation which is no longer postponed. The only change from the exposition which occurs in the recapitulation is the omission of the chorale-like transition theme which is replaced by motivic themes from the first theme which go directly to the second. A long coda in four sections concludes the movement. The first "act" of this is constructed out of the second theme, the second "act" out of the transition theme, now no longer a chorale but a bugle-call motif; the third section is reached via an accelerating transition, is marked *presto,* and is concerned with the closing theme; and the fourth section is made up of forceful cadences and chords.

For the orchestra used in the last movement, Beethoven felt the need of more power and brilliance and added three trombones, a contrabassoon, and a piccolo. This is one of the first times the trombones were used in a symphony, although they were regularly employed in theater and church music. Imagine the opening of this last movement if it were scored only for two trumpets and two horns! Even four horns could not supply the weight and majesty required — a situation tailored for the trombones.

Now let us examine the work as a whole. The unity of this symphony is one of its most striking features. It is brought about by two factors, the first of which is the use of an emotional program — the progression from darkness to light, or from struggle to triumph. This is not exactly a straight line progression in the music, nor is it in life, but rather compounded of moments of triumph in a gradually improving context of conflict. A more obvious unifying device, one which is strikingly successful, is the quotation in all of the movements of the motto theme from the first movement. Many Romantic composers will imitate Beethoven here, but few achieve the economy of utterance and the balance of form of this symphony. The use of a transition between movements is also new. This work would still be powerful and successful if Beethoven had not written the transition, but with it, the contrast is so heightened and the progression of mood made so explicit that, having heard it once, the symphony is unthinkable without it. It is one of the gratuitous gifts of genius — something that did not *have* to happen, but *did* as a result of this composer's uncommon insight.

OTHER SYMPHONIES

Time and space do not permit a detailed examination of the remaining four symphonies, but a few words concerning them are necessary. The Sixth, Op. 68, called the "Pastoral" Symphony, was written at about the same time as the Fifth, and represents the alternation between heroic and lyric symphonies that marks the work of Beethoven in this form. Symphonies No. 1, 3, 5, 7, and 9 tend toward the heroic, while numbers 2, 4, 6, and 8 are more lyric and personal. As we have mentioned, it is to this Sixth Symphony that the programmatically inclined Romantic composers point in justification for their descriptive symphonies. But Beethoven is here more inclined to the description of feelings rather than imitation of natural sounds, although these do occur in the last movement of the work. The first movement is inscribed, "The awakening of joyful feelings upon arrival in the country." It is a long, lyric movement that flows evenly from beginning to end with no surprises. The slow movement is entitled "Scene by the brook," and whatever might be construed as imitative in the musical figures describing either the flowing water or the bird-calls at the end is immediately assimilated and made part of the substance of the music, retaining no really marked descriptive characteristics. The next sequence of movements is played without pause and includes the two most descriptive movements of the symphony. The third is entitled "A jolly gathering of country folk," and corresponds to a scherzo with trio. Here Beethoven indulges in some kindly humor at the expense of the bassoon in the village band. He was probably familiar with such groups, for in his long walks in the country surrounding Vienna he must have often come upon gatherings such as he describes here, complete with the rustic band to furnish dance music. At any rate, the bassoonist of this band has only three good notes on his instrument, and uses them wherever and whenever he can make them fit. The trio has a properly rustic sound, and is followed by a drastically shortened version of the scherzo, which in turn flows directly into the fourth movement which describes a storm with appropriate effects of rain, wind, thunder, and lightning. A bridge passage, during which the storm moves away, leads to the fifth movement, the real finale of this gentle work, entitled "Shepherd's song, Joyful and thankful feelings after the storm." The most overtly descriptive section, then, is the storm; artistically, it functions as dynamic relief from the prevailing lyricism, for the scherzo by itself, even if the repetition were of the usual length, would not have enough excitement to balance three long, quiet movements. One might wonder if the storm section owes its existence to the artistic necessities, or was it conceived without consideration of them. One can hardly hold the latter opinion after having listened to even a few works of this composer.

The Seventh Symphony, Op. 92, is a large essay on rhythm. Each of the movements has a distinct rhythmic idea which furnishes the basis for the structure. Themes are almost unimportant, especially in the two outer movements, and consist of simple patterns such as broken chords and scale sections. Those of the first movement are possibly the most distinctive. This movement has a long, rather slow introduction. The two middle movements are quite individual, melodically. The second movement, which had the distinction of being applauded and encored upon its first public performance, is a set of variations on two themes arranged in a rondo pattern: A-B-A-(C: Development)-A-B-A. The A section, in minor, is march-like, and is based upon a chord sequence; the B section is in major and serves as relief from the rhythmic element of A. The scherzo is an active, bright movement with two trios arranged thus: scherzo-trio-scherzo-trio-scherzo. The two trios are identical, and pose almost static harmony against the motion of the scherzo. The key relation between the scherzo and trio is that of a third, F to D. The finale is again an idealized dance, and matches the first movement in motion and length. This symphony is a large work, just as concentrated in its way as the Third, but with a different purpose. The unifying factor here is rhythm and its manipulation, which provides an inner and more subtle coherence to the separate movements than program or theme quotation. And it is a predominantly cheerful work, easily accessible to the listener.

The Eighth Symphony is an idealization of the earlier classic symphony, and for this reason was misunderstood and criticized by concert-goers from Beethoven's time through the first half of the Romantic period. It is short and economical of material, but not terse and serious. Rather it represents Beethoven in a good humor and contains some of his most witty writing. The first movement is formally clear, uses some typically Beethovenian rhythmic devices, and concludes with a long coda. The second movement, a sonatina marked *allegretto scherzando* (rather fast and in good-humored manner), has a legend attached to it. That tyrant of piano students, the metronome — a mechanical instrument for accurately beating time — had recently been invented by a man named Maelzel. Beethoven, who knew the inventor, good-humoredly poked fun at him in the words and music of a canon, and imitated the ticking of his device in the slow movement of this symphony. In any case, the movement is charming and exceedingly well constructed. The minuet and trio might have been written by the Beethoven of the First Symphony, so typical are they of that phase of his style. The final movement is noteworthy for its humor and conciseness — at least as far as the coda, for this latter section is almost as long as the foregoing sonata-allegro. No attempt is made to unify these movements, except for the style and precision of writing. True, the treatment of rhythm and rhythmic figures could have been done by no one but Beethoven. If the work is unified it is because it was written by this master.

To briefly sum up the gigantic Ninth Symphony — the symphonic work representing Beethoven's third creative period — is an impossible task, so we shall content ourselves here with only a few remarks about it. It is written in the traditional four movements, but with the scherzo as the second and the slow movement as the third in the sequence. Each of the first three movements proposes a philosophy of life to oppose the antagonist of Beethoven's — and every man's — life: Fate. In the first movement, the inexorable problem is stated; in the second, energy, the creative force of life; in the third, sublime contemplation, mysticism; in the fourth these are summed up one by one in the introduction and rejected; the wonderful theme symbolizing joy, the answer to Fate, is chosen, and the chorus and soloists sing a variegated hymn to joy in the words of Schiller. Beethoven had long cherished the idea of setting these words, so idealistic, so near to his embracing love of humanity, and in the choral finale to this most profound of the symphonies he expresses not so much the actual meaning of the words as his interpretation of their meaning. Here the extreme of musical sophistication of his time, as exhibited in, say, the scherzo, contrasts with the naivete of the "hero's march," one of the variations of the finale. Or was Beethoven indulging in that sympathetic humor that laughs at the follies of man while still admitting his greatness? Many interpretations are possible, not only of this little section of "Turkish Music," but also of various other parts of any of the movements.

Formally, the first movement is a vast yet thematically economical sonata-allegro, the second a driving scherzo and trio in which the timpani have thematic importance; the third movement is a set of developmental variations on two themes, one of the most sublime movements in all symphonic literature, and the finale is, as we have said, a series of choral variations preceded by an important introduction. Beethoven here uses a large orchestra — the same one employed in the finale of the Fifth Symphony plus various percussion instruments, and four horns instead of two.

It is in this last symphony that Richard Wagner will find his justification for the combination of voice with orchestra in a symphonic manner. It was — and still is — a monument to classicism, for Beethoven explored and inhabited the forms and ideals of classicism completely, leaving no further development possible. In a sense he precipitated the Romantic movement in music, for none could surpass him, and weaker personalities could only imitate — except for his Viennese compatriot Schubert, who was too profoundly original in his own way to merely copy. Beethoven wrote "The End" to an era.

### THE CONCERTO

Beethoven wrote five piano concertos, one violin concerto, a triple concerto for piano, violin and cello, and a hybrid, concerto-like piece called the *Choral Fantasy* for piano, orchestra, and chorus. Of the piano concertos the fourth in G-major, Op. 58, and the fifth, the so-called "Emperor" concerto in E♭, Op. 73, are the most frequently played. The violin concerto in D major, Op. 61, is one of the standard works in the literature of that instrument. The *Choral Fantasy*, Op. 80, is seldom performed, as is the case of the triple concerto, Op. 56.

As might be expected, these works follow in the main the standard form evolved by Mozart. But the symphonic ideal of development, and the fusing of the solo part with the orchestra became features of Beethoven's works in the form. At times they seem to be symphonies with solo *obbligato* rather than concertos. In spite of this, they are grateful works for the soloist, brilliant and expressive — and certainly not easy. Both the fourth and fifth piano concertos begin with an introduction by the solo instrument before the orchestral exposition, short in the fourth, more extended and powerful in the fifth. In both of these the middle movement is connected to the last by means of a bridge passage. Beethoven evidently mistrusted the improvisational ability of performers, for he composed cadenzas for all his concertos, leaving nothing to chance.

### THE CONCERT OVERTURE

Beethoven was one of the first master composers to write music for the spoken drama. Overtures to operas were common, and were seldom detached from the stage presentation at this time; but the overture to a play is apt to be performed in the concert hall without the play, giving rise to what we now call the *concert overture*. Soon composers of the Romantic era wrote descriptive overtures not intended to preface stage works, but to exist on their own merits. In this they followed Beethoven's lead. He composed four overtures to plays, of which the ones to *Coriolanus* by von Collin and *Egmont* by Goethe are the most moving. In them he sums up the central idea of each play. One need not read *Coriolanus* to know that it is concerned with heroism and tragedy. The four overtures to his opera *Fidelio* are frequently heard, especially the so-called "Leonore No. 3 Overture." There are three "Leonore" overtures after the first name of the opera, which was subsequently changed to *Fidelio,* and we have one overture thus entitled.

In his overtures, Beethoven sums up the main idea of the play, opera, or celebration. This was one of the difficulties with the "Leonore No. 3" overture, which anticipated the climactic scene of the opera so clearly that the scene itself was greatly weakened. Hence the other attempts to find a good curtain-raiser — one which would not give the plot away.

In form, these works are all sonata-allegro. The baroque French overture had earlier given way to the Italian *sinfonia* — which was roughly the equivalent of a three movement symphony — and eventually that dwindled down to only the first movement, hence the use of the classical form. Beethoven's works in this field are among the most powerful of his compositions, partly because of his skill in transforming ethical ideas into musical symbols, and partly because of the concentration of material in a rather short movement.

### THE PIANO SONATA

The expressive potentials of Beethoven's own instrument were greatly realized in the thirty-two sonatas which he wrote for it. The piano sonata is the vehicle for some of his most intimate, heroic and profound thoughts from the beginning to nearly the end of his creative life. He began with the sonata as inherited from Haydn and Mozart:

three or four-movement form, rather transparent sonority, chord diffusion by usual means (broken chord figures) — in a word, classic in the sense that the First Symphony is classic. He expands the range, using higher and lower tones than had been employed before; the sonority becomes thicker in the middle period, then often thins out in the third period. The dynamic possibilities of the instrument are exploited; new pianistic idioms are invented and exploited, including new accompaniment figures which are often thematic, and polyphonic textures of his own unique brand. The use of contrasts — the energetic first movement followed by the prayerful, almost static, *adagio* becomes a usual sequence. Let us sum up in outline form the salient characteristics of some representative piano sonatas from all three periods.

*Sonata No. 1, Op. 2, No. 1, F-minor*

1. Transparent texture; fluid passage work, chords normally spaced (*i.e.,* rather close together), center of keyboard largely used (Example 56), idiomatic piano style, traditional in approach.
2. Homophonic texture: expressiveness result of melody, especially in second movement. Dynamic shading important.
3. Typical classic compound and single forms used. No dislocation for expressive purposes.

*Sonata No. 8, Op. 13, C-minor ("Pathetique")*

*First Movement.* Intense dramatic expression from the very beginning (Example 57). Thicker, darker sonority, more dynamic contrast, bold use of chord masses and colors, dissonances. Original sonata-

EXAMPLE 56.

Adagio.

MENUETTO.
Allegretto

Prestissimo.

EXAMPLE 57.

FIRST MOVEMENT

Sonate N.º 8.

Grave.

attacca subito il Allegro.

Allegro di molto e con brio.

SECOND MOVEMENT

Adagio cantabile.

THIRD MOVEMENT

**RONDO.**
Allegro.

allegro form dislocated by return of dramatic introductory material. New key relations (third-relationship). Changes of tempo within the movements.

*Second Movement.* Typical song-like slow movement, richly and satisfyingly harmonized. Offers relief from energy of first movement. Lower middle register of piano used, resulting in sonority not as thick as in first movement, but less transparent than in Op. 2, No. 1. A B A C A in form.

*Third Movement.* A finale, not minuet or scherzo. More "classical" in piano treatment than might be expected from the preceding movements. Return to thinner sonority. Substitutes energy of motion for dramatic *Sturm und Drang* style of first movement. Uses suspense of instability; employs simple polyphony. Symmetrical rondo in form.

### Sonata No. 23, F-minor, Op. 57 ("Appassionata")

*First Movement.* Form is sonata-allegro with three important themes, each contrasting with other two (Example 58). Dramatically expressive, using all registers of the instrument, sudden shifts in dynamics, thematic accompaniment, assimilated polyphony, headlong energy (Example 58). Note motto from Fifth Symphony.

*Second Movement.* Theme and variations in form of "doubles." Note thick sonority, rhythmically static beginning. Each variation pitched in a higher region of keyboard, returning to low region at conclusion; gradation of sonority from thick to transparent, then return to thick. Note dramatic use of deceptive cadence, forming substance of bridge to final movement.

*Third Movement.* Idiomatic theme in lower register, thick sound, but clear. Use of chord "punctuation" in rhythmic figures over flowing theme. Energetic. Expressive polyphony which implements motion and sonority rather than impeding it. Brilliance of effect.

### Sonata No. 28, A-major, Op. 101

*First Movement.* Lyric, fresh, gentle (Example 59). A return to transparent sonority, but with a different sound from that of the first period due not only to increased economy — everything is thematic! — and more advanced expressiveness, but also to the arrangement of chords and spacings between high and low registers of keyboard. Intimate work, no surprises. Gentle rhythmic imbalance, not

EXAMPLE 58.

## SECOND MOVEMENT

## THIRD MOVEMENT

shocking. Fluid, small sonata-allegro form, typical of third period: dissolution of boundaries between sections.

*Second Movement.* A jaunty, somewhat humorous march, using dotted rhythms and subtle syncopation. Phrases often of uneven lengths. Idiomatic piano style, but requires very careful and accurate playing: No showy brilliance, but an intimate composition. Note wide spacings between hands. Trio uses canon, but here, as always with Beethoven, it is employed in the interests of expression, not merely "counterpoint for its own sake."

*Introduction and Third Movement.* The very expressive beginning material, after being worked out somewhat polyphonically in the lower middle register, leads to a quotation of the principal theme from the first movement, which in turn leads to the beginning of the third movement. This is a fluid sonata-allegro with a fugal development section devoted to the first motive of the main theme of this movement. The recapitulation is partly rewritten, and the movement ends in a quietly humorous coda, again exploiting widely separated sonorities. The whole sonata uses the now-familiar key relation of thirds. Not all of the last sonatas are of the gentle lyricism and happiness of this once. It was chosen partly for its brevity and partly because it is an accessible introduction to the third period style.

### THE STRING QUARTET

The change from the purely social function of music in the Classic period to the increasing importance of the individual work and the trend toward "art for art's sake" is nowhere more dramatically shown than in the string quartets of Beethoven. Whereas Haydn and Mozart were commissioned to write such works by the half-dozen (six quartets

EXAMPLE 59.

**FIRST MOVEMENT**

**SECOND MOVEMENT**

INTRODUCTION AND THIRD MOVEMENT

in a group seems to be the usual order), only once, at the beginning
of his career, does Beethoven comply with this custom. The six
quartets, Op. 18 were commissioned, as were those of the next group,

Op. 59, significantly, three rather than six in number. The next nine quartets appear as individuals, although the last five, not all commissioned, but really written "for himself," form a group in that they share some thematic ideas in common, and are concerned with the communication of mystic ideas never before — or since — expressed in the language of music.

The same progression noted in the piano sonatas obtains in the string quartets — an increasing mastery of technique and idiom, moving away from the recognizably classic roots toward a unique and personal language. We regret that space limitations do not permit a discussion of these works, but if the listener has understood the other music of Beethoven which was analyzed in this chapter, he should have little trouble in appreciating the chamber music.

*Part III: Franz Schubert, 1797-1828*

# HISTORICAL AND
# BIOGRAPHICAL PERSPECTIVE

The only composer worthy and able to follow in the footsteps of Beethoven was Franz Peter Schubert, a native Viennese, and one of the geniuses of music. His life was simple and tragically short. Born into a schoolmaster's family, he received an adequate academic education. Because of his demonstrable musical ability he was accepted for training by the Imperial Chapel and there received excellent musical instruction. He studied piano, violin, voice, composition, and conducting during this period, and seems to have distinguished himself in all these fields. To escape military conscription, he served with his father as a schoolmaster for four almost unbearable years, then cut himself free from all bourgeois ties and spent the remainder of his life composing. He joined a fellow group of literary artists who, like him, retreated from the dull round of middle-class existence, and together they encouraged each other in their artistic efforts and shared the money which they occasionally received for their works. In these early days of romanticism, they were welcome at the salons of the aristocracy, and we read of Schubert's being frequently invited to improvise dance music for a party. Other times they gathered at the rooms of one of the group, or picnicked along the banks of the Danube. Schubert's music and the recitation of poetry inspired them in their artistic revolution. To these literary figures Schubert owed many of the insights and subtleties of his songs. As we have noted, his education, other than in music, was only adequate. He needed these poets to open to him the world of melodic verse and the progressive thinking of the burgeoning Romantic era. Schubert has been too often pictured as the romantic bohemian, a ne'er do well who sat around writing sentimental songs when he should have been working. Nothing is farther from the truth. Schubert was industrious in his composition. During the year 1815 he wrote 144 songs, as well as many other compositions for piano, chamber groups and orchestra. This is hardly bohemian idleness!

PLATE XXI. *Franz Peter Schubert. Pencil drawing by Kupelweiser, 1821. (Courtesy Austrian Information Service.)*

Schubert was highly undervalued by his contemporaries, even his literary associates. They felt he had talent, but that it was a comfortable talent, not the genius that we now recognize it to be, for they were familiar with only a few of his works. Many of these were played or sung once, then put away. Some of his greatest compositions received at most one performance; one of the greatest, the C-major Symphony, was never played during his lifetime.

This composer, like Beethoven, stands at the point where classicism and romanticism converge. But whereas Beethoven was little influenced by the literary romanticism of his day, Schubert, because of his wonderful melodic gift and ability to compose songs, was brought into contact with romantic poetry in an intimate way and responded to it. The romantic element is present in the delicate coloring and harmonic variety in his instrumental works, which, however, are conceived upon classical lines, and are worthy, as we have said, to stand beside those creations of Beethoven which Schubert admired so much. The genuine classical spirit of balance between form and content is present in Schubert's works. Classical form was a living part of the whole musical complex to him although his treatment of details was often highly original. We may be deceived by the easy-going lyricism into believing that the music is wandering, unguided, into any flowery meadow Schubert takes a fancy to; but except in a few cases, notably the piano sonatas, we are mistaken. It is one of Schubert's great accomplishments that he can use lyric material in the construction of traditional musical forms — for lyricism was to prove the bane of most romantic composers insofar as legitimate symphonic composition was concerned. Beethoven is not noted for his lyricism although he can write a moving melody when he wants to. But "when he wants to" is precisely when construction is not the most important element. Beethoven constructs his large *allegro* movements out of motives, and Schubert is wise enough to do so too, although the latter's motives are often lyric in nature. We must not let the lyricism and highly colored harmony fool us. It is the *balance* between the shape of the music and the material out of which that shape is created that is classical, regardless of the poetry of the language. Schubert idolized Mozart and Haydn all his life, and only came to understand and admire Beethoven during the last decade or so of their contemporary lives. He modelled several compositions after the older master with such success and originality that any connection between the model and the "copy" ceases to be of importance.

Sickness and poverty darkened Schubert's last years, together with the bitter realization of how little he was appreciated and understood. The last songs, grouped into a cycle called *Die Winterreise (The Winter Journey)* bear proof of this feeling. There is an ironic and pitiful attempt at grim humor in *"Die Leiermann"* ("The Organgrinder"), where the poet — Schubert in this case, for the music is the essential thing here — says to the half-frozen, penniless beggar, "Wonderful old fellow! Shall I go with you? Will you, while I'm singing, grind the tune for me?"

During his short life, Schubert composed nine symphonies, twenty-one piano sonatas, many short piano pieces, thirty-five works for chamber ensembles, six masses, seventeen operas, and over six hundred songs.

# The Style of Schubert

## MELODY

The melodic style of Schubert is essentially lyric and expressive This element comes to the fore, of course, in slow movements and second thematic sections of sonata-allegro forms. The melodies are often extremely simple, consisting of only a few notes, but these are arranged rhythmically in such a manner that they become expressively and emotionally appealing far beyond the means employed. For constructive themes, Schubert uses motivic ideas, presented either as motives, or contained in a lyric phrase.

## HARMONY

This element in Schubert's style is quite individual, and is indicative of the romantic trend. The chords are, in the main, fairly simple, although a certain amount of chromaticism is present, as we shall shortly see. Schubert uses the third-relation between keys to a much greater degree than Beethoven, often omitting transitions between key areas this distance apart. He prefers the sudden shift into the soft darkness of the new key, frequently achieved in one of three ways: a phrase begins in the foreign key immediately after a phrase in the old often tonic — key; or a single note of a final cadence chord is retained, and the first chord of the new key is built upon it. For example, in the final triad C-E-G, the E is retained, and upon it the chord E-G♯-B may be constructed. Or the chord a third lower may result: A-C♯-E. "Modulations" which rely upon such a procedure will be called "pivot-tone" modulations. In the third type of "modulation," an unstable chord (*e.g.,* the dominant seventh) of an established key either resolves surprisingly to a chord of the new key, or moves to a similarly unstable harmony of the new key which then follows.

Schubert occasionally uses chords one degree more dissonant than the seventh, *i.e.,* ninth chords. These often occur in passing from one chord to another, and result in a poignant sweetness and expressiveness rather than in a dissonant clash. This clash is, however, employed for the expression of anguish or despair.

It will often be read that Schubert makes the minor mode equal to the major. This is simply not true. They represent to him the contrast of light and shade, the longed-for utopia and the present harsh reality, life and death. Some of his most poignant effects are achieved by the change from major to minor, or vice versa. One of the clearest examples of this major-minor symbolism may be found in *"Der Lindenbaum"* ("The Linden Tree"), one of Schubert's most romantic songs. Whenever the poet, who is here a wanderer on the earth like Schubert, recalls the linden tree, the symbol of his home and past happiness, the mode is major. But the life of wandering, the bitter cold and unfriendliness of the world, is painted in the stark minor, made more grim by the warmth of the yearning major sections which follow. Little insight is needed to understand similar changes in the purely instrumental works. Often he uses the minor version of a chord to emphasize the major which appears after it, or again, he may oscillate back and forth between the two modes in order to prepare some far-reaching key change. But equate these two distinctly different harmonic values? Never. Schubert was too sensitive a composer to do that.

### RHYTHM

Schubert is not as forceful a composer as Beethoven. Where the latter commands, the former persuades. Therefore, in the main, Schubert's rhythmic procedures are on a smaller and more subtle scale, although from time to time, especially in the later works, a forceful rhythmic design appears. More often a rhythmic motive underlies lyric material and provides a gentle impetus which keeps the music alive and moving.

Two characteristic features, typically Viennese and of this period are found in the music of this master. One is triple-meter dance rhythm, especially of the Viennese *laendler* kind. This dance is a more bourgeois variety than the aristocratic minuet, although they are kindred. The waltz developed from the *laendler* during the course of the nineteenth century. It was this *laendler* that Schubert was so expert in improvising for his friends, and its easygoing rhythm permeates many movements of his serious works.

This was also the time of the Napoleonic Wars, and all through Franz Peter's boyhood Vienna was filled with marching troops. His music recollects the marches again and again, sometimes in large movements, such as the second movement of the C-major Symphony, at other times in short fragments, as in the first movement of the C-major Cello Quintet. The marches are usually of the "quick-march" type, and often have a jaunty rhythm.

### TEXTURE

This music is largely homophonic, although occasionally counterpoint appears, mostly in a decorative way, either providing a new "surface" to themes already heard, or supplying accompaniment motion. An "incidental polyphony" in fairly frequent, especially in ensemble works where there is freedom of individual movement among the instruments. This term refers to the motivic interplay between the outer parts, interplay which is often thematic, either rhythmically or melodically. Canons are often constructed between the highest and lowest members of the instrumental ensemble.

### SONORITY

Schubert achieves fullness of sonority without thickness. Where Beethoven often seemed to disregard the quality of his sonorities in order to achieve maximum effect, Schubert always has the poet's ear for euphony and beauty of sound. He is a superb orchestrator, and handles the color values of the various instruments with a delicate subtlety that is indicative of the romantic composer's attention to this element of music. A certain amount of color sense pervades the works of the Classical composers, of course, since the choice of instruments in an orchestral composition dictates that their different tone qualities be taken into consideration. But we feel that Schubert is more sensitively aware of tone color than the others, and uses it in a constructive way.

# FORMAL AND GENERATIVE PRINCIPLES

### CHARACTERISTIC PRACTICES

Schubert uses the classical forms with a true sense of their requirements. In some earlier works this balance had not yet been achieved, and there is a certain amount of lyric wandering, of diffuseness. Later works show an increase of discipline in handling the materials.

In some lesser works, and occasionally in some major compositions, Schubert employs repeated two-measure units for construction. For example, if we represent each measure by a letter we find: A-B, A-B, C-D, C-D, E-F, E-F — and so on. This can be annoying if the material is too obvious, although it is a way of assuring a certain amount of continuity.

In some of his later works, Schubert strives to create unity by using "motto themes," or by emphasizing some musical element, such as a simple interval or a rhythm. We shall attend to this in more detail when we discuss the B-minor Symphony.

Occasionally, this composer shortens transition sections in sonata-allegro movements almost to the disappearing point, sometimes by pivot-modulation, at other times by using a single phrase which accomplishes the purpose.

### THE GERMAN LIED

Schubert is a notable song composer, the first of any stature in German music. While most of the previous Classic and Baroque composers had written vocal literature, the styles of these compositions were almost always taken from Italian models, often the opera. This is especially true of Mozart, somewhat less so of Beethoven and Haydn. But the songs of the latter two are distinctly secondary in importance and mastery to their instrumental works. By and large, they were not vocal composers.

One of the outstanding traits of romanticism is the desire to fuse all of the arts into a successful, artistic union. To use Pater's words, poetry aspired to be music, and music to be poetry. The fusion of these two arts occured first in the German art-song, hereafter called the *lied* (pl. *lieder*) to distinguish it from folksong, operatic arias and French art-songs. The lieder composer attempts to make the vocal line expressive of the emotional content of the poetry, and to match it in feeling phrase by phrase as the song progresses. He also tries to create a piano accompaniment which will support and enhance the emotional nuances of the voice part, and to construct it musically by means of suitable motives, chord qualities, tone colors and rhythms. Schubert was successful in this from his first songs, both to texts by

Goethe, *"Der Erlkönig"* ("The Erlking") and *"Gretchen am Spinn-rade"* ("Gretchen at the Spinning Wheel"). In both of these, Schubert seizes upon descriptive elements of the text — in the first, the sound of the galloping horse, in the second, the whirring of the spinning wheel — out of which he fashions the accompaniment. Over the descriptive motion in the piano, the voice part interprets the text psychologically, laying bare to us the souls of the characters of the poem in their varied moods. In other songs, no less successfully, he merely portrays the prevailing mood, as in *"Der Doppelgänger"* ("The Phantom Double"), where the deep, dark and sinister chords provide an anxious and forbidding background to the gasping melody.

These lieder were often grouped in "cycles" according to the connection in plot or mood among the individual songs. Schubert wrote two cycles, and his publisher collected a number of later songs into a third cycle which, however, has not the inner unity of the previous two. The first of the genuine song-cycles is written to twenty poems by Wilhelm Mueller, and is called *Die Schöne Müllerin* (*The Beautiful Milleress*, or, more often, *The Miller's Beautiful Daughter*). The cycle traces the adventures of a young miller, newly released from his apprentice bonds, as he gaily sets out on his own for the first time. He follows a brook which leads to another mill, and there falls in love with the miller's daughter. He takes work there in order to be near her, courts her, successfully it would seem, but eventually loses her to another, a huntsman. After a period of despair, the young miller drowns himself, finding surcease from his yearning in the friendly waters of the brook. The second cycle, *Die Winterreise* (*The Winter Journey*), is made up of vignettes concerned with sights seen from the coach window or in various villages, and memories, romantically nostalgic, lamenting lost love, full of homesickness and the bitterness of fate. It was written, as we have mentioned, when Schubert was ill and wretched near the end of his life, and some of this tragedy is reflected in the songs. These are only a few of the six hundred or more songs which Schubert composed, many of which are unjustifiably neglected.

The forms of these songs would naturally correspond in some way to the forms of the poems used, including the emotional crescendo and climax of the story, if such is present. Generally there are three main types, although these may vary to suit the text. The ballad-like song, in which the music is the same for each stanza of the poem, has received the name *strophic* (*strophe*, from the Greek, meaning a stanza). If we let successive numbers represent the verses of the poem, and letters symbolize the music used for an entire verse, then the strophic form may be represented thus:

1 - 2 - 3 - 4 - 5 etc.
A A A A A

Occasionally a poem containing several stanzas rises to an emotional climax in an intermediate verse, after which the later verse returns to normal. When such a poem is set to music, new accompaniment is often used for part or all the climactic verse. Using our symbols as explained above, we then may have the following design for this type of lied, called the "modified," or "altered strophic" form, here with four stanzas, the alteration in the third:

1 - 2 - 3 - 4
A A B A.

A third general type of form is called *durchkomponiert,* or "through-composed." Usually this term is applied to the musical setting of a narrative poem in which the action moves continuously forward, or to one concerned with a series of emotions which develop and grow out of each other. There is often no *exact* repetition of previous musical sections, but varied and new music, sometimes in both the voice and the accompaniment, follows the progress of the poem. Usually, however, some unifying device is employed, often rhythmic in nature, in the piano part. This serves to lend musical coherence to the song without interrupting the flow. In the most successful examples, *"Der Erlkönig"* and *"Gretchen am Spinnrade,"* this unifying factor not only accomplishes its primary structural purpose, but enhances dramatically the effect of the song in its depiction of action and emotional states. In symbols, then, this kind of form appears thus:

1 - 2 - 3 - 4 - 5 - 6 - etc.
A  B  C  D  E  F

Unifying Factor:    *  *  *  *  *  *

One last consideration of the lied — these songs, and the Italian and French arias and art-songs, are always sung in the original language. This is done for several reasons. First, exact translations, insofar as accentuation and placement of vowels upon syllables corresponding to those of the foreign text, are extremely difficult to achieve. And, worst of all, they must be in good English! All too often such translations in their effort to match the structure of the original poem sacrifice sense, resulting in a halting, flowery kind of language that has been called "translationese." Then too, there are those words for which there is no short equivalent in English, not to mention those which have no counterpart at all. Most performers feel that rather than risk singing a limping or flowery translation, they would rather print the translation in the program and sing in the original language. Of late, more attention has been devoted to this problem, and we now possess a few very fine translations, mostly of operatic works. It is significant, however, that these works are all French or Italian in origin.

# M U S I C A L   E X A M P L E S

## SONGS

### *"Heidenröslein"*

Let us first examine the song literature of this composer. We shall begin with a simple and charming setting in strophic form of Goethe's poem, *"Heidenröslein"* ("The Hedge-rose"). The text is as follows:

*Strophe I:*    Sah ein Knab ein Röslein steh'n,
Röslein auf der Heiden,
War so jung und morgenschön
Lief er schnell, es nah' zu sehn,
Sah's mit vielen Freuden
    Röslein, Röslein, Röslein rot,
    Röslein auf der Heiden.

*Strophe II:*    Knabe sprach: ich breche dich,
Röslein auf der Heiden,
Röslein sprach: ich steche dich,
Das du ewig denkst an mich,
Und ich will's nicht leiden.
    Röslein, Röslein, Röslein rot,
    Röslein auf der Heiden.

*Strophe III:*    Und der wilde Knabe brach's
Röslein auf der Heiden,
Röslein wehrte sich und stach,
Half ihr doch kein Weh und Ach,
Musst'es eben leiden.
    Röslein, Röslein, Röslein rot,
    Röslein auf der Heiden.

(A lad saw a rose-bud on the hedge-rose, and ran to pluck it. He spoke, "I'll pluck thee now," and the rose answered, "If you do, I'll stick you with my thorns so that you'll always remember; and I won't be sorry." The boy broke the rose, the rose mercilessly stuck him, and he will always remember.)

The setting is extremely simple, in the manner of a folk-song, and yet it has a certain charm. Obviously Schubert did not regard this as a great emotional experience, although it has an allegorical meaning, and therefore did not provide an emotional or moody setting.

The second song is an example of the altered strophic form, one whose text is almost as artless as the preceding one. It is called *"Die Forelle"* (The Trout), and the words are by Schubart. The text is as follows:

*Strophe I:*

In einem Bächlein helle,
Da schoss in froher Eil'
Die launische Forelle
Vorüber wie ein Pfeil.
Ich stand an dem Gestade
Und sah in süsser Ruh
Des muntern Fischleins Bade
Im klaren Bächlein zu!
   (last two lines repeated)

Within a sparkling streamlet
   that sang its merry song,
I marked a silver trout
Like an arrow, speed along.
Beside the brook I lingered
And watched the playful trout
That all among the shadows
Was darting in and out.

*Strophe II:*

Ein Fischer mit der Rute
Wohl an dem Ufer stand,
Und sah's mit kaltem Blute
Wie sich das Fischlein wand.
So lang dem Wasser Helle,
So dacht' ich, nicht gebricht,
So fängt er die Forelle
Mit seiner Angel nicht.
   (last two lines repeated)

With rod and line there waited
An angler by the brook,
All eager, he, to capture
The fish upon his hook.
While clear the water's flowing,
So thought I to myself,
His labor will be fruitless:
I'm sure the trout is safe.

*Strophe III:*
*Altered Section*

Doch endlich ward dem Diebe
Die Zeit zu lang'.
Er macht das Bächlein
   tückisch trübe,
Und eh' ich es gedacht

So zuckte seine Rute
Das Fischlein zappelt d'ran,

The angler loses patience,
He stirs the stream,
And makes the limpid, shining
   water
All dull and muddy seem:
"I have him," quoth the stran-
   ger
As swift his line he cast;

*Return to*
*Music of*
*Strophes I & II:*

Und ich mit regem Blute
Sah die Betrog'ne an.
   (repeat last line)

And heeding not the danger,
The trout was caught at last.

In this song, the piano accompaniment pictures faithfully not only the flowing brook and the leaping trout, but also by means of "muddy" sonorities imitates the wily angler's trick. Again, a vignette, not too important, but enjoyable. At the persuasion of one of his friends, Schubert used the first strophe of this song as the basis for a lovely set of variations in his Quintet, Op. 114, known for this reason as the "Trout Quintet."

The third form, the "through-composed" song, is excellently illustrated by the exciting and dramatic *"Erlkönig,"* set to words by Goethe. Notice that there are four characters in this drama in miniature: the poet, who provides the introduction and coda; the father; the child; and the Erlking. This Erlking represents the force of the supernatural, and may be taken to be the devil in one of his many folk guises. Here is the text of the poem:

Wer reitet so spät durch Nacht und Wind?
Es ist der Vater mit seinem Kind;
er hat den Knaben wohl in dem Arm,
er fasst ihn sicher, er halt ihn warm.
"Mein Sohn, was birgst du so bang dein Gesicht?"
"Siehst, Vater, du den Erlkönig nicht?
den Erlenkönig mit Kron' und Schweif?"
"Mein Sohn, es ist ein Nebelstreif."
"Du liebes Kind, komm, geh' mit mir!
gar schöne Spiele spiel' ich mit dir;
manch' bunte Blumen sind an dem Strand,
meine Mutter hat manch' gulden Gewand."
"Mein Vater, mein Vater, und hörest du nicht
was Erlenkönig mir leise verspricht?"
"Sei ruhig, bleibe ruhig, mein Kind;
in dürren Blättern saüselt der Wind.
"Willst, feiner Knabe, du mit mir geh'n?
Meine Töchter sollen dich warten schön;
meine Töchter fuhren den nachtlichen Reih'n

Who rides so late through night and wind?
It is the father with his child.
He holds the boy within his arm,
He clasps him tight, he keeps him warm.
"My son, why hide your face in fear?"
"See, father, the Erlking's near.
The Erlking with crown and wand."
"Dear son, 'tis but a misty cloud."
"Ah, sweet child, come with me!
Such pleasant games I'll play with thee!
Such pleasant flowers bloom in the field,
My mother has many a robe of gold."
"Oh father, father, do you not hear
What the Erlking whispers in my ear?"
"Be still, my child, be calm;
'Tis but the withered leaves in the wind."
"My lovely boy, wilt go with me?
My daughters fair shall wait on thee,
My daughters nightly revels keep,

und wiegen und tanzen und singen dich ein."
"Mein Vater, mein Vater, und siehst du nicht dort
Erlkönigs Töchter am düstern Ort?"
"Mein Sohn, mein Sohn, ich seh' es genau,
Es scheinen die alten Weiden so grau."
"Ich liebe dich, mich reizt deine schöne Gestalt;
und bist du nicht willig, so brauch' ich Gewalt."
"Mein Vater, mein Vater, jetzt fasst er mich an!
Erlkönig hat mir ein Leids gethan!"
Dem Vater grauset's, er reitet geschwind,
er hält in Armen das ächzende Kind;
erreicht den Hof mit Müh' und Noth:
in seinen Armen das Kind war todt!

They'll sing and dance and rock thee to sleep."
"Oh father, father, see you not
The Erlking's daughters in yon dark spot?"
"My son, my son, the thing you see
Is only the old gray willow tree."
"I love thee, thy form enflames my sense;
And art thou not willing, I'll take thee hence."
"Oh father, father, he grasps my arm,
The Erlking has done me harm!"
The father shudders, he speeds ahead,
He clasps to his bosom the sobbing child,
He reaches home with pain and dread:
In his arms the child lay dead!

In listening to the song, notice how Schubert creates the mood immediately in the first few measures with the hammering octaves and the foreboding scale figure in the bass. First the poet speaks, melodically, but not too emotionally. Then the father, in the low register, where his part remains until the last, seeking to reassure the child. This reassurance is mirrored in the sturdy leap of a fourth upward with which all his lines except one begin. The rising hysteria of the child is pictured by Schubert's beginning each of the sections in which the child speaks one step higher than the preceding outcry. In addition, the outcries become louder. The wheedling of the Erlking causes a change in the music: the thundering horses' hooves are only suggested, the melody is sweeter, and the dynamic level is lower. At the end the poet returns to relate the outcome. The idea of using the ghostly recitative for the last line was a stroke of genius.

Here we have a typical romantic composition: fusion of emotions, poetry and music into one inseparable whole; the influence of the supernatural; the reliance on purely musical constructions to make the effect. This tone painting is more successful than many a grandiose orchestral work written later. Of importance is the way in which Schubert controls his material. The techniques used are exactly suitable to the subject and it is economical and unified. These are classical traits! So we find in Schubert the classicist existing side by side with the romantic element which is always slightly more emphasized.

Other wonderful songs of Schubert abound. Of these, selections from *Die Schöne Müllerin* should be heard, as well as *"Der Leiermann," "Der Doppelgänger," "Der Lindenbaum," "Gretchen am Spinnrade," "Die Junge Nonne," "Der Tod und das Mädchen,"* and *"Lob der Thränen."*

## CHAMBER MUSIC

We shall select our next example from the chamber music of Schubert. The String Quartet in D-minor, called "Death and the Maiden" after the song (also by Schubert) which forms the theme of the variations of the second movement (Example 60).

*First Movement.* The strength of the first movement is evident from the first notes, the rapid triplet figure of which unifies the entire movement. After the introductory section we hear a theme as symphonic in character as those of the Beethoven quartets. The transition, beginning with the restatement of the main material, is traditional, as is the key of the second thematic group. The first part of this is typically Schubertian in its lyricism, yet it is tightly controlled and limited to a repeated motive out of which most of the development section will be fashioned. Indeed, it is developed somewhat in the exposition. Notice how this theme provides material, both melodic and rhythmic, for the closing section, thus limiting the quantity of themes in a truly classical manner. The coda of this movement is truly a summing up and final comment by the composer, so eloquent is the expression of these last few measures.

*Second Movement.* The theme and variations recall the "Emperor" variations of Haydn, both in the chaconne quality of the theme, as well as in the decorative variations spun over this chord sequence. Schubert seldom writes a really developmental set of variations in the Beethoven manner, but they are not less interesting for that, since they make up for what they lack in profundity by presenting us with delightful sonorities achieved by inventive chord diffusion figures, and with lyric variants of the theme hitherto unsuspected. This set of variations is no exception. They might be characterized as follows:

331

*Theme:*   Chaconne-like series of chords with a rhythm of *"long-short-short,"* useful for development.

*Var. 1:*   The theme is fragmented and decorated in the first violin, while

EXAMPLE 60.

FIRST MOVEMENT: Allegro

SECOND SUBJECT

SECOND MOVEMENT: Andante con moto

FIRST HALF OF THEME

THIRD MOVEMENT: Allegro moderato

SCHERZO

8va lower

TRIO

FOURTH MOVEMENT: Presto

PRINCIPAL SUBJECT

SECOND SUBJECT

con forza

CLOSING THEME

the inner parts supply the basic harmony, lightened by the cello *pizzicato*.

*Var. 2:* A cello variation, with the other instruments providing chord diffusion patterns in rhythmic motion. Cello is in its upper register.

*Var. 3:* Begins as a chordal variation with the rhythm of the theme in short note values. Second phrase gives harmonic-melodic parts to second violin and viola while first violin and cello mark the first and third beats of the measure with sonorous broken chords: all instruments chordal at the close.

*Var. 4:* In major. A "harmony" variation with cello, viola and second violin engaged in a harmonic variation of the melody. First violin provides rhythm and chord diffusion patterns.

*Var. 5:* Another "harmony" variation, this time in minor. The duet first between the second violin and viola, later the cello has an important part, with others playing chords above it.

*Var. 6:* Less motion, slow chord movement in three lower instruments while first violin plays *obbligato* part using repeated note patterns.

*Coda:* Slightly varied version of theme, now in serene major key.

*Third Movement.* The scherzo recalls Mozart's G-minor Symphony in its syncopation and energetic motion, but in its thematic economy the comparable parallel movements of the Beethoven Third and Ninth Symphonies come to mind. The trio has a rather interesting construction. We hear first a lyric section of sixteen measures, which, for unity's sake uses a rhythmic quotation from the scherzo; then instead of a literal repetition, the lyric subject is given to the cello and viola while the first violin plays a decorative *obbligato,* and the second provides the rhythmic quotation. This varied interruption over, the trio continues in the manner of the first sixteen measures, later offering another varied repeat of a section. In effect, Schubert has indulged in variation technique where developmental work might be more expected, but the results are successful and beautiful.

*Fourth Movement.* The rather "Hungarian" finale is cast in sonatina form with considerable development occurring within each of the two important thematic sections, and a coda formed from the first theme. The first thematic material is fluid and vigorous, using frequent unison passages in sharply accented rhythms. Abrupt chord changes also occur, adding to the boldness. The second thematic group begins with accented long notes, declamatory in style, followed by a contrapuntal section employing running passages like the first theme combined with the melodic elements of the second theme. A charming and witty little closing theme rounds off the lengthy exposition, and an easily recognizable retransition leads back to a somewhat shortened version of the exposition. The coda, as we have said, uses the first theme and is fairly long. Schubert often had "finale trouble" — that is, it took him a long time to learn how to write last movements which had the perorative power of Beethoven's, the "summing up" quality that is needed for a large work. But learn it he did toward the end of his life, and the final movements of this quartet, the C-major Cello Quintet, and the C-major Symphony are powerful and conclusive.

Some of Schubert's loveliest music is contained in his chamber works; the serious student would do well to listen to the above-mentioned C-major Cello Quintet, Op. 163, the Octet in F, Op. 166, the String Quartet in A-minor, Op. 29, the Piano Quintet in A-major Op. 114 ("The Trout"), and the two piano trios, Opp. 99 and 100 in B♭ and E♭ respectively. These works are most characteristic and contain musical treasures of the greatest worth.

### SYMPHONIC MUSIC

As we have seen, the essence of the classical symphony, especially as it appears in the works of Beethoven, is the process of thematic development. This is most true of symphonic first and last movements, but Beethoven also includes it in second movements, which usually have a strong lyric emphasis. The lyric element, however, is rather static in nature, and thus forms a foil to the energetic first movements. Beethoven uses all his mastery of rhythmic flow to not only make such lyric movements progress, but also to control the more energetically inclined developmental procedures. With the B-minor Symphony ("Unfinished"), Schubert achieved the first truly romantic lyric symphony, overcoming the static element of his lyricism to create a homogeneous, unique work. In the great C-major Symphony which follows this one, he turned his back on the problem, and returned to a more classical conception of the symphony, using themes rather than melodies. It would appear, from the sketches of the scherzo and finale of the B-minor Symphony, that he had exhausted his inspiration in the first two movements of this work — not his lyric inspiration, which never faltered, but his energy and idealistic inspiration — for the sketches are quite commonplace and would in no sense complete the four-movement cycle successfully. The central experience of this work is one of romantic struggle against overwhelming odds, defeat, pessimism, and final resignation. Two movements sufficed to express this experience fully — more were not possible, even though Schubert tried to make a traditional four-movement work. But if this were intended from the beginning to be a two-movement work, the second movement would have been in B-minor or B-major, rather than its present key of E-major. But the two movements complement each other so completely that no more is needed — in fact, two more movements might have an anticlimactic effect, weakening the otherwise strong impression. Technically speaking, this is an "unfinished" symphony, since it has but two movements. Poetically, dramatically, and emotionally, however, it seems complete.

We have mentioned the idea of struggle in connection with this work. Is this not the premise of the Beethoven heroic symphonies? In what way does this work differ from them? The difference lies in the nature of the two composers and their attitudes toward life. Beethoven's strong and defiant nature we know about already. Schubert was a less aggressive person, given to moods of deep despair and a romantic feeling of alienation from life. His nature was passive, introspective, yearning, and this work is an expression of his innermost feelings under the impact of some tragic experience, possibly the death of his mother. The struggle in the development section of the first movement is fierce, as we shall see, but it ends in an elegy of defeat, not a paean of victory. Compared to the Fifth Symphony of Beethoven, a *classically* inclined work, the qualities of romanticism are here clearly evident.

Let us examine this symphony in some detail, movement by movement, and see how classic procedures are blended with romantic lyricism, expression and coloration to yield the first of a long line of similar works extending to the twentieth century.

*First Movement: Allegro moderato* (Example 61.) Introduction: Essentially, the motives of the introduction (Example 61a) provide the material for most of the other themes as well as the bulk of the development in the first movement. The scale line of three notes, ascending and descending is the most important motive, but the skip of a fourth and the rhythm of the first two measures should be remembered.

Exposition: The motion starts with a wavering figure in the strings, urged on by a rhythmic accompaniment figure. The woodwinds begin a wistful melody (Example 61b) constructed out of a downward skip of a fifth (a fourth inverted) and a three-note scale. After a

EXAMPLE 61.

FIRST MOVEMENT: Allegro moderato

a.

PRINCIPAL SUBJECT

b.

SECOND SUBJECT

c.

DEVELOPMENT

d.

e.

337

f.

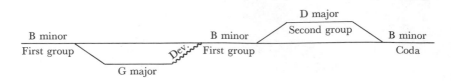

sharply accented chord, the theme is restated, expands melodically and sonorously, finally reaching a forceful cadence. One tone of the last chord is retained by the horns and bassoons, and expands into harmony which cadences in a new key: thus simply does Schubert accomplish the transition. A syncopated accompaniment begins, against which one of the most famous of Schubert's melodies unfolds. It, too, has been created out of the motives of the introduction. The first repetition is not allowed to finish, however, for, after a moment the melody breaks off and a series of harsh chords destroy the lyric tenderness. The motives of the second theme are developed against a louder version of its syncopated accompaniment, after which the yearning and wistful second theme provides a closing section. Again, it is interrupted, this time by a sudden loud octave, followed by hushed and apprehensive *pizzicato* notes in the strings.

Development: There are about seven sections in the development, all dealing with the thematic elements of the introductory idea.

(1)  Statement of the introductory theme.
(2)  Three-note scale and thematic rhythm expanded to motive of Example 61d, combined in canon. Increase in dynamic level leads to Example 61e, which becomes rhythmically compressed; tension explodes at climax.
(3)  Heavy block chords in rhythm of first two measures of introduction alternate with soft syncopated accompaniment of second theme.
(4)  Reiteration of introductory theme, fortissimo, by full orchestra.
(5)  Motto theme in brass, accompanied by slashing counterpoint in the strings.
(6)  The preceding develops into a canon between the outer parts of the orchestra, while martial rhythms appear in the brass and timpani.
(7)  A point of temporary stability is reached on a major chord, around which the scale motive plays; later the winds and strings have short decorative scale figures accompanying the scale motive. The retransition is composed of these figures, diminuendo, with motives from the first theme in the woodwinds.

Recapitulation: This section is almost the exact counterpart of the exposition except for two details. The key of the second theme is now a third above the B-minor tonic, D-major, rather than the third below, G-major, as it was previously. Thus we have the "axis" arrangement illustrated in Example 61f. The second theme is also elongated by the addition of four sequential measures in order to attain the right tonal level for the succeeding section.

The coda is another development section devoted to the introductory motives, this time concerned with their pathetic qualities.

*Second Movement: Andante con moto* (Example 62). The second movement is in sonatina form with internal development (Example 63), and expresses a mood of quiet, wistful resignation, a musical conception of the peace so ardently longed for by the romantics.

As Example 63 indicates, each of the main key areas is organized as a ternary form (A-B-A', C-D-C'), of which the central section is developmental in character. The typically irregular key-plan of the movement, not quite an "axis" relationship, is also indicated in Example 63. Thematically, this movement is closely related to the first one, using the scale motive as well as a simplification of it

EXAMPLE 62.

339

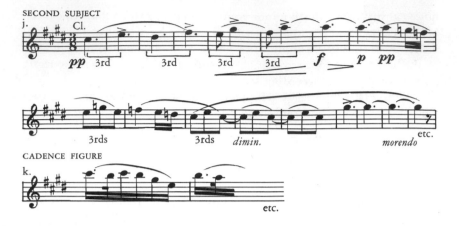

SECOND SUBJECT

j. Cl.

*pp* — 3rd — 3rd — 3rd — 3rd — *f* — *p* *pp*

3rds — 3rds — *dimin.* — *morendo* etc.

CADENCE FIGURE

k.

etc.

obtained by omitting the second note, thus creating a skip of a third. Most of the main motives are displayed in the first eight measures. The motto scale appears in the horns (Example 62g, 1) and the *pizzicato* strings (Example 62g, 2) in the first three measures. In measures three through six, two lyric ideas are presented simultaneously in the strings (Example 62g, 3, 4), all sharing in some degree the important motive. The middle section, which follows after a varied repetition of these measures, is developmental, after which there is a quiet return followed by a codetta based upon the figures of Example 62h. The transition is simplicity itself; after a cadence on the tonic chord of E-major (E-G♯-B), the G♯ is retained (Example 62i), skips up an octave, comes slowly down a triad to rest upon C♯, the tonic of the new section. A syncopated accompaniment is set up, over which the clarinet unfolds a melody consisting principally of the intervals of the third. After the beautifully shifting harmony has come to rest, the passage is repeated by the oboe in a canon with the cellos. Then follows a complex section in which the transition figure and the second theme are combined in the violins while the unchanged theme itself appears in the lower strings. The woodwinds supply the harmonic context. This passage is repeated with altered scoring, after which the C' section returns in a newly scored and somewhat changed version. It leads to a most poetic retransition, with the horns tolling like bells, and finally to a reasonably exact recapitulation.

The coda combines elements from each of the main sections and the transition. It begins with the horn motive (Example 62g, 1) over the string *pizzicato,* and is brought to a cadence with a figure from

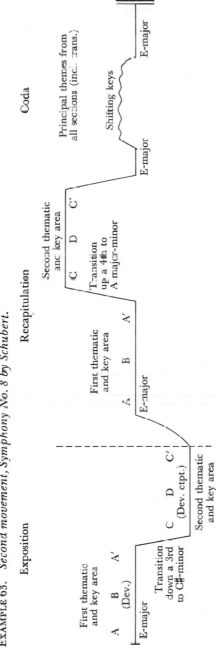

EXAMPLE 63.   Second movement, Symphony No. 8 by Schubert.

Exposition

First thematic
and key area

A    B    A'
     (Dev.)

E-major

Transition
down a 3rd
to C♯-minor

C    D    C'
(Dev. ctpt.)

Second thematic
and key area

Recapitulation

First thematic
and key area

A    B    A'

E-major

Second thematic
and key area

C    D    C'

Transition
up a 4th to
A major-minor

E-major

Coda

Principal themes from
all sections (incl. trans.)

Shifting keys

E-major

the descending part of the second theme. This is repeated with changed orchestration, followed by the transition figure in the first violins. There is a pivot modulation on the last note, shifting to an unexpected key in which the motive of Example 62g, 3 is quoted, rounded off by the cadential flourish of Example 63h. This is repeated upon a new tonal level, the cadence figures repeat, fading nostalgically away, the descending *pizzicato* scale appears under sustained woodwind and brass chords, and the movement concludes on a long-held E-major chord. The use of the woodwind instruments is especially beautiful in this coda, their intimate voices providing just the right qualities for the withdrawal from the world of this poetic movement.

## MUSIC AND THE OTHER ARTS

The artificial society of the Rococo produced only a few artists, and these were better than we might expect. Watteau and Fragonard owe a considerable debt to Rembrandt and Rubens, although they nowhere approach the passion and truth of either of those giants. The methods and organization of paintings of this time reflect those of the Baroque, but are miniaturized, refined and less vigorous. More detail, slightly less diffusion of line, fragmentation of masses into short, curved lines, more closed spatial suggestion and less action appear when we compare these paintings to those of the preceding period. But the difference is mostly one of degree, not of kind, and the choice of subject matter exerts a dominating influence similar to the importance of the melodic line in the music. When we examine paintings of these artists, such as Watteau's *L'Amour Paisable* (Plate XXII) we find scenes reflecting courtly sentiment, artificial manners, and an almost static quality. The fervor and tension of the Baroque is gone, and in its place we have delicate and restrained lyricism. The art of Boucher reveals even more clearly the elegance and formalism of the day. This artist was a favorite of Madame de Pompadour and painted many portraits of her. Chardin, as mentioned in the introduction to this chapter, illustrates the bourgeois style with his genre paintings (Plate XXIII).

Few sculptors worth mentioning appear at this time. The only one in whom interest has survived is Houdon, whose works show strong classical tendencies. He is preeminently known for his portrait busts, and has transmitted to us the expressive likenesses of Gluck (Plate XXIV), Voltaire, Rameau, Frederick the Great and others.

PLATE XXII. *"L'Amour Paisable" by Watteau. A picnic portrayed in the typically elegant style of the French rococo. (Courtesy of the Archive-German Information Center.)*

Examples of rococo architecture are numerous: the salons of Louis XV, Mme. de Pompadour and Marie Antoinette; the Sans Souci Palace of Frederick the Great in Potsdam; the Great Gallery of the Schönbrunn Palace in Vienna (Plate XXV). All of these exhibit the delicacy and grace of ornament, the elegance of color associated with the dying days of the French monarchy.

The classic element in art of this day turned to rather cold and lifeless copies of Greek and Roman architecture and sculpture. There was no vital impulse in this dubious art, and it remained academic and sterile. In this style of painting the tendency is toward realism in that the lines are sharper and more angular, and there is severe use of light and shade. All unnecessary purely decorative elements are eliminated, and the subjects are usually taken from classic Greek or Roman history. Jacques Louis David represents this style in his *Oath of the Horatii* (Plate XXVI) and other similar works.

PLATE XXIII. *"The Blessing," by Chardin. A typical genre painting extolling the pleasures of middle class life — the "bourgeois style" in art. (Courtesy of the French Cultural Services.)*

If we are to make instructive comparisons between the music of the eighteenth century and the other arts of the period, we must constantly realize that the musical style is in all cases the result of a synthesis of the many modes of expression characteristic of the various sub-cultures of the time. We must also make allowance for the changes in the rococo style when practiced by a German and in the *opera buffa* style when employed by an Austrian. While it is seldom that an entire work is written in one single style, we may find movements or sections of works in which one style is so predominant as to render the comparison with the other arts on a more nearly equal basis.

Such a movement, for example, is the first minuet of Mozart's Divertimento in D-major for Horns and Strings, K. 334. This music is almost a parody of the *style galant* and is comparable to paintings by Watteau (Plate XXII), Pater, Boucher, Lancret and Fragonard. The first and last movements belong to much the same category of popular "music for conversation" which the aristocratic patrons of these composers required. And many a finale of Haydn's sparkles with

PLATE XXIV. *Bust of Gluck by Houdon. This sculptor excelled in the portrait bust. (Courtesy of Service de Documentation Photographique des Musées Nationaux.)*

the verve and wit which have come to be the legendary qualities (possibly mythical too!) of these conversations between the intellectual elite and their princely patrons.

Mozart's *opera buffa* style has no parallel in the other arts except perhaps one of mood. Certain literary works of the time, especially plays in the comic vein, might, in the hands of accomplished actors, approach the rapid give and take of this style.

The bourgeois style, less elegant than the rococo and *buffa,* appears in the music of Haydn, usually in slow movements of symphonies, sonatas and chamber music, and in some songs, such as his setting of "She Never Told Her Love" from Shakespeare's *Twelfth Night.* In Beethoven this style becomes the basis of two rather opposed emotional states — one of humor, as exhibited in the Sixth and Eighth Symphonies, and the other a mood of mystic exaltation appearing in the slow movements of such works as the Violin Concerto, the "Emperor" Concerto, the Ninth Symphony and the B♭ String Quartet, Op. 130. Schubert's dance music, indeed much of his other music

345

PLATE XXV. *The Great Gallery in Schönbrunn Palace, Vienna. The relation of this charming rococo salon to the baroque style is plain but the heaviness, tension and architectural grandeur of the baroque is replaced by elegance, classical symmetry and lightness, both in color and in style. (Courtesy of the Austrian Information Service.)*

as well, has a lyric emotional appeal that stems from this style, an easy-going "comfortableness" in keeping with the Biedermeier furniture style of the time in which elegance was sacrificed to comfort.

The bourgeois style in the other arts, while it was not new to them, becomes of increasing importance in the time of growing social consciousness, and, while it sometimes takes on over sentimental, coarse or erotic tones, must still be included in the productions of the period. It ranges from the biting satire of Hogarth to the cheap lechery of Greuze, passing along the way the purer sentiments of Chardin and Boilly whose paintings may be used as comparable to the musical examples, although often without the depth of feeling present in the music. Works by some of the earlier Dutch genre painters as well as some by Rembrandt seem to contain more comparable expressiveness. In sculpture, perhaps the foremost exponent of the style is the French artist Houdon, who made naturalistic portrait busts of Gluck (Plate XXIV), Washington, Voltaire, Franklin, Jefferson, Fulton and John Paul Jones. And the literary works of Voltaire, Rousseau, Richardson,

PLATE XXVI. *"The Oath of the Horatii" by Jacques David. A typical painting of the classic revival in France. Note the severe, balanced treatment, the noble theme and the emotional restraint. This type of classicism is very seldom found in the music of the Classic Period. (Courtesy of Service de Documentation Photographique des Musées Nationaux.)*

Fielding, Goldsmith, Diderot and Lessing all sought middle-class readers through subject matter and style.

For examples of the "storm and stress" style in painting and sculpture we must look ahead to the Romantic era, to the works of Gericault, Delacroix, Ingres and their followers — free artists not controlled by the wishes of their princely patrons. But in the literature of the eighteenth century, in addition to some minor figures, we find the poets Herder and Schiller, and the young Goethe, all of whom produced stirring works which combined social revolt with tremendous imaginative force and agitation.

When we turn to Beethoven, the comparison with the other arts becomes more difficult, for no genius equivalent to the giant of Bonn appeared upon the contemporary scene in the plastic arts. If we make allowances, certain of the paintings of David show points for comparison (Plate XXVI). In these pictures the subject matter is of distinction, the spatial organization is clear and forceful, and the statement of the "theme" is direct: all that is lacking is the genius to breathe life into the work. One of the great forces which helped to mold Beethoven's view of life was the revival of interest in the heritage of ideals from ancient Greece. These ideals he adopted wholeheartedly and tried to make his music express them: heroism, freedom and lofty moral tone. Beethoven had to enlarge the forms and sonorities of the traditional classic symphony in order for it to contain these large ideas. In the "Eroica" we find the elevation of the heroic ideal to unprecedented heights; and in the Ninth Symphony a total view of the life of man and his battle with fate. Possibly the only other creative figure of the times to bear comparison with Beethoven is the creator of Faust — Johann Wolfgang von Goethe. Both encompassed a world view and both struggled with the demon within themselves in order to present that view with classic clarity.

### LIST OF TERMS

| | |
|---|---|
| symphonic economy | "Unfinished" Symphony |
| unified forms | "Pastoral" Symphony |
| developmental coda | "Eroica" Symphony |
| motto theme | "Choral" Symphony |
| developmental variations | concert overture |
| *obbligato* | third relationship |

LIST OF TERMS (CONT.)

| | |
|---|---|
| *fughetta* | lied, lieder |
| theme fragmentation | pivot-tone modulation |
| ethical program | ländler |
| *ostinato* | strophic song |
| lyric symphony | modified, or altered strophic song |
| germ motive | through-composed song |
| | axis key relations |

ADDITIONAL LISTENING

*Beethoven* (in addition to any of the symphonies and string quartets):

1. "Kreutzer" Sonata for violin and Piano, Op. 47
2. Septet for Violin, Viola, Cello, Double bass, Horn, Clarinet and Bassoon, Op. 20
3. "Waldstein" Sonata, piano, Op. 53
4. Piano Concertos No. 3 and 4, Opp. 58 and 73
5. Violin Concerto, Op. 61
6. Overtures to *Coriolanus,* Op. 62, *Egmont,* Op. 84, and *Leonore* No. 3, Op. 72
7. *Fidelio,* opera, Op. 72
8. Trio ("Archduke"), Op. 97
9. Two Trios, Op. 70
10. "Diabelli" Variations, Op. 120
11. *Missa Solemnis* in D. Op. 123

*Schubert*

1. Symphony No. 5, in Bb
2. Symphony No. 9, in C-Major ("The Great")
3. *Die Schöne Müllerin,* song cycle
4. *Die Winterreise,* song cycle
5. Two Trios: Op. 99 in Bb, Op. 100 in Eb
6. Quintet for Piano and Strings, Op. 114 ("The Trout")
7. Quintet in C, for Two Violins, Viola, two Cellos, Op. 163
8. Octet in F for strings, Clarinet, Horn and Bassoon, Op. 166
9. String Quartet in A minor, Op. 29, No. 1
10. Piano Sonatas Nos. 20, in A; 21 in Bb, both Op. posthumous
11. Many short piano pieces under the titles "Fantasie," "Moment Musicale," "Ländler," etc., as well as some fine piano duet sonatas

349

# VII  The Romantic
# Period, 1827-1900

## HISTORICAL AND
## BIOGRAPHICAL PERSPECTIVE

Romanticism in music generally signifies that the emotional element of a composition is foremost, often to the detriment of formal constructive logic. This emotional approach emphasizes the lyric quality, harmonic richness and descriptive ability of music. It tends to be picturesque, fantastic and experimental, qualities often achieved through lyrical or colorful instrumental effects. It opposes the concentration of classicism with a certain diffuseness, sometimes vague in harmonic movement or melodic line. It is subjective while classicism is objective, hypothetical where classicism is positive. At best, it is imaginative and progressive; at worst, it is sentimental and full of clichés.

Music is the ideal vehicle for the expression of romantic sentiments, but the movement did not start in that art until the sister discipline, literature, had explored some of the possibilities of this freer mode of expression. The trend toward a more romantic literature started during the last decades of the eighteenth century as a development of certain elements within classicism which had been held in balance by the feeling for harmonious proportion and the desire not to overstep the emotional bounds set by the manners of the century. In the decade between 1770 and 1780 a violent literary reaction to the rationalism of the Enlightenment occurred, a movement which portrayed with the most violent and fantastic means at its disposal in plays and novels the rebellion of the imagination against the strictures of eighteenth-century formality and rationalism. The movement takes its name from the title of a play by von Klinger, *Sturm und Drang,* and numbers among its literary highlights Goethe's *Werthers Leiden,* Schiller's *Die Raüber* and Lessing's *Minna von Barnhelm.* Goethe's novel caused a wave of suicides across Europe in imitation of the hero of the work, so powerfully did the story speak to the awakening sensibilities of those who were disillusioned by the failure of the Enlightenment to produce a paradise on earth. The musical reflection of this period came somewhat later, and was more rationally — that is to say, classically — presented in the middle period works of Beethoven, although these were to a great extent the results of a personal period of psychical storm and stress. As we have seen, these expressions are the result of using a heightened bourgeois style. This style, with emphasis on more Germanic and personal traits, becomes one of the great dialects of the language of romanticism.

In Germany the Romantic movement was largely literary, deeply influenced by translations of English poems and novels. Shakespeare was felt to be a supreme romantic, and with him were included such lights of English literature as Scott, with his novels of adventures far away in time and place, Wordsworth, Byron, Keats, Shelley and the American, James Fenimore Cooper, whose latest translations into German were enjoyed by Schubert during his last illness. The German Romantic composers were closely connected with the literature of the times. Schumann remarked that he learned more counterpoint from his favorite poet, Jean Paul Richter, than he did from his teacher. The writers Novalis, Rückert, Hölderlin, E. T. A. Hoffmann, Tieck and Kleist had a profound effect on German romantic expression and style in music.

In France, romanticism was revolutionary, but, the end seemingly achieved, the movement became somewhat petrified and arrived at no startlingly new results until the end of the nineteenth century. Similarly, in England the romantic poets who lived long enough to achieve middle-age drew back from the progressiveness of their youth, and became "safe" Victorians. The English produced only one composer during this period whose works are still performed, Edward Elgar.

352

Italy was torn by political, not musical, strife during the romantic century. The opera continued to occupy the forefront, while symphonic and chamber music became almost nonexistant. The plots of these Italian operas became increasingly romantic, and used stories adapted from the writings of Schiller, Sir Walter Scott, Victor Hugo and other strongly Romantic poets, dramatists and novelists. These were the years in which operas were written to exhibit the voices of virtuoso singers rather than to create meaningful musical dramas, although, to be fair, we must admit that there were some compelling scenes scattered among the clichés. The century saw the development of Italian opera from the suavity of Bellini and Donizetti to the almost Beethovian power of Giuseppe Verdi.

In the relationship between romanticism and classicism we find a repetition of that which occurred between the rising of the Rococo-Classic and the Baroque periods. The old style overlaps the beginning of the new, and an outstanding composer is discovered writing in the old style at just about the time when the new is ready to try its wings. Bach lasts well into the Rococo-Classic period, Handel even longer; Beethoven produces his most astonishing works only shortly before the first bright flowers of romanticism in the works of Mendelssohn, Schumann, Chopin and Berlioz burst into bloom. But whereas Bach was looked upon as old-fashioned and out of date by composers of the succeeding era, Beethoven became the idol and example to be imitated for many romantic musicians. Each artist differed in his interpretation of the great classicist's work, but each believed that he alone was continuing upon the path Beethoven indicated.

Let us enumerate and discuss briefly some general characteristics of romanticism. One of the most important ones is youth. Classicism is mature, rational, sober; romanticism is youthful, ardent, frequently irrational, emotionally intoxicated. Goethe was an example of the most progressive kind of romantic in his younger days, but the works of his maturity became the epitome of classical German literature.

Another characteristic of youth is its general egocentricity, and this quality imbues the whole romantic panoply of creative artists from the beginning of the movement to the very end. No longer does a composer, for example, write within a single general style, one which, like that of the classic period, sought not to invent new idioms, but rather to use the old ones superlatively well; not to attract attention by individuality but rather to belong well within a style and to create enjoyable music as needed for the social function of the art at that time. Rather, each artist sought to emphasize his personality, to demonstrate the ways in which he was different from the rest of humanity — which usually included his fellow artists. Hence all the romantic creators speak strikingly different dialects of the common language of music, or painting, poetry or prose. They unite in their ideals and techniques, however, thus making it possible to gain a general idea of the achievements of this particular style.

The romantic artist was in a constant state of yearning — longing to be somewhere else, to go back to the "good old days" of Greece, Rome or Persia, to escape from the grimy world through love, religion or some form of intoxication. These desires had varied results. They led to exploration and travel, the sciences of archeology and anthropology on the one hand, and highly imaginative literature, painting, sculpture, and music on the other. Scott's novels dealing with the Highland border feuds, medieval chivalry, or the Crusades; Delacroix's painting of Dante and Virgil in Hell, Rude's romantic sculpture, and Wagner's resuscitation of the heroes of Valhalla upon the operatic stage are all representative of the varied harvest this yearning produced.

We shall probably never know all of the artistic creations brought to life by the "grand passion." Byron, Liszt, Chopin, Schumann and Wagner owe some of their finest works to the inspiration of love, either happy or despairing, legal, or extramural. Certainly Wagner's affair with Mathilda Wesendonck affected his opera *Tristan und Isolde,* for the arrows of such experiences pierce deep. In any case, in this work Wagner has brought the romantic yearning to its highest point, expressed in the most poignant music. He has also led the romantic age to its logical conclusion by the harmonic techniques employed in this music drama particularly, but also in succeeding works.

The superficial escape from the world through religion was and still is a romantic manifestation. This does not mean the taking of monastic vows but rather the desire to belong to an age-old institution whose conservative solidity offers a refuge from the battering of experience and replaces longing with security. Needless to say, these are not true religious motives, but personal, egocentric ones. A great many Germans joined the Catholic church for just these reasons during this period.

Many romantic artists sought in the seemingly irrational processes of nature the antidote for the hampering logic with which the Enlightenment had saddled their imaginations. To them the overwhelming grandeur of mountain scenery and the primeval force of the lightning, the avalanche and the flood exalted the spirit of man by belittling the reasoned constructions of his intellect and hands (Plate XXVII). These rebels against wisdom were personified for the ardent spirits of the time by Faust and Don Juan, who sought emotional, not scientific truth. For others the enjoyment of nature became sentimental. A profusion of "nature-pieces," pictorial and musical as well as literary, were created under this mild stimulus. A more fantastic interpretation related nature to the supernatural, and the ruined abbeys and moonlit landscapes of the sentimentalists became the haunts of vampires, devils and evil spirits of men (Plate XXVIII). This is the inspiration for such notably romantic tales of horror as *Dracula, Frankenstein's Monster,* and *Dr. Jekyll and Mr. Hyde.* The forerunner of this kind of story is Goethe's *Faust,* which, of course, points to a universal truth, while most of these later works were intended simply to amuse and entertain. We find the revival of medieval folk-tales concerned with the supernatural to be popular at this time, and some of these found their way into musical compositions such as Schubert's song *"Der Erlkönig"* as well as operas little known today, *Robert le Diable, Der Vampyr, Hans Heiling,* and one which still holds the stage in Germany, Karl Maria von Weber's *Der Freischütz.*

Another of the romantic aspirations was directed toward producing a work of art in which all the arts should participate. The wealth of song literature produced by the composers of this period illustrates one aspect of this ideal, for the *lied,* as we have seen, marries the words and music in an indissoluble union. On the stage, Wagner attempted to fuse music, literature, dance, acting, painting and architecture into one grand representation, the "music drama." And as we shall see, literature was often substituted for intrinsically musical procedures in providing a formal basis for some compositions of this time, called, significantly enough, "tone poems," or "symphonic poems." Music was composed to illustrate pictures, and pictures were given musical titles (*e.g.,* Whistler's "Nocturne in Silver and Gray"). Poetry, during the middle nineteenth century, aspired more closely to music while staying within the confines of its own art. One needs only to read the verse of the Frenchman Baudelaire or the American E. A. Poe aloud to appreciate the choice of musical sounds from which these poets fashioned their works.

Finally, some varieties of musical romanticism developed a

PLATE XXVII. "The Falls of the Rhine at Schaffhausen" by Turner. A typical romantic landscape emphasizing the forces of nature — a more picturesque version of the revolt against the Enlightenment. (Courtesy of The Museum of Fine Arts, Boston.)

PLATE **XXVIII.** *"The Bewitched" by Goya. The supernatural and fantastic element in romantic art is extended here to an almost expressionistic degree. (Courtesy of the Trustees, The National Gallery, London.)*

penchant for description, not of spiritual states, for the ordinary variety of music in this era does that well enough, but of external, physical phenomena, even to the length of telling a story by means of musical syntax which imitated in some degree the action of the plot. This sort of musical narration is not new. There exists an ancient Greek melody imitating the battle between Apollo and a dragon, and as we ascend musical history we find numerous instances of this function of music. In the Romantic era it was made the basis of a whole system of composition. Richard Strauss, one of the last musicians to use the descriptive techniques of the Romantic period, once remarked, no doubt whimsically, that some day one would be able to describe an egg musically!

Consistent with their self-appointed role as leaders in the arts, the romantics caused a change in the social status of the arts and the artists. Musicians, who profited most from the change, were no longer obliged to wear the livery of an aristocratic house and compose music to order for their masters. Instead, the romantic artist owed allegiance to no one save himself and his artistic ideals. He wrote for his own self-expression, not to order, although he was usually not above dedicating the finished work to some wealthy or influential person who might reward him in some way. But "art for art's sake" was the general slogan, and the public was quick to acclaim these attractive rebels whose free acts and fiery personalities it secretly admired and envied.

In summation, then, we see that romanticism is ardently emotional, often seemingly irrational, fantastic and ambiguous. It is revolutionary, but, paradoxically, seeks the security offered by love, friendship and religion, often valuing these more for the mystic experiences which they offer than for their more enduring qualities. Romanticism is always in search of the personal, the unattainable and the exotic. It delights in the supernatural, the extremes of good and evil, the terrors of the subconscious. It is indeed no accident that the pioneering work by Freud in the exploration of the hidden side of the human mind took place during the latter years of this century. The formidable problem of the creative artist, then, was to synthesize these many aims into an understandable whole — and surprisingly enough, many of them were equal to the task!

# THE STYLE OF THE ROMANTIC PERIOD

Let us now try to summarize some of the characteristics of the music of this period paying special attention to the changes in the type and use of sonority, motion, rhythm, form and harmony compared with these qualities in the preceding era. It will be important to note that the music of certain Romantic composers exhibits wide departures from tradition in only one or two of the above classifications, that of others in almost all of them. The degree of departure is also somewhat variable from work to work among productions of the individual composer, but not so much as to destroy his personal style.

### MELODY

The composers of this era tend toward lyric melody and moods. This attitude is reflected in the great number of songs produced during this century, as well as the short piano composition, most of which might be classified loosely as "songs without words." Many of these melodies must be assigned to an intermediate classification, if indeed, they can be classified at all. They are not always *vocal* in the sense of being easily sung, yet they possess an expressive melodic quality. This quality we shall refer to as *instrumental lyricism*. The works of Berlioz and Brahms contain many examples of this kind of melody.

In this era the principal melodies — which often replace the themes of the classic style — become individualized, and serve as indicators of the structural parts of the form. The necessary *tonal* changes usually accompany these melodic sections, but tonality *as a constructive factor* is much less important than in the Classic period.

As in previous eras, many melodies are constructed from *rhythmic* motives. In the Romantic era, however, the importance of the *melodic* motive increases, not merely as a theme, appearing in the same rhythm always, but often in more or less drastically altered rhythmic form while still retaining the original melodic shape. We shall encounter this technique (theme transformation) in the works of Schumann, Brahms, Liszt, Wagner, and Strauss.

359

Finally, many of the melodies used in orchestral compositions have vague conclusions, melting into the following section rather than ending with even so much as a non-final cadence. This cadence avoidance is developed into a fine art in such works as Wagner's *"Tristan,"* and some of Strauss' compositions. The tendency goes hand in hand with the formal developments of the period.

As the search for the utmost in expressiveness continued through the period, the intervals used became less usual. Wide, angular skips to somewhat unexpected tones evoke strong emotional response, while, more intimately, chromatic intervals of narrow range appear frequently. Again, this aspect of melodic development is found to a considerable degree in operatic works, although present in many late romantic orchestral and chamber compositions.

### HARMONY

Generally speaking, the harmony of this period tends to become more rich and complex (more dissonant), and more chromatic. During the Classic period, a chord which was altered by sharping or flatting one or more of its members tended to function in much its usual way, except that the tendency to move to another chord of less tension was increased. If, as often happened in the music of the Romantic period, the chords of the whole passage are similarly altered, the tonality soon becomes weakened to the point where no chord has *any* necessity to move. In this highly charged state it is the degree of tension — dissonance saturation — of the chords which is important, causing those of greater tension to move to those with less. The ultimate results of these changes are discussed below.

1. The sense of key becomes weakened. For example, the key of C-major is composed of the notes C-D-E-F-G-A-B-C, with no sharps or flats. Now if even one sharp, F♯, is introduced, the sense of finality of the note C is greatly weakened. If, in addition to F♯, G♯ and D♯ are included, our previous tonic is further weakened. If these are introduced harmonically — that is, as altered notes of otherwise familiar and functional chords, such as IV, V, and I — the sense of the tonality of C-major completely disappears.
2. Cadences, as we have seen above, become much less decisive. They tend to be points at which the dissonant tension of the harmony relaxes to some degree. It need not relax fully, but only to harmony less tense. *Harmonic tension crescendos* may be created by just the opposite procedure, leading usually, to climactic sections.

Not only as a result of the above tendencies, but because of the desire on the part of the composer to create a continuously flowing fabric of sound, non-final cadences become more important than final ones, and many technical tricks are resorted to in order to avoid or elide cadences. One of the romantic ideals is to have a unified, continuously developing musical flow, comparable to "stream of consciousness" literature. Like this literature it avoids punctuation.

Harmonic color — that is, the sound quality of a particular musical aggregation of tones, dissonant or not — is often exploited for its own sake (but always in the service of the expressive aim of the whole composition). The static "Prelude" to Wagner's *Das Rheingold* is an example of this, as are some of Debussy's Preludes for piano, and certain of Chopin's Etudes and Preludes.

## MOTION

This title refers to the quality of movement in any composition, and includes such contributory phenomena as meter, tempo and rhythm. Romantic music does not always have continuity of tempo, as is the general rule with music of the Baroque and Classic eras. Since much of romantic music is intended to reflect emotional states, meters and tempos may change within the individual movements. In other words, the contrast of tempo that occurred between the individual movements of the classic symphony now moves to the interior of each of those movements. This discontinuity of motion is most often found in the first movements of romantic symphonies at the point where the second thematic area is introduced in the exposition. In order to enhance the lyric quality of this theme and to contrast it more acutely with the first theme, a new, slower tempo is often established. But other areas, such as the dramatic development section, reflect this attitude also. Here, instead of relaxing the tempo, the tension due to motion is frequently increased by acceleration of the metric pulse, and an increase in excitement results. This might be termed a "motion crescendo."

Except for music where a steady pulse is essential to the type of composition (*e.g.,* a march), certain of the romantic compositions often have very indistinct meter, and flow rather amorphously. This effect is created by extensive syncopations in the individual instrumental parts, the total effect of which is not the rhythmic shock of Beethoven, but a sliding around and between the metric pulsations,

Again, portions of Wagner's music drama *Tristan,* particularly the "Prelude" and *"Liebestod,"* demonstrate this almost "unmetric" flow.

Often the dictates of expression cause sharp contrasts in rhythmic motion within smaller sections of compositions. Clusters of short notes appear before and after slower-moving tones, suggesting impulsive "stop-and-go" emotional states. Often the basic metric pulse is uniform, although probably not clearly expressed; it is the time-values of the individual notes which create the effect. The beginning of Liszt's B-minor Sonata for piano is an eloquent example of this discontinuity of motion.

Related to this impulsive quality of motion is the flexibility and variability of the so-called *tempo rubato* (literally, "robbed time"). This is the style of performance we are accustomed to hearing in jazz, particularly in the free and elastic relationship of the melodic part to the steady metric pulse of the accompaniment. By holding back or moving ahead of this metric beat, the singer or instrumentalist can give an improvisational flavor to the melody which is thus more expressive than if it coincided squarely with the beat. Such performers as Hoagy Carmichael and Dinah Shore use *rubato* in the most natural way. In the Romantic era, *tempo rubato* was employed almost entirely by solo performers, rarely in ensembles where it would be difficult to control, although it does appear in some orchestral works (*cf.* Berlioz, *Symphonie Fantastique,* second movement). Indeed, it is part of the performing tradition of the piano works of Chopin and Liszt.

Rhythmic characteristics include increasing rhythmic imbalance due to syncopation, odd phrase lengths, accents within the measure stronger than the metric accent. Rhythmic motives are not always of the exciting variety in construction, but may, in slow movements, for example, be rather long in extent. The Wagnerian *leitmotiv* often has an overall rhythmic shape as well as an important melodic contour. Motion is intensified due to repetition of motives, sometimes rhythmic in character, but more often melodic. This repetition is usually accompanied by a parallel intensification in unstable harmony, leading to an eventual climax (see "dynamic curve" under Forms).

### SONORITY

In the music of the Romantic period, tone-color and sonority become integral parts of the formal design. In the music of Debussy they become almost more important than themes and rhythms.

The romantic solo instrument *par excellence* is the piano, and many of the most progressive composers of this era developed a characteristic way of writing for it according to their various sound-ideals. Chopin, Liszt and Brahms treated the possibilities of the instrument in individual ways, and each developed a piano style which advanced the concept of the instrument.

A piano comparable to the modern grand piano was developed in the early years of the nineteenth century. This instrument, which Beethoven had in mind when he wrote his last five piano sonatas, was heavier in action and more sonorous. It was provided with a pedal which raised felt mufflers from the strings not directly in use, allowing them to vibrate sympathetically with the harmonics of the struck strings. By deft manipulation of this pedal, effects of tone color impossible to the so-called "Mozart piano" could be achieved. Beethoven did not explore this technique, but Schumann, Chopin, Liszt, and a host of now-forgotten virtuosi experimented with these coloristic effects to create subtle and refined nuances on this otherwise monochromatic instrument.

As we advance through the century we see the orchestra expanded in all choirs. In the works of Wagner, woodwinds are increased to three and four of each kind, allowing chords of one tone color to be sounded. The brass section is augmented by increasing the numbers of each kind of instrument. Both sections are enlarged by the inclusion of new instruments, such as the "Wagner tubas," as well as by higher or lower-pitched members of the families already present, such as the E♭ clarinet, English horn and bass flute. In addition, brass instruments were provided with valves, and the woodwinds with improved key systems during this century — improvements which rendered them both more flexible, accurate, and useful.

This new orchestra can, obviously, create a greater volume of sound, but one of its most important functions lies in almost the opposite direction. With the multiplication of instruments, the color possibilities in either solo usage or in mixed combinations of instruments are greatly increased. The colorful and varied expressiveness of the orchestral works of Berlioz, Wagner, Strauss, Mahler, Debussy and Schönberg is one of the great achievements of the period. There exist two general types of scoring for the orchestra developed during this century, perhaps best exemplified by the opposing styles of Berlioz and Wagner — French and German. The French style prefers the bright, unmixed orchestral colors obtained by using solo instruments, whereas the German style more often doubles these at the unison or in one or more octaves, thus obtaining mixed sonorities which, while stronger, are often less characteristic in tone color. There are often gaps between choirs in the French scoring, resulting in brilliance and transparency, while in much German music the orchestral mass is filled in solidly to attain richness, warmth and density, often with some loss in brightness. Typical of the French style is also a rather high center of orchestral mass — achieved by the avoidance of extremely low tones — which adds to the clarity and brilliance of the ensemble. Many works scored after the pattern which Wagner emphasized have a rather low center of orchestral mass: the typical sound, therefore, is rich, full, often dark in quality, frequently impressive in mass. If not entirely successful this kind of scoring may turn out to be thick and muddy sounding. These characteristics must be understood in a general sense, for not all works of even Berlioz and Wagner adhere to these sonorities consistently in a single work. But as overall generalizations, the foregoing are useful in evaluating the sonority of a composition.

In contrast to the composers of the Classic period, including Beethoven, to whom the tone language was more important than its sonority, we now witness the rise of what we have called earlier in this book *non-functional,* or *"color" orchestration.* Indeed, some composers appear who have little to say, yet whose virtuosity with the orchestra insures their popularity. On the other hand, the scoring of Brahms, which is subdued and not especially colorful, was long derided by critics unable or unwilling to listen to it in terms of pure music.

### TEXTURE

The predominant texture of the period is homophony, either appearing as plain chord progressions in block or diffused style, or as polyphonically created harmonic motion in which the individual voices are not as important as their harmonic result. This latter variety appears most frequently in the orchestra, and for that reason we shall term it *orchestral polyphony.* It may be heard frequently, in the music of Richard Strauss, somewhat less so in that of Wagner. Real polyphony is rather rare in this period of extensive harmonic exploration, and is found largely in the compositions of Brahms, although Berlioz, Liszt and others often begin sections fugally without intending to pursue a polyphonic course for very long. And often the rich scoring defeats the clarity of the contrapuntal movement, subverting it to what sounds like complex chord diffusion patterns.

# FORMAL AND GENERATIVE PRINCIPLES

### THE EFFORT TO CREATE NEW FORMS

The problem of form in the music of this period was a critical one for two reasons. First, many of the composers were revolutionaries who did not want to use the traditional molds, but sought something new and experimental to suit the nature of the emotionally exciting music they were writing. Secondly, many realized that Beethoven had expanded the size and content of the classic forms to the breaking point, and that their own musical speech, less firmly controlled than that of Beethoven, would be neither suitable nor containable in the inherited classic forms. In this dilemma the romantic composer looked to the other arts for solutions to his problem, and in literature seemed to find one. The narrative quality of literature, which offered a sequence of events and/or emotions, was adaptable to music in at least two ways. On the purely subjective plane, the music could express, section by section, the changing emotional states of its literary model. On the more objective level it could portray characters and action by means of suggestive musical description, enhanced, as always, by the omnipresent emotional content of the tone combinations. In such a work, the story or program served as the unifying force, binding together what might otherwise be disparate and even incoherent musical parts. Thus was born the symphonic poem, or tone poem, usually a grandiose composition which called into play all the colorful and exciting possibilities of the expanding orchestra. We have already met, on a small scale, the model for this kind of work in the dramatic through-composed lied, of which Schubert's *"Erlkönig"* is a splendid example. The Beethoven concert overture is also an important ancestor of the tone poem. But first let us see how the composers attained musical coherence and unity in their works in addition to that afforded by the use of the program.

### THE EFFORT TO UNIFY THE FORMS

In striking out upon these new paths, many romantic composers felt the need of some principle to replace the classic logic of tonal and thematic construction in these large-scale works, and sought techniques and ways of achieving the self-sufficiency of the classic form. As so often happened, they turned to Beethoven, the composer whom they felt to be the godfather of romanticism, and examined his highly successful ventures toward symphonic unification, particularly in the Fifth and Ninth Symphonies. From the Fifth, especially, they derived the idea of quotation of a main theme from time to time during the work. With constructive logic, however, they did not stop there, but chose a theme representative of some central figure or force in the literary plot for quotation. Thus, Berlioz' *Symphonie Fantastique,* the program of which is based upon the love of a young man for an unattainable woman, uses the theme descriptive of this *femme fatale* as the unifying agent. The young man sees her in various surroundings and guises, each of which provides the scenario for the movements of the work. The theme is easily recognizable throughout, and is largely unchanged, except for meter and rhythm, upon each appearance. Berlioz called this theme the *idée fixe.* Such a work is called a *cyclic* symphony, implying that each revolution of the musical "wheel" brings round the same material to our attention, and closes the gap between the first and last movements, thus creating a circle. Similar cyclic works are found in the symphonies, sonatas and chamber music of Schumann, Brahms, Tchaikovsky and Franck, with the exception that in some of these works the "motto" theme has no descriptive or extramusical connotations, but is a purely musical pattern designed for the express purpose of unifying the compound form of the music.

But the dry repetition of such a group of tones at intervals throughout a piece of music would be a monotonous and inartistic way of using this material: variety is needed, and to supply this the technique of variation is used in a rather special way which has received the name "theme transformation." This technique was first exploited in important orchestral works by Franz Liszt. He did not invent it, for it appears in the history of music long before the Romantic era, and closer to it in the last quartets of Beethoven. But Liszt did elevate it to the level of a constructive principle, and demonstrated that principle most convincingly. Briefly, theme transformation consists of deriving new-sounding themes from a basic theme or melodic shape by changing meter, note values, or direction of skip or step of the original. New-sounding themes may also be constructed by separating the basic notes of the theme by non essential notes, thus prolonging and changing the contour of the original idea. Or it may be fragmented — broken up into smaller particles which are then tossed about in the orchestra. In short, anything which will illustrate the composer's intention can be done to this basic material — a process of variation with highly differentiated results, which may provide contrasting main themes, subsidiary themes, and incidental and accompaniment figures. Here is unity indeed! This procedure was seized upon by Liszt's son-in-law, Wagner, for use in his musical dramas, by Strauss for the substance of his operas and tone poems, and by the northern composer, Sibelius, as a means of symphonic construction. Its effects were far-reaching indeed, and it still provides a usable technique in the music of today.

## THE EFFORT TO EXPAND THE FORMS

The musical "grand manner" of the Romantic period required space in which to flourish — harmonic space, which might be called musical depth, and temporal space, comparable to length or extent. Most orchestral compositions of this post-Beethoven time are lengthy, often requiring twice as much time to perform as the classic symphony. Theme transformation helped to make this vast expanse of music coherent and unified, but in many cases more basic thematic material was required, thus giving birth to the late-romantic sonata-allegro with more than the usual number of important themes. In such works, of which the post-romantic symphonies of Mahler offer perhaps the most extreme examples, the exposition is elongated merely by the necessity of exposing all of these themes, and the development may, if the composer chooses, be well-nigh eternal! Needless to remark, this complexity makes it difficult for the listener to identify the form of the movement without considerable listening and study.

A second means of expanding a few themes while at the same time heightening the emotional element of the music is most effectively illustrated in the music of Wagner, particularly in sections of his opera *Tristan und Isolde.*

Harmonically, these passages consist of chordal motion, often arrived at by orchestral polyphony, employing melodic motives and sometimes altering these by theme transformation. Definite cadences are avoided by deception and elision, and flow of the orchestral polyphony is insured by repetition of the melodic motives, of which there are usually several. This process often results in a characteristic gradual rise in tension, pitch and dynamic level until a climax is attained, after which the music usually subsides rather quickly. It is a typical romantic phenomenon, presaged again by Beethoven, one which occurs often enough in the music of this century to receive a name. We shall call it the *dynamic curve*. Its construction and operation will be immediately plain to anyone who listens to the "Prelude" and the *"Liebestod"* from Wagner's *Tristan und Isolde*.

### THE USE OF NATIONALISTIC IDIOMS AND FOLK MUSIC

In an effort to provide fresh, unsophisticated and attractive thematic material for symphonic works, as well as for patriotic reasons, many composers of smaller European countries collected the folk music of their native lands, or composed music much like it. Such nationalistic compositions usually appear as suites of dances, tone poems, or operas, although the folk idioms may also find their way into the more serious symphony. Foremost among the nations or regions important for nationalistic music are the Balkan countries, Poland, Russia, the Scandinavian countries, and Spain. Among the composers are Dvořák and Smetana from Bohemia, Chopin from Poland, Tschaikovsky, Moussorgsky, Rimsky-Korsakoff and Borodin from Russia, Grieg, Sinding and Sibelius from Scandinavia, and Granados from Spain. The music of these composers reflects the national temperament, is usually colorful and rhythmic, and seldom offers any problems to the listener.

### VIRTUOSITY

The nineteenth century was the epoch of the dazzling performer. Pre-eminent among these were the pianists Liszt, Rubenstein, Thalberg, Hummel, Chopin, Rachmaninoff, to name only a few of the host who beguiled concert audiences of the time. Among the violin virtuosi, Paganini led the way with his uncanny mastery of the instrument. Many of these performers were also composers, and, inevitably, we find the reflection of their abilities in the music which they wrote. At worst, this resulted in shallow brilliance and fireworks simply designed to impress. At best these superior abilities were turned toward the expression of the new moods of romanticism and the deeply communicative possibilities to be found in the improved piano. The music of Anton Rubenstein (1829-1894) abounds in shallow super-ficialities calculated to astonish by their difficulty and brilliance or appeal through sentimentality. So do some of the works of Franz Liszt. But there are many others by this foremost pianist of his time in which his incredible technical facility becomes the secondary element and the servant of the music. The volumes entitled *Années de Pelerinage (Years of Pilgrimage)* abound in beautiful and expressive music of this kind. In the works of Chopin there is perhaps more success in the maintenance of a high standard of musical worth than in the output of most other composers of this time. Brahms, too, excels in this respect, although his music is more serious and not so worldly as that of his Polish colleague.

This emphasis upon virtuosity undermines formal logic in many composers' works, especially in those where technical ability at the instrument frequently overrides constructive ability at the writing desk. In some of Liszt's compositions for piano, impromptu cadenzas and display passages often interrupt the continuity of the form, leading us to believe that we are hearing a fantasy rather than, perhaps, a sonata-allegro. In other works (better ones) Liszt manages to make these decorative passages flow more or less logically out of the emotional and thematic involvement, thus incorporating them as essential parts of the form.

In addition to the wizardry of these solo performers, the age also produced the virtuoso orchestra due, in part, to the improvements in the construction of the brass and woodwind instruments which made it possible for them to play passages which had previously been out of the question. But the new orchestra compositions of Berlioz and Wagner required a higher degree of proficiency from the player too, and conductors soon came to demand this as a matter of course. The great conductor Hans von Bülow required his orchestra at the court of Mciningen to memorize the music, and to play it while standing! Most of the outstanding orchestral composers were virtuoso conductors of necessity, and sometimes vice-versa. The roster is long — Berlioz, Liszt, Wagner, Strauss and Mahler — and, when our more specialized age arrived, the prima-donna conductor flourished as never before in the persons of Koussevitzky, Toscanini, Ormandy, Reiner, Mengelberg, Krauss, Klemperer and a host of others. And the virtuoso orchestra is still very much with us, and becoming more so in its effort to cope with the exigencies of contemporary music.

# A Survey of the Varieties of Music in the Romantic Era

### THE SYMPHONY

For most romantic composers, the example of Beethoven weighed heavily upon the musical conscience: each felt that he should at least equal that master in some way while at the same time advancing symphonic technique. Brahms went even further back than Beethoven, and remarked that it was "no joke to write a symphony after Haydn." Only one composer of the early nineteenth century, Mendelssohn, disregarded the works of Beethoven and proceeded to write in a more classic style tinged with romantic poetry and tone-colors. But for the others, the problem was very real, and they sought ways of gracefully receiving Beethoven's legacy while still retaining their personal independence. As a result, the heretofore rather unified conception of the symphony divided into several varieties.

The abstract symphony continued to be written, but now with typical romantic characteristics: a more lyrical and less dramatic style, richer harmonic content with the increased flow of motion resulting from the instability of the more complex chords, and the use of unifying devices such as motto themes which were sometimes transformed into the thematic material of the work. The movements changed in character also. The outer two remained the pillars of the work in regard to seriousness and length, but the middle two tended to be less important and more in the manner of intermezzi than did those of the Beethoven symphonies, or even those of Haydn and Mozart, in which the definite qualities of "slow movement" and "minuet and trio" were plainly apparent. To be sure, the central movements of the Schumann and Brahms symphonies *are* marked *adagio* and *vivace,* but their characters are not what we would expect from the Beethoven tradition. They lack the heartfelt outpourings of emotion or robust gay spirits with which that master endowed his second and third movements, and are, instead, lyric pieces whose "specific gravity" is much less, and those place in the total design is not as significant. Yet the four movements obviously form a single unit because of the consistent stylistic qualities throughout.

The mantle of Beethoven rested less heavily upon the nationalistic symphonists, such as Borodin and Dvořák, who incorporated into their works the folk idioms of their countries. They were content with a much simpler, although not less serious, sequence of movements than were their more self-conscious colleagues. The French composer, Cesar Franck (1822-1890), carried the use of theme transformation applied to basic motives to a new height in his compositions, deriving not only the principal themes but also the harmony and key changes from implications of the basic motives — a step toward the total use of musical materials which has been so fervently pursued in the twentieth century. Franck's harmonic vocabulary is highly chromatic, of the Wagner-Liszt variety, but instead of the stage and concert-platform as the source of his musical inspiration, the solitude of the organ-loft and the mystic subjectivity of religious experience seem to furnish the spiritual content of his music, particularly that of his single symphony. This statement could be applied with equal truth to the music by Anton Bruckner (1824-1896), the Austrian organist-symphonist. Bruckner, however, is much less sophisticated in his use of theme transformation than Franck; rather, he continues the Beethoven line of symphonic writing, using similar developmental procedures and an only mildly chromatic harmonic style. His symphonies are long — far longer than those of Brahms, his contemporary — and are notable for the use of the brass instruments in the exalted climaxes of many of the movements.

The more revolutionary composers turned, as we have said, to extra-musical sources for the formal element of their compositions, specifically to literature, although musical descriptions of nature and of paintings are also found. We may divide these progressive works into two categories, depending upon whether they use the voice (as solo or chorus) or not. Those which are purely instrumental, like Berlioz' *Symphonie Fantastique,* usually preface the music with the program, outlining the sequence of events which is to be described in the music. Those works which use the voice may employ it in a number of ways. The solo or chorus may enter from time to time to tell the story, while leaving other movements wholly to the orchestra.

371

In other cases, the vocal forces are used only in the final movement, as in the Beethoven Ninth Symphony, where the text often provides a definite expression of the ideal or goal toward which the preceding movements have been striving. This is often the case in the Mahler symphonies and in the Liszt "Faust" Symphony. Only very occasionally is the voice used continuously in all the movements of a symphony.

## THE SYMPHONIC POEM (OR TONE POEM)

We have seen how the sonata-allegro and, for that matter, the entire symphony became a vehicle for dramatic expression in the hands of Beethoven. But except for the Sixth Symphony, these are abstract dramas, still following the well-established laws of musical construction, albeit in a new and exciting way. In the third, fourth and fifth movements of the Sixth Symphony, a simple plot directs the action of the music, but only on the descriptive level, for the thematic and modulatory course of the music obeys its own logical requirements. In the concert overtures, such as "Coriolanus" and "Egmont," Beethoven presents us with the idealized essence of the drama, shorn of the literary plot: this music is more subjective than descriptive, since it does not imitate, but speaks to us of qualities such as grief, heroism or pity.

The program symphony, already discussed, is a romantic derivation of the Beethoven Sixth into which the musically unifying device of the *idée fixe* has been incorporated. There are also rather direct descendents of the concert overture, in addition to those overtures of Mendelssohn which are "scenic" rather than dramatic (in the sense of having a story). To this classification belong such works as "The Hebrides Overture," to a degree the "Overture to A Midsummer Night's Dream," and even the more literary "Calm Sea and Prosperous Voyage Overture," based upon two short poems by Goethe. To this class also belong the movements of the Fourth ("Italian") and Third ("Scotch") Symphonies by this composer. More like the Beethovenian model is the "Tragic Overture" of Brahms, while the "Academic Festival Overture" of this composer stands in the class of potpourri overtures, but very high in that class! But even this kind of work in the hands of Brahms, and of the earlier Karl Maria von Weber, takes on formal organization and emerges more or less resembling the traditional sonata-allegro. In the case of Tchaikovsky, a more literary inspiration is evident in the musical material chosen, although the formal design is usually the sonata-allegro typical of this composer. A number of other composers follow the same procedure — a dramatic presentation of the essentials of the story adapted to inherited forms. In some cases it would seem that the story is deliberately chosen with this correspondence in mind, while in others the music is written first and the story adapted to fit it! Many of the famous tone-poems of Richard Strauss, for example, are romantic adaptations of classic forms written both before and after the programs. *Death and Transfiguration* and *Don Juan* are sonata-allegros, and *Till Eulenspiegel's Merry Pranks* and *Don Quixote* are essentially variations on one or two themes. Liszt's most famous work in this form, *Les Préludes,* evolves in a loosely woven sonata-allegro design which, happily enough, fits the poem upon which the work is presumably based. It would seem that these men were musicians first and tone-poets afterwards. There are, to be sure, a few works which follow quite closely the poetic model or story. Moussorgsky's *Night on Bald Mountain* comes immediately to mind in this respect, as do Strauss' *Also Sprach Zarathustra,* Saint-Saen's *Danse Macabre,* and Dukas' *Sorcerer's Apprentice.*

How are these works different, then, from descriptive compositions of previous times? The greatest difference, of course, lies in the romantically emotional quality of the music. But the process of theme transformation is of extreme importance in the works of the most progressive composers as a strong unifying factor. Since tonality gradually becomes so "unconstructively" used (at least in comparison with baroque and classic practices), the theme or principal melody was used to establish coherence via this variation process called theme transformation. Such works appeared not only in the concert hall but also on the operatic stage, for Wagner used this technique to construct whole operas lasting several hours in length. Many sections of these may be excerpted which display all of the characteristics of independent tone poems, often of a very descriptive nature.

The tone poem, with its reliance upon the extramusical form and inspiration of literature, is a typically romantic genre, for the composers of this time were word-minded. They appreciated not only the literature of their times, but also the treasures of the past. Many were writers themselves — Schumann, Berlioz, Liszt and Wagner contributed polished articles, criticism and essays dealing with music to the magazines and newspapers. Music no longer stood alone, but was a part, if not the center, of that constellation of the arts so ardently desired by the most progressive creative musicians of the time.

### THE CONCERTO

It might easily be deduced that the concerto for solo instrument and orchestra with its combination of intimacy and virtuosity would be a favorite form with audiences of the nineteenth century, and so it was. But it suffered from exactly the two qualities for which it was prized. From intimacy — lyrical intimacy — which precluded the dramatic conflict of the sonata-allegro form, and from virtuosity which too often expanded into showmanship and lost its integrity along the way. The great romantic composers had to cope with both problems, possibly more acute in the concerto than in works for orchestra alone, and their solutions follow two diverging paths — that of the conservatives like Brahms, and that of the revolutionaries whose culmination in the concerto form arrived in the works of Liszt.

The conservative line used the last Beethoven concertos as models, and we find the clearest examples of these in two concertos by Brahms — the Second Piano Concerto, in B♭ (Op. 83) and the Double Concerto for Violin and Cello (Op. 102). These works extend and make thematic the introductory section to the exposition of the first movement which was added by Beethoven to his Fourth and Fifth Piano Concertos. Brahms' other two concertos — the Violin Concerto (Op. 77) and the First Piano Concerto (Op. 15) omit this introduction in favor of the more typical classic procedure. The concertos of Paganini, Chopin, Tchaikovsky, Dvořák and Rachmaninoff, despite some small liberal tendencies, are essentially formally conservative, although often filled with the most personal language and feeling.

The progressive Romantic composers, realizing with varying degrees of clarity the problems which confronted them as post-classical composers, moved generally toward concertos in single extended movements with single expositions in the sonata-allegro sections and functional or assimilated cadenzas. The continuity of sections in these one-movement works varies: in some cases, such as the Mendelssohn concertos, there are clearly three distinct movements linked by bridge passages, while in other works, notably the Schumann Cello Concerto and the Liszt Second Piano Concerto, the seams between the sections are almost entirely obscured. Mendelssohn was also one of the first composers to suppress the opening orchestral exposition of the first movement of the concerto, thus reducing the form to a clear sonata-allegro structure with cadenza. His example was generally followed by those composers who still revered the sonata-allegro enough to use it for the first movement or section of their concertos. But, may we note, they were not always successful in writing a good sonata-allegro because of the anti-dramatic lyricism which became a consistent feature of their music. Brahms alone seems to have seen and faced this difficulty and effected a solution.

The cadenza was also put to work by Mendelssohn. In the first movement of his Violin Concerto, the cadenza is used as the last stage of the retransition to the recapitulation rather than in its non-functional position in the classical design. Other concertos of the period, however, more often absorb the cadenza into the solo episodes either by making all of the solo interludes cadenza-like, or, vice-versa, making the cadenza less showy and more like interlude material. Structurally, these interludes sometimes become rather independent little pieces, drawing away from the thematic interplay in a manner never found in the Mozartean model.

The romantic concerto is often less wide in emotional scope than its classical prototype, and dwells frequently in a shadowy region of melancholy minor tonality from which it emerges from time to time for glittering virtuoso passages. There is little of the interplay of wit, tenderness, pathos and cheer which mark the concertos of Mozart. And only the Brahms concertos approach anything like the heroism and optimism of the Beethoven works in this form, for Liszt is really only pseudo-heroic, and the gentle Schumann incurably pessimistic, but excusably so for the sake of his lyricism.

The virtuoso element in the romantic concerto often decides the fate of the work. Because of this, the Schumann and the first Brahms concertos had cool receptions, for the composers made the virtuosity functional and subservient to the purely musical ends. Those works require expert technique to perform, particularly those of Brahms, but there is no element of display for its own sake. Other concertos, however, designed for immediate popular acceptance, often consisted entirely of shallow brilliance: fortunately these, except for a few written for the violin, have passed into oblivion. Possibly the most dazzling of the virtuoso concertos still played are those of Liszt. In them the display is so much a part of the music, and the concept of the work so clearly one that includes effect, that they are more forgivable than some others. In them, Liszt tried to employ the new and colorful romantic orchestra to its fullest symphonic extent, thus requiring more sound from the piano to secure its foreground prominence. In order to achieve this, he invented a bold new idiom for the instrument, making it match the orchestra in color and power. We must perforce admire the progressive spirit of this composer in endeavoring to achieve something genuinely new and alive in this medium.

Oddly enough, for all of the era's penchant for descriptive music, almost none of the great concertos are built around programs. Karl Maria von Weber's early one movement *"Konzertstück"* for piano and orchestra and Richard Strauss' tone-poem-double concerto, *Don Quixote* are all that remain. Berlioz' *Harold in Italy* is hardly of this class, being really a programmatic symphony with viola *obbligato*.

In addition to bona-fide concertos, the nineteenth century gave birth to many single-movement works in variation form for solo and orchestra. Strauss' *Don Quixote,* mentioned above, is such a work, as are Liszt's variations on the plainchant *"Dies Irae"* in his *Todtentanz (Dance of Death,* inspired by a medieval fresco) , Cesar Franck's *Symphonic Variations,* Rachmaninoff's *Variations on a Theme of Paganini* and Tchaikovsky's *Variations on a Rococo Theme* for cello and orchestra, to name only a few. There also were written pseudo-concertos which were disguised by misleading names, such as Lalo's *Symphonie Espagnole,* as well as potpourris of folk or operatic tunes arranged for piano (usually, although sometimes the violin was used) , of which the most prominent example is perhaps the still-played *Hungarian Fantasy* by Liszt.

The nationalist composers wrote a few concertos which were, for the most part charming and inimitable in content and conservative-to-weak in structure. That this has been no great barrier to public appreciation is attested by the vitality of the Grieg piano and the Dvořák cello concertos.

## CHAMBER MUSIC

If we should make a tabulation by composers of chamber music produced during the nineteenth century, we should discover, as might be expected, that the conservative composers lead all the rest — Mendelssohn, Schumann, Brahms and Dvořák. We find a considerable gap between the amount of chamber music produced by them — numbering in the twenties for each — and that produced by the next important composer. Tchaikovsky wrote eight chamber works, followed in descending order by Franck, Smetana, Rimsky-Korsakoff,

Borodin, Chopin and Bruckner. It is rather interesting to note the number of nationalist composers here. But this list gives no inkling of the importance of the works on the concert stage today. The piano trio and string quartet by Tchaikovsky are occasionally performed, but are certainly not the composer's best and most characteristic works. The well-known violin-piano sonata by Franck is still very popular, but his more ambitious chamber works are infrequently played. The autobiographical string quartet by Smetana, entitled *Aus Meinen Leben (From My Life)*, and the chamber works by Rimsky-Korsakoff are seldom heard. The Borodin Second String Quartet is reasonably popular, although it sounds rather dated, but the Chopin piano trio and the Introduction and Polonaise for piano and cello, along with Bruckner's single string quintet, are almost never played. Those giants of the orchestra, Berlioz, Liszt and Wagner, wrote no chamber music, except perhaps for Wagner's *Siegfried Idyll*, which is scored for chamber orchestra. Moussorgsky was too interested in Russian speech and character to work with anything but song and opera. The romantic urge to create large, powerful and colorful works inclined the composers toward the orchestra, while the appeal of virtuosity attracted them toward the solo piano or the concerto, to the neglect of chamber music.

The desire for harmonic richness in the chamber music of the time is an almost fatal disease, even in the most skillful composers, Brahms and Mendelssohn, although the latter is less at fault since his classical style allows him to move freely in the idiom. Schumann's best works in this difficult medium are generally conceded to be his piano quintet, Op. 44, and piano quartet, Op. 47, although even in these he seems unable to put any trust in the stringed instrument's ability to carry their parts, and constantly doubles them with the piano, creating a monotonous color which often dulls the senses to the real beauty of the music. Dvořák's chamber music, nationalistic to the core, is perhaps least afflicted by the romantic devotion to harmonic richness, although it is none the less persuasive. The texture is often classical in its transparency, and the music moves comfortably within the smaller framework. This is not always true of the chamber music of Brahms, avowedly the perpetuator of the chamber music tradition, but the music itself is so genuine and meaningful that the imbalance is not troubling. When the size of the ensemble is expanded to include five or six instruments, or when it employs piano, the sonority seems more adequate to the demands of the music. We must not expect the

377

chamber music of this century to possess the lucidity, transparency, elegance and directness of the best works of Mozart and Haydn, much less the personal profundity of the late Beethoven: we must judge and appreciate it on its own merits, for even Brahms, so strongly tradition-oriented, was incapable of expressing ideas which were not part of his time and culture. Only the most blazing geniuses, like Bach and Beethoven, were able to surmount their time, the first by summing up the music of his age, the second by withdrawing from that of his in order to pursue flights of an ever-developing musical imagination.

Foremost among the duo combinations, in addition to the fine violin-piano sonata by Cesar Franck, are the violin-piano and clarinet-piano sonatas by Brahms. The latter must be counted as some of that master's best music. They are late works, Op. 120, and reveal, as does the Clarinet Quintet (Op. 115), his appreciation for the bitter-sweet quality of the solo clarinet, and for the expressive dynamic range of the instrument. The duo works by Schumann include pieces for various instruments with piano, and are seldom played nowadays, except in the cases of those instruments whose solo literature is small. The same is true of most of the duo works by Mendelssohn, which, although for two instruments, strongly resemble the short piano compositions of the period in mood and form.

### PIANO MUSIC

The piano was the favorite solo instrument of the nineteenth century, and a tremendous amount of music was composed for it. Much of this music was trivial and unimportant, but many works by notable composers, especially those who were pianists themselves, have come down to us as an important part of our heritage. The importance which the piano sonata had held in the Classic period, to the virtual exclusion of smaller single-movement pieces, had now vanished. In its place were numerous short compositions, often descriptive and arranged in suites, and usually simple in form. They were given various titles, sometimes vaguely descriptive, as Schumann's *"Aufschwung"* ("Soaring"), sometimes more general, such as Chopin's Polonaises, Nocturnes and Valses. Others had elaborate names which suggested more definitely the descriptive elements of the music, such as Liszt's *"St. François d'Assise prédicant aux oiseau"* (*St. Francis of Assisi*

*Preaching to the Birds)*. Such compositions tended to replace the sonata, allowing more freedom to roam through sunny meadows of lyric effusion and to avoid the rocky crags of thematic development.

Three seems to be the magic number (or is it the point of exhaustion?) for the composers who did essay the sonata form: Mendelssohn, Schumann, Brahms and Chopin all wrote three works in this by now difficult form. We can hardly include Liszt in this group, for he made no pretensions to traditional form in his single sonata, in B-minor, but true to his prophetic role, employed the unifying device of theme transformation in his fantastic yet musically logical composition. It is an interesting commentary on the nineteenth century sonata to note those works which are still performed with any frequency: Liszt and Chopin lead, with Brahms and Schumann a good way behind and Mendelssohn on the distant horizon.

The short piano pieces are by far the most popular works, singly or grouped together in picturesque and "characteristic" suites. There are also, rather surprisingly, a number of sets of variations by these composers which are performed quite often, notably those by Brahms. The virtuoso studies (etudes), especially those by Schumann and Chopin, are also still popular, and in many cases deservedly so, for these subordinate the virtuosity to the music with gratifying results. In the case of Liszt the quality is more uneven, but it is almost impossible not to respond in some degree to the magnificence of technique required to play some of these brilliant pieces, despite the fact that the music itself is sometimes not of the best quality.

### ORGAN MUSIC

Organ music went into a decline at the death of Bach, and only began to show signs of life around 1840, when certain Bach-influenced works by Mendelssohn and Schumann appeared. During the later nineteenth century, organ-builders sought to incorporate into the instrument all the colors of the romantic orchestra. There arose a number of composers who wrote orchestrally-conceived music for this new instrument. Bruckner and Franck were famous organists, and traces of their calling are noticeable in their purely orchestral works — the evenly treading basses, the somewhat improvisational chromatic harmony and the changes from solo stops to full organ at climaxes. The music of such men, together with Alexandre Guilmant (1837-1911), Charles Marie

Widow (1844-1937), Louis Vierne (1870-1937), Max Reger (1873-1916) and Siegfried Karg-Elert (1877-1933) constitutes much of the organ literature of the nineteenth century. The works of these men paralleled the development during this century of the symphony and tone poem, resulting in large, colorful and elaborate works which exploit the color possibilities and the dynamic range of the "king of instruments" to the fullest extent. We are also indebted to Brahms for his eleven beautiful chorale-preludes which hearken to the works of Bach, but are filled with the romantic warmth so characteristic of Brahms. Even Liszt was moved to write a fantasy and fugue on the name BACH (B is B♭ and H is B-natural in the German musical alphabet), as well as to compose variations on two themes by the Baroque master. But with the late romantic organ compositions, this instrument moved out of the church and into the concert hall, and became a vehicle for virtuosity and often regrettable showmanship.

### VOCAL MUSIC: SONG LITERATURE

With the example of Schubert before them, a host of German and Austrian composers exploited the possibilities of the lied. Schumann and Brahms wrote exceptionally fine songs much in the style of Schubert. Those of Schumann, especially his cycle *Frauenliebe und Leben* (*A Woman's Love and Life*), are exceedingly sensitive and full of feeling. Brahms usually provides a mood in the accompaniment rather than the picturesque detail so often found in the songs of Schubert, although from time to time he adds pictorial touches, as in *"Der Schmied"* ("The Blacksmith"). Of outstanding importance in his song literature is the cycle entitled *Four Serious Songs,* based upon biblical texts. Hugo Wolf, like Gesualdo in the late sixteenth century, endeavored to capture the psychological overtones of the texts in the melodic and harmonic schemes of his songs. He may be compared in his use of chromaticism not only to Gesualdo, but also to the Wagner of *Tristan und Isolde*. Gustav Mahler wrote a great many songs, often mystic and medieval in tone and text, reverting to a sophisticated treatment of the Austrian folksong. His cycles *Des Knaben Wunderhorn (Youth's Magic Horn), Kindertotenlieder (Songs on the Death of Children)*, and the final great cycle for tenor and contralto, *Das Lied von der Erde (The Song of the Earth)*, show his melodious and nostalgic art at its best. Richard Strauss also contributed notably to the repertory of the lied, numbering many single songs as well as the rich, autumnal *Four Last Songs* in his output.

The French art song has a long history, extending back to the motets and chansons of the medieval period. In the Romantic era, as then, the emphasis lay upon the text, which was set to a refined melodic line and supported by carefully-chosen harmonies of a sensitive character. There is usually more effort to establish mood than to describe action or illustrate the text. Among the foremost composers of the art song are Gabriel Fauré (1845-1924), Henri Duparc (1848-1933) and Claude Debussy (1862-1918).

### SACRED CHORAL MUSIC

In the Baroque era there was no difference between sacred and secular music, and we find much this same attitude in the eighteenth century, although a growing separation started to occur then as manifested in the "learned style" which seemed to belong rather with the tradition and age-old liturgy of the church than in the operatic and rococo secular style. Nevertheless, most eighteenth-century sacred music is not too different from that presented upon the operatic stage, save for the texts and an occasional fugue. But the separation reached real proportions in the nineteenth century, partly because of the researches of musicologists who brought the music of Palestrina and his contemporaries to light and upheld it as the "true" style of church music, and partly because the sensibilities of the Romantic musicians caused them to feel that there *should* be a difference. Several solutions were tried by various composers with usually mixed results. Some went back to plainchant for thematic material which they used in typical romantic fashion, thus often negating the implied return to the severity of the old music. Others drew upon those stylistic characteristics of Bach and Handel which they were able to assimilate into their romantic manner, and produced, not pseudo-baroque music, but rather restrained romantic compositions. Possibly the most successful of these are the two oratorios by Mendelssohn, *St. Paul* and *Elijah*. Here we find recitatives, arias and fugal choruses all done in the typical Mendelssohn style, often with more dramatic effect than we usually associate with him. Anton Bruckner perhaps reached the summit of romantic church composition among Austrian and German composers through a naïvete, simplicity and sincerity all too uncommon at this time. He rises above the personal and ecstatic quality of romanticism to a universality not often matched. The Brahms *German Requiem* stands as a monument to this composer's deep religious feeling and sincere artistry. Not Catholic and not really Protestant, he selected Biblical passages for the text of this work and set them in an austere and subjective manner for chorus and orchestra, with short solos by baritone and soprano voices.

French religious music of this time reaches a low ebb, except for the music of Franck, which, however, also suffers slightly from the two diseases of nineteenth century French music generally: sentimentality and bombast. Afflicted by the first, the music of Gounod has not lasted. That of Berlioz, the *Requiem* and the *Te Deum,* belong to the category of concert-music, not sacred, for they summon up the composer's entire arsenal of effects, and result in works which are not truly religious, but rather personal and ecstatic.

In Italy there had been no cultivation of any kind of music other than opera for almost two centuries. Therefore it is only natural that the religious works of Rossini and the great *Manzoni Requiem* of Verdi should be operatic — a factor which has nothing to do with their sincerity and piety. We should expect no other style.

Most romantic religious music is scored for chorus and orchestra, thus preventing adequate performances in most churches, and relegating this supposedly sacred music to the concert hall. Many of these compositions also require well-trained choruses and soloists of above average ability. The romantic mania for size and effect well-nigh defeated itself in the realm of sacred music.

## SECULAR CHORAL MUSIC

The nineteenth century was also marked by the production of a large amount of choral music intended for performance by the numerous *singakademie* and choral societies which sprang up in Germany, Austria and England. Much of the music was of only passing interest, but a number of composers wrote some of their best works for just such groups. Brahms was particularly attracted to choral music, and in addition to his *German Requiem* composed several secular works which are still performed. Among the larger of these may be numbered the *Alto Rhapsodie*, the *Gesang der Parzen* (*Song of the Fates*) and the *Schicksalslied* (*Song of Destiny*). In addition there are many folk-song settings as well as other rather short choral works by this composer. Schumann, Mendelssohn and Liszt were also active in this sphere, but time has not been kind to them.

## OPERA IN THE ROMANTIC PERIOD

A complete discussion of this subject would fill volumes. We shall limit ourselves to a partial description of the changes in German and Italian opera during this century as evidenced in the work of Wagner and Verdi.

The typical eighteenth century opera, exemplified at its most polished and elegant in Mozart's *Marriage of Figaro*, consisted of a more or less stock plot inhabited by stock characters. The lecherous Count, the sympathetic and tragic Countess, the young and attractive girl upon whom the Count has designs, Susanna, and her fiance, Figaro. All these appear, under different names, to be sure, in countless operas of that century. What makes Mozart's works superior is the quality of the music and the more surprising turns the plot takes. These operas are constructed, essentially, of two elements, *recitative* and *aria*. *Recitative* is declamation in melodic phrases to a simple chordal accompaniment by the harpsichord or piano (in which case it is called *secco recitativo*), or to a more complicated and continuous accompaniment by the orchestra (accompanied recitative, or *recitativo accompagnato*). As a general rule, the action and conversation in the opera take place in recitative, often *secco*, while the soliloquies, meditative portions, and love scenes are cast in the more melodic style of the aria, or song. This makes for a sort of "stop-and-go" action, interruptions by the arias impeding the forward motion of the plot. In some Italian operas of the early Romantic period it becomes completely ludicrous, and was beautifully satirized by Gilbert and Sullivan in their light operas. But as the style of the century develops, and particularly in the works of Giuseppe Verdi (1813-1901), we find an increasing assimilation of both the recitative and aria into the dramatic structure. The recitative is no longer accompanied by the piano, but always by the orchestra, and is composed so cunningly as not to remind us that it *is* recitative! This is accomplished either by a discontinuous, interjected orchestral accompaniment, or by a continuous background of sound from the orchestra against which the increasingly melodic phrases of recitative are projected, finally flowing without a break into the aria proper. In this style of opera, each scene is a large unit, whereas earlier it was composed of smaller, distinctly separate parts.

An outstanding characteristic of most Italian operas of the nineteenth century, and those of Verdi in particular, is the treatment of the characters of the drama. We feel that these are real people, experiencing understandable emotions in the situations of the plot. Never does a person in these works become merely a symbol. Verdi characterizes his *dramatis personae* by the music he gives to them, but more important to him is their reaction to what is happening to them — in a word, emotion. He makes little effort to unify his operas symphonically by repeated use of the same thematic material, as does Wagner. There *are* quotations of melodies heard before, to be sure, but only when they accomplish a stunning dramatic stroke, as in the last scene of *Rigoletto*. The orchestra in the early works of this composer is often relegated to the merest accompaniment, but in his last works it becomes a powerful dramatic force which, never contesting the supremacy of the voice, underlines the emotional poignancy in a most personal manner.

Stemming from much the same root — for eighteenth-century opera in Germany and Austria was Italian and under the control of Italian composers — German opera veered in a different direction during the Romantic period. The tendency of the Teutonic spirit toward mysticism and symbolism came to the fore, and operas became expositions of philosophical truths rather than adventures of human beings. This is as true of the so-called first German opera, Mozart's *Magic Flute,* with its outwardly ridiculous, but inwardly deeply symbolic plot, as it is of the supernatural *Der Freischütz* of Weber, or the Wagnerian *Ring* music dramas. The tendency toward more homogeneous construction by suppressing recitative-aria distinctions appear in these later operas also, but is accomplished in a somewhat different way with predictably different results.

In the *Magic Flute,* Mozart was still interested in his characters as people, although he realized their symbolic significance at the same time. Each person is characterized by the *kind* of music he sings, without attaching a definite musical theme or "tag" to him to make recognition easy. After all, one presumes that the audience *is* watching the stage! Weber is the first Romantic musical dramatist to employ this "theme music" for his characters, but he does it in a rather unsystematic way. Unfortunately for German opera, he died before he had thoroughly developed this approach, and so the responsibility devolved upon one of the most original and forceful geniuses of this century of geniuses — Richard Wagner. This complex personality sought to accomplish the most grandiose of artistic schemes: to combine in a single dramatic work all of the arts as well as philosophy and history — the so-called *Gesamtkunstwerk*. The ideas which he developed concerning this goal he put forth from time to time in essays and critical articles. Let us examine some of these thoughts.

First of all, Wagner felt that such an art work should be universal in its appeal. As story material, the myth or legend, with its atavistic memories buried deep in the subconscious of the human race, provided heroic drama universal in scope and symbolic in action. So, from the outset, we have nonhuman, superhuman characters who symbolize philosophical ideas, rather than real people, with their complex personal mixtures of good, bad and indifferent. But this German did not choose the lighthearted, almost human gods of Greece for his leading roles, but rather the grim, inhuman gods of Norse and Teutonic mythology, the Wotans, Fafners, Erdas, Lokis, and Valkyries, who were essentially symbols of man's struggle with an unusually hostile Nature.

Secondly, Wagner, as he progressed in operatic technique, felt more and more the undramatic quality of the recitative-aria opera, and tried in his own works to create a continuity of action and music to form large musical sections of the whole work. To accomplish this he created what he called "endless melody" and the leading-motive, or *leitmotiv* (plural: *leitmotive*). By "endless melody" he meant melodic phrases with weak cadences, usually non-final, which moved continuously forward, establishing long melodic curves which finally cadenced, probably on a deceptive note, and were ready to soar again. To match this melody, the harmonic support must also be unstable and employ frequent nonfinal and deceptive cadences. Now endless melody cannot merely wander. If it does, we lose interest. It must be internally organized by means of melodic or rhythmic motives combined into phrases. These phrases are the *leading motives,* which have another important and utilitarian function. The *leitmotiv* is a short section of "theme music" which serves to identify characters, objects and ideas in the story much like Berlioz' *"idée fixe."* For example, in the *Ring* operas there are identifying themes for such things as the ring, the Rhine River, Siegfried's sword, and the magic fire; for such people as Wotan, Siegfried, Brünnhilde, and Erda, the earth-goddess; for such concepts as the curse on the Rhinegold, the curse of the Volsungs and Brünnhilde's love. So the endless melody includes the *leitmotive* appropriate to what is transpiring on the stage. But there is more to it than that. The orchestral accompaniment is constructed symphonically, using not only the *leitmotive* of the things visually apparent to the audience, but also the appropriately transformed *leitmotive* of other elements in the plot which may have a bearing upon the stage action at that point. To sum up this function of the orchestra, in short, it comments on the present action, and makes reference to past and future persons and events by quoting their *leitmotive,* usually in the orchestral polyphony which accompanies the singing.

Wagner uses a large orchestra in these music-dramas, for so his *gesamtkunstwerke* came to be called. To him, the voice is another instrument, so he weaves it into the polyphonic web of *leitmotive,* matching it against the rich sound of the instruments. To make the contest more even, singers with large voices are required. These have received the qualification "heroic," as in "heroic tenor," or are called *Wagnerian* voices, in order to distinguish them in quality and stamina from the lighter, more lyric Italian opera voices.

So the essential difference between the German opera and that of Italy is the emphasis of the latter on humanity, of the former upon legend and symbolism. French opera of this time was constructed on the plan of the Italian works, but tended toward spectacular effects and size. This was the real "grand opera." Another variety which admitted spoken passages was not allowed at the Paris Opera, but played at another theater, the *Opera Comique,* and developed toward the Italian ideal, but with typical French refinement of vocal line, harmonic quality, and orchestral writing. Bizet's masterpiece, *Carmen,* belongs to this category, while to the almost forgotten and infrequently performed roster of grand opera belongs Rossini's *William Tell,* the overture of which still survives.

# EARLY ROMANTIC COMPOSERS

For our survey of the composers and music of this bewildering period of individualism we shall adopt a double system, combining chronology and stylistic analysis, in order to define the position of important composers within the nineteenth century. The early Romantic composers, influential during the first half of the period, are Berlioz (1803-1869), Mendelssohn (1809-1847), Chopin (1810-1849) and Schumann (1810-1856). Those who matured musically during the middle of the century are Liszt (1811-1886), Wagner (1813-1883), Verdi (1813-1901), Franck (1822-1890), Brahms (1833,1897) and Tchaikovsky (1840-1893). The late Romantic composers, often called *post-romantic,* are Mahler (1860-1911), R. Strauss (1864-1949), Sibelius (1865-1957) and Rachmaninoff (1873-1943).

The stylistic classification largely depends upon the attitude toward program, or descriptive music, plus an additional division for nationalistic composers. Excluding the latter for a moment, there would seem to be three rather clearly defined categories based upon the use of literary programs:

1.  Composers who do not use literary programs, nor write obviously descriptive music as evidenced by the titles of their compositions. Abstract titles, such as Symphony No. 4, or those indicative of a dance (*e.g.* mazurka, valse, polonaise) or belonging to a miscellaneous classification (*e.g.* nocturne, intermezzo, caprice, fantasy, impromptu) are all indicative of a non-literary attitude on the part of the composer. Such composers as Chopin and Brahms are representative of this group.

2.  Composers who are poetically inspired by any of the common sources for the Romantic composer, such as scenes of Nature or works of literature, endeavor to capture the essential elements of the inspiration in their music but purposely give the work a rather vague title which *suggests* rather than dictates to the listener what the composer is trying to communicate. Mendelssohn and especially Schumann belong to this category. Tchaikovsky also partially fulfills these requirements, as evidenced by his comments on his music, which give sufficient programmatic indications to warrant his inclusion.

3.  Composers who use not only the most exact musical descriptive devices they can create, but also base the musical form of their compositions upon a literary model. In this division we find Berlioz, Liszt, Wagner and Strauss, among others.

We must also realize that each of these composers has occasional "falls from grace," and sometimes writes music which is outside our usual classification for him: our judgments must therefore be based upon what seems to be the usual procedure for that composer.

The remaining composers belong to the nationalist group, more or less strongly influenced by the folk melodies and rhythms of their native lands, and dedicated to the patriotic, expressive and musical exploitation of these materials in compositions which often tell a story, legend, or myth. Others of these works may not be so literal, and may reflect only the composer's love for his country in musical landscapes. There are three main groups: those from the Balkan countries of the Austro-Hungarian empire, often collectively called Bohemia — Bedrich Smetana (1824-1884) and Antonin Dvořák (1841-1904) ; the Russian nationalists, most colorful and influential upon music of their day and of modern Russia — Alexander Borodin (1833-1887), Modeste Moussorgsky (1839-1881), and Nicolai Rimsky-Korsakoff (1844-1908); the Scandinavian countries represented by Edvard Grieg (1843-1907) from Norway, and Jan Sibelius (1865-1957) from Finland. Spain was late to join the ranks, for Spanish music had always been so colorful and self-sufficient as not to need symphonic treatment; nevertheless the works of Enrique Granados (1867-1916) are welcome additions to this group. The Italian style, of course, need hardly be mentioned, for it had ruled the operatic stage throughout most of the eighteenth century and was still powerful in the nineteenth. It became so stylized that there was no need to quote folk songs and rhythms to identify the country of origin.

Having, we hope, brought some sort of order out of the multitude of composers of the nineteenth century after Beethoven and Schubert, let us now examine representative compositions by them, and build up a composite aural impression of this music beginning with early Romantic composers of abstract music.

### ABSTRACT MUSIC: FRÉDÉRIC FRANÇOIS CHOPIN (1810-1849)

Chopin was the child of a French father and a Polish mother; traits of both nationalities are strong in his music. Chopin himself could be reckoned as French except for the Slavic melancholy and passion in his music. He was one of the great originals of the era, and developed music for the piano in terms of lyricism and sonority far different from those exploited by Beethoven. Chopin's harmony is most unique, offering interesting effects in color and unexpected progressions combined with the most sophisticated melody that ever graced Parisian salons or awakened the pangs of patriotism in a Polish emigré. This art of the piano is intimate in the extreme, for the most part, although, as Schumann said, there are often "cannon under the flowers," and

PLATE XXIX. *Frederic Chopin. A rare daguerreotype made in 1849 shortly before Chopin's death. (The Bettmann Archive.)*

certain compositions can roar with the best of the romantic virtuoso pieces. The forms are usually sectional, with contrasting melodies and keys; dances with multiple trios are frequent, as are simple three-part forms. There is much repetition, but it seldom becomes wearisome for Chopin usually adds fascinating and unexpected decorations in the form of dazzling figures in rapid notes, different for each return of the material. *Tempo rubato* is an essential part of this style, lending not only rhythmic flexibility and interest, but also intimacy to the melodic line. These compositions sound, and are intended to sound like improvisations, tossed off on the spur of the moment. They give no hint of the patient polishing process which kept them on the composer's desk sometimes for years after their initial creation. Chopin once wrote to a friend that he felt that he had some small talent for piano composition, and that he would do his best to realize it. Succeeding generations of concert audiences have proved him right.

### *Valse, Op. 64, No. 2, in C♯-minor*

This typical waltz of Chopin's is deservedly popular, combining a certain Polish quality with French elegance and grace. The Slavic feeling is found in the first section, melancholy, and somewhat coquettish. The second section, in the same key, represents a kind of refrain in that it occurs more frequently than the other two sections, and that it follows each of them. Its airy grace calls for careful playing and absolute accuracy on the part of the pianist. The third section, which follows, is in the parallel major key, and consists of a sensitive melody twice played, the second time with embellishments. What is most characteristic about it is the halting, hesitating way in which it moves, as if unsure of itself. The harmony under it is mildly chromatic and unstable, and the section moves into the "refrain" over a slender bridge of unstable chords. The refrain over, the first section returns, dissolving into thin air with a gossamer scale. If we let B represent the "refrain," then the form may be indicated by AB CB AB.

### *Nocturne, Op. 9, No. 1, B♭-minor*

A nocturne is music to be played at night, and represents night-time moods ranging from amorous to despairing, sometimes a combination of several. The genre was not invented by Chopin, but many of his most characteristic works are to be found among the nineteen compositions so titled. This one, cast in a rather large ternary form, illustrates several typical traits of this composer's musical imagination. The meter is duple compound — 6/4 to be exact — which lends a slow swaying quality to the music, further enhanced by the wide-spread broken chords used in the accompaniment, a typical Chopin technique for securing sonority as well as rhythmic harmonic diffusion. At the first repeat of the opening phrase we are introduced to Chopin's manner of embellishing an otherwise simple melody with rapid notes grouped so as not to coincide with the notes of the accompaniment. For example, upon the first repetition of the opening phrase, the right hand plays eleven notes against six in the left hand; later there are seven against six, nine against six, and twenty against six, the latter in the third section of the work. The middle section is more brooding in character, with a less fluid melodic line, and exploits some interesting instabilities in harmony which lead to surprising resolutions in keys far removed from the tonic major of this section. This part is also discontinuous in motion, and exhibits a wide range of dynamic fluctuation. The third section is an embellished return of the first material with a few measures of coda added for cadence purposes.

### Nocturne, *Op. 27, No. 2, D♭-major*

This composition consists of a set of variations on a lyric melody already somewhat ornamented with groups of rapid notes. But Chopin's restless, passionate nature is revealed in the warmth developed in the second half of the theme and each variation. This piece is a real study in Chopinesque *fioratura* (lame translation: "floweryness"). The harmonic accompaniment is the favorite widespread arpeggiated chord, and the harmony itself is most imaginative, but rather unobtrusive, concealed under the brilliance of the melodic material.

### Nocturne, *Op. 48, No. 1, in C-minor*

In this piece we sense the iron will behind the gracefulness of the preceding works. The opening, while subdued, seems to proclaim something less of the salon and is more epic in its forthrightness. Even the melodic decoration has a certain seriousness. The first section of this three-part form gives way to a sonorous chorale in massive block-chordal style; an octave figure in triplets interrupts the phrases of the chorale, and gradually brings the section to a dynamic and rhythmic climax, after which the first section returns, now permeated by the triplet rhythm which appears in the accompaniment and clashes rhythmically with the duple subdivisions of the original theme. This is a composition in which the virtuoso element is apparent, but subservient to the musical intent.

### Ballade, *Op. 23, G-minor*

The Ballade might be called Chopin's answer to the challenge of the sonata-allegro form. An *answer* because this composer was unable to harness his inspiration in the way demanded by that most classic of classic forms, and was never completely successful when he set out to conquer this essentially alien territory. But in the ballade, where he felt no traditional restraint, Chopin created a fluid, kaleidoscopic, developmental form as right for his genius as the sonata-allegro was for Beethoven. The form is sectional in that it contrasts various melodies in their keys, developmental in that sections are often varied upon their return, and unified in that one section and its key returns from time to time, often rather unexpectedly. Most of the elements of Chopin's style which we have discovered in the foregoing works are found here.

### The Etude

The word *"etude"* means a *study;* in music, a composition devoted to the development of performing skill which usually concentrates upon a single difficult problem and repeats the passage involving this difficulty throughout the piece. As might be expected, the number of dull etudes is legion! But Chopin raised this kind of composition to a high art, without, be it noted, departing from the original premise of etude. Number 6 (Op. 10, No. 6) poses for the pianist the difficult problem of playing rapid passages in parallel thirds smoothly with the right hand. This etude is probably one of the most difficult in Chopin's entire series of compositions of this kind.

POETICALLY INSPIRED MUSIC: FELIX MENDELSSOHN, 1809-1847

With Mendelssohn we turn to those composers whose music often was founded on poetic inspiration. This gifted musician was born into a wealthy Jewish family in Hamburg, and spent his boyhood in Berlin. In a social stratum and an era which presupposed a high degree of general culture, Felix excelled. He was provided with an excellent education, and his musical studies were given the utmost encouragement, even to the provision of an orchestra — small, to be sure, but still an orchestra — for the performance of his early compositions. These included an Octet for strings and the still bewitching music to Shakespeare's *Midsummer Night's Dream,* written in part at the age of seventeen with a most assured hand in the tempered romantic style that was to stay with him all his life. Through his teacher he developed an interest in the music of Bach, and his revival of the *St. Matthew Passion* in 1829 inspired him to compose his two oratorios, *St. Paul* and *Elijah.* He was highly appreciated in England, but returned to Leipzig to make his home and to found the conservatory as well as to conduct the famous *Gewandhaus* orchestra which he made one of the best in Europe. He

PLATE XXX. *Felix Mendelssohn. (The New York Public Library.)*

composed five symphonies, a number of concert overtures of which the "Hebrides Overture" (sometimes called "Fingal's Cave"), *Ruy Blas,* and *Calm Sea and Prosperous Voyage* are well known, two piano concertos which are infrequently played and a violin concerto which is a standard in the literature for that instrument, a goodly amount of chamber music and a series of piano pieces called *Songs Without Words.* Mendelssohn's style is classicistic — that is, it is no longer the genuine classic product, but resembles it closely in technique and form. Indeed, to his contemporaries Mendelssohn seemed to have solved the problem of uniting traditional forms with romantic contents. But when we compare his most finished works side by side with those of the Classic period, we see that he is able to make the classic gestures but that they are those of an actor playing a part, rather than of a first-person experience. Nevertheless, the polish and refinement are extreme and the music flows with the freedom of the best classic models, filled however, with a sentiment somewhat too delicate and feminine, rarely moving us deeply as do Haydn, Mozart, and Schubert, not to mention the giant of Bonn. Mendelssohn remains the romanticist in the somewhat melancholy tone of some works, the tendency to darker colors, and the elevation of sentiment. At his worst, in some of the *Songs Without Words,* he is cloyingly sentimental; at his best, as in the Fourth Symphony, he is brilliant and delightful. Unlike so many of the romantic composers, Mendelssohn was not at war with his world or himself. He was able to pursue the life that he wanted, and achieved a certain clarity and sobriety in his art through his power of organization, intellect and refined taste.

One particular type of music at which he excelled is the fairy-like scherzo, examples of which occur in the *Midsummer Night's Dream* and some of the chamber works. The light touch of these movements reveals a mastery in the use of the instruments and a felicitous expressive power seldom to be met with in this era. Their only rival is the "Queen Mab Scherzo" from Berlioz' *Romeo and Juliet* symphony. The Fourth Symphony, called the "Italian" is the musical outcome of a journey to that country in 1830-31. The only overt reference to Italy is made in the last movement which is a native Italian dance, the *saltarello;* but the joy and freedom and "sunny skies" of the first movement depict the ideal Italy dreamed of during the bleak German winters. The first movement flows with grace and conviction, but the dramatic duality of the classic sonata-allegro is missing. Rather, here is a series of pictures, all lovely and interesting, not a drama. But this does not detract from the value or enjoyment to be gained from the music. The second movement is slow, almost Bachian in the construction of the opening subject. The colors of the woodwinds are handled beautifully in this "chamber-music" piece. The third movement is flowing, like neither a minuet nor a scherzo, but indicative of a certain happy tranquillity. The finale is, as mentioned above, a saltarello in duple meter which in certain respects resembles the "fairy" scherzos. There is interesting rhythmic variation between the compound duple meter with which the movement opens and the simple duple time which recurs throughout the piece.

The Violin Concerto in E-minor is one of Mendelssohn's most notable works. It departs from the classical concerto forms in not having a separate orchestral exposition, by making the cadenza functional in that it serves as the retransition in the first movement, and by linking together the three movements. The lyricism and brilliance of the solo part of this work have made it a favorite with audiences and violinists from Mendelssohn's time to ours.

PLATE **XXXI**. *Robert Schumann. Daguerreotype taken in the early 1850's. (The Bettmann Archive.)*

POETICALLY INSPIRED MUSIC: ROBERT SCHUMANN, 1810-1856

More true to the ideals of romanticism, more original, but less polished and refined in handling the problem of form was Robert Schumann. As a youth he vacillated between literary and musical pursuits; a short session of law study at the University of Leipzig convinced him that his destiny lay with music. He studied piano and composition, and aimed for a career as a virtuoso, but ruined his right hand by exercising it with a contrivance of his own invention intended to strengthen the fourth finger. Thus frustrated in this career, he turned to composition and developed rapidly. He became one of the first music critics, and his warm appreciation of much of his colleague's work encouraged them in their musical pursuit of the romantic ideal. He announced Chopin to the music world with, "Hats off, gentlemen! A genius!," and befriended Johannes Brahms during the early part of his career. After a courtship similar to that of Robert Browning and Elizabeth Barrett, he married Clara Wieck, the daughter of his music teacher and one of the most distinguished woman pianists in history. Beginning in 1851, a mental disorder appeared, affecting his personality and his music and becoming fatal five years later.

Schumann is a lyric poet, sensitive and reflective, with a strong literary turn of mind. He is at his best in his rather short piano works where the intimacy of the moment is captured in movements offering no great formal problems. In the large works he is less successful, with the possible exception of his piano concerto. He realized, in this work, that the classical form and manner of treating the piano were entirely unsuitable for a romantic concerto, and so used the solo on equal terms with the orchestra, combining them with an intimacy of expression that had never before existed in this medium. Up to the time he felt the need to compose symphonies, Schumann was the Shelley of music, eternally young, eternally seeking. In the effort to become "universal" in the sense that Mozart and Beethoven are, Schumann hastened the pathological breakdown of his faculties. He had realized long before this that his was a divided personality, but this was true of most romantic artists to some degree, a kind of symptom of the various ideals the period sought to achieve. Schumann even had names for multiple identities: Florestan, the man of action; Eusebius, the dreamer; and cool-headed Dr. Raro, wise and even-tempered. In some of his piano works, movements bear these names as titles, and in some of the orchestral works the alternation between active portions and meditative sections makes it clear which of them has control.

Schumann wrote four symphonies, two of which are often identified by their subtitles; No. 1 is the "Spring" Symphony and No. 3, the "Rhenish" Symphony. Perhaps the most characteristic and unique solution of the romantic symphonic problem is furnished by his Fourth Symphony, Op. 120, in D-minor. It was written only a short time after his First Symphony, and was first entitled *Symphonic Fantasy*, but was withdrawn from subsequent performance and reworked, appearing later with the present number designation. There are five movements in this work, Introduction, Allegro, Romanze, Scherzo, Finale, which Schumann directed to be played without pause from beginning to end. This procedure, of course, enhances the outward unity, but the composition has considerable inner unity also. The themes of all the movements are derived melodically from motives exposed in the introduction, sometimes very freely, sometimes very strictly (Example 64). In addition, Schumann applies other devices

EXAMPLE 64.

BASIC MOTIVES

INTRODUCTION
Ziemlich langsam

I. FIRST MOVEMENT: Lebhaft

II. ROMANZE: Ziemlich langsam

Str.        etc.

MIDDLE SECTION: VARIANT OF THE FOREGOING

Vl.
Vlc.        etc.        etc.

(NOTE HARMONY)

III. SCHERZO: Lebhaft

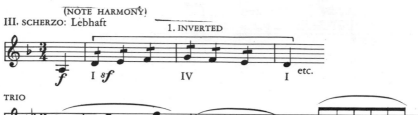

_f_        I _sf_        IV        I   etc.

TRIO

Vl. _p_   (See middle section of Romanze, above.)        etc.

TRANSITION:

Langsam        1.

Vl. _pp_   2.        etc.

IV. FINALE: Lebhaft 3        IMPORTANT MOTIVE

Ww., Br.  I        IV  I
Str.   _ff_        Vla.,        2.        1.        2.        1.
        Vlc.   2.   1.

_f_        _p < >_        _f_        _p < >_   etc.

_mf_        etc.

to secure closer unity among the movements of the work. These are:

1. The use of a bridge passage between the last two movements, similar in effect to that in the Fifth Symphony of Beethoven.

2. The highly irregular sonata-allegro form of the first movement, which omits the recapitulation, suggesting that this movement is not a complete unit, but only part of a large organization. This feeling is enhanced by the appearance in the final movement of thematic material from the exposition of the first movement — a delayed recapitulation, as it were. Schumann here realizes, obviously, that as one begins to unify a work in this manner, the various movements begin to lose their separate identities to become parts of a larger single structure. This mode of formal reasoning will lead, in the twentieth century, to the highly organized "symphony in one movement," of which the Third Symphony of Roy Harris and the Seventh Symphony of Sibelius are outstanding examples.

In the Schumann Fourth Symphony, the unification gained creates a new species of symphony, worthy to follow the great works of the classic past; here the content has a decisive influence upon the form, making it quite different from the traditional symphony. That Schumann realized this is demonstrated by his reluctance to call it a *symphony* upon its first appearance.

Schumann's creations in the intimate field of lieder are some of his finest works. The year of his marriage has been called his "year of song," and from that time onward date his 200 lieder and cycles of lieder. Schumann fuses the piano part, which is in these songs much more than accompaniment, with the melody and words in such a way that they are inseparable. He often precedes and follows the vocal part with a few measures of commentary in the piano, all the more expressive because it speaks in pure musical tones. The cycle *Frauenliebe und Leben* (*Woman's Love and Life*) is one of the most moving sets of lieder in the literature of the form.

Schumann delighted in complex rhythmic structures involving cross-rhythms, dotted rhythms, and subtle combinations of polyrhythm (this term signifies the use of a subdivision of the same pulse into a certain number of smaller beats in one performing part and into a different number of smaller beats in another; a simple example of this on the piano would be the playing of two notes per beat in the right hand while performing three per beat in the left hand). In the later works, however, the rhythmic play becomes obsessional, and the variety and interest wane.

This composer provides us with a truer example of the Romantic

artist than does Mendelssohn, who was able to travel comfortably
the middle of the stylistic road between the classical and romantic concepts. Schumann could not do this, and therefore encountered difficult problems, largely in the construction of symphonic forms. He
was too original to compromise, he felt the urge of romanticism too
strongly to accept blindly what others had accomplished, and he was
too sensitive to withstand the forces with which he had to cope. But
in his own realm of romantic piano music he is a strong and successful
composer. In comparison with Chopin the sonority is darker, thicker,
and lower-pitched, the movement less light and elegant, the chordal
structure more massive. In addition to the rhythmic imbalance often
present, Schumann delights in harmonic instability, often devising his
progressions so sensitively that the only tonally stable chord occurs
at the end of the composition. Because of the clearness with which
the mood is projected, Schumann's compositions often have a more
immediate emotional impact than those of Chopin, in which the
listener is sometimes more bedazzled by the virtuosity and sonority
than by the musical meaning of the work.

## DESCRIPTIVE MUSIC: HECTOR BERLIOZ, 1803-1869

The firebrand of French Romanticism is largely remembered by three
works: his *Symphonie Fantastique,* his *Treatise on Orchestration* and
his *Autobiography*. Each of these three reveals a portion of the personality of this coolly impetuous exponent of *program music*. In a
sense, the *Symphonie Fantastique* is autobiographical in that it discloses
a segment of Berlioz' life — that of his courtship of the Shakespearian
actress, Harriet Smithson, who later became his wife. The episodes
and movements of the symphony make plain both musically and programmatically the emotional stress of those days. But the emotion,
however molten from the heat of his passion, is not allowed to flow
uncontrolled. By a suspicious "accident" the programmatic sequences
occur in relationships which mold the music into more or less classical
shapes. Thus, we find a sonata-allegro first movement, a waltz with
trio second movement, the third movement a set of variations, the
fourth a march with trio, and the finale a sectional form harkening
back to the baroque fantasy and fugue! This in the music of romanticism? Yet we must keep in mind the rational Gallic temperament,
here demonstrated by the keen mind of one of the first virtuosi of the

PLATE XXXII. *Berlioz and Liszt. Drawing by Kriehuber, Vienna, 1846. A gathering at Liszt's which includes, from left to right: Kriehuber, Berlioz, Czerny, Liszt and Ernst. (New York Public Library.)*

orchestra, and one of its consummate masters. Berlioz played no instrument well enough to perform in public. His instrument was the orchestra, and his keen imagination struck sparks of originality in so many ways that most of the great orchestral writers from Wagner to Rimsky-Korsakoff acknowledge him — if tacitly, the music shows its debt — to be their orchestral guide.

The mind whose curiosity sought out from performers the secrets of their instruments and reduced them to logical and rational procedures in his orchestration book was similarly capable of casting its musical impulses into easily recognizable forms. These bear a thematic relationship to the forms of previous eras, and sometimes a tonal resemblance. But the essential balance, straightforwardness, and unity of the classic design — its "personality" — is missing. Instead of drama we have dramatics, instead of development we find contrasting

401

episodes, and instead of unity of spirit we find a self-conscious unity of material. Nevertheless, the music is projected with such fire and compelling brilliance that we do not miss, or even look for, the classic essentials. Here is music which exists upon a different plane, music which establishes its own criteria and, if we believe the *Autobiography,* music which was cruelly misunderstood in its time. But we must take Berlioz' elderly bitterness with a grain of salt, for, by contemporary reports, he was very popular in Germany, Austria and Russia. But in France? No. The fire of the Revolution had gone out, and all that remained of the pathbreaking ideals which fostered it were mummified in the academic hearts of second-rate composers without the imagination to write an original measure. And these persons were in power at the *Opera,* at the *Acadèmie,* and at the *Conservatoire,* allowing no art to be heard which would endanger their positions. And in league with them were the newspapers, the critics, the little musicians, brought up on a diet of musical pabulum, and, therefore, by and large, the public. In his impetuosity, Berlioz kept trying for public success, even to the extent of financing his own concerts. But his Parisians turned their backs upon him. Not so his colleagues in other nations. Wagner, Liszt, even Schumann, who disliked French music in general because of the prevailing superficiality, praised his compositions, and, while sometimes finding fault, were not above imitating some of the effects, or even stealing a scene, as did Wagner.

So, in the music of Berlioz we find an impetuous romantic imagination linked with a rational yet poetic intelligence. The same characteristics pervade the other music of this French romantic: the "symphony with viola *obbligato,*" commissioned by Paganini, *Harold in Italy;* the dramatic symphony, *Romeo and Juliet;* the various overtures; the scenes from the *Damnation of Faust;* the *Requiem,* and the orchestral songs, *Nuits d'Eté.* All are sensually and excitingly romantic, yet planned with coherence and unity, and accomplished by means of a most expressive use of the orchestra. Berlioz almost always tries to achieve a sense of unity in his larger works, frequently by restating an important theme in each of the movements or sections. This procedure is very plain in the *Fantastique,* and occurs as a result of the literary program adopted. The plan of the work revolves around the love of a young musician, and, egocentrically, the effects of disappointments upon him. The pervading character, aside from the musician who is communicating in the music, is the beloved woman, and to her is assigned a theme — more than a theme, a complete melody some forty measures long. This is the *idée fixe,* a term used by the composer which might well be translated as the "obsession." Since the beloved, or her phantom, appears in each of the movements as dictated by the literary program, a kind of "quotational" unity is achieved. But Berlioz goes a step further and varies the *idée fixe* in a manner suggested by the program: in the second movement, a scene at a ball, the theme is transformed into a graceful waltz; in the witches sabbath of the final movement, into a grotesque caricature of its previous self.

Let us examine the programs of the various movements one by one, followed by the music. Here is the situation in Berlioz' words:

A young musician of extraordinary sensibility and overflowing imagination in a paroxysm of despair caused by unhappy love has poisoned himself with opium. The drug is too feeble to kill him, but plunges him into a heavy sleep accompanied by the weirdest visions. His sensations, emotions, and memories, as they pass through his diseased brain, are transformed into musical images and ideas. The beloved one herself becomes to him a melody, a recurrent theme *(idée fixe)* which haunts him everywhere.

*First Movement:* "Reveries, Passions: First he remembers that weariness of the soul, that indefinable longing, that somber melancholia and those objectless joys which he experienced before meeting his beloved. Then, the volcanic love with which she at once inspired him, his delirious suffering, his return to tenderness, his religious consolation."

The introductory section materializes out of thin air, beginning with soft accompaniment figures for two measures, after which a fragmentary theme, later to become part of the main theme of the movement, is stated by the strings. It is spun out in a brief, quiet section, then rhythmically transformed in an animated variation. The remainder of the introduction consists of contrasting variations upon the theme, illustrating the reveries and passions of the program. After several dramatic measures which close the introduction and prepare for the allegro, the main theme — the *idée fixe* (Example 65) — is stated in its entirety (40 measures) by the first violins and flutes, to which are added increasingly agitated accompaniment parts as the theme progresses. Note the various melodic motives which the theme contains, especially the opening one, and the sequences which lead to the emotional climax of this typically Berliozian melody. The transition is a contrasting and brilliant modulatory section which flows into the second key and thematic area so smoothly that it is difficult to ascertain when that section really begins. It is made doubly uncertain

EXAMPLE 65.

I. IDÉE FIXE–PRINCIPAL THEME: Allegro

II. VALSE: Allegro non troppo

Entire IDÉE FIXE quoted, as above, 3/8 meter.

## III. Adagio

OPENING DUET

b.

cresc. poco a poco

c. Fl. & Ob.

IV. Allegretto non troppo

Vla., Vlc.& **ff**
Cb.

dim.

*p*

Br. & Ww. *f*

IDÉE FIXE

Cl. *pp*

*ff* Pizz.

V. IDÉE FIXE: Allegro

a.   Cl.

*ppp*

by the fact that the second thematic idea is a transformation of part of the *idée fixe*. The music flows smoothly into the development section also, the beginning of which is signalled by the first motive of the *idée fixe* given to the low strings in a rising sequential pattern, increasingly agitated in nature. The accumulated tension due to the sequence and the chromatic movement is released in a dynamic climax, followed by a short section of the second theme in the winds, answered by the strings, which leads to a series of ascending and descending chromatic scales, each "wave" of which crests on a higher pitch. Again the tension explodes in a climax, followed by a silence of almost four measures duration. The entire first theme is now quietly presented in the dominant key over an accompaniment fashioned out of the interval of the opening of that theme. The non-final cadence of this section, produced by the strong chromatic scale in the cellos and bassoons, leads to a development of the concluding section of the *idée fixe,* at first rather simple in nature, later decorative and brilliant.

The cellos now announce part of the second theme as the subject of a fugal section which grows to climactic proportions, followed by a tranquil development of fragments from the last part of the *idée fixe,* descending through each division of the string section after the inital statement of them by the woodwinds and horns. The cellos and basses reverse the direction of the motive, providing a link to the next section which consists of a new-sounding transformation of the *idée fixe* — actually a reassembly of motives from it — given to the oboe. Before the first phrase is finished, the cellos and violas begin an alternating rising sequential pattern consisting of the first seven notes of the *idée fixe*. At the peak of the climax thus developed, the recapitulation begins with the main theme, tonic key, accompanied boisterously by syncopated chords in the brass and scale figures in the upper strings. The cellos and basses are busy at the same time with a fragment from a later part of the theme: thus we hear both halves of the *idée fixe* simultaneously. The following section, ostensibly the transition, does not lead to the second theme, which never appears, but rather to new variants of the main theme. The climax which concludes the recapitulation is again prepared by slowly rising harmonic sequences. The coda begins quietly with a sustained tone in the oboe to which the violins and violas add motion by rocking back and forth upon expansions of the opening interval of the *idée fixe*. The first phrase of this theme is then stated softly by the violins, followed by organ-like chords in the winds and strings, suggesting by their plagal nature the "religious consolation" mentioned in the program.

During the entire movement the motion is discontinuous, with sections of contrasting tempo. The scoring emphasizes brilliance and often pits opposing sonorities against each other, much as Beethoven did, but with more emphasis on instrumental color. The general feeling is one of nervous intensity.

*Second movement:* "A Ball: At a ball, in the midst of a noisy, brilliant fête, he finds the loved one again" (Example 65II). This is a French waltz, rather fast, elegant, and graceful. The introduction is one of the earliest symphonic compositions to use the harp, and, as might be expected, Berlioz employs it brilliantly. The *idée fixe* does not appear until the trio, and is later brought back in the coda. The waltz section flows into the trio without a break, and, similarly, there is no pause between the trio and the resumption of the waltz.

*Third movement:* "In the Country: On a summer's evening in the country he hears two herders who call each other with their shepherd's melodies. The pastoral duet in such surroundings, the gentle rustle of the trees softly swayed by the wind, some reasons for hope that had lately come to his knowledge, all unite to fill his heart with long-missed tranquillity, and lend brighter colors to his fancies. But

SHE appears anew, spasms contract his heart, dark premonitions appear to him. What if she proved faithless? One of the shepherds resumes his rustic tune, the other does not follow. The sun sets — far away there is rumbling thunder — solitude — silence."

This movement is one of the offspring, more or less legitimate, of the Beethoven Sixth Symphony, the "Pastoral." Such nature-pieces tend to be purely descriptive in the Romantic era, whereas in the Beethoven work, the first, most of the second, and all of the final movement are absolute music — "more description of feeling than tone-painting." And given the above program, little is needed otherwise to provide the music: pastoral duets, the beloved-plus-agitation, and the return of one part of the pastoral duet (now a solo), rumbling timpani, and there we have it. But within this rather trite framework is room for the most subtle and telling artistry, much as the Renaissance painters of the Madonna exercised their imaginative and coloristic skill in the depiction of the much-painted subject. The statement of the theme of this set of variations is preceded by an introduction, a conversation between the male voice of the English horn and the female tones of the oboe (Example 65, IIIa) : the symbolism is plain, and the melancholy and pensive mood is established. Now the theme appears (Example 65, IIIb), introduced by the first violins and a flute in unison. It is approximately thirteen measures in length and is constituted of transformed motives from the *idée fixe*. The first variation is simple, and consists of nothing more than the addition of parallel harmony a third above the melody. After an extension of the chromatic cadence figure of this variation and a small developmental flurry, the second variation, with the theme in the violas and cellos, ensues. Above the melody is a running accompaniment in the violins and rhythmic punctuation by the woodwinds. The melodic line begins to resemble the *idée fixe* more closely, and finally, after an agitated climax, that fateful theme does appear (Example 65, IIIc), interrupted and accompanied by expressive gestures in the low strings. When this excitement has subsided, the very soft third variation follows. The *pizzicato* violas and violins begin a rapid, decorated version of the theme, aided by the clarinet and flute playing clarifying outlines and motives. More rhythmic figures are superposed, the theme is given intact to the second violins and more woodwinds join the original two. There follows a short climax and a bridge passage which leads to the fourth variation, a varied statement of the theme combined with an increasingly important thematically derived figure. A codetta formed out of the downward leaps of the *idée fixe* closes the variations, and a coda based upon the introduction is now heard. The English horn's solitary musing, now unanswered by the oboe, the distant thunder produced by four timpani, and the closing sigh of the strings produce effectively the mood of melancholy solitude suggested by the program.

*Fourth Movement:* "March to the Scaffold: He dreams he has killed his loved one, that he is condemned to death and led to the execution. A march, now gloomy and ferocious, now solemn and brilliant accompanies the procession. Noisy outbursts are followed without pause by the heavy sound of measured footsteps. Finally, the *idée fixe*, like a last thought of love appears for a moment, to be cut off by the fall of the axe." In the opinion of this writer, we have here the most realistic piece of music ever penned which is still susceptible to the title "music." The orchestration abounds in new and amazing effects, like the sneering of the muted horns in the few introductory measures, the ghostly gibbering of the bassoon as a countermelody to the gloom-laden, dragging footsteps of the main march theme, or the incisive chord which interrupts the *idée fixe*, followed by the low string pizzicato which brings irresistibly to mind the picture of the severed head falling into the basket. And during the "brass band" trio sections, one can easily visualize Madame LaFarge imperturbably knitting as the tumbril rolls by (Example 65 IV).

*Fifth Movement:* "Dream of a Witches' Sabbath: He sees himself at a Witches' Sabbath surrounded by a fearful crowd of spectres, sorcerers and monsters of every kind, united for his burial. Unearthly sounds, groans, shrieks of laughter, distant cries, to which others seem to respond! The melody of his beloved is heard, but it has lost its character of nobleness and timidity. Instead, it is now an ignoble dance tune, trivial and grotesque. It is SHE who comes to the Sabbath! A howl of joy greets her arrival. She joins the diabolical orgy. The funeral knell, burlesque of the *Dies Irae*. Dance of the Witches. The dance and the *Dies Irae* combined."

In this movement, Berlioz shows that without a doubt — if one existed before — that he is a Romantic composer. The unholy rites celebrated by evil and supernatural beings was a favorite subject of the Romantic era. Numerous musical compositions — Moussorgsky's *Night on Bald Mountain,* and Saint-Saens' *Danse Macabre,* to name only two — together with stories such as *Frankenstein's Monster, Drac-*

*ula,* and, of course, the grandfather of them all, *Faust,* demonstrate this penchant. Musically, too, the audacious combination of a witches' dance with the Latin chant for the dead from the Requiem Mass — "*Dies Irae, Dies Illa. . . .*" "Day of wrath, day of judgment" — here is another romantic trait. Formally, as we have noted, this is a large fantasy and fugue — actually a double fugue, since it has two subjects, the witches' dance and the *Dies Irae,* which are combined in the latter part. The introduction establishes the eerie mood in a fine piece of tone painting — establishes it so well that the burlesque of the *idée fixe* sometimes comes as a considerable shock (Example 65 IVa). The fantasy section proper is devoted to the exposition and development of this theme. Then a foreboding descending passage by the bassoons, cellos, and double-basses ushers in the funeral knell and the grim tune of the Latin mass (Example 65, IVb). It is stated in long note values in the tubas and bassoons first, a version twice as fast in block chords by the brass follows, and then the *pizzicato* strings parody the theme in a typical rapid 6/8 rhythmic pattern. The next section is devoted to the exposition of the witches' theme (Example 65, IVc), which, under different circumstances might pass as a rather guileless Italian *tarantella.* It is introduced fugally, after which a contrasting episode drawn from the introduction appears, and this in turn is followed by another fugal exposition of a chromatic version of the dance theme. Then the *Dies Irae* is combined with it, the two are loosely developed, along with some previous material, and the movement ends with an orthodox authentic cadence.

The orchestra which Berlioz employs in this composition is large, calling for, in addition to the double woodwinds and four horns, two cornets, two trumpets, three trombones, two tubas, two bassoons in addition to those usually employed, bells, bass drum, four timpani, and "extras" such as piccolo, clarinet in E♭ and English horn. Only in the final movement are all used, but the augmented brass section functions as a "band" in the "March to the Scaffold."

Now what is epoch-making about this work? First of all, the mere sound of it. It was performed in 1830, three years after Beethoven's death, and represents a view of the orchestra undreamed of by the older master, for in it tone-color supplants purely musical logic in a way comparable to the replacement of draftsmanship by color in the work of many Romantic and Modern painters. Were one to play this symphony on the piano, he would get an entirely distorted view of the work. It was *written for the orchestra* and it must be heard in the orchestra. Much of the piano music of the Classic and Baroque eras can be orchestrated without loss of essential values, and the orchestral compositions may be similarly reduced for the piano: but not the music of Berlioz, and romantics like him. The tone-colors of the instruments, and the ways in which the orchestra functions are of the utmost importance. This is non-functional orchestration — type-casting, if you will, suiting the role exactly to the instrument.

Secondly, the audacity and originality of this conception of the orchestra, and the functions of its parts — soloistic, opposed, *en masse,* the exploration of mutings of the brass, the materials of drumsticks, the use of the string mutes — these point forward toward the emancipation of the orchestra, and the formation of the modern symphony orchestra.

Thirdly, the use of a unifying theme, and the derivation of other themes from it. Berlioz is usually given credit for only the first half of the above statement, reserving the latter half for Franz Liszt. But, it would seem, Berlioz employed it first, not as thoroughly as Liszt was to use it, to be sure, but to a degree which pointed a way. We have noted Schumann's tendencies in the same direction — without a program, however, to suggest such a procedure.

Fourthly, the use of a definitely stated literary program which presumably dictates the episodes of the form. In this work, literary "accident" and musical logic approach, so that no violence is done to the classic format, although, to be sure, this is far from a classic symphony in form as well as content! The "fantastic" nature of the program is also an innovation of some importance, opening the door to this aspect of romanticism. Did someone say "Is the program necessary — cannot we listen to this music without knowing in advance what it tries to portray?" The answer? Listen to it — and decide for yourself.

Berlioz wrote many other works well worth hearing, if only for the purely musical experience. We may oppose the lovely and expressive *Romeo and Juliet* dramatic symphony with the mighty *Requiem,* with its four brass bands, symphony orchestra and large choruses, or the *Damnation of Faust* with the pellucid *L'Enfance du Christ.* One day we may hope to hear some of the operatic works, for the reputation of Berlioz among present-day listeners is rapidly growing. And as our reaction against the nineteenth century wanes, we may come to appreciate the truly original and worthwhile qualities of this full-blooded Romantic of the first generation of his century.

# LATE ROMANTIC COMPOSERS

## ABSTRACT MUSIC: JOHANNES BRAHMS, 1833-1897

Certain composers, inclined by nature or training to a more sober view of the art of music, decried what they felt was the gaudy and meretricious debasement of Beethoven's heritage. Not for them were the easy virtues of program music, but rather the abstract symphonic path, difficult and overshadowed by the giants of the past. One composer of the nineteenth century stands as a solid monument to this conservative and responsible point of view, and that is Johannes Brahms. This intensely self-critical composer filled the most truly classic forms of his time with a romantic language of lyric and constructive charac-

PLATE XXXIII. *Johannes Brahms. Photograph about 1895, previously unpublished. (From the author's collection.)*

413

ter. He understood that one of the perils which beset the Romantic artist was that of the loss of form. Rather than fill the empty classic shell with his music, or endeavor to create new forms, Brahms, like the sturdy peasant stock from which he sprang, began with the tradition and exerted himself to continue it in the same direction, applying evolution instead of revolution. He felt the responsibility of tradition: his first symphony was finally completed only after he was forty years old. But he also felt the responsibility to himself, and rigorously criticized, discarded and rewrote his works until they satisfied him. It would not be going too far to say that in point of technique, no composer of the Romantic era rivals him. But this is exactly what his contemporaries objected to. "All technique and no invention, no melodies" they cried. We find this hard to understand, for to modern ears, Brahm's music is full of satisfying lyricism, balanced with enough development to give depth, and combined with a sober, yet rich orchestration.

Brahms composed four monumental symphonies. The first, hailed as the "Tenth" — or worthy to follow Beethoven's nine — is in C-minor, and is a truly serious and uncompromising work. It contains some of this composer's most beautiful lyricism. The Second Symphony in D-major, is a more genial work, sunny and serious by turns, Brahm's "Pastoral." The Third, in F-major, is cast in a more nostalgic, darker shade, and is the shortest of the four. With the Fourth in E-minor, a new realm is reached, one in which the fusion of classicism and romanticism have achieved a mystic balance. Four concertos which are part of the standard repertoire are the work of Brahms. Two are for piano; the first, in D-minor is perhaps the more difficult to appreciate, the second in B♭-major is more lyric and is easily accessible. The violin concerto is one of the great three for this instrument, the others being those of Beethoven and Tchaikovsky. Brahms also wrote a double concerto for violin, cello and orchestra which is frequently performed. Among the other works are two overtures — the Academic Festival Overture, which is based on student songs, and the Tragic Overture — two serenades, a set of *Variations on a Theme by Haydn,* much vocal and choral music, piano music, and chamber music.

Before going further, let us examine the general qualities of Brahm's style:

*Form:* Brahms employs an expanded version of classical forms in most of his works. In the piano works, binary and ternary forms abound. Among the vocal and choral compositions, sectional forms (strophic and altered strophic) as well as through-composed are found. In the larger choral works such as the *German Requiem,* traditional movements in fugal forms occur. Brahms showed no interest in the descriptive forms adopted by Berlioz and Liszt, but resumed the large symphony as written by Schubert (the Seventh and Eighth). Here we find lyric themes becoming the dominating characteristic of each particular section rather than significant key changes, although the tonality does change at the appropriate places, but often so gradually as to be difficult to hear. There also occurs development within expository sections, causing considerable expansion of those areas. In fact, Brahms often develops a theme while presumably exposing it.

*Techniques:* Construction is economical, using as simple material as possible, achieving length by development. Polyphony is used as a method of achieving smoothness of parts as well as a developmental tool. There is little emphasis on the "Beethoven surprise" element, but instead logical progression to climactic points rather than sudden shocks. Brahms, while interested in the coloristic possibilities of the orchestra to a degree, uses largely functional orchestration. His orchestra is conservative in the extreme, being limited to the instruments which Beethoven used, and in the quantities found in the Fifth or Ninth Symphonies.

*Romantic Qualities: Rich harmony,* imaginatively used for expressive purposes. It is usually dark in sonority, for Brahms preferred instruments of this quality, such as the cellos, violas, clarinets, oboes and horns. Structurally it contains many intervals of the third and sixth which do much to create the characteristic sonority of this composer's music.

*Lyricism,* especially in the second themes of sonata-allegro forms, and the material of the middle movements of the symphonies.

*"Motto" motives,* used to a considerable degree, are particularly noticeable in the Second and Third Symphonies. They are usually stated clearly, but then tend to perform secondary inconspicuous roles. Sometimes, as in the Second Symphony, the motto is of so basic a shape as to be virtually impossible to exclude from themes and melodies. There is one basic motto which Brahms seems to use consciously in many works. It begins the Third Symphony, and here consists of the ascending line of notes, F-A♭-F. Variations of this shape may be discovered in many in other works.

*Complicated rhythmic patterns,* often superimposed upon each other, are a particular delight to this composer. They are often achieved by the use of syncopation — (here giving a gentle elongation to melodic parts rather than a plainly unstable or a shock effect), and by the division of beats or groups of beats into three parts instead of the usual two. For example, in a 4/4 measure, each of the beats may be subdivided into three smaller pulses. Or, the first two beats may be replaced with three which occupy the same time duration, and achieve a kind of syncopated effect. The music of Brahms is full of these subtleties, which are not indulged for their own sakes, but to impart flow and interest to the texture.

*Continous flow* of music within a structural section, and close attention to the lengths of these sections in order to make balanced structures are important features of Brahm's music. Brahms is a master of cadence elision, or avoidance, often prolonging the end of a phrase by rhythmically varied repetition of the last few notes until the expected cadence point has been passed.

## MUSICAL EXAMPLES

*Symphony No. 3, Op. 90, in F-major*

Without going into great detail, let us examine the Third Symphony of this composer in order to demonstrate some of these qualities, and to form some idea of Brahm's conception of the symphony.

*First Movement — sonata-allegro:* The opening statement of the motto is followed by the main theme, a two part structure of which the first element is made up of descending broken triads, and the second of upward-striving figures which culminate in different descending broken triads (Example 66 I). Most of this rather short section is accompanied by the motto theme in longer note values. The transition passage begins on the final cadence note of the preceding section, and consists principally of a rhythmically divided, rising scale figure, and chords decorated with arpeggio passages in the strings and woodwinds. The rhythmic figure has definite thematic characteristics, and is not derived from any previous material. The meter changes now from duple compound to triple compound, and the graceful second theme is sung by the clarinet (Example 66 I). This theme is typical of

EXAMPLE 66.

I. Allegro con brio

SECOND SUBJECT

*A is important three-note scale figure.

## II. PRINCIPAL SUBJECT: Andante

Ob.

Cl.

## SECOND SUBJECT

Cl.

## CLOSING MOTIVES

Str.

## III. PRINCIPAL SUBJECT: Poco allegretto

Vlc.

## SECOND SUBJECT

Fl.

IV. PRINCIPAL SUBJECT: Allegro

Brahms' lyricism in that it continually returns to its beginning note. After a repetition in the oboe and violas, a tiny, march-like figure begins the codetta of this section, followed by a developmental version of the second theme which leads to a repetition of the motto theme, thus beginning the closing section of the exposition. Actually, this is a developmental section devoted to the inversion and fragmentation of the first theme, and a rapid variation of the second theme, together with references to the motto theme. The exposition does not close with a cadence, but with a whirlwind of development devoted to the first theme. Out of this syncopated flow emerges an agitated variation of the second theme, given to the bassoons, violas and cellos, the last few notes of which are fashioned into a repetitive figure to extend the period and delay the cadence. When it comes, it is deceptive in character, and the upper strings take over the thematic work. The period is again extended by the same means, this time for half a measure longer, and cadences at the entrance of the march-like figure belonging to the codetta of the second theme. This is developed, and, in the course of this, shortened from a three-note figure to a two-note, and finally to a one-note figure which seems to slow down as it descends. It is the unstable rhythm which causes this effect, plus, at the lowest point of the scale, longer note values — a "built-in" *ritard.*

A quiet section follows in which the horn expressively declaims the motto theme against a background of strings, with the bassoons and contrabassoon adding depth and richness to the sound. The retransition begins by hesitantly announcing a somewhat fragmented version of the first theme which dissolves into a descending scale in the rhythm of the theme. This in turn feeds into the motto theme, stated as at the beginning of the movement, but more fully scored, and the recapitulation now begins. This section is perfectly regular, repeating everything which was present in the exposition, with the proper change of key for the second theme, so that it now appears in the tonic. The coda of this movement is rather long, and is a development of both parts of the first theme, ushered in by the motto theme. The motto appears again against a rising variation of the first theme, which is then stated quietly in its original form to close the movement. The techniques of cadence-weakening and avoidance are beautifully demonstrated in this composition, as well as the special characteristics of Brahms' lyricism, harmonic richness, dark sonority and developmental procedures.

*Second Movement:* This is a very subtly written sonata-allegro, strongly lyric in character, which emphasizes the tone-colors of the clarinets and bassoons in particular. The main theme consists of five phrases separated by short passages in the low strings (Example 66 II). A developmental repetition of figures follows from this theme, with animated quasi-melodic decoration in the strings, which subsides by gradually shortening the back-and-forth figure of the theme, as well as giving the tones longer note-values. This developmental section acts as a transition, and brings us to the hesitant second theme, again in the clarinets and bassoons (Example 66 II). It includes a three note figure — a triplet, occupying one beat of the meter — which gives rise to very expressive polyrhythmic passages later on. The closing idea is derived from the first theme, and flows without a cadence into the development which consists largely of manipulations of the first theme, and works up to a climax of considerable power and eloquence. The first half of the development uses the triplet figure against duplet ("two") motion in the melody — although it is difficult to determine which of the two is the melody. In the second half of this section, the triplet motion gives way to quadruplet — four notes per beat (thus back to simple subdivision of the metric pulse, rather than compound, as with the triplet), and this motion is maintained for some time, the figures serving as accompaniment for the main theme in the recapitulation. This section of the form is quite irregular, since the second theme, in only fragmentary form, appears after a soaring, ecstatic portion which otherwise would seem to be the coda. The coda proper is fashioned out of the main theme. There is a slight reference by the horns to the motto theme just before the "soaring" theme in the recapitulation, but it is so momentary as to escape notice easily. Though this movement is marked *andante,* which signifies a less than moderate tempo, and though it is highly lyrical and expressive, a certain sense of "slow movement," as typified by the Beethoven symphonies, is lacking. Somehow, the specific gravity is not as great as in the case of the older master, the sense that the movement is an important and significant statement after the first movement is not felt, and the conviction that this is the only thing which could have happened at this point — the inevitability — is somehow not present.

*Third Movement:* The same thing seems true — to this writer, at least — about the third movement (Example 66 III), which is a melancholy ternary form in triple meter, with a coda which returns to fragments of the second (B) section, but combines these fragments in such a way as to suggest the first theme. In the middle of the B section there is a very arresting development by the strings of the two measures immediately preceding it — a development so different sounding that it at first appears to be something new.

*Fourth Movement:* This is a "massive" sonatina, with a long autumnal coda. There is a great deal of internal development within the exposition and recapitulation, and the transition and closing section of the latter are much reworked. The main theme, whose motives furnish an extensive amount of expansive material, is announced in rather ominous, hushed tones at the beginning of the movement (Example 66 IV). A chorale, featuring the trombones, and combined with motives from the first theme, characterizes the transition. The horns and cellos announce the fanfare-like second theme, with compound division of the duple meter, thus opening the possibility for polyrhythmic combinations. The sequence of themes in the recapitulation is regular, but more development is present, and new accompaniments are added. The coda begins with a curiously winding variation of the first theme in compound division of the measure, and played by the violas. Little by little the strings are muted, and play wavering broken chordal figures, while above them we hear variations of the first theme, the motto theme, and finally, in slow, solemn tones, the chorale from the transition section, now expanded in note values. Near the end of the movement the motto theme returns, combined with the motive from the first theme of this movement, now in the cellos; and during the last, long drawn-out tonic chord, the upper strings echo the first theme of the first movement bringing the whole work to a cyclic conclusion.

Now that we have heard the whole work, we may note points of resemblance among the materials used for the several movements. One of the basic motives of this work, aside from the more obvious motto theme, is a three-note scale figure, which may be found ascending or descending in many of the themes. This could be accidental — but if one is familiar with the subtleties of Brahms, he is more inclined to feel that it was done knowingly with the aim of unifying the total work. Again, the rhythms used have something in common, especially the compound division of a primarily duple meter. This is particularly noticeable when the two outer movements of the work are compared. The first is largely in 6/4 meter (with an interior change to 9/4 for a section) — that is, duple compound. The fourth movement is 2/2, or duple simple, but is frequently subject to compound subdivision of its two basic pulses, giving the equivalent of duple compound. The fact that the two movements have certain emotional and expressive elements in common ties them together even more firmly. The complexity we have found in this symphony is characteristic of most of Brahms' work, whether it be a small piano composition, or a large choral or orchestra work. He *can* be disarmingly simple, but seldom lets it go at that — preferring to introduce subtle complexities little by little during the course of his seeming simplicities.

## Chamber Music

One of Brahm's lifelong interests was chamber music, and, although he was not the only composer of this era to cultivate the medium, his efforts are the most noteworthy and most frequently performed nowadays. The clarinet was always a favorite orchestral instrument of Brahms, but, until he met the virtuoso Richard Muhlfeld he had not written any chamber music including this instrument. In 1891, at the age of fifty-eight, he composed the Clarinet Quintet, Op. 115 and the Clarinet Trio, Op. 114, and later, in 1894, two sonatas for clarinet and piano, Op. 120. In each of these, the bittersweet tone-quality of the instrument reflects the autumnal nostalgia and resignation of Brahms' later years. We shall examine the Clarinet Quintet in B-minor. The only noteworthy predecessor of this composition is Mozart's work for the same combination, written some one-hundred years before. Both works reflect a similar attitude on the parts of the composers and both owe their existence to the happy chance that the composers had come into contact with excellent clarinetists.

The first movement of Brahms' composition opens with a lyric motive in the violins, a sort of revolution around one note (Example 67, Ia). This basic shape becomes a unifying motive throughout the work, although Brahms often disguises it rhythmically or by making unessential melodic changes. Another unifying motive, still more basic in design, appears next (Example 67, Ib). It is the descending half-step, which is immediately inverted, and the combination of the two form the substance of the next two measures. Under them, as though this were a tiny exposition of the most elemental ideas to be used, appears a syncopated rhythm alternately in the viola and cello. While not the only syncopation that the composer uses in the work, it may be taken to suggest the kinds of rhythmic figures to be expected. Both the turning and the half-step figures are exploited in the first key area (Example 67, Ic), after which a more rhythmic figure introduces the transition (Example 67, Id). When this subsides, the second key area (D-major) is devoted to a dialogue between the clarinet and first violin with polyphonic accompaniment, in which the theme becomes increasingly developed, followed by a rhythmically halting section (Example 67, Ie). The development resumes and finally, as

EXAMPLE 67.

424

## II. Adagio

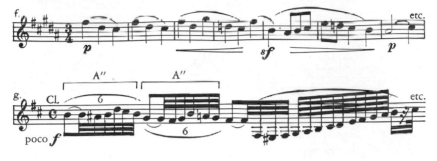

## III. Andantino

## Presto non assai

a sort of closing theme, states the first phrase of the second theme, once in the second violin, then in the clarinet, followed by the turning motive which provides a preparation for the repeat of the exposition (which ends at this point), or for continuity into the development. A description of this exposition is difficult, for the technical mastery of a subtle composer is here exploited in forming a section of "artless complexity," in which thematic fragments and development seem so effortlessly intertwined as to defy simple analysis, and yet the parts are there. The development unfolds, lyric and expressive, followed by a rewritten recapitulation. The sequence of themes is the same, but accompaniments, leading instruments, and developments are altered. The coda is somewhat more orchestral in the use of *tremolo* and double-stops in the strings, since Brahms here wants more sound than simple playing would supply, but it is not at all offensive in the sense of chamber music style. The movement ends with the quotation of the two motto themes.

The second movement, ternary in form, is in B-major. The first section consists of a lovely melody and its gentle lyric development (Example 67, IIf). The second section recalls Brahms' fondness for Hungarian gypsy music, probably dating from his youthful tours with Remenyi, the Hungarian violinist. Here the strings have held notes, or more emotional *tremolos,* while the clarinet declaims cadenza-like passages (Example 67, IIg). Many of these begin with figures reminiscent of the "turn" which begins the first movement, thus hinting at a unifying factor where one might least expect it. The first section returns in a rewritten form.

The third movement might be called a scherzo with slow introduction. Possibly Brahms felt that a transition in tempo was needed between the *adagio* second movement and the *presto non assai* scherzo. In any case, the latter movement begins lyrically, *andantino,* and retains this tempo for a section of considerable length. The theme is a simplified version of the "turn" theme of the first movement (Example 67, IIIh), and the section is in D-major. The scherzo which follows is not regular in form, but rather like a rondo, ABACABA (Example 67, IIIi, j, k). The quality is here intimate, purest chamber music style, and the texture quite polyphonic in the romantic manner. The A theme is a variation of the half step theme of the first movement, but so compressed rhythmically as to sound quite different.

The fourth movement is a set of five developmental variations with coda. The theme is binary, but only the second section is repeated (Example 67, IVl). The use of the "turn" motto from the first movement is fairly obvious throughout the theme, and in some of the variations. During the latter, the rhythmic shape of the motto is often altered. The half-step motto appears in many less important places, seeming quite incidental in its use. The coda is noteworthy, for here Brahms quotes a version of the beginning of the first movement, with the motto themes "out in the open." This quotation is most effective, both structurally and poetically, for, besides binding the cyclic form together, it seems to sum up everything that has gone before, and express Brahms' sentiments and resignation.

From our explorations in these two compositions by this late Romantic master, we have seen clearly the sources from which he draws his forms, and the personal quality of his lyricism, textures and orchestration. We have found that he was not a slavish imitator of the forms of the Classic period, but altered and developed them in accordance with his own musical conscience. Whether he may be said to have continued the work of Beethoven is not important. He is one of the monuments of the Romantic age, and a composer of universal importance and appeal.

POETICALLY INSPIRED MUSIC: PETER ILYITCH TCHAIKOVSKY,

## 1840-1893

The professional life in music of this composer began late, at the age of twenty-two. Previously he had had several music teachers, but none of these discerned any signs of genius in their pupil. Upon making the decision to be a musician, Tchaikovsky applied himself to the study of musical theory with such good effect that after three years Nicholas Rubenstein engaged him as professor of harmony at the newly estab-

PLATE XXXIV. *Peter Ilyitch Tchaikovsky. Painting by Kusnezoff. (Courtesy of The Tretiakov Gallery, Moscow.)*

lished Conservatory in Moscow. From this time on his musical career progressed rapidly. In 1876 there began a strange friendship with Nadejda von Meck, the widow of a wealthy railroad magnate, who found great emotional satisfaction in Tchaikovsky's music. She began by commissioning works from him at generous fees, and in 1877 settled on him an annuity of 6,000 rubles. In spite of their warm friendship as evidenced in their letters to each other, the two met only twice and by accident, and never shared each other's company. In 1878 he resigned his teaching position, and used his time to compose and travel. From 1887 on he began conducting concerts of his own works, although he was extremely shy and nervous, and, in 1891, came to America, where he conducted concerts in connection with the dedication of Carnegie Hall in New York, as well as others in Baltimore and Philadelphia. In the last year of his life he composed his Sixth Symphony, the "Pathetique," and, shortly after conducting the premiere of that work in St. Petersburg, drank a glass of unpurified water and fell victim to a cholera epidemic then prevalent.

Tchaikovsky's music mirrors the man. Shy, irritable, neurotically emotional and pessimistic on one hand, and on the other exhibiting a childlike delight in the ballet and fantasy pieces, this composer reveals again the typical dual personality of the Romantic composer. In all of his music there appears this ambivalence, but the extremes may be typified by his symphonic music, on the side of emotional instability, and the music of his ballets such as *The Nutcracker* and *The Sleeping Beauty* on the other. Sometimes they mingle, as in the second movement of the Sixth Symphony, and the contrast is heightened, but not resolved. The emotionalism of his serious music, with its dark, brooding sections and almost hysterical climaxes, is easily understood by even the untutored listener, and has often caused the musical highbrows to regard him with disdain. But if one of the criteria used in judging a composer is his ability to communicate with his audience, then Tchaikovsky ranks high. Of course, there must be taken into account the value of what he is communicating — and for Tchaikovsky each listener must decide upon this point for himself. About one facet of his music there can be no doubt: Tchaikovsky is a great melodist. True, his melodies are not of the same expressive types as those of Mozart, Beethoven, Brahms or Bach, but then he is interested in expressing other things than they were. There is often a touch of Russian folk-song in Tchaikovsky's melodies, although he was not a self-conscious Russian composer, as were his contemporaries Moussorgsky and Borodin. His colorful orchestration is always effective and as simple and straightforward as circumstances will permit. He revels in shattering climaxes, but his use of the lower instruments of the orchestra is notable, particularly when he is exploring the darker emotions of pessimism and melancholy. All in all, it is very simple music, but with the simplicity of genius.

Despite a number of compositions in the realms of chamber music, song, and piano pieces, Tchaikovsky's real habitat is the orchestra. Here he ceases sounding like a salon composer of pretty dainties, and reaches his full stature. Of the six symphonies which he composed, the last three are standard concert fare; the first three are infrequently played. His concerto for the violin is a standard in the literature of that instrument, as is his first piano concerto in B♭-minor. The second and third piano concertos are seldom played. He composed a number of symphonic poems and overtures inspired by literature and history, among which the favorites are *"Francesca da Rimini"* (after Dante), *"Romeo and Juliet"* (a so-called "fantasy-overture"), and the *1812 Overture*, based upon the defeat of Napoleon in Russia that year. A *Marche Slave*, and the *Capriccio Italien* are often heard, as are movements from the *Serenade* for string orchestra. He composed seven operas but the only one performed with any frequency outside of Russia is *Eugen Onegin*, after a story by Pushkin. Occasionally an aria, *"Adieu forets"* from *Jeanne d'Arc* appears on recital programs as does his song *"Nur wer die Sehnsucht kennt"* ("None but the Lonely Heart") on words by Goethe. The ballets *Swan Lake*, *The Sleeping Beauty* and *The Nutcracker* are in the repertory of practically every professional company the world over.

### Overture-Fantasy Romeo and Juliet

Let us now take a closer look at the music of this composer, keeping in mind that he is the contemporary of Johannes Brahms, whom we have just studied, as well as of Liszt and of Wagner, whose music we shall deal with shortly. Probably the best work for introductory purposes is the Overture-Fantasy *Romeo and Juliet*, since it contains in a rather short movement — compared with the symphonic works, at least — the essential qualities of Tchaikovsky's style: dark colors, intense climaxes, clear and effective orchestration, his personal brand of lyricism, and his way of treating a literary program.

First, there is a long introduction which consists of a series of rather short variations of the thematic material stated in the first two of the sections (Example 68a). There are about eight of these in all, the last serving as a transition to the main thematic and key area of the work. The function of this introduction is to establish atmosphere and mood, and introduce a theme to be used later on. Some commentators relate it to Friar Lawrence of the play, but let us discuss the implications of that after we have heard the music.

The first thematic element of the sonata-allegro form — Tchaikovsky style — which follows is rhythmic and rather abrupt in manner,

EXAMPLE 68.

INTRODUCTION: Andante

PRINCIPAL SUBJECT: Allegro guisto

SECOND SUBJECT: Allegro guisto

431

and Tchaikovsky gives it length and substance by developing it in a manner which leads with increasing intensity to a full-scale climax complete with cymbal crashes (Example 68b). There follows a codetta which has the effect of closing off this thematic area into a self-contained unit. The tempo slackens, and a preparation is made for the key of the next section, which, after B-minor of the first section might be expected to be the relative major, D-major, or possibly the dominant, F♯-major. But no, Tchaikovsky has decided that a key farther away is the right one, and we find ourselves in D♭-major. Possibly he wishes to show by this choice how much the lovers — for this is undoubtedly love music which follows — are in a beautiful world of their own making, far away from the B-minor strife of the first theme. At any rate the composer now gives us one of his finest melodic inspirations, one which expresses the longing and tenderness of the lovers (Example 68c). This is developed in much the same manner as the first theme to produce an entire and complete section. This procedure is typical of the way Tchaikovsky regards the sonata-allegro form, together with the habit of slowing the tempo for lyric sections. The development is devoted largely to a quasi-contrapuntal treatment of the theme of the introduction and the first theme of the exposition, building the dynamics little by little to the climactic entrance of the main theme in the recapitulation. Aiding in this crescendo are syncopated chords, rushing scales, and excited passages in rapid notes through which the trumpet calls pierce. The recapitulation having been gained, Tchaikovsky does not slow down now to create complete sections — the drama must rush to its tragic conclusion. The intensity of the first theme subsides to the lyricism of the second, but this too builds to an ecstatic climax. The first theme is brought back as a closing section — one which corresponds to no similar place in the exposition — and, after an exciting series of syncopated chords and much fireworks, the final phrase is entrusted to the basses and cellos, after which a dramatic timpani roll ushers in the coda. This coda is one of the great summations in all romantic symphonic literature. It is developmental, to be sure — but it is much more than that. It seems to utter from the profoundest depths of human sympathy and feeling a summation of the noble brief and sublime tragedy embodied in the story of the "star-crossed lovers."

Whether Tchaikovsky meant themes and sections to illustrate certain episodes in the story is uncertain. What is certain is that he seized upon the essence of the story and transmuted it into music understandable in terms of any tragedy. The play must use characters, but the music has no need for these, and approaches universality more nearly. The parlor game of assigning themes to each of the episodes is harmless, but not really necessary — the music speaks for itself, as it should. To argue about Tchaikovsky's use of the sonata-allegro form in this work would be pedantic. It is a successful employment of the basic parts of that musical organization, and that is what is important. It probably would not be so right for Brahms, or Schumann, or Mendelssohn — but this does not matter, except for purposes of comparison in order to gain insight into the musical personalities of those composers. The balance of sections, the choice of keys, the changing tempos — all combine with Tchaikovskian lyricism and orchestration to form a musically compelling work.

## Symphony No. 6, in B-minor

Let us now turn to Tchaikovsky's Symphony No. 6, probably his finest composition, revealing as it does his romantic view of life, full of melancholy, hopeless struggle and fatalism. It is indeed remarkable that with such an outlook this man could compose music, and no small tribute to his strength of character that he wrote masterpieces. In a revealing letter to Madame von Meck he says that work is the saving force in his life, work and the almost trancelike state into which his musical inspirations cast him. Beethoven called such a state a "raptus." When this happens, the world recedes into oblivion, and nothing exists save the musical fever in the brain translating the inspired sounds into notes on paper. The awareness of time ceases to exist and bodily discomforts are not felt. One part of the composer's brain often seems to stand aside, watching and wondering at the process. Tchaikovsky said that he could plunge himself into such states at will by beginning to write, using craftsmanship, and the state of inspiration would come gradually. At such times, he said, everything he wrote was good. The Sixth Symphony is probably largely the product of such inspirational states.

*First Movement:* With the example of the *Romeo and Juliet* overture so fresh in mind, we shall experience little difficulty with the first movement of the Sixth Symphony, for the two resemble each other quite closely. Both have slow introductions, quite independent first and second thematic sections in contrasting tempos, cumulative developments which rush headlong into the recapitulations and codas which

summarize the movement's emotional qualities. The symphonic movement is somewhat more tightly constructed, since it employs a germ
theme which is introduced in the *adagio* (Example 69a) and transformed or incorporated into the principal theme (Example 69b),
the second subject (Example 69d) and the closing material (Example
69e, f). In addition to this unifying idea, a secondary germ theme is
also introduced in this movement, but does not become really important until the third movement. It consists of the plain or decorated
interval of a fourth, either ascending or descending, and is first exposed
at the beginning of the transition between the first and second thematic
areas (Example 69c), a position whose relation to the second theme is
somewhat analogous to that of the primary germ theme to the first
theme. Similarly, it is incorporated into the second measure quoted of
the second theme. Another useful motive is the half or whole step,
which appears in the primary motto as well as in its inversion during
the second half of both the main and second themes, and in other
movements of the symphony.

*Second Movement:* The second movement is formally quite clear,
ABA-coda. But it has other interesting features. One of these is that
it is written in quintuple meter — 5/4 — subdivided in two beats
plus three beats. This gives it somewhat the aspect of a waltz, especially
since the melody is of that type (although upon conducting or counting the meter, one finds that waltzing to it might be difficult!). The
graceful melody begins with two rising phrases each of which is composed of the first three notes of the germ theme used twice (Example
69g). The following phrases descend similarly, although not so closely
adhering to the three-note figure. The A part is in binary form, of
which the second section begins with a particularly charming development of the melody. In other surroundings this might be some of
Tchaikovsky's best ballet music. The orchestration is apt and characteristic for we find the ubiquitous scale passages adding their simple
decoration to the more involved melodies. The trio (B section) offers
contrast to the first section, for it is in minor, and has a brooding
melancholy, as though Tchaikovsky beckons us to look under the
surface gayety to find grey thoughts. The descending melody (Example
69h) exploits the descending whole or half step which first appeared
in the primary germ theme, and the complementary ascending melody
which follows progresses in short scales outlining successive intervals
of the fourth (Example 69i). By means of a transition in which he

434

EXAMPLE 69.

I. INTRODUCTION: Adagio

a.

PRINCIPAL SUBJECT: Allegro

b.

c.

SECOND SUBJECT: Andante

d.

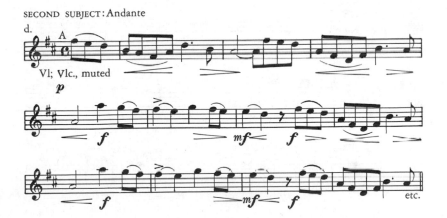

Moderato mosso

e. Fl. & Fg.

*p*

f.

Ww.

*f* espr.

II. Allegro con grazia

g. Vlc.

*mf*       3                    *mf*       3

*f*

*ff*

TRIO

Vl. 1 & Fl.

h.                    STEP              HALF-STEP              STEP              STEP              etc.

Vl. II    *p*

i. later              4TH                    4TH                    4TH

Str.  *p*

4TH              PRIM. MOTTO    Ww.              Str.

*pp*              *p*              *mp*              etc.

436

## III. PRINCIPAL SUBJECT-PART 1: Allegro molto vivace

j.

*p* Str.

Ww.   Str.   Cl.   etc.

### PART 2

k.

Str.

*p*   etc.

*f*   SCALE   etc.

### IMPORTANT MOTIVES

4TH   + SCALE

### SECOND SUBJECT

l.

Cl.   4TH   4TH   4TH   4TH   4TH   4TH

*p*

4TH   4TH

etc.

## IV. PRINCIPAL SUBJECT: Adagio lamentoso

SPAN OF 4TH

m.

Str.   *f*   *mf*   *p*

introduces the rhythmic figures of the A section, Tchaikovsky leads
us out of the shadows and back to the quasi-waltz. But the sobriety of
the trio returns in the coda as if to remind us that reality still lurks
at our elbow.

*Third Movement:* The third movement is a combination of scherzo
and march, but so subtly are the two woven together that it is difficult
to tell "which came first." The form resembles that of a sonatina
quite closely, but Tchaikovsky chooses to wink at tradition in the
exposition, for he introduces the march theme together with the first
theme of the scherzo (Example 69j, k). Of course we do not realize this
except in retrospect. The principal germ theme may be found in
this movement, but it plays no obvious part. For example, the second
half of the scherzo theme with which the movement opens may be said
to be constructed of units of the germ theme. But it goes by so rapidly
and with so little emphasis on the germ theme shape, that we hardly
notice the construction. What *is* important in this piece is the interval of
a fourth, for it is the basic interval out of which the "bugle call" theme
of the march is constructed (Example 69l). In addition, the scale
plays an important part in this movement — at one point scales run
riot as Tchaikovsky uses them to maintain a high pitch of excitement
before the final march section. This excitement continues until the
very end of the movement, and provides a bright spot in an otherwise
rather somber symphony.

*Fourth Movement:* The final movement, a sonatina form marked to be played *adagio lamentoso,* opens with a cry of despair. Musically this is formed out of a descending scale figure of five notes which turns back one note at the end, thus resembling an expanded and inverted version of the primary germ theme while at the same time using the interval of a fourth between the first and last notes of the phrase (Example 69m). Orchestrally, its strange and passionate color is the result of crossing of the string parts in such a way that the first violins alternate with the seconds in the descending scale. A little later, the woodwinds have a sequenced and inverted version of the more familiar three-note germ theme, and after a repetition of the main theme a short transition brings us to the second theme (Example 69n). The accompaniment begins first, a hesitant rhythmic figure in the horn, and over this unfolds a theme of noble resignation and mourning. It is essentially the same theme as the first subject, but now in even, rather slow notes, without the despairing passion of the previous one. As it progresses, carried by the strings, it rises higher and higher, developing dynamically, and increasing in tempo until a full-orchestra climax arrives, from which the strings cascade in ever faster descending scales until brought to an abrupt halt by a percussive chord. All of this development has been concerned with the descending scale theme, either first or second subjects, and the syncopated accompaniment pattern which, at the climax, is taken over by the whole brass and woodwind section.

The next section returns to the tempo of the second theme, and, using the first phrase of that theme, establishes the dominant chord in preparation for the recapitulation. This comes with a struggling upsurge of the strings to the first note of the theme — a procedure which is quite frequent from this point on. The material is developed to another climax, at which level it remains for some time, in an excess of despair, then quiets down in a bridge passage notable for its use of low brass harmonies. The second theme now sounds like coda material, its nobility departed, leaving only resigned melancholy, descending lower and lower in pitch until it fades away in the blackest regions of the orchestral range.

The balance of sections is interesting in this movement. In the exposition, the noble second theme is developed, while in the recapitulation it is the sorrowing first theme. Surely this is done on purpose with the intention to leave the listener with the pathetic, hopeless feeling rather than the "so be it" of the second theme. The unity of

439

this movement could hardly be improved upon, since the melodic design of the two themes is almost identical. And the fact that both are derivations of the germ theme helps to connect the movement musically with the others. The emotional connection between the finale and the first movement hardly needs pointing out. Indeed, the whole symphony coheres emotionally and artistically in a remarkable degree, even if it does not lift the spirit. Perhaps the *katharsis* of the ancient Greeks — the purging of the emotions by tragedy — is at work in this symphony, where we share Tchaikovsky's terror, hopelessness and fatalism.

## DESCRIPTIVE MUSIC: FRANZ LISZT, 1811-1886

Liszt is, in many respects, the Byron of music. He revealed in his compositions a temperament fiery and bold, a pioneer spirit in that movement called the "music of the future" which opposed the conservatism of Brahms so violently. He was the foremost pianist of his day, and the friend and benefactor of many of his colleagues, among them Berlioz, Chopin and Wagner. Himself a none too stable union of opposing tendencies, he typifies the best in progressive romanticism, as well as the worst in oversentimental and gaudy vulgarity. It is unfortunate that many of his weaker compositions have gained popularity through their shallowness and superficial brilliance, for Lizst also composed many sensitive and expressive works. He realized, like Schumann, but more keenly, that the new music needed new forms, and during his career sought solutions for this problem. He adopted Berlioz' transformation of the *idée fixe* in principle, making it generally applicable to the development of thematic material, whether the basic *idée* had programmatic significance or not. Thus, we frequently find in the music of Liszt a series of sections, each devoted to a particular mood and using as thematic material a transformation of the basic theme suited to the prevailing sentiment. This kind of sectionalism replaces the classic idea of development so firmly held and exploited by Brahms. In essence, theme transformation is a kind of melodic variation rather than development, although in the music of Liszt and others development occurs as well. As we shall see, Liszt reasoned parallel to Schumann, matching the "total sonata-allegro" construction of the Fourth Symphony with a similar form in his First Piano Concerto. He was a superlative performer of Beethoven's piano works, by all accounts, and undoubtedly had delved deeply into that master's formal procedures, adapting those which suited his style, theme transformation among them.

Liszt was fully equipped to carry the romantic banner to new heights but for one element which was lacking: genius of the searching and universal kind, the variety possessed by Beethoven, Mozart and Bach. These were whole men, whereas Liszt was not. The fatal romantic ambivalence divided him between worldliness and religion. Repeatedly Liszt announced his retirement from the concert stage and his retreat to meditation and institutional security. This ambivalence is found in his music, some of which reflects the vulgarity of the concert showman; in other works we find a purely musical romanticism of the most refined kind.

Liszt wrote a great amount of piano music as a matter of course. In these works he developed a piano style similar to that of Chopin, but more varied in figuration and sonority, and more impetuous in temper. For Liszt, the piano matches the orchestra, and he manages to secure almost orchestral sounds from the instrument. His music is less straightforward than Chopin's and often progresses impulsively, breaking into cascades of rippling cadenza-like figures at emotional climaxes. Among his more worthwhile compositions are the volumes entitled *Années de Pèlerinage* (*Years of Wandering*) in which he describes or tells stories in music about what he saw, heard and felt during his travels in Switzerland and Italy. Other piano works include the *Hungarian Rhapsodies*, based on gypsy music, the *Harmonies poetiques et religeuses*, the *Transcendental Etudes* after Paganini, and many miscellaneous compositions. Liszt also devoted much time to the transcription of vocal and orchestral literature for the piano. Many Schubert songs were thus treated, usually in sensitive and pianistic renditions. The *Symphonie Fantastique* of Berlioz is available in a Liszt transcription, as are many of the orchestral compositions of Richard Wagner, who was, by the way, Liszt's son-in-law.

## "Petrarch Sonnets" (Piano Solo)

Let us choose several representative works of Liszt for our examination. The three "Petrarch Sonnets" from the *Années* exhibit his composition and pianism at its most refined. The sonnets were addressed to his beloved and unattainable Laura by Petrarch, and of the series, Liszt chose to transmute into music those numbered 47, 104, and 123.

However, one does not need the poems to appreciate the music, for there is no program in any of them for the composer to follow. Rather, here are protestations of love, complaints of the pangs of love, and similar states of passion for which Lisztian music is the ideal expression. Each of the compositions has a short introduction, and then proceeds to present a melodic theme which is treated sectionally in various ways, breaking out now and then into cadenza-like passages. Liszt's use of non-final cadences is interesting, as is the chromatic accompaniment in many spots. There is typical discontinuity of tempo and motion resulting from the varying emotional states of the music, but thematic unity due to the use of theme transformation.

### Les Préludes, Tone Poem for Orchestra

In the realm of orchestral music, the name of Liszt is usually associated with the *tone poem,* or *symphonic poem,* although it does not originate with him. In a composition of this kind, the music consists of sections whose moods match those of the verses, and is constructed out of transformations of a basic melodic motive. Such a work is the most famous of the Liszt tone poems, *Les Préludes,* after a poem by Lamartine. However, as we shall discover, the general outlines of the music also roughly conform to a species of purely musical architecture — that of the sonata-allegro. The poem begins, "What is life but a series of preludes to that unknown song the first solemn note of which is sounded by death? Love is the magic dawn of every existence, but where is the life in which the first enjoyment of bliss is not dispelled by some tempest? . . . Yet no man is content to resign himself for long to the mild beneficent charms of Nature; when the trumpet gives the alarm, he hastens to the post of danger, so that he may find in action full consciousness of himself, and the possession of all his powers." Quoted here are the sections most meaningful to the understanding of the music.

The composition begins quietly with two *pizzicato* notes in the strings, after which the melodic motive is announced by them (Example 70a). The important part of it is the first three notes, C-B-E, a motive which is subjected to a great number of transformations. The introductory section has considerable discontinuity of motion, now hurrying forward, now slowing down. After a long dominant preparation, the main part of the work begins with the motive in the trombones, sounded out against chords in the winds and *arpeggios* in the

EXAMPLE 70.

Andante

a.

Andante maestoso

b.

c.

Allegro ma non troppo

d.

Allegro tempestoso
e.

Allegretto pastorale
f.

Allegro marziale
g.

strings (Example 70b). Transferred to the basses, the motive moves forward, and arrives at a quiet lyric section, undoubtedly signaling the "magic dawn of every existence." Shortly thereafter the motive is transformed almost out of recognition in a version given to the horns (Example 70c), then transferred to the whole orchestra, and built up to a climax which subsides to a few questioning chords created from the motive and given to the upper woodwinds. The "tempest" begins ominously in the low strings, which sound the motive and attach to it a chromatic scale figure (Example 70d). Again a climax builds, this time using, among other devices, the chromatic scale we heard in the *Symphonie Fantastique*. The tempo accelerates, the motive is hurled out by the low brass (Example 70e), a martial rhythm develops, and then the dynamics die down, the tempo slackens, and a pastoral section ensues (Example 70f). This symbolizes the retreat — so dear to the romantics — to nature, away from the world. The motive is present here, and various chamber-music textures and sonorities employ it as an incidental figure. The love music reappears and expands, but a sharp rhythm in the brass "gives the alarm," and the last section of the work develops and transforms the motive into a series of military calls (Example 70g). The long dominant preparation heard previously is brought back, and leads to the last part, ostensibly the coda, which ends the work in a blaze of glory.

We have seen how the music matches the poem; but notice how it resembles also the general plan of a large sonata-allegro — exposition — motive in its first forms provides the first thematic and key area (C-major): the "love music" constitutes the second thematic area, and is in the key of E-major: development — the "tempest": recapitulation — the "love music" is brought back first, then the section which repeats in somewhat altered form the part devoted to the motive in the exposition; and finally, coda. It departs slightly from the normal, but resembles the sonata-allegro nearly enough to provide a more traditional framework for the piece. The music is not descriptively realistic in the same way as Berlioz' symphony, but still furnishes a number of clues as to what is transpiring. This work contains some of Liszt's most poetic ideas, as well as others which are bombastic and rather empty. Here we have the man, mirrored in his music.

### Piano Concerto No. 1, E♭-major

The next large work to be examined is the Piano Concerto No. 1, in E♭. Here Liszt is not bound by a program, but must use abstract musical architecture for the construction. This is not a traditional concerto, but is more like the Schumann Fourth Symphony. The concerto consists of three movements, the last two of which are linked together. This is the sequence of sections in the first movement:

Section 1: Motto theme (Ex. 71, Ia) stated by orchestra.
Section 2: Display passages by the piano, culminating in a cadenza marked *grandioso.*
Section 3: Orchestra repeats motto theme.
Section 4: Piano interrupts with a lyric theme (Ex. 71, Ib), joined by the clarinet and strings in chamber music sonorities.
Section 5: Recapitulation of the motto theme and cadenzas (sections 1 and 2 above).
Section 6: Coda.

EXAMPLE 71.

I. Allegro maestoso

a.

b.

II. Quasi adagio

III. Vivace

445

The second movement is devoted almost entirely to the melody heard at its beginning, first in the orchestra, then in the piano (Example 71, II). A double-trill in the piano part connects the two movements. The first part of the last movement is a scherzo (Example 71, III) which begins with the famous triangle solo for which Liszt was so harshly criticized. The scherzo material is developed until the return of the motto signals a general recapitulation of all important material. The beginning of the first movement is reviewed, then that of the second movement, then the scherzo; and finally, at the end, the motto theme in cadenza style in the piano part supported by the orchestra brings the work to an emphatic close. So, we see that, like Schumann, Liszt here uses a grand recapitulation in order to bring all the themes to our attention one last time, and so create unity.

Here we have the first important cyclic piano concerto, establishing in this medium what had already been consummated in the symphony. It might have been more effective had the work been longer — as it is, it lasts about eighteen minutes, far shorter than any but the classical concertos. But it indicates the way in which Liszt regarded the problem, and a possible solution. Certainly, it fits Liszt's style, which, in its showiness and improvisatory quality requires something less rigorous than the classical form. In harmony, cadential practices, and use of the orchestra it resembles closely the music of this composer previously heard, although it is admittedly less programmatic than those works.

## RICHARD WAGNER, 1813-1883

This composer is preeminent in the Romantic era for the development of new harmonic and orchestral techniques as well as for the creation of the music drama. His influence was so great that composers of the latter half of this century found it necessary to take sides for or against him; thus arose the Brahms-Wagner opposition. We have already discussed Wagner's theories concerning the opera, and mentioned his use of the orchestra, contrasting it with that of Berlioz. It now remains to be seen and heard how those theories and ideas, as well as the technique of chromatic harmony which Wagner developed, are used in the music. Many discussions and synopses of the operas and music dramas are to be found on the shelves of any library, so we will not recapitulate them here. We have chosen to illustrate Wagner's

446

PLATE XXXV. *Richard Wagner. (New York Public Library).*

techniques in excerpts from three of his music dramas: *Die Walküre, Die Götterdämmerung* and *Tristan und Isolde.* The first two of these are from the opera cycle *Der Ring des Nibelungen (The Ring of the Nibelungs)*, which is made up of four operas, *Das Rheingold (The Gold of the Rhine), Die Walküre (The Valkyrie), Siegfried* and *Die Götterdämmerung (The Twilight of the Gods).*

### "Magic Fire Music"

From *Die Walküre,* the "Magic Fire Music" is a frequently played selection. While this is a section of the opera and includes voices, it is often heard as an orchestral transcription, resulting in a species of tone poem. Here, instruments replace the voices. Two of the drama's leading characters are involved: Brünnhilde, the Valkyrie, and Wotan, her father, king of the gods. Brünnhilde has aided a mortal in battle

447

against Wotan's orders, and, to punish her, he condemns her to everlasting sleep. But she is his favorite daughter, so, moved by her entreaties, he changes the sentence: she will become mortal, and will sleep on a mountain-top surrounded by a circle of magic fire until the kiss of a hero brave enough to defy Wotan and go through the fire awakens her to be his bride. All of this has been preordained by the three Fates, or Norns, who spin out the thread of existence.

As the music opens, we hear the "sleep" motive (Example 72a) softly in the orchestra as Wotan places the sleeping Valkyrie under a fir-tree on the mountain-top, and covers her with her shield. The music descends into the low register, and the sinister "fate" motive (Example 72b) appears twice. Then Wotan strides solemnly to the center of the stage, points with his spear to a large rock. Here the brass sound (Example 72c), reminding us of his promise to his daughter. He calls upon Loge, the fire-god (in concert versions the voice part is usually taken by trombones at this point), and a chromatically rising harmonic complex is heard as Loge draws near. Wotan strikes the rock three times with his spear, and upon the third stroke a flash of flame issues from the rock, symbolized by a rapidly mounting chromatic scale which culminates in the music of Example 72d. Wotan directs the fire with his spear, and it surrounds the mountain-top. We hear now the "sleep" and "magic fire" motives combined as the god takes a last farewell of his daughter, and directs that "he who fears not the spearpoint of Wotan shall cross the fire." As this occurs the *leitmotiv* of "Siegfried the Volsung," appears in the music, combined with the "sleep" and "magic fire" motives (Example 72f). Wotan then turns and departs, and the music comes to a conclusion as the stage curtains slowly close.

## "Siegfried's Rhine Journey"

Our second example, "Siegfried's Rhine Journey," occurs one opera later than the "Magic Fire Music." The intervening drama has introduced us to Siegfried, the hero, and we have followed his growth from boyhood to young manhood. During this time, he has forged a magic sword and with it slain the dragon who guarded the ring made from the accursed Rhinegold. He is accosted in one of the later scenes by Wotan, and shatters that god's spear with his sword, thus presaging the downfall of the gods (to be accomplished in the last opera *Die Götterdämmerung*), as well as fulfilling one of the require-

448

EXAMPLE 72.

SLEEP
a. Langsam

FATE
b.

$pp < pp$

WOTAN'S PROMISE
c. Mässig bewegt

$f$

Trmb.

etc.

MAGIC FIRE
d. Mässig bewegt

Str.

$mf$

Ww., Br.

etc.

SIEGFRIED, SLEEP
e.

$f$

etc.

ments for the awakening of Brünnhilde, which occurs in the last act of the opera *Siegfried*.

As *Götterdämmerung* opens, the three Fates are seen spinning, and when their thread breaks, dire catastrophe is foretold. They vanish, and at this point the music with which we are concerned begins. We hear the "fate" motive (Example 73a), after which Wagner paints an orchestral picture of dawn in a short section. During this, and immediately after, we hear the motive of "Siegfried the hero" in the brass, followed by that of Brünnhilde (Examples 73b and c). The latter motive is used to spin out a section which is noted in the score as "sunrise and the transition to full daylight." The conversation between Siegfried and Brünnhilde is omitted in the concert version, but in it Brünnhilde sends him forth to new deeds of valor. The concert version skips at this point to the motive of Siegfried the hero, but in a developed, boisterously syncopated version which appears in the opera after the vocal section. He sets out on his journey toward the Rhine, and is soon out of sight of the audience, but Brünnhilde (Example 73c) follows him with her eyes; she hears the adventurous

EXAMPLE 73.

BRUNNHILDE'S LOVE

SIEGFRIED'S HORN: ADVENTURE

MAGIC FIRE RECOLLECTION, SIEGFRIED'S HORN

THE RHINE

RENUNCIATION OF LOVE

h, Rasch

RHINE-MAIDENS AND RHINEGOLD

i, Rasch

RHINEGOLD

LATER:

452

sound of his horn in the distance (Example 73e), and muses on their love (Example 73d). The curtain is now lowered, and the music which follows acts as an introduction to the main portion of the music drama which ensues. During this music we hear recollections of *leitmotive* introduced in the "Magic Fire Music" in which the fire motive is combined with that of Siegfried's horn (Example 73f). As the hero approaches the river, the Rhine motive rises sonorously through the orchestra (Example 73g). When the gold was stolen from the Rhine, a curse was put upon it, and it was stated that if the possessor of the gold would renounce love he should rule the world. This prophecy is recalled (Example 73h), as are the Rhine-maidens and gold (Example 73i). The motive of "renunciation of love" (Example 73h) appears again, followed by a concert ending based on the *leitmotiv* of Siegfried the hero. In the opera, the music flows into the first scene.

### "Prelude" and "Liebestod" from Tristan und Isolde

Our next two examples are drawn from the epoch-making *Tristan und Isolde,* the plot of which may be briefly stated in this way: Isolde, a young Irish princess unwillingly betrothed to the aged King Mark of Cornwall, determines to commit suicide during the sea voyage to her future home. Tristan, under whose protection she has been placed, is the nephew and trusted henchman of the king; during a previous battle he killed Isolde's lover, and in revenge she plans to poison him also. She bids her maid to prepare a lethal cup of wine, but out of affection the maid disobeys and instead prepares a love potion which has the expected result. After their arrival in Cornwall, their guilty love is discovered by King Mark, Tristan is wounded in the fray which follows and flees to his castle followed in turn by Isolde and the king. When she arrives, Tristan is dead. King Mark comes upon the scene and, after hearing of the love potion, forgives them. In the closing *"Liebestod,"* Isolde imagines a vision of Tristan, alive and transfigured, and ecstatically vows a deathless love as her spirit departs to join his.

The predominant emotion of this opera is that of longing — the desires of love, and the desire for death and union in death — and Wagner's basic problem was that of transmuting his feeling into music. He accomplished it by the use of complex chromatic harmony. The chords are continually seeking resolution, but the cadences, when they finally arrive, are apt to be deceptive, thus postponing any sense of finality, and prolonging the motion. The complex chords add rich-ness of sonority to the music, as well as instability to the harmony. In much of the opera, orchestral polyphony provides the background for the voices, using as its material the various *leitmotive*. The sonority of the orchestra is predominantly dark as befits a tragedy in which night and death play such a large part. Let us listen to two sections of the work, the "Prelude" and the *"Liebestod"* (*"Love-death"*) of Isolde. The first is played before the curtain opens, of course, and is woven out of the motives to be found in Example 74 where they are listed in order of their appearance in the music. There are many points of resemblance among them, which, weakening their individuality, add to the unity and coherence of the work. Wagner realized this, and by resemblances in motive detail suggests the relations between these ideas and things. Incidentally, it is noteworthy that Isolde and Mark do not possess *leitmotive,* and the sole one for Tristan, "Tristan the hero," appears only in the last scene of the first act, so important are the *psychological forces* and their *symbols.* In this opera perhaps more than in any other, Wagner's orchestra is the psychological interpreter of the stage action; the drama lives more fully in the music than on the stage. In the "Prelude," a structure appears which we have encountered only in its formative stages in other music. This is the *dynamic curve,* a term which will be used to describe the gradual crescendo from a very soft beginning to a loud climax in which the whole orchestra takes part. Such a form is this "Prelude," and our next example, the *"Liebestod."* Both of these subside rather quickly after the climax, another frequent feature of this formal design.

The motives for the *"Liebestod"* are to be found in Example 74 and include also the first two listed for the "Prelude." This excerpt is often played in a concert version without the voices, but to be appreciated to the fullest extent, it should be heard with the voice of Isolde mingling with the magnificent motivic polyphony. Wagner treats the voice in two ways: the traditional manner, as a singing voice predominant over the orchestral accompaniment, and as an instru-ment of the orchestra, the way it is used in the *"Liebestod."*

*Tristan und Isolde* provoked violent reactions among its hearers. Many, of course, felt that it was sublime. But Berlioz wrote, "Wagner is evidently mad," and many shared his feeling. As an example of the most advanced harmonic technique, it has had incalculable results. The style was imitated and developed by later composers such as Schönberg in his tone poem for string sextet, *Verklärte Nacht*

EXAMPLE 74.

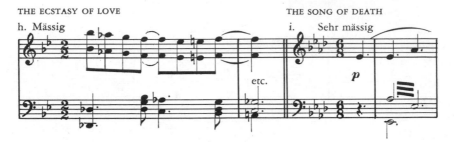

(*Transfigured Night*). And it gave rise to the atonal, or twelve-tone system of composition evolved by this composer. The reactions were equally strong among those who did not like Tristan — and in the revolt impressionism was born. We of this century have no idea what a burning issue Wagnerianism was in the latter half of the Romantic era and how valiantly the composers of the early twentieth century struggled to free themselves from its influence.

# NATIONALISM

During the Romantic era, a wave of music whose roots were the folk idioms of the Balkan, Slavic, Scandinavian, and Iberian peoples spread over Europe. The nations of these regions had been on the outer edge of a musical culture led by the Italians, Austrians, Germans and French since the sixteenth century. Now they produced composers who for several reasons employed the native resources of their individual countries for musical composition. These new and fresh materials were rooted in the rhythms of dances and folk songs, the scales and harmonies to be heard in the music of the people, and in the composer's feeling for the spirit of his native language and the genius of his people.

We have seen that the Romantic artist was interested in anything new, strange and exotic. Folk music supplied this need with hitherto unsuspected riches. Legends and stories upon which musical compositions could be based existed in the folklore, waiting to be dramatized. The sounds of native instruments could be imitated or introduced into the orchestra for new effects. All that was required was a composer "of the people" who could recognize the worth of these materials, and who had the ability to assimilate them into his personal musical language and then employ them.

### BOHEMIA

Two such composers emerged from the Balkan part of the Austro-Hungarian Empire, that section usually called Bohemia. They were Bedrich Smetana (1824-1884), and Antonin Dvořák (1841-1904). Hardly a work exists by these composers which does not use folkloric materials. Smetana is best known for his folk-opera *The Bartered Bride,* and his tone-poems, *The Moldau* (a Bohemian river) and *From Bohemia's Forests and Meadows,* both of which belong to a series of such works entitled *Ma Vlast (My Fatherland)*. His string-quartet entitled *"From My Life,"* is sometimes heard. A very personal work, this composition incorporates in it the continuous high note which Smetana heard ringing in his ears during his later years when he was becoming deaf.

Antonin Dvořák's principal claim to fame in America is his Fifth Symphony, subtitled "From the New World." Though it was largely composed during a visit to this country, it contains little that is native American: the subtitle is correct, for it is a composition *from* the New World, not *of* it. The other symphonies are also Czech in spirit as are the *Slavonic Dances,* the "Carnaval Overture," and the chamber music, which often incorporates in its construction a lament called a *"Dumka."*

RUSSIA

In Russia, a new form of nationalism developed. The Bohemian composers were content to capture the idiom of the people in music constructed and harmonized in the more-or-less accepted fashion of European music. Not so the Russians. Out with German academicism! Out with all European influences! The less technique the composer knew, the better — *then* he would write Russian music from his heart. He would evolve new forms, ideas, musical textures and sounds from the richness of the Russian heritage, both of the folk and the church. The group of five composers who set themselves up as the standard-bearers of the Russian music despised German compositional technique, and went blundering among the sharps and flats hoping to discover, by intuition it would seem, masterpieces which surely must be lurking just around the next corner. That they *did* discover some is to be marveled at. The group of "The Mighty Five" consisted of Mily Balakirev (1834-1910), the leader, Cesar Cui (1835-1918), Alexander Borodin (1834-1887), Nicholas Rimsky-Korsakoff (1844-1908) and Modeste Moussorgsky (1839-1881). Of these, only three, Borodin, Rimsky-Korsakoff and Moussorgsky, rose to musical eminence. Only one became a professional musican in the sense that he derived his living from music: Rimsky-Korsakoff, who was first a naval officer, and who later became an inspector of naval bands as well as a professor in the conservatory. Borodin was a medical chemist, and Moussorgsky, the only real genius among them, had a minor post with the government for a time, lost it, and devoted his time to composition and drinking. He died an alcoholic, mourned by his compatriots as one whose ineptness would never win for him a place in music. All except Rimsky-Korsakoff despised their famous colleague, Tchaikovsky, for they felt that he had succumbed to the German musical poisons then being spread by Wagner, Brahms, Schumann and Mendelssohn. That Rimsky-Korsakoff did not agree entirely with them is shown by his later decision to study musical theory, using Tchaikovsky's text on harmony and counterpoint as a guide. He was appointed to a teaching post at the conservatory, and, in his charming autobiography, *My Musical Life,* says that he was the best student the conservatory ever had, studying diligently to keep ahead of his students.

Both Borodin and Rimsky-Korsakoff exploited the exotic element in Russian folklore, frequently employing scales and melodic idioms which more nearly resembled those of Asia than their native Moscow and St. Petersburg. Borodin's opera *Prince Igor* is notable for the brilliant orchestration and choral writing, which mirrors the barbaric splendor of the camp of this early Russian chieftain. His tone poem, *On the Steppes of Central Asia,* is similarly but more soberly colorful, while his "First Symphony" in B-minor reflects in more formal surroundings the same inclinations. His string quartets are infrequently played, although they contain many pleasing moments. Rimsky-Korsakoff is even more exotic in his use of oriental materials. Best known, perhaps, is the symphonic suite *Scheherezade,* a set of four tone poems related to the *Arabian Nights.* Also frequently heard in concert are the suites drawn from his operas *Tsar Saltan,* and *Le Coq d'Or (The Golden Cockerel).* More Russian is his "Russian Easter Overture," while the *Capriccio Espagnol* exploits Spanish themes in a brilliant virtuoso-piece for orchestra. All of the Russian composers seemed to be born with brilliant orchestral sense, resembling Berlioz rather than Wagner in their use of color and solo instruments. They explored many new coloristic combinations and exerted thereby considerable influence upon later composers, particularly those of the impressionist group. For them this development of orchestral color was almost a necessity. We have seen a little of the intellectual side of developmental procedure in the music of Brahms: lacking the training disciplines of counterpoint, variation and strict formal writing, the Russian composers found the development of a theme almost beyond their powers and resorted to repetition. In order to make these repetitions interesting they sought new instrumental combinations and colors, new accompaniments, and unique rhythmic and percussive effects. Their music is, therefore, rather easy to understand, but it does not often wear too well. In pursuit of this coloristic ideal, Rimsky-Korsakoff wrote a text on instrumentation and orchestration, drawing the examples from his own works, presuming, one supposes, that any student would be familiar with them. The book is now of limited usefulness because only a few of the compositions are heard or recorded nowadays.

Modeste Moussorgsky is the most Russian of all. He tried to capture the rhythms and intonations of everyday speech in his music, avoiding everything that seemed artificial and unnatural. He sought dramatic material in the folk-legends and history of old Russia, as well as in the lives of his own class of people. These were all captured and distilled into some of the most profoundly original music of the nineteenth century, his opera *Boris Godunov*. Far different from either the philosophic, symbolic music-dramas of Wagner, or the individualized tragedies and comedies of Italian opera, this vast work has as its hero the Russian people — not necessarily noble or heroic, but plain, honest and not-so-honest folk caught up in political events not of their own making. Czar Boris, the tragic figure who serves as a focus of the drama, while important, is not the hero in the usual sense. Great choral scenes in which the modal music of the Russian church mingles with typical folk song point to the real protagonist — the common people of the country. In using these folk materials, Moussorgsky stumbled on some amazing and fascinating effects. One of the most memorable is the "Coronation Scene" near the beginning of the opera. Here, the key sense is obliterated by the chords used to imitate the bells, followed by modal choral music from the Russian Orthodox Church. The combination is magnificent in its color and impressiveness. Moussorgsky is represented on our concert programs by only a few works, the tone poem *Night on Bald Mountain,* a depiction of a witches' sabbath after an old legend, and some music from the unfinished opera, *Kovanstchina.* The suite for piano *Pictures at an Exhibition* has been brilliantly orchestrated by Maurice Ravel, and is frequently heard in that form as well as in the original piano version. In song recitals, his *Nursery Songs, Sunless,* and *Songs and Dances of Death* are finding an increasing popularity. Because of what he considered Moussorgsky's musical illiteracy, Rimsky-Korsakoff revised many of the works which his friend left upon his death. It is in these revisions that we know Moussorgsky. One wonders how much of them is original and how much the result of Rimsky's well-meaning tampering.

460

SCANDINAVIA

The Scandinavian countries are represented by two composers whose music is still well-known, Edvard Grieg (1843-1907) from Norway, and Jan Sibelius (1864-1957) from Finland. This is not to say that there were no other composers in these countries. There were, composers whose momentary fame may have outshone the two mentioned, but in the United States these are almost the sole representatives of their countries. Grieg was a miniaturist, at his best in short piano pieces, songs, or small orchestral movements such as those of his *Peer Gynt Suite*. His only successful venture into sterner waters is the popular Piano Concerto in A-minor. In all of these works, Grieg reveals himself to be a sensitive and subtle harmonist with an ear for typically Norwegian turns of musical phrase. His scoring for orchestra is delicate and imaginative. Many of his compositions are descriptive of the customs of his native land. Jan Sibelius was a composer of a different nature, imbued with the gloomy grandeur of the epic poem of legendary heroes and gods of the north, the *Kalevala*. These he depicted musically in many tone poems such as *Lemminkaiinen, Pojhola's Daughter* and *The Swan of Tuonela*. Even his purely symphonic works are marked with a northern atmosphere, in some works overpowering and dark, in others brilliant and glistening. He wrote seven symphonies, more or less in the Brahms tradition, but with interesting ventures into new formal procedures. The Second Symphony is popular, and uses gay folk-tunes and rhythms from the province of Karelia. In addition to these, he wrote a violin concerto, a string quartet, and many separate single compositions. Well known among these are *Finlandia* and *Valse Triste*.

SPAIN, ENGLAND AND FRANCE

Spain contributed a few composers who used their national idioms to advantage in music reflecting the passion and excitement of that country. Enrique Granados (1867-1916), Isaac Albéniz (1860-1909) and the more modern Manuel de Falla (1876-1946) have faithfully recorded in their music the colors and rhythms of Spanish folk and popular music.

Other countries participated to some degree in this nationalistic movement. Many, like England and France, had no strongly marked characteristics in their folk music to make it immediately recognizable and representative. The twentieth-century English composer, Ralph Vaughan Williams has come as close to expressing English traits as anyone. He accomplished this by using real folk-songs as material, and by a partial return to the styles of the Elizabethan period, a time when the national idiom was more clearly defined. France, with its heritage of refinement and stylization in music, had even less chance than England in this respect. We may name any number of composers who exhibit in their music marked "French" characteristics, but there is no group of composers who set out with nationalism as a goal. There are a few compositions using folk tunes — D'Indy's *Symphony on a French Mountain Air* is an example — but no pre-eminent composer comparable to Smetana or Moussorgsky. Perhaps one might say that all French composers are nationalistic, since they all express their nationality so clearly in their musical style!

## POST-ROMANTIC COMPOSERS

This title applies to composers who formed their styles within the nineteenth century and conform to the accepted musical language of that period, choosing Brahms or Wagner as their model, or writing in the style of some other contemporary whom they admired.

Richard Strauss (1864-1949) followed the stylistic manner of Wagner, after a passing interest in that of Brahms. A virtuoso of the orchestra, Strauss wrote seven tone poems of a descriptive nature, and many operas, the most famous of which are *Elektra, Salome* and *Der Rosenkavalier (The Cavalier of the Rose)*. He employs in both opera and tone poem the *leitmotive system,* with theme-transformation and development. His music is less dark than Wagner's, full of brilliant rapid modulations and easily understood melody. The instrumental polyphony is often profuse in his orchestral textures, but never obscures the main thematic line, and is apt to be thematic itself in construction. The most popular of his tone poems are *Till Eulenspiegel's Merry Pranks, Don Juan, Death and Transfiguration, Thus Spake Zarathustra* (after Nietzsche) and *Don Quixote.* He frequently employs a very large orchestra and the voices needed for his operas are Wagnerian in character.

462

Gustav Mahler (1860-1911) is the most modern of the post-romantic composers in his concept of music and in handling of the orchestra. His music is full of antithetical elements — bitter-sweet, almost Schubertian passages contrast with convulsive climaxes and ironic wit. There are military trumpet calls, little marches, imitations of the sounds of nature, and Viennese waltzes imbedded in this *fin de siècle* art. The nine Mahler symphonies are extremely long works (the first movement of the Third lasts some forty-five minutes), and they frequently use vocal soloists and/or chorus. The texts of these passages are often drawn from the writings of medieval mystics and visionaries, and deal with Nature, the sinfulness and redemption of man and God's forgiving grace. They contain many pages of surpassing exaltation and beauty, but often there appear seemingly arbitrary discords and passages of bitter irony. The form of these works at times resembles that of the traditional classical models expanded to monstrous proportions, but there occur about as frequently movements whose formal design is lost in the effort of the composer to communicate his visions. Also a virtuoso conductor, Mahler was a consummate orchestrator. Each instrument in his orchestra sings, and his combinations within the larger instrumental framework often resemble those to be found in contemporary music. Among Mahler's works are numbered many beautiful songs with piano or orchestral accompaniments. Music for combinations other than these and the symphonies is negligible in Mahler's production.

Sergei Rachmaninoff (1873-1943) was famous during his lifetime as a great pianist as well as a composer, who, within the Russian style as exemplified by Tchaikovsky, exhibited considerable individuality He wrote four piano concertos, of which the second is the most popular. His symphonies number three, but are seldom played. Possibly his best work is the *Variations on a Theme of Paganini,* for piano and orchestra. Many composers used this Paganini *Caprice* as material for variations, among them Brahms and Liszt. Also, in one of the later variations, Rachmaninoff introduces the *"Dies Irae,"* last heard in the *Symphonie Fantastique* of Berlioz and the *"Totentanz"* of Liszt. Rachmaninoff is well known as the composer of many works for solo piano, among which are the famous Prelude in C#-minor, and the Prelude in G-minor.

### FRENCH POST-ROMANTIC COMPOSERS

A number of French composers, certainly less famous than those singled out above, have produced fine works in the post-romantic tradition. Gabriel Fauré (1845-1924), is remembered for his sensitive and deeply-felt *Requiem* as well as for numerous piano pieces and songs. Vincent D'Indy (1851-1931), Henry Duparc (1848-1933) and Paul Dukas (1865-1935), are all to be encountered on programs of French romantic and post-romantic music. Their music is notable in its refinement of melody, the use of discreet and unusual harmony, and the employment of coloristic effects which often rely upon the woodwinds. Their national characteristics of clarity, wit and good taste are evident in the music. There are, however, lapses from grace when the music becomes stickily sentimental and precious. Someone once said that "every French composer has a bit of Massenet in him," a remark as true today as in the nineteenth century. Many fine composers narrowly skirt the edge of this precipice, saving themselves only by a dissonance or unexpected turn of phrase.

### OTHER POST-ROMANTIC COMPOSERS

In Germany we encounter the song composer Hugo Wolf (1860-1903), in England Sir Edward Elgar (1857-1934) of "Pomp and Circumstance" fame, in Hungary the original and modernist composer Leos Janáček (1854-1928), and in Italy the opera composers Ruggiero Leoncavallo (1858-1919), Giacomo Puccini (1858-1924) and Pietro Mascagni (1863-1945).

# THE ROMANTIC STYLE IN THE OTHER ARTS

Music was preeminently *the* romantic art because of the directness and power of its appeal to the emotions, but its sisters, literature and painting, were not far behind. In each of the important art media of this period certain similarities may be noted in the use of techniques which emphasize emotional quality. But when the term "emotion" is used, we must not always infer agitation and excitement: quieter moods of tenderness or melancholy are equally genuine. All music was not after the pattern of Berlioz' "March to the Scaffold," not even all of Berlioz' music. Nor was all painting a swirling pattern of motion as in many works of Delacroix, for there was also the calmness of Corot and Turner.

Foremost among the techniques used to heighten the emotional impact of this art was the use of color. We have seen how the Classic composers used it in much the same ways as the classic artists, such as David, for whom drawing — the clear delineation of forms and their arrangement — was primary, and the use of color secondary. We must realize that color *was* used, however, but that it was not the constructive element which it became in the nineteenth century. One need only play the *Symphonie Fantastique* on the monochromatic piano, or look at black and white reproductions of the paintings of Gericault, Delacroix, Corot and Turner to realize the importance of color in this art. In literature we need only quote the word-music of two outstanding poets of this century to show the importance of the vowel and consonant sounds themselves as well as the imagery in the creation of effects of color in language. The first example is the opening stanza of Byron's poem, *The Destruction of Sennacherib*.

> The Assyrian came down like a wolf on the fold,
> And his cohorts were gleaming in purple and gold;
> The sheen of their spears was like stars on the sea
> When the blue wave rolls nightly on deep Galilee.

The second is from *Ulalume* by Edgar Allen Poe (although the *Raven* might do as well). Notice the difference in color connotations from those of Byron's work.

> The skies they were ashen and sober:
>    The leaves they were crisped and sere —
>    The leaves they were withering and sere:
> It was night in the lonesome October
>    Of my most immemorial year;
> It was hard by the dim lake of Auber,
>    In the misty region of Weir —
> It was down by the dank tarn of Auber,
>    In the ghoul-haunted woodland of Weir.

The tendency of poets to rely increasingly upon verbal music and color led to the "modern" poetic practice of combining words for their sound values alone, disregarding the sense of the result. This verbal "orchestration" at its height is exemplified in poetry in the works of the symbolist poets Mallarmé, Baudelaire and Yeats, and in some of the prose of James Joyce, Paul Valéry, Marcel Proust and Thomas Wolfe. Later, meaning was reintroduced by the use of "color" words associated in such a way as to suggest other levels of meaning impossible to traditional combinations, thus enriching literature by a new dimension.

The reading of the above poetic excerpts suggests another device of romanticism: the fusion and continuity of parts, here demonstrated by the commas, dashes and semicolons, which allow the flow, urged on by the rhythm, to reach only non-final cadences within the stanza. This weakening of conclusive devices is shared in music, as we have seen. It is reflected in painting by the use of less sharply defined lines and by the use of curves which transfer to one another so that the eye

PLATE **XXXVI**. *"Oriental Lion Hunt" by Delacroix. Not only the exotic subject, but also the motion, which almost creates an abstract design, proclaim the romanticism of this painting. In color the effect is greatly enhanced. (Courtesy of The Art Institute of Chicago, Potter Palmer Collection.)*

is caught up in continuous motion, excellently illustrated in Delacroix's *Lion Hunt* (Plate XXXVI). Such continuity and diffusion may be compared to the orchestral polyphony of Wagner, in which there is a constant fusion of one *leitmotiv* with another.

There is also a constant play of dynamic values, of loud and soft, light and shadow, assonance and dissonance in these art works. In the music and painting, details are often sacrificed for overall effect — the preference for the broad canvas and the orchestra rather than the miniature and the string quartet. And as we have shown above, poetry linked together unusual and unexpected words in order to form richer total effects than might be secured by more traditional procedures.

The strong projection of the individuality of the artist is also felt by the listener or beholder of this art. The creative artist is the conscious interpreter of the real or dream world which he presents to us, whether he be the Berlioz of the witches' orgy, Constable before

PLATE XXXVII. *"A View of Salisbury Cathedral" by Constable. An early romantic, quasi-impressionistic treatment of landscape. (Courtesy of The National Gallery of Art, Washington, D.C., Mellon Collection.)*

Salisbury Cathedral (Plate XXXVII) or Poe and his raven. Most important, he interprets this world in his own images and symbols in highly personal and inimitable forms and arrangements. "The style is the man" was never before more true, for the element of psychology entered the romantic arts and began shaping the course of music and painting particularly, toward the styles of the twentieth century which are termed expressionism and surrealism. The researches of Freud, it might almost be said, were rendered historically necessary by the romantic cult of the individual.

Perhaps one of the most obvious unifying threads that ran through all of these artistic endeavors was the choice of subject matter — what the music, poem, novel or painting was "about." As we have seen earlier in the chapter, distance in time or place had great charms for the romantic. The escape from the world which was becoming "too much with us" became highly important to the romantic individual who saw the death of imagination and fantasy in the realistic world of the industrial revolution. He fled to the opera house to hear Gounod's *Faust*, Wagner's *Tristan und Isolde* or Marschner's *Der Vampyr*. Or he attended concerts of such works as Berlioz' *Damnation of Faust* or Wagner's "Faust Overture" or Liszt's *Faust Symphony*. Or he mused on German folksong and on Teutonic musical profundity in the symphonies of Brahms or Mahler. Perhaps he picked up a book which spirited him back to the middle ages, such as *Ivanhoe*, or to America with *The Last of the Mohicans*, or chilled his blood with *Macbeth* (for to this century Shakespeare was a supreme romantic) or with *Dracula* or *Frankenstein's Monster*. He may have gone to an art gallery to see Delacroix's illustrations for *Faust*, or his oriental scenes from North Africa; perhaps he was pleasantly scandalized by Ingre's harem women and *odalisques*, or, at the other extreme, admired the rather sentimental portraits of English beauties by Lawrence and Reynolds, or their French counterparts as pictured by Ingres or Renoir. Or, to get some fresh air, he may have walked to the construction site of a new cathedral — or library, college building, postoffice or railway station — in the genuine Gothic style, such as St. Clotilde in Paris, or St. Patrick's in New York. "Anytime but now, anyplace but here" seemed to be the watchword.

But this was not wholly true, for painters like Daumier, novelists like Zola, dramatists like Ibsen and composers like Mascagni, Leoncavallo and Puccini turned away from these escapes and faced the often ugly reality of their times (Plate XXVIII) . Some of their observations

468

PLATE XXXVIII. *"The Third Class Carriage" by Daumier. An example of realism by an artist, like Zola in literature, dedicated to exposing the seamy side of life to the attention of the public in order to hasten social reform. (Courtesy of The Metropolitan Museum of Art, New York, The H. O. Havemeyer Collection.)*

were real protests, shocking in their truths, while others sugar-coated the unpalatable and turned it into works which appealed to the upper middle class, who were delightfully scandalized at the stage violence and immorality. But in some works the psychological insight penetrated uncomfortably deeply, causing real shock and a moment's glimpse of motives usually hidden within the subconscious.

To sum up, then, we find that the arts of the nineteenth century shared several comparable techniques whose purpose was to induce an emotional response, and that those techniques which accomplish this best became highly developed. We find also that the arts shared subject matter which attempted to escape reality, or which delved into the subconscious; or which faced reality and interpreted it in an emotional way. The arts most cultivated were music, literature and painting, with sculpture and architecture far behind and largely devoted to works in the Gothic revival or the oriental genre, without the marked advancement in techniques which occurred in the other arts. We shall see, in the next chapter, how this advancement and refinement led to the impasse out of which the art of the twentieth century slowly emerged.

### LIST OF TERMS

classicism
romanticism
lyric melody
instrumental lyricism
complex harmony
harmonic tension crescendo
discontinuity of motion
French scoring
German scoring
functional orchestration
non-functional orchestration
orchestral polyphony
programmatic symphony
dramatic symphony
choral symphony
tone poem, symphonic poem
cyclic symphony
motto-theme

theme transformation
dynamic curve
nationalistic music
short piano piece
virtuosity
recitative and aria
*secco* recitative
accompanied recitative
*gesamtkunstwerk*
*leitmotiv(e)*
music-drama
literary program
nocturne
etude
*idée fixe*
non-functional harmony
chromatic harmony
post-romanticism

### ADDITIONAL LISTENING

*Mendelssohn*
Overtures:
"The Hebrides ("Fingal's Cave")
"Calm Sea and Prosperous Voyage"
*Ruy Blas*
Incidental Music to Shakespeare's
*A Midsummer Night's Dream*
Symphony No. 3 ("Scotch")
Symphony No. 5 ("Reformation")
Octet for Strings
*Elijah* (oratorio)

*Schumann*
Symphonies Nos. 1, 2, 3
"Manfred Overture"
Concerto for Piano and Orchestra
Symphonic Etudes, for piano
*Carnaval Suite,* for piano

Song Cycle: *Frauenlieben und Leben*
Individual songs:
*"Die Beiden Grenadieren"*
*"Ich grolle nicht"*

*Chopin*
Piano Concertos Nos. 1 and 2
Various piano compositions:
valses, mazurkas, polonaises
impromptus, ballades, scherzi, sonatas, etudes, nocturnes, preludes

*Berlioz*
*Romeo and Juliet,* dramatic symphony
*Requiem*
*L'Enfance du Christ* (oratorio)
*Damnation of Faust*

## ADDITIONAL LISTENING (*Continued*)

*Harold in Italy,* for Viola and
  Orchestra
Overtures:
  *Roman Carnival*
  *The Trojans*
  *Benevenuto Cellini*

**Brahms**
  Academic Festival Overture
  Tragic Overture
  *Variations on a Theme by Haydn*
  *Variations on a Theme by Handel*
  Symphonies Nos. 1, 2, 4
  Violin Concerto
  Piano Concerto No. 1
  Double Concerto for Violin and Cello
  *German Requiem*
  Piano Quintet in F-minor
  Clarinet Sonatas
  *Liebeslieder Waltzes*
  Various piano compositions, espec-
    ially those of Op. 116, 117, 118,
    and 119

**Liszt**
  *Faust Symphony*
  *Hungarian Rhapsodies,* for piano
  Sonata for Piano, B-minor
  *Transcendental Etudes,* for piano
  Piano Concerto No. 2 in A-minor

**Wagner**
  Overtures and excerpts:
    *Tannhäuser* (Venusberg scene)
    *Lohengrin*
    *Flying Dutchman*
  Prelude to *Die Meistersinger,* and
    Act II
  *Die Walküre,* Act I

**Tchaikovsky**
  Piano Concerto in Bb-minor
  Violin Concerto
  Symphony No. 4
  Symphony No. 5

Overtures:
  Francesca da Rimini
  1812
  Suite for String Orchestra

**Antonin Dvořák**
  Symphonies 2, 4, 5
  Concerto for Cello and Orchestra
  Slavonic Dances
  String Quartet F-major, Op. 96
    ("American")

**Bedrich Smetana**
  *The Moldau*
  *From Bohemia's Forests and Meadows*
  String Quartet (*"Aus Meinen Leben"*)
  *The Bartered Bride* (opera)

**Alexander Borodin**
  Symphony No. 1, B-minor
  *Prince Igor* (opera)
  "Polovtsian Dances," from
    *Prince Igor*
  *On the Steppes of Central Asia*
  String Quartet No. 2 in D-major

**Nicholas Rimsky-Korsakoff**
  Russian Easter Overture
  *Capriccio Espagnol*
  *Scheherezade,* symphonic suite
  *Tsar Saltan,* symphonic suite
  *Le Coq D'Or*

**Modeste Moussorgsky**
  *Night on Bare Mountain*
  *Boris Godunov* (opera)
  *Nursery Songs*
  *Songs and Dances of Death*
  *Pictures at an Exhibition*
    (piano solo, or orchestral version)

**Edvard Grieg**
  Piano Concerto in A-minor
  *Peer Gynt Suite*
  *Norwegian Dances*

471

## ADDITIONAL LISTENING *(Continued)*

*Jan Sibelius*
  Symphonies 1 through 7
  *Finlandia*
  Violin Concerto


*Richard Strauss*
  Tone Poems:
    *Don Juan*
    *Death and Transfiguration*
    *Till Eulenspiegel*
    *Also Sprach Zarathustra*
    *Ein Heldenleben*
  Operas:
    *Elektra*
    *Salome*
    *Der Rosenkavalier*
    *Die Frau Ohne Schatten*
    *Capriccio*
  *Four Last Songs*
  Symphony for Wind Instruments
  *Burleske,* for piano and orchestra

  Suite from *Le Bourgeois
    Gentilhomme*

*Gustav Mahler*
  Symphonies 1, 2, 3, 8
  *Das Lied von der Erde*
  Songs from "Youth's Magic Horn"
  *Kindertotenlieder*

*French Romantic and Post-Romantic
    Composers:*
  Fauré: *Requiem*
  Chausson: Poem, for Violin and
    Orchestra
  Chabrier: *España Rhapsody*
  Dukas: *Sorcerer's Apprentice*
  D'Indy: *Symphony on a French
    Mountain Air*

*Edward Elgar*
  "Enigma" Variations
  *Falstaff,* tone poem

# VIII   The Modern

# Period, 1900~

## HISTORICAL PERSPECTIVE

Toward the end of the nineteenth century, technology began to accelerate, and as scientific discoveries multiplied, man and the humanistic expressions which had formerly revealed his soul were forced to hurry along with them. But the inner growth does not necessarily proceed at a rapid rate just because its external surroundings are quickly changing, and so the arts — that is, man himself in his role as artistic interpreter of his world — either fell behind in expressing the present, or by fantastic efforts and experiments tried to reveal the essence of the contemporary culture.

In a rapidly industrializing England, Victoria was queen. The tentacles of empire had extended to perhaps their greatest degree, and Kipling wrote of India while explorers and colonists ventured further and further into Africa. The Boer War occurred in 1899. Italy had become a nation in 1861 and was undergoing the birth pains common to such events, while in 1871 Germany finally became a united empire. In the same year, Darwin published *The Descent of Man* and Louis Sullivan erected the first skyscraper. After the great Paris Exposition in 1889, for which the Eiffel Tower was erected, the Wright brothers proved that man could fly (1903), Einstein published his first papers on relativity (1905), Henry Ford turned out the first mass-produced automobile (1908) and Marconi demonstrated that the continents could be linked by radio. The Curies discovered radioactivity, Roentgen, the X-Ray and Edison invented the electric light and the phonograph. And in 1914, in the obscure little Austro-Hungarian village of Sarejevo, the match was touched to an explosive train of gunpowder which resulted in the catastrophe of World War I, the event which, more than any other, signalled the definite end of the unique culture of the nineteenth century.

The tensions brought about by the industrial revolution had reached their breaking point all over Europe in 1914: political and social conflicts had been increasing since early in the century. But yet, on the eve of an apocalypse, the greater part of humanity danced, laughed and sang to the music of Johann Strauss, Offenbach and Victor Herbert, ignoring the prophets of doom who put into their plays, novels and music the unrest and psychological reality of the times. The arts were like molecules in a steam boiler about to explode; the activity and desire for release into a new atmosphere was enormous. And the decade after the war was largely powered by the impetus of the prewar years. Most of the significant breakthroughs, as they are now called, were accomplished in those agitated years: impressionism, cubism, dadaism, expressionism, surrealism, atonalism, primitivism, functionalism — the list of "isms" is long and not entirely confined to the arts. But through these prewar years there was also the sense of the passing of an age of security and peace — the "good old times" — and its replacement by a nostalgic, weary and pessimistic kind of boredom which required ever new experiences to stimulate it. We hear it in the music of Mahler particularly, a man too chained to his century to see very far beyond it, but also one who had glimmerings of the future. But the weariness had to give way to the energy of those who felt it within their power to shape the arts of the new century: let us see how it was accomplished.

## Part I: Impressionism

Two important transitional styles in music developed during the end of the nineteenth and the beginning of the twentieth centuries. These were impressionism and expressionism: diametrically opposed, they stemmed both from the revolt against and the continuation of Wagnerism. Impressionism developed first, coming into full power during the period between 1890 and 1910, whereas expressionism flourished between 1910 and 1930. Impressionism was a passing style, however important, and we shall examine it first in this chapter in that light; whereas the ideas and techniques developed by expressionism have proved to be increasingly important up to our own time, and will be considered later in our survey.

Both styles derived their names from the sister art of painting, and their disparate aims are made clear by referring to representative examples in that art (compare Plates XXXIX and XLIII). Expressionism seeks to reveal the reaction of the soul of the artist to the experiences which befall him. Not only the lithograph by Munch, but also the vivid paintings of Van Gogh are expressionistic in nature. On the other hand, the impressionist deals not with emotions, but rather with the *appearance* of reality, without trying to interpret it in any way. Such art is not without feeling, but it is apt to be sensitive to small nuances, delicate, withdrawn, objective. It was a revolt against the grandiosity and emotional excess of the music of Wagner and his followers, and if we reverse the tenets of Wagnerism, the result is a rather good definition of the aims of impressionism.

Yet musical impressionism is a logical outcome of the development of the romantic style: it is descriptive, colorful, harmonically exploratory, eager for the exotic and new, and requires unique, nonclassic forms in which to contain its ideas. Instead of exploring an emotional situation thoroughly, as, for example, the *"Liebestod"* in *Tristan und Isolde* does, this technique seeks to capture fleeting images, often necessarily (and preferably) vague, relying upon color and dynamic rather than clear draftsmanship. It avoids Teutonic thematic development, substituting transformation and fragmentation. Impressionistic views of the world are essentially static, the unmoving view of an "action

475

PLATE XXXIX. *"House of Parliament, Westminster" by Monet. Here we see the deliberate vagueness of impressionism: only the general outlines of the subject appear. The painting is, of course, much more effective in color, but the essential quality is preserved even in black and white. (Courtesy of The Art Institute of Chicago, Mr. and Mrs. Martin A. Ryerson Collection.)*

shot," a moment of motion frozen. Monet shows the Houses of Parliament partially visible for an instant through the swirl of fog (Plate XXXIX); and Rodin captures in stone the moment when, out of a formless mass, the hand of God begins to shape humanity (Plate XL). The capture of this instantaneous quality in music required the development of new techniques; the man who rose to the task, uniquely fitted for it in temperament, was Claude Debussy (1862-1918), (Plate XLI). An examination of his innovations is necessary before proceeding with the music of the later twentieth century.

PLATE XL. *"The Hand of God" by Rodin. Here is the impressionistic technique adapted, insofar as the medium will allow, to sculpture. It depicts a moment in creation: we have an impression of fluid, unfixed forms taking shape out of the amorphous mass of the uncut marble. (Courtesy of The Metropolitan Museum of Art, gift of Edward D. Adams, 1908.)*

# THE STYLE OF IMPRESSIONISM

### MELODY

Melodies are apt to be short, almost fragmentary and are frequently instrumental in character. They often do not have clear-cut cadences, nor are they of the antecedent-consequent variety, for this would presuppose some length of melodic line and tonal harmonic function. Since most of the compositions have titles, the melodies often reflect some aspect of the title.

A composer often wishes a melodic line to stand out clearly against its background accompaniment: to achieve this, he may add one or more instruments playing the same melody in unison or at some interval above or below the original melodic line. The most common interval used is the octave, but any interval is possible, lending to the composite sonority the quality particular to the interval, from the "open" sound of the fifth or fourth to the sweet richness of the third or sixth or the dissonant bite of the seventh or second (*c.f.,* Chapter III, Medieval period, parallel organum). The impressionist composers used such doublings to create atmosphere: note the mystery, distance and serenity of Debussy's *"Nuages"* ("Clouds") from the *Three Nocturnes* for orchestra, or *La Cathédral engloutie* (*The Engulfed Cathedral* for piano. *Multiple* doublings, which create masses of parallel chords, are sometimes used. Such chords are said to be "gliding" or "planing," and, since they are melodic doublings, are usually largely nonfunctional in character. It must be recognized that such a procedure is not an harmonic process, but rather a melodic one; hence the dissonances are integral to the sonority and need not resolve to consonances. Such a point of view achieves a considerable simplification of the otherwise exceedingly complicated harmonic structures which abound in this style. Such doubling creates a vagueness of outline and tonality, a diffused quality analogous to the use of light and color in impressionistic painting.

## HARMONIC STYLES AND MATERIALS

The harmonic structures used by Debussy are quite characteristic of late romantic music: they consist of triads to which the dissonances of the seventh and the ninth have been added, rarely going beyond that degree of complexity except for special effects. But it is the manner in which these chords are used and their relatively greater frequency which distinguishes impressionist harmony from that of Wagner, for example.

We have already encountered unresolved dissonances resulting from the multiple doubling of melodic lines: these sonorities were employed for their color value, and, by logical extension, one such chord could stand alone as a sound "pigment," without the necessity of moving to a less complex chord. Hence, *dissonance became an integral value in itself,* freed from the traditional bondage of consonance. Debussy's refined taste and fastidious use of sonorities made these

478

sounds acceptable, but this revolution opened the way for many ca-
cophonous compositions of the 1920's as well as for the differently
controlled sonorities of the midcentury.

In his effort to create new sonorities, Debussy explored much
exotic or infrequently used basic musical material. The old modal
scales of the Medieval period (Chapter III) and the devices of organum
are exploited in his music. Modal harmony has relatively weak chord
progressions in regard to defining the keynote of the scale, and just
this kind of vagueness appealed to Debussy. Such harmony appears in
his String Quartet and in other music, often that intended to recall
bygone ages, such as the prelude "The Dancers of Delphi" (Example
75).

But Debussy also sought other scale material, often using the pentatonic scale which we associate with the orient. (One version of this
is composed of the five black keys within any octave of the piano.)
Another scale sometimes employed contains only whole steps between
its members and is thus called the "whole-tone" scale (*e.g.,* C - D -
E - F♯ - G♯ - A♯ - C). Neither of these scales has a tonic note, other
than that chosen by the composer and suitably emphasized to give

EXAMPLE 75. *Debussy: "The Dancers of Delphi." Planing.*

it tonic importance. Nor do the chord progressions define a key-note, for those of the pentatonic scale are mild and vague, and those of the whole-tone scale pungent but static. The former appears melodically in "Pagodes" (Example 76) and in "The Maid with the Flaxen Hair," while the whole-tone scale is used in *"Voiles"* (Example 77). The chromatic scale (Example 78, *"Prelude à l'après midi d'un faune"*) as well as the major and minor scales also appear in impressionistic music, but are usually used in such a way that they bear little resemblance to previous styles which employed them.

In order to bring one of these airy creations to earth on some relatively satisfying final tone, should this be desired, impressionist composers resort to various means of emphasizing that tone. One of the simplest is that of repetition of the tone or the chord based upon it. Another consists of using the tone as an organpoint (see Chapter V), either in the treble or, more importantly, in the bass. Sometimes such

EXAMPLE 76. *Debussy:* "Pagodes." *Pentatonic scale.*

SCALE USED

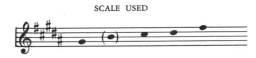

EXAMPLE 77. *Debussy: "Voilcs." Whole-tone scale.*

Modéré

SCALE USED

EXAMPLE 78. *Debussy: "Prelude à l'après-midi d'un faune." Chromaticism, color.*

Molto moderato

a pedal is doubled at the fifth above, creating something like a bagpipe drone, which firmly anchors all of the wayward sonorities above it. More complex doublings of the organpoint may be used, resulting in chordal complexes which, however, often produce too diffuse a sound to emphasize a tonic note. But chords moving above such a multiple organpoint provide wide coloristic possibilities, and are found very frequently in this music.

## MOTION

No real generalization can be made here which will distinguish this music from romantic music in general. It is often discontinuous in motion, and sometimes has clearly marked rhythms and metric pulse; at other times both of these are missing.

## SONORITY

The sound-value, like the harmonic-value, becomes an absolute element in this style, sharing with the chord in importance. The impressionistic use of tone-color raises this element to an importance equal to those of rhythm, melody and harmony. The style brings to perhaps the highest point of refinement and sensitivity the tendency which began early in this century with Berlioz. The generally soft dynamics, the use of muted brass and string sounds, the refined voices of the woodwinds, and the richness of the harp combine to give the impressionist orchestra a luminosity, a clarity, and a sensuous appeal different from any previous music.

In addition to exploring a whole new world of sound in the orchestra Debussy created a new technique of writing for the piano, the first development in this area since Chopin and Liszt. The impersonal, delicately shaded tones of the piano were most appropriate to this coolly objective musical style. The shimmering sounds created by rapid notes in the upper register, the bell-like sonority of all tonal regions of the keyboard, the percussive accents which were possible, and the intimacy of the medium were all attractive, not only to Debussy, but to all impressionist composers. The compositions follow in the tradition of the short piano work, and almost always have titles which are not too precise, often suggesting qualities to be expected in the work.

# FORMAL AND GENERATIVE PRINCIPALS

### MUSICAL PONTILLISME

Once again we must depend upon paintings for analogies. A technique developing from impressionistic uses of color and light was invented by the post-impressionist French painter, Georges Seurat (1859-1891), who composed his paintings of myriad spots of color, combining them scientifically so that at a distance the color spots merged into shimmering effects of light. This can be examined in his paintings "Sunday Afternoon on the Island of La Grande Jatte," and *"La Parade"* (Plate XLI). This technique, called *pointillisme*, was transferred to music, replacing the color spots with fragments of melody, chordal masses and instrumental sonorities. The music is no longer entirely made up of logical sequences of melodic and harmonic

PLATE XLI. "La Parade" *by Seurat. Pointillism is best seen in color but the photograph does show the multitude of tiny dots which gives the technique its name. (Courtesy of The Metropolitan Museum of Art, bequest of Stephen C. Clark, 1960.)*

material, but of purely arbitrary elements chosen according to the artistic taste of the composer. It might be compared to the construction of a mosaic out of tiny colored fragments of glass or tile. At close range the total design is less important than any small section momentarily in the line of vision, and, of course, this is the way we hear the music — a small piece at a time. This mosaic technique replaced the formal phrase logic of previous music, just as the color values of the chords replaced the old chord-progression concept. When thematic fragments are extended to form larger phrases, development by means of theme transformation is often used. In some cases the mosaic fragments are gradually combined to form "themes" as the music progresses.

### FORM

The total form is often sectional, the three-part form — or, more accurately, three section form — still retaining its validity. Sometimes these sections are increased in number, giving sequences resembling those of the rondo, although some resemble the more contemporary "arch-form," ABCBA. The function of tonality in creating form has, of course, been weakened almost to the vanishing point: few composers do more than pay it occasional lip-service.

In any case, the new forms created in this style are many times the direct result of the interplay of tone-colors, harmonic colors, dynamic qualities, and melodic materials. In this form-building function the interdependence of structure and contents resembles that of the Baroque and Classic eras, but most often without the clear organizing force of tonality used in those styles. Debussy frequently employs the devices of theme transformation and fragmentation to provide lyric material: this practice is quite evident in early works, but is also found in his more mature compositions.

## IMPRESSIONIST COMPOSERS

### CLAUDE DEBUSSY, 1862-1918

*Preludes, Book I* (for piano)

"*Danseuses de Delphes*" ("The Dancers of Delphi") (Example 75): This piece was suggested by a fragment of a frieze from a Greek temple which Debussy saw in the Louvre. It exhibits planing, nonfunctional harmony and exploitation of veiled piano sonorities.

*"Voiles"* ("Sails, or Veils") (Example 77): This piece employs ternary construction, the first and last sections using the whole-tone scale, the middle part written in the pentatonic scale It is essentially static in feeling. Note the color splashes of rapid notes, and the active rhythmic quality. Both are needed to breathe life into the motionless quality of the harmony derived from these scales. Also note the frequent use of organpoint.

*"Des pas sur la neige"* ("Of Footsteps in the Snow"): This melancholy little vignette uses the repetition of a rhythmic-melodic motive to hold it together. This motive appears almost continuously throughout, providing the harmonic background in many places, and supporting fragments of melody above it. The piece is written in the Aeolian mode, but uses chromaticism to introduce richer chords than occur naturally in that scale.

*"La fille aux cheveux de lin"* ("The Maid with the Flaxen Hair"): This poetic composition uses the pentatonic scale melodically. Harmonies are not pentatonic, and are sometimes functional. Planing occurs, most notably about two-thirds of the way through. Parallel fourths appear at the cadence.

### *Preludes, Book II* (for piano)

*"Feux d'artifice"* ("Fireworks"): piano sonority, techniques. Dissonant color splashes, nontonal. Possibly a Bastille Day celebration — listen for the fragment of the *"Marseillaise"* at the end.

### *"Prelude à l'après-midi d'un faun"* (*"Prelude to the Afternoon of a Faun"*)

This was one of Debussy's early successes, inspired by a poem of the Symbolist poet, Mallarmé, published in 1876 with illustrations by Manet. In the music, Debussy sought to evoke "the successive scenes in which the longings and desires of the faun pass in the heat of the afternoon." The scene is, presumably, ancient Greece, and the faun, half man, half beast, lies in the shade during a warm afternoon. He drowses, and thinks he sees (or does he dream?) nymphs bathing in the stream. He dreams on. This work is a tone poem, but the painting is anything but literal, either in description or in sequence of events.

PLATE XLII. *Claude Debussy. (The Bettmann Archive.)*

To us, it owes more to tradition than do some other compositions of Debussy, but to the people who heard it at the first performance in 1894, it was a revelation, and not always a welcome one. Nothing like it had been heard before. The sonorous yet transparent orchestra was more like Berlioz than Wagner yet the nervous brilliance of the earlier Frenchman was not there. Each instrument provides a specific color which is used with all the care of a painter to capture just the right effect of light and shade. The low, exotic tones of the flute at the beginning of the piece, the answer by the muted horns, the piercingly sweet voice of the oboe — these as well as the colors attributable to various harmonic groupings are handled with the utmost finesse. Theme transformation is used, rather than (horrors!) Germanic development, and section follows and flows into succeeding section with purely sensory logic, disregarding the traditional tenets of musical structure. Many of the characteristics of Debussy's later style are present in this composition.

*La Mer (The Sea)*

This, the longest of Debussy's orchestral works, resembles in some respects a three movement symphony, although the middle movement is scherzo-like rather than a slow movement. There is more sharing of themes among the movements than in other works of this composer, but in the atmosphere here created, this thematic transference seems of little significance. Debussy's marine experience consisted of two crossings of the English Channel — hardly sufficient, one would think, to impress him enough to compose a work like *La Mer*. He wrote to his publisher in 1903 from Burgundy, where he was at work on the composition: "You will say that the ocean does not exactly bathe the Burgundian hillsides — and that my seascapes might be studio landscapes; but I have numberless stores of memories and, to my mind, they are *worth more than a reality which often deadens one's thought.*"

The first movement of the suite is entitled *"De l'aube à midi sur la mer"* ("From Dawn to Noon on the Ocean"), and has a curious static quality, perhaps reflecting the essentially unchanging face of the ocean, despite the small squalls which appear from time to time. The primeval undulation of the waves, the gradually clearing atmosphere and a glimpse of the green depths all are here, painted with the utmost subtlety in the orchestra. Notice the mysterious beginning, as the sea begins to become visible, the woodwind figurations, the mosaic of patterns, the parallel chords in the muted lower strings, and the many ways the thematic materials are transformed to provide "mosaic tiles" of various shapes and colors.

The second movement, *"Jeu de vagues"* ("Play of the Waves"), presents us with the same seascape, but with a fresh wind blowing, whipping the surface into small whitecaps. There is a certain element of the fantastic to be noticed here, largely resulting from the rapidity with which the orchestral colors shift, and the qualities of those colors.

The third movement, *"Dialogue du vent et de la mer"* ("Dialogue of the Wind and the Sea"), depicts a stormier ocean scene. Themes from the first movement are recalled, transformed, and the brass "chorale" returns for a climactic section. But, as always, "the whole is more than the sum of its parts," and all the technical tricks are only means to evoke this ideal view of an ocean of the mind.

*Iberia*

This work is a tone painting of Spain in three movements by Debussy, who never set foot in that country. Yet the Spanish composer Manuel de Falla called it the most authentic musical portrait of his country ever painted! The first movement, entitled *"Par les Rues et par les Chemins"* ("Through the Streets and Byways"), is a brilliant, rather rapid movement evoking the Spanish atmosphere by its use of typical rhythms, castanets and melodic fragments of Moorish character, akin to that found in much Spanish folk music. The mosaic construction, parallelisms and other devices of impressionism are easily recognized. This is also true of the second movement, *"Les Parfums de la Nuit"* ("The Perfumes of the Night"), but a slower tempo and a darker sonority give this music a more sensuously emotional quality than is usual in Debussy's works. The second movement is joined to the third by a transition which gradually introduces the brighter coloring and faster motion appropriate to *"Le Matin d'un Jour de Fête"* ("The Morning of a Festival Day"). Here we find the counterpart of the first movement in bright sonority and mosaic construction. One notable orchestral effect is the use of the entire string section, *pizzicato,* in the manner of a huge guitar. And, as in the first movement, the *portamento* slides of the brass instruments are novel and delightful.

*Three Nocturnes*

Debussy intended the title to mean that these were "to designate . . . all the various impressions and the special effects of light that the word suggests." The first movement, *"Nuages"* ("Clouds") "renders the immutable aspect of the sky and the slow solemn motion of the clouds, fading away in grey tones tinged with white." One of the notable characteristics of this movement is the planing harmony, and the especial harmonic color of those chords, obtained by omitting the third of the chord. The second Nocturne, *"Fêtes"* ("Festivals") "portrays the restless dancing rhythms of the atmosphere, interspersed with abrupt scintillations; the episode of the procession passing through the festive scene and becoming merged in it. But the background remains persistently the same: the festival . . ." The last movement, *"Sirènes"* ("Sirens"), "depicts the sea and its innumerable rhythms; then amid the billows silvered by the moon the mysterious song of the sirens is heard; It laughs and passes." In this last movement, Debussy added to the orchestra a chorus of women's voices which does not sing words, but vocalises upon various vowel sounds. This is one of the earliest examples of using the voice as part of the orchestra, a practice which the motion pictures have frequently adopted in musical scores.

## MAURICE RAVEL, 1875-1937

This countryman of Debussy's was early influenced by the impressionist style, but developed individually in the direction of clearer forms, more sharply defined melodic lines, and the expression of a witty and ironic personality. The vagueness disappears in Ravel's music, replaced by a diamond-hard clarity. He is anti-romantic in many ways, often viewing the emotional excesses of that era with ironic humor. He was a master of the orchestra, but toward the end of his life there seems to develop a feeling of disinterest in music for music's sake, and a corresponding interest in the dazzling technique he had developed in handling the orchestra. For this reason, many of his later works seem shallow and meaningless despite their bejeweled settings. Of more lasting interest are:

1. The omnipresent *Bolero*, which is a study in the redemption of melodic and rhythmic monotony by brilliant orchestration.
2. The music drawn from the ballet *Daphnis et Chloé* and arranged into two orchestral suites. The second suite is the more popular, and contains a description of dawn and a "General Dance" that are quite compelling.
3. The suite, arranged from the suite for piano, *Ma Mère L'Oye (Mother Goose Suite)*, which shows his dazzling orchestration at its best. Some of the moments here are definitely impressionistic but without the vagueness of line and contour associated with that style.
4. *La Valse*, a rather gaudy and bombastic glorification of the spirit of the waltz, especially the Viennese variety.
5. A string quartet, piano trio, and "Introduction and Allegro" for harp, flute, clarinet and string quartet. Ravel's clarity of formal design combined with sharpness of musical ideas make these works highly successful. They often evoke feelings of the earlier French composers of the Renaissance and Baroque, especially in the dance movements.
6. Many piano pieces, among which *Jeux d'eau (The Fountain)*, "Pavan for a Dead Princess," the suite *Miroirs*, the *Sonatine*, and the difficult and frequently impressionistic *Gaspard de la nuit* suite are frequently played.
7. Two piano concertos — the first, in D for the left hand alone, was composed for Paul Wittgenstein, who lost his right hand in World War I;

the second, in G, for the usual complement of hands, was first performed in 1932.
8. *Rhapsodie Espagnole* for orchestra is one of Ravel's numerous works using Spanish rhythms and melodic elements.

A number of other composers may be numbered among the impressionists, none of whom attained the stature of Debussy or Ravel. The Englishman, Frederick Delius (1862-1934), the American, Charles T. Griffes (1884-1920) and the Alsatian, Charles M. Loeffler (1861-1935) are all notable for having written individual and interesting music. Some of the early works of the Spanish nationalist, Manuel de Falla (1876-1946) are impressionistic in atmosphere (*Nights in the Gardens of Spain*), while those of his Italian compatriot, Ottorino Respighi (1879-1936), are somewhat too bombastic and richly romantic in tone to qualify as impressionistic, although many techniques which Debussy invented are employed in the music.

*Part II: Expressionism*

The harmonic style of Wagner's *Tristan und Isolde*, together with its expressive aims, was continued and developed by a number of composers of many countries with important results. The dissonant style of Strauss in *Elektra* and *Salome*, as well as the comparatively milder works of the French Wagnerians resulted from explorations of the style. But the work carried on by a group of Viennese composers proved to be of the utmost significance for the coming development of music. Foremost, and mentor of the group, was Arnold Schönberg (1874-1951) (Plate XLIV), who, in various compositions such as

PLATE XLIII. *"The Cry." Lithograph by Edvard Munch, one of the early German expressionists. Note the emotional quality which is conveyed by the deliberate distortion and the composition. (Courtesy of the Archive-German Information Center.)*

*Verklärte Nacht (Transfigured Night)* and the enormous *Gurrelieder (Songs of the Dove)*, pressed the *Tristan* chromaticism and psychological expressiveness to the limits of the technique. He began to realize very clearly that the use of such a high degree of chromaticism negated tonality, and, after pondering the problem, set out to discover if there were any method of organization possible for nontonal music. His thinking and experimentation led to the establishment of what he called "the composition with twelve tones related only to one another," which is usually shortened to "the twelve-tone technique." His students and associates played an important part in the evolution of this system, and constitute with him the so-called "Viennese atonalists." Those who emerged as important composers in their own right were Alban Berg (1885-1935) and Anton von Webern (1883-1945).

The method of composition is as follows. The composer invents a theme, one which uses all twelve of the chromatic tones of the scale only once, and which, in the original plan, employs no formation within the series which resembles any triad. The fact that each tone may be used only once in the series and that no triad is admitted prevents

PLATE **XLIV.** *Arnold Schönberg. (Vogue photograph by George Platt Lynes.)*

the establishment of a tonic note. The series may now be manipulated into other shapes by inverting it, playing it backward (retrograde) and by playing the inversion backward; these all preserve the relationships between the adjacent tones, and thus retain the integrity of the series.

The series now furnishes the melodic material upon the application of metrical values assigned by the composer. Grouped into clusters of three, four or more tones, the row furnishes harmony for itself. Thus, the twelve-tone system exhibits the same relationship between melody and harmony that obtains from the use of the major-minor system. Since Schönberg's establishment of this technique in the 1920's, more sophisticated manipulations of the row as well as the serialization of rhythmic values, dynamics and articulation (the manner in which the tone is played, *e.g., staccato*) have been developed so that such music may be said to be totally organized.

Many musicians and critics, as well as laymen, have felt that this is too mechanical a process to produce good music, but we must realize that just such a system operates in traditional music of the major-minor scale variety. The only difference lies in the fact that the latter evolved through use over a long period of time, whereas the twelve-tone system required only somewhat over a decade for its formulation. Then too, we must realize that the composer is in control of the construction of the row: if he chooses intervals which do not sound chromatic, for example a number of perfect fourths or fifths, the result will be music whose harmonic style, based upon those fourths and fifths, will sound more open, less Wagnerian than that using a row in which the half step predominates. The initial choice lies with the composer, as it always has, and, within the system, he is still free to exercise his musical imagination.

The Viennese twelve-tone composers emphasized the expression of psychic states in their music to a high degree by employing not only the power of chromaticism, but also an enormously refined orchestral technique which sought out color possibilities of a more full-blooded kind than those exploited by the impressionists. In the use of these sonorities, as well as in the distortion of melodic lines by the employment of large and unexpected intervals and in the prevailing use of dissonant harmony, these composers were felt to be allied to the expressionist painters of the time, men such as Schönberg's friend Oscar Kokoschka, Edvard Munch (Plate XLIII), Vasily Kandinsky (Plate XLV) Paul Klee and others of the *"Blaue Reiter"* group (*c.f.,* also El

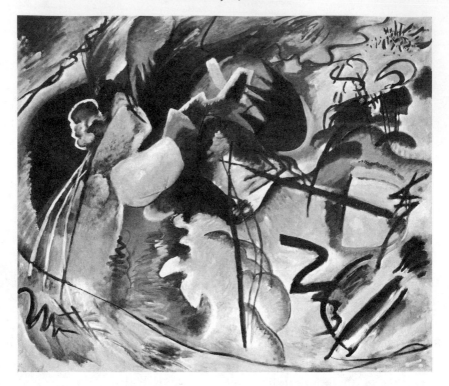

PLATE **XLV.** *"Painting with White Form, No. 166" by Kandinsky (1913). This is an example of abstract expressionism. Here Kandinsky, without preparation, paints the feelings that come to him, now abstracted and freed from the necessity of portraying real subject matter. (Courtesy of The Solomon R. Guggenheim Museum.)*

Greco, Plate XII, and Van Gogh, Plate XLVI). Hence, the application of the name *expressionism* to this musical style.

# THE STYLE OF EXPRESSIONISM

It must be realized that the twelve-tone technique is not the only means whereby expressionistic music may be created: a free use of the chromatic scale can accomplish the same thing, but is not as a rule organized to the extent that most composers wish. And so there are all varieties of expressionistic composers, and this variety extends to even the twelve-tone expressionists, no two of whom sound exactly alike. In describing the style we must remember again that these are generalizations

### MELODY

Expressionistic melody tends to move in angular leaps of considerable span, non-vocally, and usually possesses considerable tension because of this.

### HARMONY

The chromatic harmony, often composed of a number of major and minor seconds, usually has a high degree of dissonance saturation. The combinations of instrumental sonorities, however, control to a surprising degree the dissonant effect of this music, sometimes increasing or decreasing the clash of the intervals.

### RHYTHM

The rhythm of expressionistic music is usually complicated, with impulsive movement that adds to the tension of the melodic and harmonic elements. The movement is often discontinuous, with pauses, ritards and *accelerandos*.

### TEXTURE

The textures of these compositions are comparable to those of traditional music, mixing homophony and polyphony. In many works the *leitmotiv* technique is employed, resulting in a rather polyphonic texture.

### SONORITY

As mentioned above, most expressionistic composers seek for new and exciting sonorities which they feel will help them to more immediate communication with their listeners. To this end they have explored a wide variety of instrumental combinations, some delicate and impressionistic in quality, others rich, sometimes brutal in their stridency. The extreme registers of instruments are often brought into play, as are refinements of performance technique such as string harmonics, flutter-tonguing on the brass and woodwinds, solo violin or cello, and unusual percussion effects.

# FORMAL AND GENERATIVE PRINCIPLES

Foremost among these is, of course, the manipulation of the series. But by transposition to other degrees of the scale, analogous to changing key in the tonal system, or by introducing a new series or re-arranged fragments of the initial series, forms which originally derived from the interactions of tonality may be employed. Thus we find sonata-allegros, rondos, etc. Schönberg's principle of continual variation often obscures the return of themes or sections, however, and makes it difficult to recognize the various forms.

# EXPRESSIONIST COMPOSERS

## ARNOLD SCHÖNBERG, 1874-1951

*Verklärte Nacht (Transfigured Night)* (1899)

This work was originally composed by the twenty-five-year-old Schönberg for string sextet, but later he transcribed it for string orchestra, which is the medium used for most performances. The piece uses the chromatic harmony of *Tristan* so continuously and intensely in expressing the essence of the poem which inspired it, that the impossibility of developing this style further is almost as plain to the listener as it was to the composer himself. The music was inspired by a poem of Richard Dehmel (1863-1920) in a cycle called *Woman and the World,* and has been rendered into prose by Henry Krehbiel as follows:

PLATE XLVI. *"Starry Night" by Van Gogh. The painting is expressionistic in that the artist shows his feelings about the starry night. Note the emotional effect of the upward leaping cypress tree. (Courtesy of The Museum of Modern Art.)*

Two mortals walk through a cold, barren grove. The moon sails over the tall oaks, which send their scrawny branches up through the unclouded moonlight. A woman speaks. She confesses a sin to the man at her side. She is with child, and he is not its father. She had lost belief in happiness, and longing for life's fullness, for motherhood and mother's duty, she had surrendered herself, shuddering, to the embraces of a man she knew not. She had thought herself blessed, but now life had avenged itself upon her by giving her the love of him she walked with.

A man speaks. Let her not burden her soul with thoughts of guilt. See, the moon's sheen enwraps the universe! Together they are driving over chill waters, but a flame from each warms the other. It, too, will transfigure the child, which she will bear to him. For she has inspired the brilliant glow within him and made him, too, a child. They sink into each other's arms. Their breaths meet in kisses in the air. . . . Two mortals wander through the wondrous moonlight.

Anything much more romantic — and Freudian — than this is hard to imagine. Schönberg sets these erotic and guilty emotions in music using the *leitmotiv* technique of his great model, Wagner, and, through the typical uses of nonfinal cadences and chromaticism, manages to convey the searing emotionalism of the poem. This is, by the way, the first tone poem written for a chamber music ensemble.

### *Pierrot Lunaire* (1912)

This work marked a further step away from traditional chromaticism toward the twelve-tone techniques. Like *Verklärte Nacht,* it has a literary inspiration, but here the poems are declaimed by the voice as part of the music. The poems, originally in French, are by Alfred Giraud, but, as used by Schönberg they appear in the German translation of Hartleben. These "thrice seven poems" devoted to the moonstruck private reality of Pierrot, are recited by a speaking voice whose musical modulations and inflections were suggested by the composer by writing approximate pitches on a staff in the score. This notation also defines the time-relationship between the voice, called *sprechstimme,* and the instrumental parts. Each poem is a miniature, scored for some combination derived from the following chamber group: piano, flute (interchangeable with piccolo), clarinet (interchangeable with bass clarinet), violin (interchangeable with viola), and cello. The scoring is often extremely tenuous, suggesting more than it states, and the technique is that of free chromaticism, with a high saturation of dissonance. The work is extremely difficult to perform, and required forty rehearsals before the premiere performance in 1912. Each of the twenty-one poems deals with an adventure of Pierrot, expressionistically vivid but elusive in meaning, and often poignantly nostalgic in mood. The most sophisticated techniques are applied to create purely musical forms, the structures of which are often not at all apparent to the listener.

### *String Quartet No. 4, Op. 37* (1936)

Schönberg completed this twelve-tone work after coming to America. It is very strictly organized, but the flow of the rhythmic patterns makes it seem almost improvisational. It is one of this composer's most accomplished works, one in which his freedom within the system allows him to create formal movements corresponding to those of the classic string quartet. The first movement is reminiscent of the sonata-allegro, the second a kind of minuet, the third a slow movement which includes two unison recitatives, and a complex final allegro related to the rondo structure.

## ALBAN BERG, 1885-1935

Alban Berg was once called "the finest of Schönberg's works," so a word about him at this point will not be out of place! This gifted composer arrived at an advanced harmonic style very early in his career, but never became a strict twelve-tone composer. Rather, he incorporated into his work romantic influences as well as twelve-tone techniques, leaning rather far toward the expressive element, which to him was of the utmost importance no matter what musical devices were necessary to accomplish it. For this reason his music is often easier for the listener to understand than that of his teacher. Three of his works are heard frequently enough in concert to warrant mention here.

### The Lyric Suite, for string quartet (1926)

This work, in six movements, marks Berg's first essay in the twelve-tone technique, although it is not used consistently throughout the composition. The fast and slow movements alternate, the fast ones becoming faster and the slow ones becoming slower as the work progresses. Berg uses almost all of the "trick" effects possible on stringed instruments, but the sounds produced are always closely related to what he is trying to communicate.

### Violin Concerto (1935)

Berg wrote this concerto "to the memory of an angel," the young daughter of Alma Mahler, whose death affected the composer profoundly. He chose a twelve-tone series containing triads so as to mitigate the harshness of the twelve-tone construction, and, since triad harmonization was thus rendered possible, inserted in the finale a Lutheran chorale whose text ("It is enough. Lord, if it pleases Thee, measure out my days.") reflected upon the tragedy. Berg completed the work in such a short time that certain commentators feel that he had a premonition of his own death a few months later. The work was commissioned by the American violinist Felix Krasner.

## *Wozzeck* (1914-1921)

In this opera Wozzeck, a poor soldier, is tormented by three people: by his superior officer, the Captain; by a sadistic physician to whom he surrenders himself for medical experiments in order to get money to support his mistress, Marie, and their child; and by the Drum Major who vaunts his superior physical ability by beating up the seemingly helpless and inoffensive soldier. The brutal Drum Major finally seduces Marie, and when Wozzeck, after torturing uncertainty, has convinced himself of her infidelity, he stabs her, and subsequently drowns himself in remorse.

This expressionistic psychological drama is set with extreme realism by Berg in an opera of three acts duration, arranged by him from Büchner's drama. Each act is cast in a purely musical form. Thus, the five scenes of the first act are the movements of a suite: rhapsody, military march, lullaby, passacaglia, and rondo. The second act is a symphony in five movements: sonata-allegro, fantasy and fugue, largo, scherzo, and rondo. The third act consists of a series of pieces each of which exploits a single musical concept. They are entitled "inventions," and in this act are based upon a theme, a tone, a rhythm, a chord, a key, and on steady eighth-note movement. Despite this formal approach, the opera moves fluidly and dramatically, not stiffly, as might be imagined. Atonal and tonal writing are mixed, according to the dramatic effect desired. This work is undoubtedly one of the history-making compositions of our century.

### ANTON VON WEBERN, 1883-1945

This student and disciple of Schönberg wrote in a rarified idiom in which the twelve-tone row was broken up into its component notes (fragmented) and sounded in widely separated time relations and pitch registers. There is often no traditional sense of continuity, form, or organization in the sound of this music. It may be called "athematic" in the sense that no themes are heard as such, although it is usually very strict in its employment of the tone-row. Webern is regarded as the musician of the future by the more advanced composers.

## TOTAL SERIALIZATION, CHANCE MUSIC AND MUSIQUE CONCRÈTE

The techniques of Webern have been adopted and further organized by certain contemporary composers, prominent among whom are Pierre Boulez, the Italian Luigi Nono and Karlheinz Stockhausen, although the latter is more notable for his electronic music, an outgrowth of the twelve-tone system. These composers have sought to totally organize their music not only by using serial technique in regard to the pitches, but also by applying this concept to the metric flow, the dynamic variation and the articulation of the pitches (*i.e., staccato, legato,* etc.). For example, a metric row like the following might be applied to the tone-row:

Superposed upon these might be the dynamic and articulation rows:

Each of these may be manipulated in the same ways as the tone-row, except, of course, the problem of inversion and transposition becomes more or less arbitrary in many cases. The music thus resulting is said to be totally organized.

Freeing themselves from the confines of the twelve-note chromatic scale and the limited dynamic scheme of instrumentally-produced music, Stockhausen and others have adopted electronic tone-generating devices to produce their music. The pitch and time elements are notated on a graph, together with the dynamics and the mixture of overtones needed to produce the desired sonority. The whole complex is recorded on tape. The possibilities are well-nigh limitless, for the electronic devices are capable of producing an infinitely variable pitch spectrum and a similar dynamic range, and the durations of these sound complexes can be minutely controlled. The technique is as yet in its infancy: whether it will produce music understandable and meaningful to the laymen remains to be seen.

A technique opposed to the logic of totally organized music, popular among some composers of whom John Cage (1912-) is notable, has been termed "chance" or "random" music. It is analogous to certain practices of the painter Jackson Pollock (1921-1956) who dripped paint from his brushes in interesting random patterns upon a canvas. In one of Cage's compositions, twelve radios are placed in a semicircle upon the stage. Each is tuned to a different station and provided with an operator who controls the dynamic level and the choice of station at the signal of a conductor armed with a stopwatch and a time-chart giving the temporal relations of each of the radios. The nature of programs tuned in on the radios does not matter: in this lies the chance element. Various other compositions of this kind have been created by Cage and his colleagues. Very probably they are useful as experiments which jar us out of our complacency, and some of them may yield valuable results in the investigation of subjective time.

In addition to percussion music — Edgar Varèse (1885-) is the pioneer here — Boulez, Otto Leuning, Vladimir Ussachevsky and others have explored the possibilities of the manipulation of tape-recorded natural sounds. By varying the tape speeds (hence the frequencies of the sounds) and the use of multiple recording, they have produced what has so far received a name only in French: *musique concrète*. This is not a random procedure, since the sounds are chosen and manipulated, but a modern electronically sophisticated echo of the "noise music" or "Futurism" which followed the First World War.

These varieties of experimental music have considerable value, and not only as "shock treatments." They are certainly more representative of our present culture than are instruments whose shapes and techniques were old centuries ago. But, it seems, this music has yet to find its Haydn — or better yet, its Perotin.

# Part III. Neoclassicism

Neoclassicism stems in part from the various anti-romantic passing styles which proliferated during the years from about 1910 to 1930. Among these was Futurism, which advocated the use of noise as music, Primitivism, the return to the artistic culture of the savage, and the various tongue-in-cheek parodies of the romantic manner and the glorification of the often cheap and vulgar popular song by the French group called *Les Six*. Neoclassicism, however, is non-romantic rather than anti-romantic often returning to pre-romantic styles for source material. It is a modern classic manifestation because it (a) strives for a balance between form and material, (b) it is carefully controlled in emotional expression, (c) it tries to attain classic clarity of thought and presentation by the adoption of modest means of performance and transparent, often non-blending textures, (d) it adopts polyphony as a cardinal element and (e) it uses formal ideas from earlier periods, adapting them to modern concepts of tonality, melody, harmony and rhythm.

We shall find many varieties of neoclassicism in our survey of the style, for each individual composer utilizes those concepts of classicism which are most native or important to him in accordance with his musical background. In the case of Stravinsky, it would seem that the intellectual concept of music as an objective sounding structure in time, with no intrinsic emotional content, together with the detachment typical of his personality, have combined to produce the non-romantic compositions of the period from 1923 to 1950. Bartók, on the other hand, exhibits an essentially romantic musical temperament with a strong nationalistic bent in his use and development of forms arising out of the Baroque and Classic eras. The third prominent neoclassic composer, Hindemith, is as Teutonic as Bartók is Hungarian, but the German style has been so prominent for so long that this nationalistic element in his music usually passes without comment. Hindemith's music is written in a less objective style than that of Stravinsky, and admits of emotional communication. In structure, however, the connection with the classic, baroque and even renaissance and medieval styles may be noted. American neoclassicists are equally individual in their approaches, some including nationalistic or romantic elements,

PLATE XLVII. *"The Lovers" by Picasso. The return to neoclassic simplicity, grace, and naturalness is seen here. (Courtesy of The National Gallery of Art, Chester Dale Collection.)*

while others pursue more objective and less emotional style. But before we examine the works of these individual composers, let us note certain general characteristics of the neoclassic attitude, always keeping in mind that it is the classic ideals which are important, regardless of complex innovations in harmony and rhythm which may momentarily obscure the main point.

# THE STYLE OF NEOCLASSICISM

### MELODY

About the only safe generalization to make about melody in this style is that it tends to be rather constructive in quality, often containing workable rhythmic or melodic motives. It does not usually contain triad motives or other strongly chordal elements, and it often tends toward thematic inconclusiveness rather than melodic completeness.

### HARMONY

The neoclassic composer finds his scale and, therefore, harmonic material in the major-minor system, the modal scales of the Middle Ages and of folk song, and in so-called "artificial" scales which he may devise in accordance with some expressive intent. The harmonies derived from these scales may be summarized as follows:

*Tertian harmony,* traditional chord-building procedures, using the third as the basis of construction, and extending the chord up to the thirteenth above the bass (Example 79a). Also chromatic alterations of these chords.

*Quartal harmony,* built upon successive fourths rather than thirds (Example 79b). Such construction allows of a chord containing all of the twelve tones of the chromatic scale, although in normal practice only three or four tones are usually used.

*Secundal harmony* is built upon the whole or half step (the second), and is apt to be more dissonant than those mentioned above (Example 79c). The clusters have a way of sounding like triads when they contain several tones, and therefore are most effective when the number of notes is limited to three or four.

EXAMPLE 79. *Examples of modern harmony.*

a. TRIADIC HARMONY     b. QUARTAL HARMONY     c. SECUNDAL HARMONY

TRIAD   7th   9th   11th   13th

Two other kinds of chords also appear in modern music which may be analyzed as belonging to one of the above systems, but which do not necessarily sound as different or as complex as they. The first is the usually tertian chord (especially the simple triad) with an added dissonant tone (*e.g.,* C-E-F♯-G). The most frequent added tones to the triad are the second, fourth and sixth notes above the bass of the triad. The second type is called a *polychord,* and is formed by combining two triads, usually foreign to each other, as in Stravinsky's ballet *Petrouchka* where the tonic chords of C-major (C-E-G) and F♯-major (F♯-A♯-C♯) are combined. The choice of chords governs the total dissonant (or consonant quality).

It must be realized that much neoclassic music also employs a considerable amount of chromaticism: this element is so controlled in these works, however, that they do not resemble expressionistic compositions. All in all, most neoclassic harmony is apt to have a considerable degree of dissonance present. But once within the private world created by one of these composers, dissonance ceases to shock us and becomes a more normal quality.

### RHYTHM

If the special realm of the Romantic period was harmony, that of the contemporary period may be said to be rhythm. In order to eliminate the monotony of the regularly recurring strong metric pulse at the beginning of each measure — the so-called "tyranny of the bar-line" — various new techniques were invented, some simple, others quite complex. And the research in rhythmic techniques still goes on, especially in the field of electronic music where the ordinary time elements of musically notated rhythm and meter are far too coarse to be used.

The simplest way to shift the metric accent is to change the meter. In other words, metric signatures might vary with every measure, a procedure called "changing meters." Or the same result may be obtained by retaining the one meter throughout, but shifting the stresses by means of accents written in the music. Both have been used, the latter by many conservative composers like Brahms, the changing meters most notably by Stravinsky and Bartók.

Such changing meters give the effect of prose rhythm, as compared to the poetic rhythm of traditional music. A variety of this broken metric rhythm is that called additive rhythm. In this technique the meter signature of each measure adds or subtracts one pulsation from the number contained in the preceding measure, *e.g.*, 4/4, 3/4, 2/4, or the reverse. These are sometimes called "Stravinsky rhythms" from his use of them in *Le Sacre du Printemps*.

Another modern rhythmic procedure consists of subdividing smaller pulses within an ordinary measure into repetitive groups of two and three. For example, in 4/4 meter the eight eighth notes might be divided *1 2 3 1 2 3 1 2*. Or in 6/8 meter the old device called *hemiola* may be used, alternating two groups of three eighth notes with three groups of two eighth notes.

Rhythmic counterpoint, fostered by the interest in percussion instruments, has developed steadily, using the above devices alone as well as in polymetric combinations of considerable complexity to Western ears, but of childish simplicity to the Javanese and Indians whose rhythmic systems are far more subtle than ours.

### TEXTURE

While both polyphony and homophony appear in the music of our times, there is a definite tendency toward polyphonic writing. The principal aim of modern counterpoint is to emphasize the individuality and freedom of each of the lines. This type of polyphony has been named "linear counterpoint" in order to distinguish it from the more harmonically oriented counterpoint of the romantic and previous eras.

### SONORITY

Along with the return to greater formal clarity in the construction of the music, there has been a return to the modest ensemble and clear sonorities of the earlier times. Depending upon the aim of the composer, such groupings may yield rich or thin, warm or cool sonorities without becoming overpowering in the manner of the gigantic late romantic orchestra, and always retain a certain classic reserve due to their size.

# FORMAL AND GENERATIVE PRINCIPLES

## TONALITY AND MODALITY

Most neoclassic composers employ some extension of the tonal (or modal) systems. There are several ways of accomplishing this in a modern context, one which is flexible enough to allow for the varieties of harmony.

In order to weaken the sense of keynote in either tonal or modal systems, sometimes the harmony is kept deliberately non-functional, much like the modal procedures of the late Medieval period. There is usually little dissonance in this music, but the unexpected harmonic progressions and the clarity of the major and minor triads of which the music is largely composed make up for the loss.

A more dissonant idiom which still retains many of the advantages of the tonal system is polytonality (or polymodality) which employs two or more keys on separate planes simultaneously. The planes may be caused to clash sharply, or to have only a few mild collisions, depending upon the choice of keys. The harmony consists, of course, of polychords, mentioned earlier. This technique admits of functional harmony in its separate parts. It was exploited by Stravinsky in *Petrouchka* and *Le Sacre du Printemps,* and has formed an important element in the music of the French composer Darius Milhaud.

One of the simplest systems makes use of all chord-building possibilities — tertian, quartal or secundal — of the major or modal scales, usually with little or no chromatic alteration. Functional, key-defining harmony is avoided, but since the materials consist only of the notes of the particular scale, the importance of the tonic as a rest point is preserved. This technique is known as *pandiatonicism.*

A method allied to the above pandiatonicism, yet differing from it in allowing more chromaticism, is that which we might call "tonal-axis" composition. Here the composer establishes a tone which he wishes the listener to feel as the tonal basis of the music by various devices of emphasis — repetition, cadences, organpoint, etc. Foreign chords and melodic lines, chromatic or not, are heard in reference to the important tone, thus creating in the listener's mind a clear distinction as to what is passing and what is more important. Much of the later music of Hindemith and Bartók relies upon the subtle use of this technique.

### UNIFYING DEVICES

Many modern works employ the cyclic devices invented during the Romantic era — mottos, thematic quotation and theme transformation. Others rely only upon stylistic unity to achieve coherence. In the first division are many of the works of Bartók — his Concerto for Orchestra and Sixth String Quartet are notable — while the greater number of compositions of Stravinsky and Hindemith do not make use of such techniques.

## THE OSTINATO

This old device came into prominence again during the first years of the twentieth century and has remained as an important element ever since. Simply stated, an *ostinato* is created by the repetition of a harmonic or melodic musical figure. In its simplest form it may be merely a repeated chord. Melodically, such a figure may be of any length, but it is probably most effective when relatively short. It may be derived thematically, and may appear in a single voice or imitatively. It may be a structural element also, in that sometimes an *ostinato* resembles an activated organpoint, creating a more or less static situation or emphasizing a tonic note.

## DEVELOPMENTAL TECHNIQUES

In modern musical compositions there is a greater tendency to vary the thematic material more boldly than there was in the pre-romantic times. It is now common practice to expand or contract an interval of the theme in order to suggest new ways for that theme to grow. Inversion of the basic idea, rhythmic transformation, retrograde and mirror inversions are all to be met with frequently. Distortion is also employed if it is consistent with the expressive purpose of the music.

## PARODY

Some neoclassic and antiromantic compositions parody the procedures of bygone musical eras. The intent may be ironic or humorous, as in the *Divertissement* of Jacques Ibert, nostalgic and charming, as Prokofiev's *Classical Symphony* is, or a modern adaptation of thematic material from the classic period in the manner of Stravinsky's use of themes by Pergolesi (1710-1736) in his ballet *Pulcinella*. Much of the neoclassic music of the 1920's was parodistic in that it imitated the manner of an earlier time in regard to form, objectivity and rhythmic drive, while still employing modern concepts of harmony and melody.

Examples of this, such as Stravinsky's *Concerto for Piano and Wind Instruments* and Ernest Bloch's two concerti grossi, illustrate the point amply.


### FOLK MUSIC

Probably as a result of the nationalistic movements during the latter part of the nineteenth century, many modern composers have worked with music derived from folk sources. They have used it intact sometimes in the manner of Ralph Vaughan Williams (*e.g., Three Norfolk Rhapsodies*), or, more importantly for purely art music, distilled the essence of their researches in the field, combined it with their personal style, and presented us with music which is often more universal than either of its sources. The outstanding example of this synthesis is to be found in the music of Béla Bartók, especially in such works as the Divertimento for String Orchestra, the *Allegro Barbaro* for piano and the final movement of the wonderful *Music for Strings, Percussion and Celesta*.


### TENSION MODULATION

Just as the melodic aspects of contemporary music reflect the tensions of our time, so the harmonic practices support these melodic ideas with vertical tone-clusters of varying tension. We have seen that impressionist harmony accepted dissonance as an entity which required no explanation, no resolution to consonance. The modern composer has almost wholly adopted this attitude, but is more likely to use gradations of dissonance in order to use the structural implications of this musical tension. With such tension modulation he can achieve harmonic climaxes, an interesting ebb and flow of chordal structures within a work, and devise strong and satisfactory cadences.

EXAMPLE 80. *Tension modulation.*

Briefly, tension modulation is accomplished by the addition or subtraction of dissonances in a chordal complex (Example 80). A dissonance, in modern thought, consists of the intervals of a major second (C to D), a minor second (*e.g.*, C to D♭) and their inversions (minor seventh: D up to C; major seventh, D♭ up to C). These are combined with other intervals in chord structures. As they are added or eliminated the tension of the total structure changes. The cadences in Example 81 use tension modulation on a purely structural level, and may often be classified as final or non-final, as well as emphatic devices to create a tonic tone.

EXAMPLE 81. *Modern cadences.*

## NEOCLASSIC COMPOSERS

It would be well to recollect at this point the fact that within any of the historical styles with which we have dealt there have been rather different personal idioms and dialects. In the Baroque, for example, were the four quite contrasting personal idioms of Corelli, Vivaldi, Bach and Handel. It was thus in impressionism and in expressionism, and will be found to be increasingly so in neoclassicism, even to the point of inclusion of other strong styles within the neoclassic framework. And, as usual, each of these composers passed through stages of development in which he experimented with various materials. Stravinsky, for example, began as a nationalistic impressionist before establishing a neoclassic norm; and both Bartók and Hindemith went through periods when the expressionistic element was important in their music. So let us make these allowances: composers are human beings, after all!

### IGOR STRAVINSKY, 1882-

This pathfinder of modern music was born in Oranienbaum, a suburb of St. Petersburg, Russia. The son of a bass singer of the Imperial

Opera, he was raised in a musical atmosphere, and became a proficient pianist at an early age. It was not until 1901, when he met Rimsky-Korsakoff, that he decided to study composition seriously. After six years of preparatory work, he became a private pupil of the older Russian master. During this time two works of his gained some success: a "Fantastic Scherzo" and a tone painting called "Fireworks." These came to the attention of Sergei Diaghilev, the impresario of the Ballet Russe in Paris, who commissioned the young composer to write a score for a ballet, *The Firebird,* based on a Russian legend. With the success of the composition, Stravinsky was commissioned repeatedly by Diaghilev for ballet scores, the results of which were *Petrouchka* (1911), *The Rite of Spring* (1913), *L'Histoire du Soldat* (*The Soldier's Tale*) (1918), and *Pulcinella* (1920). During this first period, extend-

PLATE XLVIII. *Igor Stravinsky. (Photo by Columbia Records, courtesy of Boosey and Hawkes.)*

ing from *The Firebird* in 1910 to the opera *Mavra* in 1922, Stravinsky produced music which was distinctly national in character, based upon Russian literature and history. At this time he also made the acquaintance of American jazz and composed a few works in which the jazz influence is strong: *Ragtime* (Armistice Day, 1918), and *The Soldier's Tale* of the same year.

With the composition of the Octet for Wind Instruments, Stravinsky inaugurated his neoclassic period, which was to extend to approximately 1950. Many aspects of this work indicate the way he was to take during this time: clear-cut motives, "tick-tock" rhythmic accompaniments and syncopated rhythms, clear and unemotional orchestration for unusual combinations of instruments, coloristic use of dissonance, *ostinati,* and oblique references to jazz. Of the numerous works composed during these years, the following stand out: the Octet for Wind Instruments (1923), the Concerto for Piano and Wind Instruments (1925), the ballets *Apollon Musagète* (1928) and *Le Baiser de la Fée (The Fairy's Kiss)* (1928), the *Capriccio* for piano and orchestra (1929), the oratorio *Oedipus Rex* (1927), the *Symphony of Psalms* (1930), the Symphony in C (1940), the Symphony in Three Movements (1945), the ballet *Orpheus* (1947), and the opera *The Rake's Progress* (1950), after the series of etchings by Hogarth.

After about 1950 Stravinsky turned toward more abstract techniques, and since then has written a number of works using the serial technique. These works are not expressionistic, however, but are still neoclassic in an idiom, austere, severe, and somewhat forbidding. Among them are numbered *In Memoriam Dylan Thomas, Agon* (1957), an abstract ballet, and the *Canticum Sacrum* (1956) which was written for the Cathedral of St. Mark in Venice.

## The Russian Period

The ballets which Stravinsky wrote for Diaghilev between 1910 and 1913 effectively ended the romantic era in a blaze of glory. The first of these, *The Firebird,* is more obviously impressionistic in style, but the techniques of doubling, free use of dissonance, complex chord structures (almost always tertian), exploitation of orchestral color and fragmentation of thematic material are also common to the later works, *Petrouchka* and *Le Sacre du Printemps.* Combined with the still novel inventions of impressionism were some rather new techniques, ones which seem to be characteristic of Stravinsky throughout most of his career. Many of these are found in *Le Sacre* (as it is familiarly known) and we shall trace them in that work. A detailed analysis of this gigantic and epoch-making work is beyond the scope

EXAMPLE 82.

of this book, however; so we must be content with indicating a few points of interest as we journey through the first part of the work.

There are two large episodes in the ballet, the first entitled "The Adoration of the Earth," and the second "The Sacrifice." The action depicts the celebration of the coming of spring by a pagan Russian tribe in the dawn of history. To insure the fertility of the earth, a maiden is chosen to be sacrificed; after preparatory rites she dances until she is dead.

*Part I, Introduction:* The bassoon, in its extreme high register, announces a plaintive theme composed of only a few notes (Example 82a) which are rhythmically varied upon repetition. An impressionistic section follows which sets the Neolithic scene, grows to a climax, then subsides with a recollection of the opening melody. This section is not marked by strong rhythms and employs almost entirely the colors of the wind instruments.

*Dance of the Adolescents:* This section is introduced by a fragmentary *ostinato,* one of Stravinsky's frequent devices, after which a percussive series of polychords assigned to the strings — not the brass or percussion — provides an exciting series of sections in additive rhythms separated by more angular figures in the bassoons and cellos. A motive outlining the interval of a fourth appears and eventually becomes a primitive scale melody of narrow range (Example 82b). This is followed by a more rhythmically active section, still exploiting the *ostinato,* during which the horns announce a variant of the previous melody, still narrow in range and primitive sounding (Example 82c). This version is presented with increasing force and instrumentation, always against multiple *ostinato* figures. Such repetition, typical of Russian composers, bears Stravinsky's hallmark in that it is usually rhythmically varied by shifting the theme so that the metric accents fall upon different notes.

*The Play of Abduction:* This is an active polytonal section which presents a bright theme characterized by leaping fourths in somewhat the fashion of a fanfare (Example 82d). Although they are heard with difficulty, changing meters and unequal subdivision of the measure add their excitement to that of the highly dissonant sonority. In a sense, there are not themes in this impressionistic section but only scales and *arpeggios* derived from the basic polytonal chords. The interval of the fourth again has an important place in the figures.

*Round Dances of Spring:* This section presents varied repetitions of two themes, again primitively constructed against a plodding *osti-*

PLATE **XLIX**. *African Mask from Itumba, The Congo; "Les Demoiselles d'Avignon" by Picasso. Examples of primitivism, genuine and imitated. Note the use of the primitive style of the mask by Picasso in the two faces at the right. Note also the distortion in representing the noses as well as other features of the other figures. (Courtesy of The Museum of Modern Art.)*

516

*nato* which appears first in the low strings. The horns play a colorful version of the theme doubled at the fifth, minor sixth and the octave (Example 82e). Later, a rapid section brings back the theme of the previous Play of Abduction, developing it athletically with changing meters and massive chordal interruptions. A quiet solo in the alto flute doubled two octaves higher by the E♭ clarinet leads to the next scene.

*Games of the Rival Tribes:* Here we find *ostinati,* changing meters, antiphonal exchanges between choirs of the orchestra, and splashes of woodwind color obtained by parallel triads moving in rapid scale figures. The strings again act as percussion instruments. The first melodic ideas are related to those based upon the fourth which were heard previously; these are now followed by a more lyric theme, still narrow and repetitive, which emphasizes the interval of the third both in its shape and in its doubling (Example 82f). It is handed around the orchestra, interrupted by impressionistic fragments and finally returned to prominence in *stretto* imitations.

*Procession of the Sage:* A short section of highly dissonant, *ostinato*-saturated impressionistic writing in which a bugle-call fourth again comes to the fore.

*Dance of the Earth:* This is the concluding section of Part I, and is essentially choreographic in nature, containing many figures which through energy or direction seem to imply physical motion; these are called "gestic" motives. It is notable for the combination of not only different *ostinati,* but also for the combination of several decorated versions of the same figure. There are added-note chords, fragments of whole-tone scales, doubling at the fifth and octave, and rhythmically compressed versions of the primitive scale theme based upon the fourth.

Part Two consists of an "Introduction," "Mysterious Circle of the Adolescents," "Glorification of the Chosen One," "Evocation of the Ancestors," "Ritual Activity of the Ancestors," and concludes with the "Sacrificial Dance." Much of the same kind of treatment of similar themes takes place here. There is perhaps more obvious use of changing meters, especially in the "Sacrificial Dance," but after being guided through Part I, the listener will find no new problems in Part II.

In summation, then, we find the free use of dissonance, parallel chord movement and doubling at intervals other than the octave, sophisticated rhythmic procedures, polytonality, unusual orchestration and use of instruments, and frequent *ostinato.* Many of these become more refined, some eliminated entirely, in the second creative period.

517

## The Neoclassic Period

With the composition of the Octet for Wind Instruments, Stravinsky began his neoclassic period which extends roughly from 1923 to 1950, although certain traits of this style persist in the serial techniques adopted increasingly during the fifties. We shall direct our attention to two compositions: the Octet and the *Symphony of Psalms*. During this period Stravinsky adapted the inward essentials of the classic and baroque forms to his music, creating concerto grosso types (Concerto for 16 Instruments, the so-called *Dumbarton Oaks Concerto* 1938), the oratorio (*Oedipus Rex*, 1927), the classic symphony (Symphony in C, 1940), and the eighteenth-century "numbers opera" (*The Rake's Progress*, 1950).

In each of these works the tonal basis is very clear, although bitonal passages occur with reasonable frequency; the *ostinato* and rhythmic tricks are still present, although not emphasized to the degree of *Le Sacre*, the gestic motive is plainly in operation as the clear-cut thematic element, and the orchestration is mercilessly transparent, allowing every line and rhythm to be heard. During this time, Stravinsky did not lose his interest in the ballet, as evidenced by several scores written for that art form. Important among these are *Apollon Musagète* (1928), *Perséphone* (1934, a choral ballet, and one of the very few works by this composer which is homophonic throughout), *Jeux de Cartes (The Card Party*, 1937) and *Orpheus* (1947). Note the preference for subjects based upon classic mythology.

*The Octet for Wind Instruments:* This work is in three movements, *Sinfonia, Tema con variazioni,* and Finale. The basis is baroque rather than classical style, and the work is scored for flute, clarinet, two bassoons, two trumpets, and two trombones. The *Sinfonia* is prefaced with an introduction in a slower tempo, consisting first of a series of ornamental cadences around a held tone — almost rococo in sound — which serves to establish the tonal center. There follow cool sonorities in contrapuntal texture created out of somewhat repetitive figures which answer back and forth, and the introduction concludes with trill figures. The main body of the movement which follows forcefully announces the angular theme at the octave and unison (Example 83a). This theme is developed imitatively, accompanied by countersubjects. It becomes rhythmically shifted to off-beats of the measure, and its intervals become progressively changed.

Example 83.

FIRST MOVEMENT: Allegro moderato

a.

b.

cant. tranquillo

c.

1 Fl., 8va higher.

SECOND MOVEMENT: Andantino

d. THEME 8va

Fl. & Cl. 2 8ves apart

Trpt.

e. FIRST THEME

SECOND THEME
f.

A second theme (Example 83b) announced by the trumpet now appears, more lyric, although it contains two skips — one of a fifth upward, the other a major seventh. Out of the counterpoint to this theme as it develops, flows a third section (Example 83c), the main material of which is a chromatic scale theme, an angular "chain suspension" figure which resembles those used in the Baroque period, and a rhythmic motive. These are developed, after which the B theme returns, followed by A, which closes the work. There are *ostinato* elements, the texture is reasonably polyphonic, always propelled by interesting rhythms, and the clarity of intent and coolness of emotional atmosphere is truly neoclassic. Formally, the plan is: Introduction:

A B C B A. This is the so-called "arch" form which appears with some frequency in the music of the twentieth century.

The theme of the variations of the following movement is lyric, and, from beginning to end, covers a wide span (Example 83d). Prominent among its features is the favorite Stravinskyan device of oscillating between major (C♯ down to A) and minor (C♮ to A) thirds. Indeed, the whole movement might be termed "variations on an interval," so important a part do the major-minor thirds (and their inversion, the minor-major sixths) play in the construction of the angular melodic and contrapuntal lines. The other prominent interval is that of the seventh, already encountered together with one species of third in the theme of the A section of the first movement! The sequence of variations is rather interesting: after the theme has been stated, Variation A ensues, consisting of rapid scale figures over a bold statement of the M-m thirds in the trombones. This is followed by Variation B, a ternary structure with a balletic central section, which requires somewhat less than twice the time of Variation A to perform. A now returns, followed by Variations C and D whose total length is somewhat greater than three times the length of A. Variation A again returns, followed by Variation E, lasting a little less than four times the duration of A, which leads to the finale by means of a short cadenza for the flute. Here we see the principle of additive rhythms applied to formal procedures according to the following plan: A-2A-A-3A-A-4A-finale. The last movement must be considered in the plan as the goal toward which the whole middle movement is directed. No trace of this calculation is audible in the music, however, which sometimes takes on a fantastic character (A), or a somewhat humorous cast (B).

The Finale might be termed a "sonata-allegro without recapitulation," or possibly a movement resembling the baroque orchestral concerto in which two themes are presented and developed. In any case, two themes are clearly stated, the first one in the bassoons, one instrument having the theme while the other plays a C-major scale accompaniment (Example 83e). This theme sounds like a good fugue subject, but it is never employed as such. The second theme arrives shortly, stated expressively by the trumpet (Example 82f). It is to be noted that these themes are consistent with those of the other movements in that they include thirds and sevenths — indeed, at times these closely resemble some of the other themes. After the exposition of the second theme, the first one returns in an exact repetition of most of the beginning section of the movement. This leads to a development of various parts of this theme by rhythmic compression, interval alteration, fragmentation, simplification and association with new accompaniment figures. The downward second interval of the second theme is also used in an extended fashion during the development. A rhythmic motive develops out of the contrapuntal accompaniment, and leads to the coda, a series of block chords which are gently syncopated, resulting in a rhythm reminiscent of some of the South American dances. Recurring from time to time in this section is the opening theme of the *allegro* of the first movement. Despite the lack of recapitulation, the form seems fulfilled and complete: the use of the C-major tonality in the beginning and final sections may have something to do with this.

*Symphony of Psalms:* If one were to judge the second period of this composer's works solely by the one just mentioned, one might think that Stravinsky had lost the elemental power so in evidence in *Le Sacre* and had become a composer of pleasing small works in a strictly neoclassic style. Such a judgment would be confounded upon hearing the *Symphony of Psalms,* for here one is confronted with a mighty evocation of the religious attitude of an earlier age. This work is such a complete fusion of the medieval and modern that the two become inseparably one. It is austere, yet moving, and has a kind of elemental simplicity for all the modern sophistications of rhythm and harmony it contains.

The work was completed in 1930 and was composed "to the glory of God, and dedicated to the Boston Symphony Orchestra on the occasion of its fiftieth anniversary." The orchestra used is novel: 4 flutes, piccolo, 4 oboes, English horn, 3 bassoons, contrabassoon, 4 horns, high trumpet, 4 ordinary trumpets, three trombones (including bass trombone), tuba, timpani, bass drum, harp, 2 pianos, cellos, double-basses, and mixed choir, preferably of men and boys. The text consists of Latin verses of Psalms 38, 39, and 150, taken from the Vulgate Bible. According to Stravinsky's comments concerning the setting of words, he chose the Latin text precisely because it is a "dead language," and therefore largely meaningless to his auditors. Thus, it will have no emotional connotations, and become only a sounding vehicle for the voices. This view of the function of the text is supported by others of his works, with the exception of his opera. In the case of the *Symphony of Psalms,* however, one cannot help feeling that the emotion is con-

EXAMPLE 84.

FIRST MOVEMENT: Tempo ( ♩ = 92)

a.

b.

c.

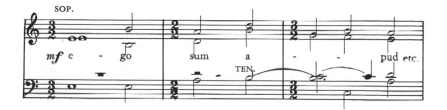

h.

Lau - da - te E - um se - cun - dum

mul - ti - tu - di - nem ma - gni etc.

tained in the music, and that some sort of spiritual communication is intended.

The first movement begins with a percussive E-minor chord, scored in such a way that its dissonant quality is emphasized, followed by angular arpeggios in the oboes and bassoons built upon the dominant seventh chords of two tonalities, E♭ and C-major (Example 84a). This process is repeated twice, after which a few measures prepare for the entrance of the voices. The altos enter alone, singing a chant composed of only two tones, E and F, reminiscent of Gregorian chant, but less melodic (Example 84b). Somewhat later, after this narrow range melody has been repeated and the tenors and sopranos have forcefully declaimed a phrase in octaves, another theme, angular in contour, is announced and developed in the chorus against various *ostinato* figures in the orchestra (Example 84c). The movement cadences on G and is linked to the following one. The text of this first movement begins: "Hear my prayer, O Lord, and give ear unto my cry: . . . O spare me, that I may recover strength before I go hence, and be no more."

The text of the second movement is a testimony to the power of God: "I waited patiently for the Lord: and He inclined to me, and heard my cry." In form this movement is a double fugue. The angular subject of the orchestral fugue is announced first by the oboes, and answered in turn by the first flute, the second flute, and the second oboe, after which an episode follows (Example 84d). The orchestral fugue subject is then announced in the cellos and basses, while the sopranos state the choral fugue subject, somewhat less angular, as might be expected, beginning with the downward leap of a fourth

(Example 84e). The orchestra and chorus develop their subjects complementarily. A *stretto* of the choral subject arrives, unaccompanied by the orchestra, then the development continues, with the first four notes of the orchestral fugue subject repeated in *ostinato* fashion while the chorus reaches a climax and a sudden hush at the end of the movement.

The third movement is devoted to singing the praise of God and begins with an alleluia, followed by the words *"laudate Dominum"* ("Praise ye the Lord") (Example 84f). These words are heard frequently during the movement — each sentence of the Psalm text begins with *"laudate."* The movement is divided into three clearly defined parts by thematic and tempo differences. The first and last sections are slow and impressive, the middle is rhythmic and faster. The first A section is built on a modal cadence figure in the choral parts which is developed against an *ostinato* in the orchestra. The faster second section employs rapidly repeated chords in the brass instruments against an *ostinato* in the pianos and low strings (Example 84g). An unexpected touch is the "tearing" chromatic scale highlighted by the trumpet color which appears from time to time. The chorus enters after considerable time has been given to the orchestra, and, while not imitative, the entrances are staggered, beginning with soprano followed by the alto. The melodic line is very like that of the first movement, and consists of two notes only for most of the phrase. The altos and tenors now chant rhythmically, using the repeated chord figures we have heard only in the orchestra up to now. Then the basses begin a striding theme with wide intervals which progresses upward (Example 84h), answered by a slower inverted version of the orchestral fugue subject from the second movement. Then the voices move more homophonically while the orchestra supports their sound with various *ostinati* figures. There is an interruption in slower tempo for an "alleluia," after which a recapitulation of the first part of this middle section ensues, with the chorus used rhythmically rather than polyphonically. Now a return to the tempo of the first A section occurs and an upward-striving disjunct, dotted-note theme is used in the chorus against a sustained background. This is not of long duration, however, for an even slower tempo is soon established with a solemn, bell-like *ostinato* in the orchestra against which the chorus builds a long crescendo of irresistible power. The cumulative effect of this sustained section is tremendous: its sheer weight, together with the dissonant chords in the wind instruments, makes it most impressive, The climax subsides with the repetition of the modal cadence figures on the words *"Alleluia, laudate Dominum."*

*Other Works of This Period:* Possibly Stravinsky's neoclassicism reaches its high point in the Symphony in C (1940), a strongly diatonic work in four movements whose general tempo relations are those of the classical symphony. The work is cyclic, and uses a motto theme (B-C-G) prominently in the first and last movements. The first movement is a modern sonata-allegro form, the second a three-part form, the third is scherzo in quality but more polyphonic and less sectional than its classical counterpart; the finale is close to rondo-form, with deviations of tempo as well as theme.

Stravinsky's next symphony, the Symphony in Three Movements (1945), resembles the classical symphony only in name. The first movement, marked Overture, has been called a toccata with a rhythmic drive and complexity that recalls *Le Sacre;* the second movement is slower and more like chamber music in its quiet mood; the third movement follows the second without pause, and consists of three sections which act as preludes to a final fugue. In this work, Stravinsky's pandiatonicism is widened considerably. The first movement contains no thematic development, but rather a kind of "additive" construction which regards music as consisting of clearly defined blocks which are given unity and coherence by the continuity of steadily and logically evolving organic force. This concept is demonstrated quite clearly in the *Symphony of Psalms,* as well as in the Symphony in Three Movements. Moreover, it is the basic principle, somewhat obscured by other elements, upon which *Petrouchka* and especially *Le Sacre* are constructed. One might guess that this is the sophisticated outcome of the primitive repetitive quality of the Russian composers — the preference for repetition and addition of material rather than the development of themes. Rather than the *analytical* techniques of breaking a theme down into its constituents, here we have the synthetic approach in which the theme is combined with new ideas, and grows by this addition.

*Works Since 1950*

In his later works, the musical personality of Stravinsky is still evident: the rhythmic procedures, the *ostinati,* the use of abrupt percussive chords to open a work and the characteristic preference for wind instruments are all present. But now the use of a row of tones — not always all twelve of them, nor necessarily chromatic — and the contrapuntal manipulation of this row in much the same manner as the serial technique of the Schönberg school, has replaced the more neoclassic modes of procedure. Certainly the result impresses one as "constructions in sound," which, of course, has been this composer's avowed intention throughout his career.

Such a work is the Cantata (1952), largely based upon the canonic manipulations of a series of notes — a mode of construction which goes back to the late Medieval Netherland composers. The melody, if we wish to call it that, is used in its original form, backwards (*i.e.,* beginning with the last note), inverted (*i.e.,* upward ,motion now becomes downward motion with intervals of the same size), and the backwards version of the inverted form (technically called *retrograde inversion*). This manipulation of a series of notes (hence "serial" technique) is employed with diatonic tones in this work: it remains only to introduce chromaticism and the stipulation that no repetitions of any tone occur before all twelve of the chromatic scale tones have appeared to lead us into the twelve-tone system of Schönberg. The Cantata thus serves as an introduction to Stravinsky's use of this means of composition.

This work is based upon anonymous English poems from the fifteenth and sixteenth centuries. These poems are sung by women's chorus, soprano and tenor solo voices, and are accompanied by an ensemble consisting of two flutes, two oboes. one of which is interchangeable with English horn, and cello.

The seven movements of the work consist of three long movements (ricercari) prefaced and separated by a refrain which also concludes the work: this refrain is the "Lyke-Wake Dirge," based upon fifteenth and sixteenth-century words sung at a wake for the dead: (Example 85a).

> "Lyke-Wake Dirge," Versus I (Women's chorus)
> "Ricercar I": "The maidens came . . ." (Soprano)
> "Lyke-Wake Dirge," Versus II (Women's chorus)
> "Ricercar II": "Tomorrow shall be. . . ." (Tenor)
> "Lyke-Wake Dirge," Versus III (Women's chorus)
> "Westron Wind" (Duet)
> "Lyke-Wake Dirge" (Women's chorus) Versus IV (I)

The first long movement is entitled "Ricercar I," and refers to a renaissance form in which canonic procedures were the basis of

EXAMPLE 85.

"LYKE-WAKE DIRGE"
(MOVEMENTS 1,3,5,7)

Tempo (♩ = 52)

a.

*mf* This ae nighte, this ae

nighte, E - ve -ry nighte and alle,

RICERCAR I. Tempo (♩ = 69)

A.
b.

Fl.

VOICE: The mai -dens came when I was in

Cor. Angl.

CANON INVERTED, RHYTHMICALLY CHANGED

B.

CANON INVERTED
Fl.

my mo - ther's bo - wer. VOICE: The bai -ly be -rith the

bell a - way, The li - ly, the rose, the rose I lay

Ob.

CANON, ORIGINAL FORM

c.
RICERCAR II: Tempo (♪ = 108)
C. SUBJECT
INSTS.

VOICE: ORIGINAL FORM

> ♩ (sounds 8ve lower)
To - - mor -

RETROGRADE
INVERTED

row    shall be, shall be    my dan-cing day, I would my    true

RETROGRADE INVERSION

love    did    so chance to see    the le - gend of my    play,

RITORNELLO

etc.

To call,    to    call my    true    love    to    my    dance.

"WESTRON WIND" Tempo (♩ = 136)
d.
SOP.
mp We - stron    wind,
TEN.
We - stron

we - stron    wind,    when    will    thou    blow
etc.

wind    ,    when,    when will thou    blow,

construction. It is set for soprano and the instrumental ensemble, and employs the old poem "The maidens came . . ." as its text (Example 85b).

The form ABABA (using different, although similar subjects, but in differing meters and modes), followed by a recitative beginning "Right mighty and famous Elizabeth," after which a fully accompanied prayer serves to conclude the movement. The second "Ricercar," separated from the first by a repetition of the "Lyke-Wake Dirge," is a much more complicated affair, based upon the text of "Tomorrow shall be my dancing day." The opening section states the canonic subject in the instruments, after which it is repeated by the solo tenor in its original, retrograde, inverted and retrograde inversion (Example 85c). These are not apparent to the listener since they overlap and there are no pauses between the forms of the series. The canons (often retrograde canons called "cancrizans") which follow are all based upon this series, often transposed up or down to effect key contrasts. A refrain appears from time to time which serves as a more obvious unifying factor as well as a section of less tension: this is called a "ritornello," and uses text revolving around "To call, to call my true love to my dance." The implication is religious, and the words of the refrain are altered from time to time to make sense with the preceding canon. The ritornelli make use of voice and both pairs of flutes and oboes, together with the cello, while the canons are scored for voice and only the oboes and cello. The third large movement is considerably simpler in construction, avoiding canons, although some imitation is used (Example 85d). It is a duet for soprano and tenor, using the famous poem "Westron Wind." The form might be stated as A A' A, since the procedure is quite homogeneous throughout, and the last part is a literal recapitulation of the first section. The work concludes with a repetition of the "Lyke-Wake Dirge," Verse IV, followed by the words of the first verse.

The style of this forerunner of Stravinsky's chromatic serial technique is little different in sonority from the earlier neoclassic compositions. There are the same narrow-range melodic ideas, the typical octave displacements of scale lines, the use of tonality, or rather, in this work, modality, and the expected "dry" sonorities produced by a selected instrumental body which is scored with the utmost finesse. Stravinsky is here, as always, interested in the structural problems of music; his solutions, largely in the form of canons in this work, are not obvious, for it is next to impossible to identify a retrograde or inverted canon when it is heard. In a sense, this is the "art that conceals art." Unfortunately for the intent of such works — to appeal only as abstract tonal constructions — most listeners cannot help reading into them some sort of communication or emotional attitude, a practice which has certainly had a long tradition behind it. Which way of listening will eventually prevail is yet impossible to forecast: as always, time will tell.

## BÉLA BARTÓK, 1881-1945

In our survey of the music of Stravinsky, we noted his transition from the folk-song element of the first period to the constructivist, neoclassic style of the second period, a style which adopted the forms of classic and pre-classic music, and gave no hint of national characteristics. Stravinsky had become international, if not universal. When we come to regard the works of Bartók, we find that detailed explanation of his music without consideration of the effect of folk music upon it is utterly impossible. In addition to this, we find Stravinsky firmly anti-romantic in all of his tendencies almost from the first, whereas Bartók's musical speech tends to have an expressive romantic element within it — certainly not grandiose or sentimental, but virile and firmly controlled. Thus, Bartók is neoclassic, but several degrees less so than Stravinsky and personal in his idiom and communication.

Bartók was born in 1881 in a farming region of Hungary, and from his earliest years heard the various peasant songs associated with work and recreation. His father, who was the director of an agricultural school, died when the boy was seven, and the subsequent lean years involved many removals from town to town as the job situations of his mother changed. Arduous as these must have been, they afforded acquaintance with new folk-songs for the boy. After attending various grade schools, Bartók graduated and, refusing a scholarship in Vienna, entered the Royal Academy at Budapest. Shortly after his graduation from the Academy in 1904, his interest seems to have been focused more intently upon the folk-songs of his country, and in 1905 he began, with Zoltán Kodály, a composer-companion who shared his interest, the first of his life-long researches into the unwritten music of his country. The effect of the folk-songs upon his personal style was profound. Previous to this time, his compositions had been strongly influenced by Liszt, Brahms and impressionism, and programmatically

PLATE L. *Béla Bartók. (Photo by Fritz Reiner, courtesy of Boosey and Hawkes.)*

touched by patriotic nationalism. He writes: "In my studies of folk-music I discovered that what we had known as Hungarian folk-songs till then were more or less trivial songs by popular composers and did not contain much that was valuable. . . . The outcome of these studies was of decisive influence upon my work, because it freed me of the tyrannical rule of the major and minor keys. The greater part of the collected treasure, and the more valuable part, was in old ecclesiastical or old Greek modes, or based on more primitive (pentatonic) scales, and the melodies were full of the most free and varied rhythmic phrases and changes of tempi, played both *rubato* (freely) and *giusto* (strictly). It became clear to me that the old modes, which had been forgotten in our music, had lost nothing of their vigour. Their new employment made new rhythmic combinations possible. This new way of using the diatonic scale brought freedom from the rigid use of the major and minor keys, and eventually led to a new conception of the chromatic scale, every tone of which came to be considered of equal value and could be used freely and independently."[1] From this time on we find innumerable arrangements and transcriptions of folk-songs for piano solo, or piano and voice. In addition, the folk-song idiom so permeates Bartók's thinking that it is reflected in his other compositions, little by little becoming so assimilated that it is impossible to separate this nationalistic flavor from his work.

Because of various disappointments connected with the reception of his works and the difficulty of obtaining adequate performances of them, Bartók retired from public life in 1912, and pursued his folk-song studies for five years. In 1917 the Budapest public favorably received the production of a musical play by Bartók, *The Wooden Prince,* and in 1918 there took place a performance of a similar stage work, *Duke Bluebeard's Castle.* But shortly after these promising beginnings occurred the political and economic breakdown of Hungary following the war, and any organized concert activity was impossible. Since the available areas for folk-song activity were severely limited by the treaties which cut Hungary into small sections, Bartók sought concert and recital opportunities, and undertook tours which touched most of the nations of Europe as well as the United States. In addition, he gave frequent lectures on folk music, and published many articles in this field. He worked as a member of the Hungarian Academy of Science until 1940, when, because of the increasing tension due to the Nazis, he was forced to come to the United States, his family following later. Here financial difficulties beset him which were alleviated somewhat by his recitals and a commission from Columbia University to edit a collection of Yugoslavian folk-songs. In 1942 he began to suffer ill health, and was obliged to give up lecturing. The ill-health which was due to the advancement of leukemia, caused his death on the 26th of September, 1945, in a New York hospital.

Bartók's creative life exhibits the usual three periods: the youthful works in which the influences of admired composers may be heard; the mature period of mastery of technique; and the final period in which technique becomes wholly subservient to higher expressive aims.

[1] Béla Bartók, *A Memorial Review,* New York: Boosey and Hawkes, 1950.

In Bartók's case, the first period shows the influence (by his own admission) of Liszt, Strauss, Brahms, and impressionism plus a superficial kind of nationalism. From 1908 to about 1916 he began to find a style in which folk elements were important. His middle period was more experimental than might be expected, and he developed a harsher harmonic vocabulary of almost expressionistic fervor, rather close to the style of Schönberg. This period ended about 1922 with the two violin-piano sonatas, after which the growing influences of Bach and polyphony came to the fore along with an increasing interest in formal constructive procedures. His language of the later years was mellowed and less harsh, and the techniques became wholly subservient to the demands of expression. However, a general description of the Bartók style can be discerned and is discussed in the following section.

## Scales

Bartók's music, although it may be tonal, pentatonic, modal or chromatic, tends to revolve around a key center which is often emphasized by tonal axis techniques, including cadences. Pentatonic scales are frequently used, whereas tonal scales are most often present in the minor mode, establishing a connection with the various modal scales which he employs. These are not only those of the Medieval period, but also scales which he discovered in folk music, often containing odd-sounding steps and varying in length from six to nine tones.

Bartók is fond of narrow-range chromatic themes which revolve about an axis tone or return to it frequently; but themes containing leaps are also to be found, especially using the interval of the fourth. Constructive elements in the form of melodic or rhythmic motives are almost always present and are welded together in an expressive manner, usually avoiding the noncommunicative attitude of some neoclassicism.

The harmony derived from the scales mentioned is always consistent and usually possesses a high degree of tension where this is possible. Bartók tends to build chords on close intervals such as the second rather than on wider, more open ones such as the fourth or fifth, although these do occur from time to time especially in works having a pentatonic basis. There are often compositions with a polymodal or polytonal basis, the clarity of which is at times obscured by the chromaticism of the melodic elements.

535

*Rhythm*

Bartók is a past master of all the rhythmic tricks of modern music. Some of his procedures stem from folk-song, as in the "Bulgarian" rhythms which result from unequal division of the beats of the measure. When combined with the proper melodic and harmonic factors, these rhythms are unmistakably middle-European. Above and beyond the mere fact that Bartók uses such rhythms, it must be noted that his use of them is appropriate in the last degree, and that the total effect, usually quite different from that of Stravinsky, is equally exciting. Bartók is also fond of *ostinato* figures, which are apt to be clearly melodic in shape, often drawn from a theme, and may be imitated and developed rather than merely repeated.

*Sonority*

In general, Bartók avoids the rich sound of the Romantic era, but his instrumental combinations have a different kind of richness and fullness unlike the spareness of many of the more neoclassic works of Stravinsky. One particular kind of sonority is a favorite with this composer — an expressionistic painting using impressionistic musical techniques of what have been called "night sounds." One seems to hear in these eerie moments the rustling and chirping of insects, the almost inaudible flight of night birds and the soft sounds of the wind. These movements are often rather terrifying in their intensity, and one imagines that Bartók is not describing night in general terms, but perhaps "the dark night of the soul."

Included in this section must be the mention of the kind of piano sound preferred by this composer. He regards the piano as a percussion instrument (which it is) and proceeds to treat it as such. There are occasional singing lines, but one is more often reminded of the Hungarian national instrument, the cimbalon, which consists of strings stretched across a frame, much like those of a piano, and struck with small hammers held like xylophone sticks in the hands. The sound is brilliant, the rapidity of playing astonishing, and over all hangs a haze of sound left over from previously struck strings, something like the impressionistic technique of holding the damper pedal down throughout an entire composition.

## Texture

Bartók's music shows a preference for polyphony which is usually chromatic, and often imitative in nature. It does not have the angularity nor the repetitive quality of the counterpoint of Stravinsky, but moves in much the same way as Bach's, often accumulating tension in a similar manner.

## Form

Bartók is most neoclassic in his use of traditional forms — more so than Stravinsky, for his procedures are more traditional. But this does not mean that the form is not shaped by the contents — far from it. Bartók's developments in the concepts of form are profoundly modern and original. He seems to prefer the sonata-allegro, the fugue, and the various sectional forms of which the "arch" is one. Especially in the works of his last period, when the tonal axis of each section is plain, the forms have a rightness about them which is felt immediately by the intent listener, a sense of completeness comparable only to the superb constructions of Mozart or Beethoven. Combined with these innovations in the single forms is Bartók's use of cyclic procedures developed from those in use during the romantic period and strikingly illustrated in his Sixth String Quartet and the Concerto for Orchestra.

Let us now examine some compositions of Bartók, first those in which the piano appears, then orchestral works, and finally chamber music.

### Allegro Barbaro (*1911*)

This is Bartók's first large work for the piano which bears the stamp of folk-music upon it. Here are demonstrated his use of the percussive sound of the piano and the folk-rhythms he had discovered. The piece uses the Phrygian and Lydian modes, and is devoted to the working out of two themes, the first of which appears near the beginning and the second, a kind of cadence figure, somewhat further on (Example 86a, b). The form is developmental and ternary, A-B-A'. The B section is quieter and somewhat more sustained, while the return of the A section is accomplished by means of a long develop-

EXAMPLE 86.

mental transition section employing both motives. The A' section proper is very short and consists only of the rhythmic chords in the proper mode without either theme appearing. A logical follow-up of the *Allegro Barbaro* for the interested listener is the Sonata for Two Pianos and Percussion. Space does not permit the analysis of this complex work here.

## Piano Concerto No. 3 (1945)

This is the last completed work of Bartók and, paradoxically enough, is probably one of the easiest compositions in his entire output to understand. It is cast in the normal three movements, *allegretto* (somewhat fast), *adagio religioso* (slowly, in a religious mood), and *allegro vivace* (fast and "full of life"). The first movement is a sonata-allegro, the first theme of which is announced by the piano almost immediately (Example 87a). After a short transition three short, interrelated secondary themes appear, not so plainly stated as the first theme, but smoothly spun out of the transition passage (Example 87b, c, d). The interval of a third, derived from the second themes serves as a closing figure, and the music subsides on a consonant interval in the piano. The development follows, with the solo divided between *arpeggio* and thematic passages. The recapitulation is not exact, for the themes are harmonized differently, but the sequence of events is much the same. A short coda via the same closing figure as before leads to a partial statement of the first theme in the solo flute answered by a fragment of the second theme in the piano. Altogether, this is not an heroic work but an intimate concerto movement like those of the Classic period in tone and manner, full of charm and grace.

EXAMPLE 87.

FIRST MOVEMENT: Allegretto ( ♩ = 88)

a.

*mf*

etc.

b. Allegretto

Pfte.

*p*

etc.

c. Allegretto

d. Scherzando

SECOND MOVEMENT:

e. Adagio religioso

f. Adagio religioso

g.

Pfte.

*f*

etc.

h.   Allegro vivace

Pfte.

*p*

etc.

The second movement is a ternary form combining two quite different sections. The first of these is composed of short imitative sections in the strings (Example 87e) answered by a fervent chorale in the piano (Example 87f). The central section is an example of Bartók's "night music," here more on the cheerful side than is usual. It will be noticed that many of the short motives in the piano and woodwinds are derived from the opening section of the A part. The third part finds the chorale in the woodwinds, while the piano embroiders the chords with Bachian "two-part inventions." Of particular interest are the almost impressionistic rapid scales at the cadences, which envelope the chords in a polytonal haze recalling the sound of the cimbalon. The music rises to a climax near the end of the movement with the piano developing the chorale theme, then dies away in a last echo of the beginning of the movement.

The third movement is an interestingly constructed form in which elements of the sonata-rondo and fugue are intermixed. An ascending *arpeggio* in the solo ushers in the syncopated first theme (Example 87g) which is repeated and developed to a degree. A cadence ends the section which is followed by a solo for the timpani. The second main section is composed of a fugal exposition and a portion of development. The subject is stated and answered first in the solo piano, followed in turn by the orchestral instruments. There is no touch of academic procedures here, for the fugue flows lightly and naturally. The following section reintroduces a version of the first theme which again ends in the timpani solo followed by a continuation of the fugal development, this time dealing with an inversion and later an expansion of the subject accompanied by the scale-like counter subject in the piano. The last large section begins with a rapid version of the first theme scored in such a way that an American is almost irresistibly reminded of Gershwin. Following this the coda, marked *presto* (very fast), brings the movement to an energetic conclusion using fragments from both of the principal sections. Were we to assign letters to the sections of this finale, we should arrive at something like this, understanding that A is the rhythmic first section and B the fugal section: A-B-A'-B'-A"-Coda. Essentially, then, this movement is a species of sonata-rondo with a fugal second theme — but a sonata-rondo form which all the unessential "surrounding themes" have been eliminated. The whole concerto reveals the simplicity of Bartók's view of formal procedure in his last period.

542

### Concerto for Orchestra (*1943*)

This work was written by Bartók shortly after his arrival in America. Because of the difficulties in Hungary and the upsetting conditions attendant upon his leaving that country, it is the first work written after the completion of his Sixth String Quartet in 1939. Although the experience of trying to acclimate himself at the age of sixty to a new country and life must have been very difficult, his frustrations may have been somewhat alleviated by the fact that he was composing again, and so the music is not as pessimistic as might be expected. Bartók said that the work represented "a gradual transition from the sternness of the first movement and the lugubrious death song of the third, to the life-assertion of the last."

There are five movements in the work — three important ones and two *intermezzi* separating them. But why call it a "concerto?"

EXAMPLE 88.

FIRST MOVEMENT: Andante non troppo

543

d. Tranquillo

SIMILAR ACCOMPANIMENT

FOURTH MOVEMENT: Allegretto

e.

f. Calmo

544

Accelerando al Piu mosso

g.

Cl. *mf*

FIFTH MOVEMENT: Pesante
FIRST SUBJECT
h.

Cor.
*ff*

accel. . . . . al

lunga
Str. PIZZ.

Presto
Vl. II  SECOND SUBJECT

*pp*

Vl. I

Vl. II

etc.

Let us quote further from the composer: "The title of the symphony-like orchestral work is explained by its tendency to treat the single orchestral instruments in a *concertante* or soloistic manner." But far from degenerating into a display piece for orchestra *à la* Rimsky-Korsakoff or Ravel, the thematic richness and the logical formal construction make it a modern masterpiece. The Hungarian flavor is noticeable throughout, somewhat more so than in music written before or after this piece, and is possibly the result of homesickness for his native land.

The first movement opens softly with a slow introduction which foreshadows much of the thematic material of the following *allegro vivace*, particularly the interval of a fourth (C-F) (Example 88a). The phrases of this theme are separated from each other by impressionistic *tremolo* chords in the muted strings and solo woodwind figures — a bit of Bartók's "night music" in an unexpected place. The material given to the low strings now turns into accompaniment to a new theme stated first in trumpets, later repeated in a varied manner, extended and developed by the strings. This theme emphasizes the interval of a second and has a definite Hungarian flavor (Example 88b). The *ostinato* figure in the low strings now becomes more prominent and accelerates to the tempo of the *allegro vivace*, which constitutes the main portion of the movement. In a sense, Bartók has provided us with clues in this introduction to themes and procedures which will appear in the important movements of the work — the first, third and fifth. The themes will appear in both the first and last movements, while the third movement will contain portions of the "night music" style.

The accelerating *ostinato* comes to a dramatic pause, and then the strings announce the first theme of the movement, typically irregular in rhythm, and largely constructed out of fourths (Example 88c). This theme is further emphasized in the brass, and at the end of this expository section, the trombone presents very clearly the beginning of the theme. The second thematic area begins with a rather slowly repeated perfect fifth harmonic accompaniment over which the oboe unfolds the lyric, almost static, second theme which is based upon the second theme of the introduction (Example 88d). Again, like the first theme, but in a more leisurely manner, the theme is repeated in different instrumental colors, varied, extended, and developed by imitation before this section concludes unstably in the low stringed instruments.

546

The development begins with a dash, quite noticeably developmental in the "no nonsense" air of the first string and brass figures. There follow sections devoted to soloistic passages for the woodwinds, culminating in two accompanied brass *fugatos* which conclude the development. There is a suggestion of the first theme, a full recapitulation of the second, again over repeated chords, this time in the harp, and a final repetition of the first theme in the strings and winds, concluding abruptly with the trombone statement of the head of the first theme. Here, then, we have an "arch" form sonata-allegro movement, symmetrical about the development section, thus:

First Theme — Second Theme — Development — Second Theme — First Theme

Throughout this movement there are fascinating coloristic orchestral effects which do not seem to exist only for the sake of effect, but for emphasis and variety. The varying quality of the motion is typical — romantic in essence — and the feeling is of surging vitality.

Bartók entitled the ternary second movement *"Giuocco delle Coppie,"* or a "Game of Pairs." The first section consists of a chain-like structure, each "link" of which is devoted to a like pair of woodwind instruments, and each pair is combined at a characteristic interval: the bassoons in sixths, the oboes in thirds, the clarinets in sevenths, the flutes in fifths and lastly the muted trumpets in seconds. The melodic ideas presented by these pairs are similar, but differ enough to make each section seem as though it is a variation of the preceding one. The middle portion of the movement consists of a brass chorale punctuated by interesting rhythms on a snare drum with loosened snares, a sound which was heard at the beginning of the movement and which follows the last A section. The reprise of this latter part uses the themes of the first A section, but now combines three bassoons in the first section, oboes and clarinets in the second, clarinets and flutes in the third and flutes with all the woodwinds in the fourth, while the muted trumpets are accompanied with harp *glissandi* and dissonant chordal trills in the strings. The final chord is a seventh chord which, in these surroundings, sounds perfectly consonant and final.

The third movement, "Elegia," is possibly at once the most Hungarian and the most emotional of the five. It begins with a recollection of the low string theme of the introduction to the first movement, at first interrupted by "night music" passages. These expand and progress with increasing sonority to the main body of the movement. Here are stated, with great passion, declamatory themes of typically Hungarian character derived also from the first movement's introduction. Again Bartók shows his command of the orchestra, indulging in a piccolo solo supported by an *ostinato* in one place, and a cimbalon-plus-tone-cluster accompaniment for low string themes in another. The declamatory section returns, followed by the coda of "night music" quality, a reference in the violins to the theme in fourths with which the elegy began and the movement concludes with a piccolo solo against a percussion background.

The "Interrupted Intermezzo" which follows gives us a glimpse of Bartók's humor which is almost Beethovenian in its abruptness, and far more obvious — at least in this instance. The movement begins with a flourish in the strings followed by an intriguing little theme in the oboe, emphasizing the tritone interval by means of repetition (Example 88e). A small three-part section is created by giving a version of this melody to the horns and finally returning it to the oboe. There follows a deeply lyric, folk-like theme which sounds almost too rich to be used by Bartók (Example 88f). It would not be out of place at all in a composition by Tchaikovsky, but here it is treated with reticence, appearing first in the violas then in the upper strings, and never once allowed to create a climax, as the Russian surely would have done. The first section of this ternary form is rounded off by a return to the tritone theme, again in the oboe. The low strings now play a series of fourths with accelerating pace and the solo clarinet announces a music-hall tune (Example 88g) which contrasts shockingly in its vulgar gayety with the more aristocratic themes of the previous section. The rest of the orchestra seems to think so too, for it bursts out in raucous laughter, interrupting the tune near the cadence. A disrespectful noise is made by the trombones, after which is set up a sort of barrel-organ sound, reminiscent of *Petrouchka,* which acts as accompaniment to the return of the music-hall tune. The laughter again follows, concluding the middle section. The emotional lyric theme appears first, now in the upper strings, accompanied by the harp and string *pizzicato*. It is followed by a woodwind interlude which develops portions of the tritone theme. The movement ends with a cadence phrase constructed from the beginning of the tritone tune followed by the end of the lyric theme.

The last movement is replete with dance rhythms and themes of typically Hungarian character, but these are assimilated in a complex sonata-allegro structure which testifies in its élan and flow to Bartók's mastery of his material. The two principal themes are announced within the first few measures of the movement (Example 88h). The horns immediately state the subject of much of the complicated fugal writing in the development section, and the strings begin the rapid, rushing yet melodious passage-work which some commentators have called *"perpetuum mobile,"* or "perpetual motion." There is a rather long section devoted to this material, and as it progresses dance motives in the woodwinds are combined with it. The rhythmic motion is quite exciting, and the music sweeps to full climaxes notable for the use of major chords. There follows a portion which might be called the "closing section," since the bassoon announces the first theme and a short *fugato* develops which disappears in woodwind polyphony. The development begins with the *perpetuum mobile,* followed by a pentatonic section introduced by a timpani *glissando.* A *fugato* now appears, based upon a jazzy version of the fugue subject, works its way through the strings of the orchestra first, and finally develops in the winds in all manner of polyphonic elaboration. The recapitulation brings back the *perpetuum mobile,* dance themes are added, the music grows in sonority, and finally the fugue theme emerges and is used in a brilliant brass passage. The measures following are developmental in character and form an exciting conclusion to the movement.

This work is deservedly one of the most popular in Bartók's entire catalog. Everything about it — the themes, rhythms, orchestration and form — is very clear, and the layman need not have any previous exposure to contemporary music in order to understand it. For this reason it appears on many orchestral programs and forms an excellent introduction to the style of this composer.

### *Music for Stringed Instruments, Percussion and Celesta (1936)*

In contrast with the exuberance of the preceding work, this composition is wholly serious in intent, although the last movement is typically dance-like. In workmanship and attention to detail, as well as in the thoroughly unified construction, it bears a closer resemblance to the string quartets than to the more varied and more loosely constructed (by comparison) orchestral compositions. It was written for double string orchestra, separated on the stage so that a three-dimensional effect is secured. The additional instruments are harp, celesta, piano, xylophone, timpani, and various percussion instruments including tambourines, cymbals and tam-tam. Bartók gives explicit direction concerning the grouping of the instruments.

The style of the themes is predominantly chromatic, some more so, as in the theme of the first movement, others, like the theme of the last movement, much less semitonal. The work is thematically unified, since all of the important themes of the second, third and fourth movements are derived by transformation from the theme of the first movement. Withal, the rhythms and some of the themes show relationships to Hungarian peasant music, but except for the last movement, the Hungarian style is much less obvious than in many other works. Here the process of assimilation of the folk-style into Bartók's personal idiom is complete.

The first movement has been called a fugue, but this is only generally true. No fugue was ever as tightly and continuously thematic as this. There is literally only one subject (Example 89a), and the entire movement is devoted to imitation of it, sometimes in a simple and direct way, at other times inverted or mirrored. There are no

EXAMPLE 89.

FIRST MOVEMENT: Andante tranquillo

SECOND MOVEMENT: Allegro

c. Allegro

*p* scherzando

d. Allegro

etc.

Vl. *mf*

e.

*p* leggiero

etc.

FOURTH MOVEMENT: Allegro molto

f.

*f*

etc.

g. Allegro molto

Pfte.

*p* marcato

etc.

h. Allegro molto

i. Vivacissimo

Xylophone ostinato

LATER:

episodes, and, from the statement of the subject by the violas on the
tonal axis of A, alternate imitations at the fifth above and below take
place, creating what has been called a "wedge" form (see first part of
the following diagram). When the imitations have traversed the
various fifths above and below A, they unite on E♭. From here they
retrace in inverted form the imitations back to the tonality of A
where they cadence. The return is less texturally complex and the
celesta, combined with tone-clusters in the strings, is used to throw up
a haze of secundal harmony surrounding the subject. It will be noticed
that this movement also traces a dynamic curve from the quiet beginning to the intense climax, and drops off rather rapidly after that
point. The chromatic tension of the subject assists in the dynamic
crescendo in that it creates a concurrent tension crescendo. The
diagram of the form on p. 553 shows the "wedge" form used.

The second movement, a sonata-allegro with Bartókian modifications, is based on a less chromatic transformation of the fugue
subject (Example 89c, d, e), plus other versions, and the interval of a
fourth, which becomes "stretched" to a tritone or a seventh — an

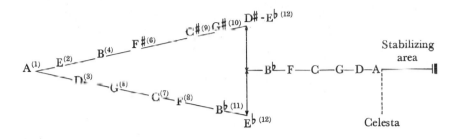

example of Bartók's thorough-going developmental procedures. The formal sections, especially those of the theme areas and the recapitulation are very clear, but the development is much too long and complex to be described here in words. Look for much imitation, sometimes in cross-rhythms between the orchestras, and exciting use of piano sonority in emphasizing rhythms. Used in this movement are two instrumental techniques very characteristic of Bartók: the *glissando* (slide) on the stringed instruments and the percussive *pizzicato* — one with such force that the string strikes the fingerboard with a snap. Notice the combined *glissandi* of the harp and piano in the coda, and the use of *glissandi* in the timpani.

The third movement is sectional ("arch" form, ABCDCBA) and is the finest piece of "night music" in Bartók's works. From the ghostly tapping of the xylophone at the beginning to its return at the end of the movement, the mood of mystery, almost of supernatural terror, is maintained with the greatest artistry. The themes are derived from the fugue subject of the first movement by drastic rhythmic transformations. The central portion of the movement is less improvisational than the beginning, and the motivic work is less elusive in character. The instrumental combinations exploited are amazing in variety and significance, always treated so as to verify the formal proceedings as well as to be communicative.

The final movement is a rondo (A-B-A-C-A-D-B-germ theme-A), extremely folk-like in the profusion of dance tunes which seem to come straight out of *Mittel-Europa*. The introduction recalls the cimbalon — although it could also be an evocation of the Spanish guitar — but the theme which follows could be nothing other than Balkan (Example 89f). It is a "straightened out" version of the fugue theme of the first movement in Bulgarian rhythm which gives way to a less straight version of the same chromatic theme. The first A section of this rondo is in itself a three part form, the second section of which follows the timpani solo (fourths), and introduces the piano (Example 89g). After this, the first section returns in altered form and reaches a pause on an unstable note before beginning the first subsidiary section of the rondo. The main section, when it returns, is first announced in a dance rhythm by the piano, and followed in the more familiar version by the strings. This section is very brief and gives way to a rhythmically marked modal (Dorian) dance tune (Example 89h) which is developed at length and merges with the theme of Example 89g harmonized in seconds in the piano. This is picked up by the other instruments and developed with increasing enthusiasm and tempo. The interval of the fourth comes in for its share of development after this, both alone and as part of the theme; then a more diatonic version of the germ theme (first movement) with its intervals expanded follows and is developed by imitation in both groups, finally reaching a climax of intense, closely packed dissonance which dissolves into a descending cello cadenza. Immediately the main rondo theme starts up, now ascending in the violas and imitated by the other sections. Its impetuosity is interrupted for a moment by a scale version of the theme in the celesta and harp, then it returns in a form more like the original. In the section which follows there occurs a passage with piano that sounds like a "jazz break," whether Bartók intended it to do so or not. Then there is a slowing down just before the final measures which are fast and conclude the movement brusquely and firmly.

This work is certainly not as easy to comprehend, even without paying attention to thematic transferences and form, as the preceding examples, but, like many difficult works it repays repeated listening a thousandfold. Together with the string quartets, it bids fair to become a modern masterpiece, one of those genuine and unique works which is as inevitable-sounding as the masterpieces of any previous musical era.

## The String Quartets

To leave a discussion of the music of Béla Bartók without at least mentioning his six string quartets would be unjust, for these works contain some of the most significant and beautiful music of the twentieth century. It is generally conceded that this composer's compositions in the field of chamber music are the most important since the last quartets of Beethoven. Certainly they are the first to strike out upon new and vital methods of chamber music composition. Furthermore, they exhibit Bartók's growth, since he wrote them at all periods of his life and was planning another one shortly before his death. These quartets are extremely unified, often cyclic, and explore the technical resources of the stringed instruments far beyond any similar works contemporaneous with them. Since any brief discussion here of these works would be woefully inadequate for reasons of time and space, the student is urged to explore Halsey Stevens' book, *The Life and Music of Béla Bartók* (Oxford University Press, 1953), which devotes considerable space to each of the quartets as well as to other compositions.

## PAUL HINDEMITH, 1895-1963

In the music of each of the two previous composers we have seen the evolution of a personal language from nationalistic beginnings, through a romantic period to mastery of the particular branch of neoclassicism each espoused. Paul Hindemith seems to have emerged with his own style from the beginning, although that style has developed somewhat as the years passed. He belongs to the traditional line of basically conservative composers such as Brahms and Reger, and was one of the very few twentieth century composers to theorize about his music in an effort to clarify and substantiate the style. Hindemith believed in the power of expressive communication of music, and bent his efforts to write music which he felt will be understood and which would fulfill the needs of modern audiences. His composition is not "art for art's sake," but a definite attempt to close the gap between the contemporary composer and his public. In accomplishing this feat, he believed that two requirements must be met: tonality must be used, and the composer must not only be an artist but also a musical craftsman of the highest order. His beliefs in this respect are presented in his book, *The Craft of Musical Composition*, the title of which emphasizes his stand on the technical part of making music. Like St. Augustine and other medieval theologians, Hindemith believed that music is the sounding symbol of a great universal spiritual and moral order, and so assigned symbolic meanings to keys and musical materials. These mystical extramusical qualities are not apparent to the listener, however, except in works with texts which explain the symbols.

PLATE LI. *Paul Hindemith. (Press-foto Köhnert, Berlin.)*

Hindemith produced a great deal of music — indeed, as a musical craftsman this would be expected. He tried his hand at all varieties of media, from chamber music to opera, with considerable success in each. He was early associated with *"Gebrauchsmusik,"* or *"music for use."* This was an early attempt to close the gap between composer and public by writing works in which the public could participate while in the concert hall by singing or taking part in the performances. Allied to this was the easy music written for amateur performance upon various available instruments. These works marked the end of an expressionistic phase in his composition extending from 1920 to 1930, during which the harsher elements of his style came to the fore in such works as the song-cycle *Das Marienleben* (*The Life of Mary,* since revised), the tragic opera *Cardillac,* and some chamber music. During the period from 1930 to 1963 the expressionist element dwindled and the harshness was replaced by an almost romantic warmth of expression and clarity of form. Works appeared such as the opera *Mathis der Maler* (*Matthias the Painter,* based on the life of Matthias Grünewald, the sixteenth-century German artist), the ballet based upon the life of St. Augustine, *Nobilissime Visione,* the piano and string orchestra variations *The Four Temperaments,* the Symphony in E♭ and the three piano sonatas of 1936. In the decade of the 1940's he produced, among other works, his fifth and sixth string quartets, the *Symphonic Metamorphoses on Themes of Carl Maria von Weber,* the *Ludus Tonalis,* which is a set of preludes and fugues for piano, a choral work with orchestral accompaniment using Whitman's poem *When Lilacs Last in the Dooryard Bloom'd,* and a Symphony for Band. He has composed concertos and sonatas for most of the orchestral instruments, as well as Concert Music for various combinations of them.

Before the last war, Hindemith was forced to leave Germany by the Nazis. He came to the United States where he taught at Yale, exerting much influence on many young composers. In 1953 he took up residence in Zurich, Switzerland, where he taught and composed, departing frequently, however, to conduct his works in concerts.

## Piano Sonata No. 3, 1936

This work is in the usual four movements, marked *Ruhig bewegt* (quietly moving), *sehr lebhaft* (very lively), *mässig schnell* (moderately fast), and *lebhaft* (lively). The first movement opens with a lyric theme (Example 90a) which the remainder of the movement develops. In order to accomplish this development the theme is broken down into the four motives of the example, each of which receives variation treatment. The movement is divided into three main sections: first, a relatively uncomplicated exposition and development of the theme as a whole, either by making it the leading part, or, later in the section, by combining upper parts with it in a modified cantus firmus technique. The second section is occupied with motive 2 principally, and presents it combined with a brilliant and rapid contrapuntal accompaniment. The third main section returns to the theme as a whole, and is a reworked recapitulation of section one, containing, however, more development of the theme. The movement ends quietly in B♭. Especially noticeable is the lyric quality of the writing, the numerous major triads which appear, and the means of establishing tonality by repetition of the key note and by cadence patterns, often derived from motive 2.

The second movement is a clear ternary form, the first section of which is devoted to the development of a rhythmic motive (Example 90b). The music reaches a very definite cadence, after which a humorous little coda brings the section to a soft close. The second section is devoted to a rapidly running figure over a repeated accompaniment (Example 90c). The theme appears first in the upper register, then in the lower register where it is extended, then again in the treble. A descending quicksilver *arpeggio* returns the music to the first section which is repeated substantially intact.

EXAMPLE 90.

FIRST MOVEMENT:
Ruhig bewegt

a.

SECOND MOVEMENT:
b.   Sehr lebhaft

c.   Sehr lebhaft

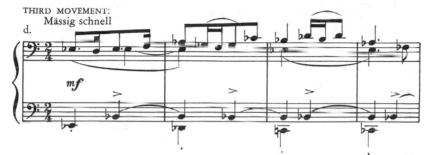

**THIRD MOVEMENT:**
Mässig schnell

d.

e.  Mässig schnell

f. Mässig schnell

g. Mässig schnell

FOURTH MOVEMENT: – FUGUE

h. Lebhaft   SUBJECT I

i. Lebhaft

j. Lebhaft

The third movement most resembles an asymmetrical ternary form, or a sonatina form with interior developments differing in the exposition and recapitulation. The movement opens with a lyric march theme in the lower middle register accompanied by a firm "baroque" bass (Example 9od). The phrasing is very clear, and a series of nonfinal cadences marks the descent from the melodic climax, at times interrupted by a curious descending *arpeggio* figure (Example 9oe) which will assume increasing importance as the movement progresses. The second theme is stated fugally, and is more cheerful and rapid in nature (Example 9of). It moves to a climax, but instead of diminishing gradually, a new section appears, entirely in the upper register, rather soft and with the wistful charm of a music box (Example 9og). This concludes with a short rhythmic motive which seems to summon the first theme in the bass register to appear, after the descending *arpeggio* leads the attention to it. The restatement of the first theme is considerably more developed and dramatic than in the exposition, and it now reaches a series of climactic points which are separated from each other by the rapid *arpeggio* figure. There is one last powerful statement of the march theme in the treble, and the music subsides to a development of the music of Example 9og. The coda makes use of the extended descending *arpeggios* and the first theme to close the movement on a luminous E♭-major chord. There is no recapitulation of the second theme, resulting in the following formal plan:

A-B developed — Closing Section — A developed — Closing Section — Coda
(d)(f)                    (g)                      (d)              (g)                  (e)

The finale is an impressive double fugue. There is an exposition devoted to each subject, after which they are briefly combined. The first subject is angular and rhythmic, and exactly suited to its task, just as are the subjects of the Bach fugues (Example 9oh). It builds up imitatively to four-voice texture, after which an episode appears, to be followed by a forceful counterstatement of the subject. A tranquil episode based on a descending scale passage which is combined with material from the subject provides dynamic relief (Example 9oi). Now there comes an exposition of the second subject which is identical to the second theme of the third movement (Example 9oj). After completing this exposition, the previous episode with the descending scale figure reappears, now combined with the second subject and followed by a counterstatement of the same subject. The final section combines the first subject in treble octaves with the second subject in augmentation (note values twice their former length) in the bass. The music then moves to a triumphant repeated cadence on B♭, using thematic motives. The texture of the fugue is rather free and employs chords when needed for harmonic support or dynamic emphasis. Nevertheless, it is an excellent example of the use of the baroque form in modern dress. We feel that there is nothing academic or forced about this fugue. It wears its modern garb comfortably, proving that it is a genuinely functional form, not a "jello mold."

It is of value to compare the piano style of this composer with that of Bartók and Stravinsky. It is immediately apparent that Hindemith has a more traditional view of both music and the instrument. His writing for the piano can be percussive and steely when he wants it to be, but there is also much lyrical and expressive melody. The harmony is full and chromatic, but firmly based on a key. The tension-modulation technique is used, often employing major triads as an element. The rhythmic treatment is less complex than that of Bartók, but not as precisely neoclassical as that which Stravinsky uses. In its contrapuntal textures we clearly discern the baroque influence, but it does not force itself upon us. Polyphony is the natural language of this composer just as it was of Bach.

*Theme and Four Variations (The Four Temperaments),*
*for Piano and Strings (1940)*

This charming work — how few twentieth-century works deserve this description — consists of variations on a theme which contains three sub-themes, according to Hindemith's musical interpretation of the four temperaments conceived as descriptive of human character by medieval man: melancholic, sanguine, phlegmatic and choleric. The variations are developmental and rather free, although the recognition of the beginning of each of the themes is rather easy for Hindemith uses a rhythmic transformation of the theme while keeping the melodic or intervallic contour intact. Each variation consists of three parts, corresponding to the three sections of the theme, and within the variations he makes full use of the possibilities of the ensemble, varying the sonority from that of violin-piano duet through string quartet to the full orchestra with piano. There are frequent passages

563

for the solo piano, sometimes rhapsodic in the style of a cadenza. The piano not only plays a leading solo role in the work, but also supports and combines with the strings in a purely orchestral manner. There are some so-called "characteristic" variations in the set — a waltz and a march — as well as others which exploit the *pizzicato* strings in fleet passages which are quite delightful. Even in the melancholic variation, Hindemith's mood is not heavy and oppressive. Above all, there is the sense of well-constructed, easily-flowing music, modern but good-natured.

### Mathis der Maler

Probably the most popular of all of the works of this composer, this symphony consists of three orchestral movements drawn from the opera of the same name. The plot of the opera concerns the life of the late medieval German painter, Matthias Grünewald, who painted the triple altar-piece in the church at Isenheim, Germany. Each of the movements of the symphony seeks to describe one of these in music.

EXAMPLE 91.

FIRST MOVEMENT: Ruhig bewegt
*"Es Sungen drei Engel"* (INTRODUCTION)

SECOND MOVEMENT:

THIRD MOVEMENT:

The first, entitled "Angelic Concert," is a modern version of the sonata-allegro form. There is first a short, tonal introduction which establishes G-major as the tonal center, during which the trombone intones a Crusader's hymn, *"es sungen drei Engel"* ("There sang three angels") (Example 91a), accompanied by unobtrusive scale figures in the strings. The chant is imitated by the horns and, with increasing background sonority, by the trumpets. The music mounts to a climax, subsides, pauses upon a mildly unstable harmony, then begins the somewhat faster main thematic section, based upon a subject characterized by a rapid descending scale figure of five notes (Example 91b). This motive is developed considerably before it slows and cadences. The second theme follows, an expressive one in B-major, whose outstanding melodic shape consists of three rising scale notes followed by the upward leap of a fifth and back, after which it descends to the region of the opening note (Example 91c). There is considerable imitation of this theme in various parts of the orchestra, after which it too comes to rest upon two long chords. The closing section contains two themes of which the first is new (Example 91d), and the second we have heard before as the first subject. This section quite properly concludes with some finality on a B-major chord in the strings. After a pause the development begins with the first theme which soon gives way to the second theme, subsequently combining the two. There is a wonderful expectancy about the way this development begins. We know at once what it is and that there are exciting adventures in store. It is not long, however, and is mostly concerned with the first and second themes. It flows without pause into the recapitulation signaled by the statement of the Crusader's hymn by the trombones in 3/2 time while the rest of the orchestra plays in 2/2 meter. When the trombones have finished, the horns continue, also in 3/2 against the orchestral 2/2. But this recapitulation contains another novelty. While the brasses are stating this theme, the remainder of the orchestra is occupied with the first and second themes in polyphonic combination with it. Even the transition theme appears for a moment inconspicuously in the bassoons! Here is symphonic economy indeed! The third repetition of the Crusader's hymn brings back the trumpets with the full orchestra, as before, but now the tempo broadens and the previous monophonic line of the hymn expands into a mighty brass chorale, still combined with the second theme in the woodwinds, but also accompanied by brilliant figuration in the high strings which bears a slight resemblance to the closing theme motive. The climax and sonority now diminish, and the section which now appears, devoted to the first theme, becomes gradually slower and more tranquil and flows into the closing section.

The end is not yet in sight, however, for Hindemith now presents us with the coda based mainly upon the closing theme, the first theme, the second theme, and a theme which up to this time we probably have not recognized as such: the three chords in strings which first appeared in the introduction (symbolic of three angels?). In retrospect, or upon rehearing the work, we shall find these three chords in several important places: the introduction, as mentioned; in the woodwinds at the close of the first thematic section; in the first thematic section in rapid notes; also near the end of that section in the strings, separated by passages based upon the first theme in the woodwinds; and twice in the closing section, first in short note-values, later in the three cadence-chords which bring the exposition to a close. Now, in the coda they reappear, first as heard before, later in a majestic "development" which consists of adding a shorter upbeat chord to each of the three long ones, and finally as cadential chords at the end of the movement.

The second movement ("The Entombment") is largely based upon the halting scale presented by the strings at the beginning (Example 91e). There are a few other themes, notably that announced by the oboe and imitated by the flute about a third of the way through the movement (Example 91f) but these are not used in any important way, and must be regarded as merely contrasting material. In this movement we have an opportunity to sample Hindemith's practice of building chords upon fourths or fifths (quartal harmony), as well as to notice tension modulation principles in action, especially near the climax of the movement about three-fourths of the way through. But on a smaller scale, passages of a similar kind occur all through the work.

The last movement is very complex formally since all of the themes bear a close resemblance to each other. For this reason there is a feeling of continuous development, even though some sections are more lyric than others. It is entitled "The Temptation of St. Anthony," which may or may not be a clue to the derivative nature of all of the sections, and begins with a dramatic, free-sounding recitative by the strings, punctuated at cadence points by short, massive chords (Example 91g). These materials are then transferred to the wind instruments. Both the nature of the recitative line and the chords turn out to be important thematically. After this introduction, the movement which follows is cast in a rather free sonata-allegro form whose complexity lies in the fact that marked tempo changes as well as far-reaching theme transformations often make recognition of previously heard themes quite difficult. In addition, there is the "family resemblance" of many of the themes, sometimes causing one to feel quite justly that they are all derived from the figures of the opening recitative! At any rate, the first section *(sehr lebhaft)* exposes a broadly melodic theme (Example 91h) which is repeated and slightly developed before it reaches climactic cadence chords through which the odd-sounding low notes of the flute sustain, providing a bridge to the following section. The next theme, presented by the oboe against a curious background of violins and cellos in bare octaves (Example 91i), is repeated and developed in much the same manner as the previous idea; interestingly enough, they both appear to be based upon the same tonal center of C♯. This second theme also reaches a climax, at which point the chord series (Example 91 g2) first heard in the introduction appears. Melodically, this series outlines a scale fragment of a descending fourth. It is followed by a cadential motive (Example 91 g3), also from the introduction, which later becomes important. After some development of these materials at a rather high dynamic level, the music arrives at a clearly-defined point of conditional stability: the exposition has been completed.

A trill high in the first violins leads to the next section, which is considerably slower in tempo and of a decided lyric quality. Its principal melodic idea (Example 91 j1) is a development, nevertheless, of the second theme (Example 91 i) by transformation; and the cadential pattern with it concludes (Example 91 j2) is clearly related to the motive (Example 91 g3) of the preceding section. This lyric interlude cadences after recollecting the introductory recitative, and the rapid tempo resumes with a development of the chord series (Example 91 g2) and a syncopated version of the cadential figure (Example 91 g3) against a busy string background. Again a massive climax is attained, after which the violas project the lyrically transformed second theme (Example 91 j1) against a light woodwind accompaniment. After the concluding figure (Example 91 g3:j2), the opening recitative is boldly recalled in freely inverted form by the brass. This leads to a recapitulation of the first subject (Example 91h), also in the brass, now provided with a brilliant accompaniment of high woodwind trills and rapid scales in the upper strings.

The coda, faster in tempo and more quiet, appears suddenly. It is a double *fugato* formed out of a rapid transformation of the first subject combined with a fragment of the recitative (Example 91 k1). It is continued imitatively, mounting in intensity and sonority as more instruments are added. After a short climax, the music subsides slightly to allow the woodwinds to present in octaves the medieval plainchant *"Lauda Sion Salvatorem"* ("Praise to Sion which shall save us").

Under this melody, the horn has an *ostinato* which consists of the first eleven notes of the introductory recitative (Example 91 kuːgi). As is usual when *ostinati* are used, the tension increases with each repetition of the pattern. When the plainchant melody has been presented in full, there is a slackening in tempo and an increase in dynamic level: at this point the unaccompanied brass choir intones *"mit aller Kraft"* (with full strength) a chordal "Alleluia" which concludes the movement in a mood of exalted joy: St. Anthony has conquered his temptations.

## Part IV: Neoromanticism

A great many composers were not persuaded by either expressionism or neoclassicism, but preferred to work out their own styles from the traditions of the past. Certain of these developed in ways quite parallel to those of Schönberg and Stravinsky, while others pursued ideals of expressivity closer to those of romanticism, especially that of Brahms, Sibelius and Franck; these have been called "neoromanticists." The melodic and harmonic aspects of their works employ many of the innovations of impressionism, expressionism and neoclassicism, but the result is usually richer in sonority, more highly subjective and, as a rule, quite easily comprehended by the average listener. The romantic unifying devices are employed, sometimes in no really different way than Brahms and Liszt used them, and a certain tendency toward frequent climaxes and highly colorful orchestration is apparent.

Many American composers write in a style which contains an element of neoromanticism, often mixed with a neoclassic or even a twelve-tone idiom, resulting in a more easily accessible musical language. The music of Howard Hanson, for example, is highly neoromantic, that of William Schuman and Roy Harris, somewhat less so. The uniquely personal style of Aaron Copland owes more to neoclassicism than to the romantic element, while the complicated chromaticism of Roger Sessions is closer to expressionism. In England neoromanticism flourishes in the music of William Walton and Arthur Bliss; in France, Olivier Messaien, André Jolivet and Henry Barraud opposed the Parisian neoclassicism; while in Germany Carl Orff, Ernest Toch and Werner Egk have established personal idioms of neoromantic quality. It is not merely the slow dying of romanticism which has caused neoromanticism, rather it is "the other side of the coin" from classicism and represents a desire in the heart of the composer to communicate his visions in subjective terms. It is important as a leavening agent in the present mixture of styles, one which will infuse the sometimes sterile mixture with a touch of life and warmth.

# Part V: Contemporary Music in America and Europe

## MUSIC IN THE UNITED STATES

During the first two-thirds of the nineteenth century, most of the music heard in the United States was imported from Europe. To be sure, there were native composers, but there was no lasting music produced by them. They were products, for the most part, of the European conservatories, principally those of Germany, and the music they wrote was German-romantic in style with all too little individuality. But these men were important because they showed that there could be American composers and because they established the study of music in the universities and colleges of the country. This group includes the names of William Mason (1829-1908) who studied with Liszt, the conductor Theodore Thomas (1835-1905) and John Knowles Paine (1839-1906) who occupied the first university professorship in music at Harvard in 1873 and whose music to Sophocles' *Oedipus Tyrannus* is sometimes heard. To this list may also be added other composers who were Paine's students: G. W. Chadwick (1854-1931) Arthur Foote (1853-1937) and Horatio W. Parker (1863-1919).

Possibly the first American to make more than a passing imprint upon the musical consciousness of the nation was Edward MacDowell (1861-1908). Born in New York City, MacDowell's talents were recognized early and carefully nurtured, first by private music lessons, later, at the age of 16, at the Paris Conservatoire where he was a classmate of a strange young man named Claude Debussy. Later he studied in Germany, and concluded his European sojourn as a member of the informal "class" which met at Liszt's house in Weimar. Here MacDowell met most of the influential men of German and French music. He returned to the United States in 1888 and lived in Boston until 1896, when he moved to New York to become the first chairman of the new music department at Columbia University. He resigned from this position in 1904 due to a conflict in ideals with the university administration, and resumed the role of a private teacher and composer. His mind gradually weakened, however, and he passed his last days in an uncomprehending, trance-like state.

Among the works which are still heard today, in addition to some

573

of his smaller sketches for piano (the omnipresent "To a Wild
Rose" was never intended by the composer to reach the public eye:
it was thrown in a waste-basket, but rescued by the composer's wife),
are four romantic, heroic piano sonatas in the grand manner and
two early piano concertos, the product of his European stay. The
Second Suite for Orchestra, based on Indian themes, is probably the
work for which he will be longest remembered. Much of his music
has a rugged northern quality, somewhat Schumannesque in its dark
coloring and rhythmic flow. The music is well made, for MacDowell
was a craftsman and aware of the latest stylistic trends of his day.
However, the sounds of impressionism were not for him; rather he
favored the conservative trend as represented by Brahms and Schumann, even though he was a member of the Liszt circle. The colony
which bears his name at Peterborough, New Hampshire, was established in his memory by his wife and commemorates his love of solitude
and nature and offers these necessities to artists and students.

A group of somewhat more familiar composers now fills the scene,
beginning with Edgar Stillman Kelley (1857-1944) and including
Henry Gilbert (1868-1928), John Alden Carpenter (1876-1951),
Daniel Gregory Mason (1873-1953) and Edward Burlingame Hill
(1872-) among others. There was an increase not only in the number of American composers whose productive years began about 1890,
but also a growing interest and pride on the part of the nation in
the efforts of these men. To be sure, many of them still found it necessary to study in Europe, but one of the most important, Charles Ives,
was taught in the United States.

CHARLES IVES, 1874-1954

Ives was born in Danbury, Connecticut, taught by his father, the
village bandmaster and organist, and at Yale by a number of instructors
including Horatio Parker. For a few years, Ives made music his voca-
tion, but in 1898 he entered business and put music aside as an active
avocation although he composed continuously until his retirement
in 1930. For the remainder of his life he wrote little, and his fame
rests upon those works composed between 1890 and 1925.

His music might be called eclectic, if it were not for the fact that
he combined musical styles in a most original and daring way. Impressionistic devices, Stravinsky rhythms, polytonality, quotation of

574

popular and folk-tunes, dissonant tone clusters and experiments with sonority are all to be found in this surprising music. And this at a time when the new music was principally confined to Paris — certainly not to be heard in staid and conservative Boston, where Philip Hale, the annotator for the Boston Symphony, wrote "exit in case of Brahms!" Ives' *Concord Sonata,* published in 1919, had to wait until 1939 for a first American performance. Technically challenging as well as difficult to understand, the work attempts to convey the spirit of transcendentalism associated with the Emerson circle at Concord. Thus, there are impressionistic pictures of Emerson, Thoreau, the Alcotts and a scherzo depicting the fantastic side of Hawthorne's imagination.

Another work which reveals clearly the inquiring mind and experimental method of this surprising man is the first of his suites for orchestra, entitled *New England Scenes,* which consists of three movements. "Boston Common," "Putnam's Camp (Redding, Connecticut)" and "The Housatonic at Stockbridge." The style of all three movements is essentially impressionistic, recalling the sounds of Bartók's "night music" to a certain extent, but scored more heavily, with divided strings. Thus a harmonic texture is set up composed of a multitude of dissonances, often at a low dynamic level. Such a combination results in opaque harmony of high tension in which no single dissonance is clearly apparent. Often a strong organpoint will seem to act as the root of this harmony, thus making it possible to achieve variety and interest.

The first movement, subtitled "Colonel Shaw and his Colored Regiment," purports to be a ghostly procession, but resembles a march only by a considerable stretch of the imagination. Against the harmonic background mentioned above, fragments of Civil War tunes and drum beats are projected. There is no clear form, and the whole movement resembles a portion of a dream.

The second movement is very much alive with the spirit of rural New England, and is, Ives tells us, a fantasy describing the dreams of a child who falls asleep during a Fourth of July outing within sight of Putnam's old camp. The movement opens with a riotous march, and continues in this vein almost throughout, slowing only once for a section of the "night music" sounds. Many familiar march tunes are quoted, among them the "British Grenadiers," "Yankee Doodle," "Columbia the Gem of the Ocean," and, although not a march, "Row, Row, Row Your Boat." In addition to these, a fragment of a sentimental song appears now and then in the lulls between marches. It is said that Ives heard the effect produced by two bands marching into Danbury from opposite directions and playing different tunes: he has here incorporated this effect into the music, creating not only polytonal combinations, but also polymetric ones of a complexity undreamed of at the time the work was composed.

The third movement again returns to the impressionistic harmony of the first, and generally recalls that movement, although in a calmer fashion. A melodic line which may be derived from a hymn appears against the dissonant harmonic curtain, but other events are not as noticeable. At the conclusion, the music rises to a climax which suddenly vanishes, leaving behind a few instruments to play a quiet and consonant cadence.

Ives also wrote a number of effective songs, among which the setting of Vachel Lindsay's "General William Booth Enters into Heaven," with its quotation of the hymn "Are You Washed in the Blood of the Lamb?" seems tailor-made to the Ives style. Other songs are settings of his own texts or those found in newspapers, and vary in length from the Vachel Lindsay poem to the brief "One, Two, Three" whose text reads:

> Why doesn't one, two, three
> Seem to appeal to a Yankee
> As much as one, two!

Ives also composed four symphonies, of which the third is the most frequently performed, four violin-piano sonatas, two piano sonatas, over two-hundred songs, chamber music, choral works and many miscellaneous piano compositions.

This composer was indeed a prophet without honor in his own land, for had he journeyed to Paris, where new artistic ideas of the time were treated seriously, he would have become one of the famous pioneers of the style of the twentieth century. But instead, he cultivated his own New England garden, and it remained for an appreciative posterity to recognize his importance.

## OTHER EARLY TWENTIETH-CENTURY COMPOSERS

The next decade brought a new group of American composers to the fore: Deems Taylor (1885-), notable for his orchestral suite *Through the Looking Glass,* as well as for his operas *The King's Henchman* and *Peter Ibbetson* and for numerous highly readable books on music and program notes for the New York Philharmonic Orchestra. Charles Wakefield Cadman (1881-1946), remembered best for his song "At Dawning," and Charles Griffes (1884-1920) already mentioned in the foregoing section on impressionism belong to this time. So also does Wallingford Riegger (1885-1961), regarded in his time as an avant garde experimenter in atonalism, but now felt to be one of the most individual composers to develop a highly personal, non-Schönbergian style of composition. A more controversial figure, Edgar Varèse (1885-), came to live in the United States in 1915, and influenced many American composers with his unorthodox music which features percussion instruments as well as devices not usually regarded as musical instruments, such as the fire-siren!

## JAZZ

During the years before the first World War a new folk-music was springing up in the southern part of the United States. Begun, some say, as improvised music to funeral processions in New Orleans, this music with its syncopations, free-for-all improvisations, new uses of harmony and care-free attitude soon came to represent the United States to the musically adventurous of Europe. This music was jazz. Several serious composers wrote pieces in the jazz idiom, but none could wholly capture the complicated rhythms on paper, for jazz is a way of performing, not a written-down style. As always, there were some who attempted to fuse serious music with the jazz idioms, usually with notable failure. Other adopted the jazz idiom whole-heartedly as an escape from the dilemmas of style and tonality at the end of the century. Such a one was Kurt Weill (1900-1950) who dropped his atonal writing entirely and, with Bertolt Brecht, wrote the biting satires *The Threepenny Opera* and *Mahoganny,* as well as the later Broadway show *Lady in the Dark.* But perhaps the most successful practitioner of jazz was a native American who, so to speak, cut his teeth to the accompaniment of the jazz band.

George Gershwin (1898-1937) first emerged as a musical personality in the field of popular song and the Broadway musical comedy. His music for these has become a part of the heritage of America. In 1924 the movement to combine the jazz idiom with serious concert music was at its height. Paul Whiteman asked Gershwin to write something especially for a concert by his band entitled *Experiment in Modern Music*. The result was the now famous *Rhapsody in Blue* for piano and orchestra, scored by Ferde Grofé. The piece was an immediate success, and Gershwin was launched as a composer of more "serious" music. Damrosch, conductor of the New York Symphony Society, commissioned Gershwin to compose a concerto for piano and orchestra in 1925, and later, in 1928, requested the ballet *An American in Paris*. A Second Rhapsody, written in 1932, was not as successful as the first, but the folk opera *Porgy and Bess* won instant and deserved enthusiasm, and has continued to do so all over the world. The jazz of Gershwin's time seems dated to us now, but in its natural habitat — the music of the colored inhabitants of "Catfish Row" — it sounds completely natural and authentic. More than any other American opera, this one has gained continued popularity.

In the wake of Gershwin's success in grafting the jazz idiom onto the trunk of serious music followed scores of imitators, all less able to synthesize the two than he was. But more important for later music, many composers grew up more or less surrounded by jazz, absorbed its important features and assimilated them into a more serious and personal musical expression. It would probably not be amiss to say that every American composer has in his music some of the rhythmic or harmonic effects of jazz, usually refined to the point where recognition of these elements as jazz is almost impossible.

Most of the composers born in the 1890's are still alive and highly influential in the music of our time. Let us examine some of them more closely for that reason.

### WALTER PISTON, 1894-

Piston began as a neoclassic composer of the linear counterpoint school, but has since developed a warm and less obviously neoclassic style in which emotion, though controlled, is very much present. Nevertheless, the dry sonorities and rhythmic energy of his First String Quartet are still attractive. He has seven symphonies to his credit, two of which, the third and the fourth, won a Pulitzer Prize and the Naumberg Award respectively.

The Third Symphony is a good example of Piston's communica-

PLATE LII. *Walter Piston. (Associated Music Publishers.)*

tive style. His analysis, printed in the program notes of the premier performance is so clear that quotation of themes is unnecessary. Piston says:

I. *Andantino,* 5/4: based on three thematic elements: the first heard as a melody for the oboes, the second, more somber in character, played by bassoon, clarinets and English horn; the third, soft chords for brass. These ideas are developed singly and in combination to form a prelude-like movement. Tonality C.

II. *Allegro,* 2/4: a scherzo in three-part form. The theme, stated by violas and bassoons, is treated in contrapuntal, imitative fashion. The middle part is marked by the melody for flute, accompanied by clarinets and harp. Tonality F.

III. *Adagio,* 4/4: the movement has four large and closely connected sections, or rather "phases" of musical development. The first of these is the statement by strings of the theme, which is in three parts (part one by the violins, part two by violas, part three by all except basses). The second section is a variation of the theme with woodwinds and harps predominating The third section, starting with bases and celli, builds up to the climax of the movement, and the final section returns to the original form of the theme, played by solo viola, the closing cadence recalling the variation by clarinet and bassoon. Tonality G.

IV. *Allegro,* 4/4: a three-part form similar to that of a sonata form movement. There are two themes, the first being developed fugally in the middle section. The second theme is march-like, first heard in oboes and bassoons over a staccato bass, and later played by full brass at the climax of the movement. Tonality C.

In addition to his orchestral music, Piston has written considerable chamber music, of which the charming Sonata for Violin and Harpsichord and the solid Piano Quintet are good examples.

### ROGER SESSIONS, 1896-

The music of this composer is atonal but does not belong to the twelve-tone serial technique. Rather it is a personal style which uses chromaticism freely to portray emotional states. Often the music sounds like that of the Viennese school of Schönberg because of aspects of the scoring such as much use of muted brass, clarinet and bass clarinet *arpeggios,* and solo violin. Anyone accustomed to the style of Schönberg and Berg will not find this music difficult. Sessions has not written a great deal of music, but that which has reached the public is consistent in style, ranging from the early *Black Maskers* suite through two operas, much chamber music, four symphonies and two concertos. His Second Symphony is available on records and provides an example of his style. It is in four movements, scored for standard orchestra with the addition of English horn and bass-clarinet. The themes quoted in Example 92 are hardly sufficient in themselves to give an idea of the work, for the orchestral coloration and busy

PLATE LIII. *Roger Sessions. (Courtesy of the BMI Archive.)*

accompaniment and motivic work, especially of the woodwinds, are almost as important as the themes themselves.

The first movement, *molto agitato,* resembles a sonata-allegro in form. The first section introduces several fragments of thematic material which are subsequently developed (Example 92, a, b, c, d). These are presented twice, comparable to the repetition in the corresponding section of a classical sonata-allegro. The second thematic section introduces less material, but the character of the themes is more elusive. The principal element is presented by the solo violin, accompanied by woodwind and string figuration, sometimes derived from the first theme of the preceding section. Development follows, after a brief pause, dealing largely with themes a and b. The latter

EXAMPLE 92.
FIRST MOVEMENT: Molto agitato

e.

Ob., Cor. Angl.

*p*

THIRD MOVEMENT: Adagio, tranquillo ed espressivo

f.

Muted Vla.

*pp*

poco cresc.

FOURTH MOVEMENT: Allegramente

g.

Trpt. *ff*

etc.

heralds what would seem to be the recapitulation of the second theme, followed by a return of most of the material from the first thematic section. The movement comes to a quiet close.

The second movement, *allegretto capriccioso,* is a wry little scherzo, cast in a rondo form. The interludes are short and serve only as contrasting sections to the principal theme (Example 92e).

The third movement is an elegaic, expressive *adagio* of extremely involved lyricism which uses devices of theme transformation, inversion, retrograde and fragmentation, thus making recognition of formal sections exceedingly difficult (Example 92f).

The final movement is a rondo-like structure whose recurring element is the gay and rhythmic succession of triads noted in Example 92g. The direction of this triadic stream is sometimes inverted, but it is still easily recognizable.

## HOWARD HANSON, 1896-

Hanson is a neoromantic composer who is at his best in those orchestral compositions especially suited by program or text to displays of orchestral color, such as *The Lament for Beowulf, Three Poems from Walt Whitman* or the *Cherubic Hymn.* He has written five symphonies to date, the most popular of which are the First, or "Nordic" and the Second, or "Romantic." His opera, *Merrymount,* based upon an event in the early history of Puritan New England, was produced by the Metropolitan Opera in 1934, and from it the composer extracted a suite of movements which is often performed. In later years, Hanson has been interested in artificial scales, both as a means of understanding certain historical styles of music as well as providing consistent stylistic materials for the modern composer. The *Cherubic Hymn,* which we shall examine, makes use of this technique. In recognition of his extraordinary service to the cause of American music as educator and conductor, he has been the recipient of many awards and honors.

PLATE LIV. *Howard Hanson. (Photo by Ouzer, courtesy of Howard Hanson.)*

### Symphony No. 2, "Romantic"

Let us examine his Symphony No. 2, subtitled the "Romantic Symphony." This work was written for Serge Koussevitsky and the Boston Symphony Orchestra at a time when audiences sought re-assurance amid the din of experimental music that there were still composers who were writing understandable symphonies. Hanson made a definite effort to emphasize romantic qualities in this work.

EXAMPLE 93.

MOTTO THEMES

a. Adagio

FIRST MOVEMENT: Allegro moderato

c. Allegro moderato

d. Lento

Cor. *mf*

Str. (harmony also)

etc.

SECOND MOVEMENT: Andante con tenerezza

e.

Ww. *p*

THIRD MOVEMENT:

f. Allegro con brio

*ff* Cor.

etc.

g.

Cor. 8va lower.

*ff*

etc.

etc.

h.

Vlc. *mf* espr.

+ Cor. Angl.

etc.

*First Movement:* The first movement is a rather free sonata-allegro which opens with an introduction in slow tempo based upon a chromatic motto theme (Example 93a). The sequential treatment of this motto, with accumulating instrumentation, traces a dynamic curve to a climax, after which it subsides.

The *allegro moderato* section is ushered in by a brass fanfare built on fourths, after which the horns proclaim the principal theme against a motivic background (Example 93b). The theme is developed somewhat at a rather high dynamic level. The lyric transition theme now appears in the solo oboe (Example 93c). It undergoes considerable development by imitation and both rhythmic augmentation and diminution before it cadences.

The third important thematic section of the *allegro* actually contains two themes presented simultaneously, one by the horn, the other by the strings (Example 93d), in a most romantic and poetic fashion. A bridge, leading from the end of this section to the development, makes use of a fanfare figure based on the motive of the transition theme, first presented by the muted trumpets, then taken up by the woodwinds.

The principal theme, now lyric rather than forceful, occupies the development section, projected by the winds against tranquil background harmonies emphasizing the interval of the fourth.

The development flows without a break into the rewritten reprise of the principal theme, followed, as expected, by the lyric transition subject. This leads, not to the second theme, but rather to the introduction, which is then followed by the second theme, climaxing in grandiose fashion. The final short section cadences softly and thematically.

*Second Movement:* The second movement begins with a refreshing change of color, and is almost entirely based upon one theme (Example 93e), although the motto theme and the horn theme from the first movement (Example 93d) appear during the middle of the movement.

*Third Movement:* This movement contains only a small amount of new thematic material, for the themes of the preceding movements are recapitulated in part and are used developmentally. The first theme (Example 93f) bears a strong resemblance to its counterpart in the first movement in the use of fourths, besides being a fanfare. The motive of the second movement intervenes, after which the horns present a new theme (Example 93g) whose scale pattern becomes useful developmental material.

Next, the fanfare which occurred in the first movement between the introduction and the first theme becomes elevated to the stature of an important theme, followed by another theme, now emphasizing fourths (Examples 93h), first in the cellos, later in the winds. This theme is extended by repetition, ending with a short coda built out of the main theme of the second movement.

A faster section now begins with the syncopated rhythm of the low strings played *pizzicato* and using a short scale line derived from the main theme of the second movement, over which a fanfare figure in the horns develops. The dynamics mount, more instruments are added to both the *pizzicato* accompaniment and the fanfare, and this section reaches a climax on the main theme of the second movement, now proclaimed by the trumpets, extended, imitated by the horns, and amplified by the addition of the other wind instruments. At this point, the strings and trumpet recall the first theme of the first movement, now in a more ample rhythmic form, while the woodwinds are occupied with the scale figure heard before in the *pizzicato* strings. The whole section is played at a high dynamic level, and presses onward with considerable power. It cadences expansively, with a decrease in tempo, upon the horn subject of the second theme, first movement, followed by the triplets of the string subject with which it was associated. The movement halts, and after a short silence, a solo string quartet softly repeats the triplet figure. This is used in sequence, together with a new scale subject (Example 93i) to build a final climax during which are heard the first themes of the beginning and second movements.

### Cherubic Hymn

The *Cherubic Hymn,* with text from the Greek Orthodox liturgy of St. John Chrysostom, was composed in 1949, when Hanson was doing research for his book which deals with what we have called artificial scales. As we have seen in the case of the pentatonic and whole-tone scales, the harmonic possibilities of a scale are regulated by the intervals which occur in it. Hanson devised a way to analyze scales for their intervallic content, and then, by the opposite process, to synthesize them according to what intervals were desired to predominate, thus giving the resulting scale a very characteristic sound. This procedure provided the material for the *Cherubic Hymn:* here Hanson wanted to use material which would suggest the quasi-oriental splendor of the Byzantine ritual and accordingly synthesized scale forms which contained a predominance of colorful intervals of Near Eastern feeling. These, combined with appropriate orchestration, suit the subject without making it another romantic oriental fantasy. The choral writing is diatonic despite the chromaticisms which occur in the scale and is very singable. The thematic materials are very simple, elemental, in fact, since they consist for the most part of scale fragments — a characteristic which makes for extreme unity, far beyond that obtained by theme transference in the symphony. Here Hanson has achieved an exciting setting of the text without detracting from its solemnity — indeed, the glory of St. John's vision is more clearly revealed.

## ROY HARRIS, 1898-

The best music of this composer seems highly representative of pioneer America in its rugged and rough-hewn quality. This is true of the early Piano Sonata, the Overture "When Johnny Comes Marching Home" and the fine Third Symphony. Other works are not as vital, although Harris at his dullest still gives the feeling that he is imparting something profound. He writes with great facility, and has produced many works. His reputation rests largely on the works mentioned above, however, together with a few chamber compositions such as the Piano Quintet.

The Third Symphony (Example 94) is a one-movement work cast in five main sections which differ from each other in themes, sonority and tempo. The first section, with which the work begins, has been characterized by the composer as "tragic — low string sonorities." The long-breathed melodic lines are combined in counterpoint which relies heavily upon the intervals of the fifth and fourth, and which, when sufficient lines have accumulated, creates nonfunctional modal har-

PLATE LV. *Roy Harris. (Courtesy of the BMI Archive.)*

mony (Example 94a). The motion quickens, the sonority brightens, and Section II: "Lyric — strings, horns, woodwinds" arrives (Example 94b). Section III: "Pastoral — woodwinds with a polytonal string background." In this section (Example 94c) muted strings play over-lapping *arpeggio* passages, accompanying the solo woodwinds. Here Harris has created an entirely new sound, never before heard in the orchestra. Section IV: "Fugue — dramatic" (Example 94d) consists of three subsections: (1) Brass and percussion predominating; (2) Canonic development of materials from Section II, providing a back-ground for continuation of the fugue; and (3) Brass climax employing a rhythmic motive derived from the fugue subject. The fifth section, "dramatic — tragic" first restates some of the thematic material of Section I, while the brass and percussion continue with the rhythmic motive of Section IV. This is followed by a coda built over a constant metric beat in the timpani. The thematic material is derived from Sections I and II (*i.e.*, the long melodic lines of Section I appear throughout this entire last section). This work is most convincing in its unity, variety and coherence, and provides one of the more successful examples of the one-movement symphony written in the twentieth century.

EXAMPLE 94.

FUGUE SUBJECT: ($\sigma = 112$)

RHYTHMIC MOTIVE:

## AARON COPLAND, 1900-

This composer was early influenced by jazz, and used it in some of his works — "Dance Symphony" (1925), "Music for the Theater" (1925) and Piano Concerto (1926). Since about 1937, however, he has consciously turned toward increased simplicity and a certain use of folk-like materials (the ballets *Billy the Kid, Rodeo, Appalachian Spring, El Salon Mexico;* and concert music *Symphonic Ode, Statements, Lincoln Portrait,* Piano Variations, Clarinet Quintet, Third Symphony). He has also written several fine film scores of which those for *Our*

PLATE LVI. *Aaron Copland. (Photo by John Ardoin, courtesy of Boosey and Hawkes.)*

*Town* and *Of Mice and Men* have been outstanding. He uses modern versions of traditional forms very clearly, so that there is usually little problem in analytical listening. His scoring is always appropriate and skillful.

A good example of his present style is his Third Symphony. It is a work in four movements.

*First Movement (molto moderato):* The key is E-major; arch form is employed, using three themes (Examples 95, a, b, c) of which (a) and (c) are heard in later movements of the work. Theme (a) is typically intervallic and wide-spaced, b♯ is more lyric and not so widely spaced, although it still uses thematic intervals; and (c), which first appears in the trombones, consists of triad formations connected by scale passages of a few notes. The three themes are presented in an expository section, developed and recapitulated, although (c) does not appear in the recapitulation.

*Second Movement (allegro molto):* The movement consists of a scherzo and trio. The main thematic element of the scherzo is a fanfare figure (Example 95d) whose rhythm is as important as the melodic pattern. There are three varied statements of this theme followed by short developments before the trio is reached. In contrast to the climax which precedes it, the trio is quiet and lyric, built on a flowing and only slightly angular theme (Example 95e), first stated in the oboe. It is developed in free and imitative counterpoint, after which the scherzo gradually returns by way of a passage of increasing rhythmic motion marked by the use of the celesta (sometimes piano) at first, later by fragmentary development of the scherzo theme and increasing force. The return of the scherzo is abbreviated and recomposed.

*Third Movement (andantino, quasi allegretto):* This is the slow movement of the work, and employs theme c of the first movement as the subject for the introduction and coda, between which there is a continuous, close-knit series of four variational sections, each of which seems to grow organically out of the preceding one. The theme of these variations (Example 95f) is typically angular, tonal and suited to some of the additive rhythmic sections included in the animated variation.

*Fourth Movement (molto deliberato* (Fanfare) — *Allegro risoluto):* The fanfare (Example 95g), with which this movement opens

EXAMPLE 95.

FIRST MOVEMENT. Molto moderato-with simple expression

a. Vl., Fl. *dolce.* *p*

etc.

b. Molto moderato
Vla. *p*

etc.

c. Molto moderato
Trmb. *f* *marc.*

SECOND MOVEMENT: Allegro molto

d. Cor. *f* *marc.* *sf* *sf* *sf*

LATER

etc.

593

without pause after the preceding one, is first stated softly in the flutes and clarinets, followed by a forceful repetition in the brass. After this introduction, the main body of the movement, essentially a sonata-allegro, follows. The first theme (Example 95h), a repetitive, rapid note pattern, is stated in the oboe, joined contrapuntally by the other woodwinds and finally by the strings. The theme is thoroughly developed, during the course of which the harmonic-lyric second theme (Example 95i) is presented. The development of the fanfare and the first theme continues, coming to a climax on a shrill, dissonant chord which signals the close of the development section, after which the first theme (h) in the piccolo is combined with the fanfare theme (g) in the bassoons. Somewhat later, the two harps, piano and celeste are given rapid scale figures against which the solo horn plays the fanfare theme (g), after which the violins and later the trombone state the opening theme of the first movement (a). The second theme of the finale then appears in even note values in the horns after which the second theme of the first movement (b) is used in the horns and trombones to form the closing section of the finale. Interestingly enough, this symphony which began in E-major ends in D-major.

## WILLIAM SCHUMAN, 1910-

The saga of the films has come true for Schuman, for he began as a Tin-Pan Alley composer of popular songs, and later served a number of years as the president of the Juilliard School of Music. The early days in the "Alley," however, have left their impress on his lively rhythmic sense which is apparent in every page he has written. His style is neoclassic, but without the stylization of Stravinsky, the introspective chromaticism of Bartók or the Germanic quality of Hindemith. It is economical and spare, typically American in its verve and brilliance. One of his most popular works is his Third Symphony, and his "American Festival Overture" is frequently played.

The Third Symphony of Schuman is divided into two large movements, each of which consists of two sections. The neoclassic tendency toward baroque formal patterns is evident here, for the first movement is a passacaglia and fugue, and the second is formed by pairing a chorale and toccata.

The passacaglia theme (Example 96a), a rather angular melodic line covering nearly two octaves in span, is first stated in the violas and

595

PLATE LVII. *William Schuman. (Courtesy of the BMI Archive.)*

imitated seven times, each entry a half step higher than the preceding one (*cf.* Bartók: first movement of Music for Strings, Percussion and Celesta, page 548). At the conclusion of this canonic section, the thematic idea is developed simultaneously in the strings, trumpets and trombones, concluding with a passage for the brass alone. The following sections are devoted to development and transformation of the theme, not as a ground bass, as in baroque style, but as a melodic element.

The fugue subject (Example 96b) is announced by the unison horns and *pizzicato* strings, and followed by the violins, violas and cellos, basses and tuba, woodwinds, trombones and trumpets. After the first imitation, there is a short episode between the succeeding entries, each of which is a half step higher than the preceding one. A climax is accumulated, not only dynamically, but also because of the increasing number of instruments participating, followed by a brilliant canonic passage based on the subject and played by the four trumpets. A quiet section employing the woodwinds ensues to which the strings add their sound, again reaching a high point at which the timpani has a variant of the fugue subject. During the rest of the movement, strings and woodwinds supply developmental backgrounds to thematic motives in the brass: the passage culminates in a statement of the subject in augmentation (long note values) by the horns

EXAMPLE 96.

PART I
PASSACAGLIA

FUGUE:

PART II
CHORALE:

d. TOCCATA (♩ = 108-112)

Snare drum
*pp* 3

etc.

( ♩ = 108-112)

B. Cl. *p*

etc.

e. B. Cl. ( ♩ = 108)

Vlc. *fff*
> accelerando
a tempo

which leads to the coda where similar procedures bring the movement to an impressive close.

   Part II, Chorale and Toccata, begins with a set of chorale variations on a theme (Example 96c) first presented by the trumpet after a rather polyphonic introduction by the low strings. The variations work up to a considerable climax, subside to a low, sustained B♭ and lead to the statement of the rhythmic toccata theme by the snare drum (Example 96d). The bass clarinet in its low register invests these rhythmic fragments with pitch contours (Example 96d) which chase each other in various transformed patterns throughout the movement. As befits the title, the movement is a rhythmic display piece for orchestra. There is an interesting passage for the cellos which introduces a new theme (Example 96e), briefly worked out before the movement gathers momentum and rushes toward its conclusion.

## SAMUEL BARBER, 1910-

This gifted composer grew up in cultured surroundings, affected by the influence of the concert and operatic stage in the person of his aunt, the singer Louise Homer. He writes for the most part in a warm neoromantic idiom, although certain experimental works such as the *Capricorn Concerto* reveal somewhat Stravinskyan neoclassic tendencies. His works have been well received and among those frequently heard in concert are the *Adagio for Strings, First Essay for Orchestra,* "Overture to the *School for Scandal,*" *Music for a Scene from Shelley* and the First Symphony. His opera, *Vanessa,* written to a text by his friend, Gian-Carlo Menotti, has been produced by the Metropolitan Opera Company.

## GIAN-CARLO MENOTTI, 1911-

Born in Milan, Italy, Menotti came to the United States in 1928. He has composed some purely instrumental works, but is best known for his operas, of which *The Medium* and *The Consul* have earned him international renown. He writes not only the music for these works, but also the text, and is singularly successful and imaginative in operas in the romantic Italian *verismo* tradition of Mascagni, Leoncavallo and Puccini. The *Saint of Bleeker Street* falls well within this classification, but some other works, such as the Christmas opera for television, *Amahl and the Night Visitors,* and the madrigal comedy, *The Unicorn, the Gorgon and the Manticore,* show a more fantastic and sympathetic side of his nature. He is the organizer of the Festival of Two Worlds in Spoleto, Italy, which is devoted to the production of new musical works.

There are a good many more American composers than we have mentioned here, and any kind of examination of their work would necessitate a volume at least as long as the present one. Many of these younger men are in a sense traditional, following the paths opened up by those composers we have mentioned. But others are more pioneering in spirit, widening the boundaries of tonal and rhythmic manipulation; these composers include Elliott Carter (1908-), Hugo Weisgall (1912-), Leon Kirchner (1919-), Ross Lee Finney (1906-), John Cage (1912-) and others. And there are many more who exhibit stylistic assimilations ranging somewhere between the extremes. Most of these men are well-equipped technically: it remains to be seen whether they can meet the demands of the twentieth century spiritually and provide our culture with masterpieces that are unique and significant.

Our nation is coming of age musically at a time when a definite twentieth-century style is beginning to take shape out of the chaos of "isms" and "neos." The younger composers will benefit from the stylistic unity forged by their elders in such works as we have mentioned above, together with those of the pioneers — Stravinsky, Bartók, Hindemith and Schönberg. Within the next few decades the style of the first half of the century will probably exhibit a unity that we are as yet unable to discern, and may then be studied in the way we have examined the Baroque or Classic periods. Let us do our part as interested, intelligent, informed and tolerant listeners to aid in this development, making the music of our era as important and meaningful in our lives as are those scientific advances which are reported each day. The spiritual side of man must keep pace with his accomplishments in the physical world, or we shall gradually become robots. Bernard Rogers, a distinguished American composer, made an apt comment which bears upon this point: "Religion and art are synonymous: they both attempt to civilize, to convince people that there is something above what we see and touch."

# TWENTIETH-CENTURY MUSIC IN OTHER COUNTRIES

Of course, Americans are not the only active composers of today, for European composers since the turn of the century have been producing music characteristic of their countries and times simultaneously with the works of Stravinsky, Bartók, Hindemith, Schönberg and the Americans just examined. Let us review some of the more important of these from France, England, Germany and Italy.

### FRANCE

During the years after the first World War, a number of Parisian composers sought to throw off the influences of romanticism and impressionism. They came under the influence of Erik Satie (1866-1925), u twentieth-century composer born before his time, and Jean Cocteau, who through esthetic observations and writings persuaded not only these men but also the public of the validity of his ideas. Almost by chance, a group formed which a journalist called *"Les Six."* These composers, Darius Milhaud (1892-), Arthur Honegger (1892-1955), Francis Poulenc (1899-1963), Georges Auric (1892-), Louis Durey (1888-) and Germaine Taillefaire (1892-), were not all in sympathy with each other's ideals, and ultimately the group disbanded. Only the first three became notable composers of serious music, although the characteristic flippancy of much of their work (with the exception of that of Honegger) might seem a challenge to the term "serious." For it was through the cultivation of the artfully banal or impertinent in music that they sought to destroy Wagnerism, the passionate romantic emotionalism, and the vagaries of impressionism, substituting for them a healthy vulgarity at times, an objective and sometimes ironic approach. Milhaud slowly outgrew this tendency, especially when it was no longer needed, and reverted to a lyric style often employing polytonality. Poulenc's music is still witty, but in a more refined way than that of the early years. He has become the foremost exponent of the modern French art song, in addition to composing chamber music and more serious operas. Honegger, on the other hand, was oriented from the first toward romanticism and never veered away. His compositions are serious in intent, and, while employing many devices of the new music, retain a romantic fervor. Most popular is his oratorio *King David*, but another work in this vein, *Joan of Arc at the Stake*, is equally powerful and more stylistically consistent.

Jacques Ibert (1890-1962) and Jean Francaix (1912-) share the French predilection for charming and witty music. The *Divertissement* of Ibert is devastating in its sarcasm, directed, as might be expected, toward romantic styles. But other works, such as *Escales* and the *Suite Elizabethaine*, are full of more serious charm and color. Francaix is notable for his typically light touch with woodwinds, and his chamber music for such combinations is pleasant listening.

Of sterner stuff are Olivier Messaien (1908-) and his pupil, Pierre

Boulez (1925-). Messaien's style derives from Gregorian chant, Hindu chant, impressionism and mysticism, especially in regard to the musical aspects of nature, the bird song, a field in which this composer has done much research. His theories of rhythm have had an energizing influence upon many of the younger generation of composers. Pierre Boulez, in an effort to totally organize his music, has turned to serial techniques in rhythm, dynamics and articulation as well as in pitch (*i.e.,* twelve-tone technique). A disciple of the Webern style, he has moved away from the use of instruments toward *musique concrète,* which employs electronically controlled and varied natural sounds as its material.

### GERMANY

Music in Germany and Austria had hardly recovered from the first World War when the Nazi blight appeared, thoroughly blocking attempts to advance musical style beyond that of late romanticism. Certain composers, however, did manage to exist through these times, either by remaining quiet or by emigrating to more liberal environments. Carl Orff (1898-), Werner Egk (1901-) Boris Blacher (1903-) and Gottfried von Einem (1918-) came to world notice only after the second war, while Ernst Křenek (1900-) and Kurt Weill (1900-1950) made successes in the United States during the thirties and forties. Those who stayed became the teachers of the new generation and represent the conservative neoclassic or neoromantic composers of the country. The younger German composers are almost without exception disciples of the twelve-tone gospel, especially as interpreted by Webern, and some have extended the boundaries of this technique into the realm of electronic music. Members of this avant garde generation include Rolf Liebermann (1910-), Giselher Klebe (1925-), Heinz Werner Henze (1926-), and perhaps the most striking, Karlheinz Stockhausen (1928-), the leader of the electronic group.

### ITALY

The music of Italy, in general, has also become twelve-tone. Here too, two generations of composers exist corresponding to the situation in Germany: Gian Francesco Malipiero (1882-), Alfredo Casella (1883-1947) and Ildebrando Pizzetti (1880-), for all their connections with the "modern music" movements early in the century, are basically romantics of the Italian lyric variety. The younger group is headed by Luigi Dallapiccola (1904-), whose music shows a personal lyric style fused with the twelve-tone technique. Luigi Nono (1924-) is a thorough-going twelve-tone composer who has also written electronic works, and Bruno Maderna (1920-) and Luciano Berio (1925-) both share in the post-Webern style as applied to both conventional and electronic music-producing apparatus.

### ENGLAND

England, without a notable composer since the Baroque, slowly came to life musically during the late nineteenth century, producing Edward Elgar (1857-1934), Ralph Vaughan Williams (1872-1958), Benjamin Britten (1913-) and William Walton (1902-). Elgar has been called the "English Brahms," and his music does have some of the qualities of that composer; but it also unites two rather opposed qualities in the color and orchestration reminiscent of Richard Strauss with a thoroughly British musical temperament. Vaughan Williams is equally English in his bluff and forthright way, a nationalism reflected in his fondness for the modal harmonies derived from English folksong as well as other techniques which were an important part of Elizabethan music. But he advanced during his lifetime, spanning the turn of the century and the entry into "modernism" with a youthful and forward-looking spirit. Benjamin Britten, who possesses an eclectic musical style, is most notable for his operas. Especially successful were the full-length works *Peter Grimes, Billy Budd* and *The Turn of the Screw*. He has also written many songs, orchestral works and chamber music. William Walton is most famous in the United States for three works: his early music, *Façade,* to accompany poems by Edith Sitwell, his Viola Concerto, and the setting of the biblical story of *Belshazzar's Feast* for chorus and orchestra. He has the romantic's love of drama, color and lyricism — qualities that make his music easily understood and popular.

### RUSSIA

Music in Russia has had a curious history in the twentieth century. Relatively late in emerging as a musical entity, the Russian composer has been alternately encouraged and discouraged by political forces in the expression of new techniques. The composers after the famous nationalists, guided in their studies largely by Rimsky-Korsakoff and his associates, had formed their musical habits along nationalistic lines, all quite committed to the post-romantic style. Of the four important ones in Russia at the time of the revolution in 1918, three, Sergei Rachmaninoff (1873-1943), Alexander Glazounov (1865-1936) and Serge Prokofiev (1891-1953), left their native land for either security or more peaceful surroundings in which to work. The other, Reinhold Glière (1875-1956), remained and shared in the shaping of the new generation. While Rachmaninoff and Glazounov never returned to Russia, Prokofiev did so for various reasons in 1934. The younger Soviet composers whom he joined are, at least in part, quite familiar to Western concert-goers — Dmitri Shostakovich (1906), Aram Khatchaturian (1903-), Dmitri Kabalevsky (1904-) and Tikhon Khrennikov 1913-).

In the 1920's, new and experimental music was welcomed and encouraged by the revolutionary government. But with the advent of Stalin, a sterner, more socialistic control of the arts was instituted to the end that each of the artistic disciplines was to provide popular culture for the people; that is, products which, without ceasing to be art, could be readily comprehended by the untutored. In addition, of course, the subjects were to be strongly nationalistic, and the treatment of them carried out in such a way as to glorify the ideals of the state. The artist was ordered to submerge his individuality in the national character. Such a program had the effect of discouraging musical progress, although from the scoldings administered by the government to the above composers we can guess that their curiosity often led them into socialistically unacceptable bypaths. After the death of Stalin, the strictures were relaxed to a considerable extent, and a new spirit of individualism — in art, at least — has appeared.

The early music of Prokofiev was highly individual, anti-romantic and dissonant, but these qualities became mellowed upon his return to Russia, and the subsequent style became no less individual, but more lyric and less harmonically spicy. The music of Shostakovich is typically Russian in its broad gestures and brilliant orchestration. More nationalistic through the use of folk materials is the music of Khatchaturian, Kabalevsky and Khrennikov. The fertilizing influence of the twelve-tone technique has not been evidenced in the music of the Soviet Union as of this writing.

## THE SMALLER NATIONS

Nationalistic music from the smaller European states also entered the twentieth century: we have already noted the place of Bartók in this scheme, but the name of Zoltán Kodály (1882-), Bartók's collaborator in the collection of folk material, should be mentioned. Much less progressive than Bartók, Kodály's music is strongly tonal and uses typical romantic elements. The folk element is present in simple form, not in the assimilated synthesis of Bartók. The *Rumanian Rhapsodies* of Georges Enesco (1881-1955) appear quite frequently on concert programs, as do the evocations of Spain in rather modern terms in the music of Manuel de Falla (1876-1946). For most people, Ernest Bloch (1880-1959) speaks most eloquently for the Jewish race, although now that there is a Jewish nation, he is already being followed by some talented young composers of whom Paul Ben-Haim is outstanding.

## LATIN AMERICA

Until the end of the nineteenth century, the nations of South and Central America imported their music from Europe. To be sure, there were native composers of songs and theater pieces, but these works were couched in the international romantic styles of France, Germany and Italy, and made almost no use of the folk resources of these colorful people. The popular music, sung on street corners and in taverns, however, amalgamated the imported music with the already present mixture of native Indian and Negro folk idioms, resulting in a strongly rhythmic and characteristic quality, easily recognizable as generally "South American." Two composers were mainly responsible for the development of nationalistic music in their own countries, a development which has spread by imitation into many of the states of Latin America. These men were Heitor Villa-Lobos (1887-1959) in Brazil and Carlos Chávez (1899-) in Mexico. The music of Villa-Lobos is richly romantic, evoking comparison with the lush tropical vegetation of his nation. It employs folk elements and especially folk instruments of the percussion variety. Because the composer was so prolific, the quality is uneven, but most of it is rhythmically and sonorously exciting, highly individual. The music of Chávez lies at the other extreme, severely neoclassic, highly dissonant, and, partially because of the Indian folk element, rather stark and primitive-sounding. Both of these men have been highly influential in the cause of music education in their countries, a program which is now paying dividends in the appearance of a new generation of Latin-American composers.

# THE MODERN STYLE IN THE OTHER ARTS

It is a commonplace to state that the culture of the twentieth century has been strongly influenced by the machine, but like most commonplaces, it is profoundly true. That influence dates from the advent of the first Model T Ford in 1908, which introduced mass-production; from the erection of the Wainright Building, the first skyscraper, 1871, by Louis Sullivan in St. Louis; from the invention of the radio by Marconi in 1909; and, most important for the citizen of the middle of the century, from the moment the Wright brothers lifted man into the air in 1903 and Einstein began to lift man's imagination and finally man himself into space with his first papers on relativity in 1905.

Creators in the arts developed similar points of view, most of them rather different from purely mechanistic representations, although there were a few of those, too: Léger's paintings of imaginary machinery have a certain relation to George Antheil's *Ballet mécanique* (written to accompany a Léger experimental film of the same name); Honegger's composition *Pacific 231* exalts power in the form of a great steam locomotive and "noise music" became a passing fad after World War I under the imposing title "Futurism." But most of the artistic products of the twentieth century have tended to recreate their various views of experience upon the purely technical terms of each art: they have sought to give a meaningful expression to the culture and values of their particular time, and to seek ever more powerful means of bringing these ideas before their contemporaries.

Each of these works — a painting, a sculpture, a piece of music, a poem — creates a small private world of its own in which certain forces and tensions prevail which may seem strange to the outsider — the beholder, the listener, the reader — until he overcomes his reticence or prejudice and steps into this new microcosm. If he will accept

PLATE LVIII, *"Mont St. Victoire" by Cezanne. This painting is a forerunner of geometrical abstraction and cubism. Note the reduction of natural objects to quasi-geometrical forms. (Courtesy of The Philadelphia Museum of Art.)*

it on its own terms — just as he would accept the flora and fauna of a new planet — he may be able to make delightful or significant discoveries about that world or about himself. But, presented with such an opportunity, he must take the first step. Let us leave the museum of historic masterpieces and go exploring.

The arts, especially painting and music, responded quickly to the arrival of mechanistic culture. We have seen how the impressionist painters, profiting by advanced researches into the nature of light, learned new ways to handle the application of paint to canvas, and similarly how composers gained a like freedom in the use of tone-color and dissonance. But both impressionistic art and music were representational: each had a rather close association with physical reality, although certainly once removed from the almost one-to-one correspondence of David's classicism or the late romantic tone poems of Strauss. This representational romantic trend was continued in the primitivistic style of the early years of the century — for what was this but a further manifestation of the romantic longing for far places and new and exotic sensations? The African masks which influenced Braque and Picasso so profoundly (Plate XLIX) and the Polynesian

PLATE LIX.  *"Man with a Guitar" by Braque. A typical cubistic reassemblage of the features of the subject. (Courtesy of The Museum of Modern Art.)*

neoprimitivism of Gauguin had their reflection in the *Rite of Spring*, Falla's *El Amor Brujo* (*Love the Magician*), and certain other nationalistic works in which the primitive folk element was deliberately presented in a rather unsophisticated state.

From the geometrical simplifications of primitive art, together with the theories of Cézanne that everything could be represented as modifications of the sphere, cylinder and cone, the style known as cubism arose (Plate LVIII — Cézanne; Plate LIX — Braque). While the melodic angularity of some contemporary music offers a reasonable counterpart in sound to such design, certain practices which the followers of cubism developed have closer parallels in musical procedures. These artists broke down the figures in their paintings into a myriad of cubes. Realizing that in a three-dimensional drawing of a cube all sides are visible, they showed in these cubes, and later without them, the various sides of the subject simultaneously: the paintings of this period by Picasso show, on a two dimensional surface, the eyes, or even the half-face of a figure represented in profile next to it. In Picasso's painting "Girl Before a Mirror" (Plate LX), the artist demonstrates this "spatial simultaneity" on three levels: the picture, which also employs a certain amount of distortion, is intended to portray the subject clothed, nude and X-rayed. And the total effect is often one of abstract design rather than objective portrayal, especially when viewed in the original colors rather than black and white.

Such procedures in painting are akin to Stravinsky's use of rhythm, both in the distortion through syncopation or changing meters, and in the use of rhythmic variation applied to the repetitions of a melodic line, such as appears in the opening bassoon solo of the *Rite of Spring*. Another parallel may be made to the constructive methods of twelve-tone composition in which the row appears melodically (horizontally) as well as harmonically (vertically) at the same time. And, of course, the various versions of the row — original, retrograde, inverted and the retrograde inversion — may all appear simultaneously. But these manipulations are not usually heard — indeed, they are not usually intended to be obvious — as those of the paintings are seen, so the analogy is one of technique rather than of experience, so to speak.

Meanwhile, another style of art which employed distortion was developing in middle Europe, a style reminiscent of the fantastic imagination of German Gothic painters such as Heironymous Bosch, a style which used the symbols of the new psychology of Freud painted in vivid, unreal colors to express the anguished or exalted moods of

PLATE LX. *"Girl Before a Mirror" by Picasso. An example of post-cubistic distortion and presentation of several views (clothed, nude, X-rayed) simultaneously. (Courtesy of The Museum of Modern Art.)*

the human soul. These were the expressionists, and although the style was predominantly German, it included Van Gogh and the Viennese Kokoschka as well as others. In music, it was exemplified by Strauss's two experiments in psychopathology, *Elektra* and *Salome* — experiments which he did not repeat, but fell back on the more publicly acceptable style of *Der Rosenkavalier;* and, of course, Schönberg and his disciples carried to the utmost the ideals of this style in works such as *Pierrot Lunaire* and *Wozzeck.* These composers and some painters, however, eventually tried to create a more abstract, less overtly symbolic art by departing from the use of a "subject" (*i.e.,* in painting, the model, still-life or landscape which the artist depicts). In music, this meant the abandonment of tonality, for what is classic form but the embodiment of tonality given recognizable and memorable features by melodic, thematic and rhythmic contours? The paintings of Kandinsky (Plate XLV) exemplify abstract expressionism, as do the non-programmatic works of many atonal composers, such as Berg's *Lyric Suite,* or the Fourth String Quartet of Schönberg, or Webern's Five Pieces for Orchestra.

Other creative artists abandoned representations of reality for those of the dream-world, valuing the fantasies of the subconscious as more real than experiences of wakened awareness. This movement was surrealism. We are almost all familiar with the works of Dali, de Chirico, Chagall and Klee, but how often do we recognize the surrealist quality in some of the compositions of Mahler (*Das Lied von der Erde*)? Significantly, music, "being the stuff that dreams are made of," usualy requires a non-musical "explanation" to make clear that its intention is surrealistic, and so, many scenes from operas and ballets as well as the all-too-often trite "dream sequences" of the motion picture often employ surrealistic music. Here the techniques of either or both impressionism and expressionism are called into play in the use of tone-color, distortion and fragmentation of themes and unstable harmony. Such is the case in Bartók's opera, *Duke Bluebeard's Castle* and Ravel's *L'Enfant et les sortilèges,* while in Prokofiev's opera, *The Love for Three Oranges,* a surrealistic story is set to often brittle and sardonic music. The bread-machine and the trance of Baba the Turk in Stravinsky's otherwise quite neoclassic opera, *The Rake's Progress,* are surrealist elements introduced by the libretto. Recently, the modern American composer Gunther Schuller (1925-) has composed a rather delayed essay in surrealism, *The Twitter-Machine,* a musical counterpart to Klee's whimsical *Zwittermaschine.* In literature, the surrealistic quality occurs frequently, most obviously in the works of certain stream-of-consciousness writers such as Joyce and Gertrude Stein, but also more unexpectedly in stories by authors less given to these techniques, such as in "Death in Venice" by Thomas Mann.

The neoclassic style of the twenties made itself felt in the production of the original or rewritten Greek dramas, especially in France, by the abandonment of distortion in painting, as exemplified by certain works of Picasso (Plate XLVII), and the simplification of musical textures as well as the borrowing of techniques from earlier, pre-romantic times, as we have already heard in compositions by Stravinsky. Even Debussy, shortly before his death, perhaps influenced by the spare style of Satie, composed certain works in which he tried to return to the clarity and elegance of the French harpsichord composers and the Grecian ideals of restraint and grace. His *Six Epigraphes Antiques,* as well as Ravel's *Tombeau de Couperin (Tomb, or Memorial, to Couperin)* and Satie's *Gymnopedies* are examples of this attitude. Prokofiev's famous *Classical Symphony* is a witty evocation of the eighteenth century accomplished with modern sophistication. And Stravinsky's oratorio, *Oedipus Rex,* powerfully sets forth the old Greek tragedy in a somber and impersonal style which emphasizes the implacability of fate.

Perhaps more than any others, Picasso and Stravinsky personify the seeking spirit of the first half of the twentieth century. They are much alike in their use of the whole historic range of artistic material which they use in contemporary fashion, not "filling old bottles with new wine," but making new bottles out of the old. Each has revolutionized his art and contributed greatly to it. They are comparable at many periods of their creative lives: each has produced primitive, neoclassic and constructivist works of great value. And they and all the other creative artists who kept their integrity during difficult times have enriched our lives by producing works representative of the times in which we live. Let us permit this enrichment by giving them our attention and curiosity; let us enter private worlds and learn that they are our worlds too, inhabited by creatures like ourselves. Only thus will we be able to perceive our relations to the outer and inner worlds in which we exist.

## LIST OF TERMS

impressionism
expressionism
neoclassicism
neoromanticism
tension, tension-modulation
pandiatonicism
*ostinato*
functional, non-functional harmony
functional, non-functional
   orchestration
quartal harmony
secundal harmony
tonality
polytonality
modality
polymodality
polychord
atonal, pantonal
twelve-tone
Stravinsky rhythm
mosaic construction
diatonic

complex harmony
free dissonance
dissonance, consonance
dissonance saturation
"night music"
changing meters
additive rhythms
whole-tone scale
gliding or planing harmony
pentatonic scale
Bartók *pizzicato*
post-romanticism
post-impressionism
stylization
*glissando*
artificial scales
chromaticism
free chromaticism
doubling
escaped chords
organpoint (pedalpoint)

## ADDITIONAL LISTENING

### GERMANY

Carl Orff (1895-)
  *Carmina Burana*
  *Carmina Catulli*
Karlheinz Stockhausen (1928-)
  *Kontra-Punkte*
  Piano Piece XI
  *Zeitmasse*

Jean Françaix (1912-)
  Wind Quintet
Jacques Ibert (1890-1962)
  *Suite Elizabethaine*
  *Divertissement*
  *Escales*
Oliver Messiaen (1908-)
  *Banquet céleste*
  *Bergers*
  *Turangalila Symphony*

### FRANCE

Darius Milhaud (1892-)
  *Scaramouche,* Suite for Two Pianos
  *La Création du Monde*
  *Suite Provençale*
  *Les Choéphores*
Francis Poulenc (1899-1963)
  *Sextuor* (Sextet for Winds and
    Piano)
  Mass in G

### SWITZERLAND

Arthur Honegger (1892-1955)
  *Joan of Arc at the Stake* (oratorio)
  *King David* (oratorio)
  Symphony for String Orchestra
    (1941)
Frank Martin 1890-)
  *Petite Symphonie Concertante*
Ernest Bloch (1880-1959)
  Concerto Grosso

## ADDITIONAL LISTING (Cont.)

*Schelomo*, Hebrew Rhapsody
  for Cello and Orchestra
String Quartets Nos. 1 and 2
Piano Quintet

HUNGARY
  Zoltán Kodály (1882-)
    *Psalmus Hungaricus*
    Sonata for Unaccompanied Cello
  Leos Janácek (1854-1928)
    Sinfonietta
    *Taras Bulba*
    *Youth*
  Bohuslav Martinu (1890-1959)
    Serenade
    Partita for String Orchestra
    Concerto Grosso

ITALY
  Gian Francesco Malipiero (1882-)
    *Rispetti e Strambotti*
    (String Quartet)
  Luigi Dallapiccola (1904-)
    *Il Prigionero*
    *Quaderno musica de Annalibera*
  Luigi Nono (1924-)
    *Polifonica, Monodia, Ritornica*

RUSSIA
  Prokofiev (1891-1953)
    *Peter and the Wolf*
    *Lt. Kijé*
    *Alexander Nevsky* (cantata)
    Piano Sonatas
    Toccata for piano
    Symphonies Nos. 1, 5, 7
  Dmitri Shostakovitch (1906-)
    Symphonies Nos. 5 and 6
    Piano Quintet
    Piano Concerto

Dmitri Kabalevsky (1904-)
  *Gayne*, ballet suite
  Suite from *Colas Breugnon*
Aram Khatchaturian (1903-)
  Piano Concerto

ENGLAND
  Ralph Vaughan-Williams (1872-1958)
    *Variations on a Theme by*
     *Thomas Tallis*
    Folk-Song Suite
    "London" Symphony
    Fantasy on "Greensleeves"
  Benjamin Britten (1913-)
    Three Sea Interludes, from
     *Peter Grimes*
    *Sinfonia da Requiem*
    Serenade for Tenor and Horn
    A Ceremony of Carols
  William Walton (1902-)
    Concerto for Viola and Orchestra
    *Belshazzar's Feast* (Choral)
    *Façade*
  Edmund Rubbra (1901-)
    Symphony No. 1
    String Quartet No. 2

BRAZIL
  Heitor Villa-Lobos (1887-1959)
    *Bachianas Brasilieras* Nos. 2 and 5
    *The Little Train of the Caipira*
    String Quartet No. 6

MEXICO
  Silvestre Revueltas (1899-1940)
    *Cunahuac*
    *Sensemaya*
  Carlos Chávez (1899-)
    *Sinfonia de Antigone*
    *Sinfonia India*

# Appendix I: Glossary

## TEMPO

*Presto.* Very fast

*Vivace.* Lively

*Allegro.* Fast, often followed by a qualifying term of which the following are the most common:

    *Allegro vivace.* Somewhat slower than *vivace* alone, still very fast.

    *Allegro molto.* Very fast, but not as rapid as *presto*.

    *Allegro assai.* Very quick

*Animato.* Animated, less rapid than allegro

*Allegretto.* Literally, a "little *allegro*", -etto being a diminutive suffix.

*Moderato.* At medium speed.

*Andantino.* Again a diminutive suffix, -ino, thus meaning "a little *andante*."

*Andante.* Literally, "going," less fast than *moderato*.

*Adagio, Lento, Largo* and *Grave* signify increasingly slow tempos, often qualified by *molto* (very), *assai* (extremely), or the comparative and superlative suffixes, -issimo (*largissimo*, "most slowly") and -ississimo (*largississimo*, "most slowliest").

## EXPRESSION

Very often one of the tempo indications given above is modified by another term in order to convey to the performer the manner in which the piece is to be played. Such words are:

*Affettuoso.* With warmth, affectionately.

*Agitato.* Agitated, excited.

*Appassionata.* Impassioned.

*Con brio.* With spirit.

*Cantabile.* In a singing manner.

*Capriccioso.* In a humorous or capricious manner.

*Dolce.* Sweet and soft.

*Dolente, Doloroso.* Sadly, dolefully.

*Frenetico.* Frenzied.

*Giocoso.* Playful.

*Grazioso.* Graceful.

*Lamentando.* Mournfully, lamenting.

*Leggiero.* Light and graceful.

*Lusingando.* Flattering, coaxing, intimate.

*Maestoso.* Grandly, with majesty.

*Marziale.* Martially, march-like.

*Ma non troppo.* Not too much so (*e.g., Allegro ma non troppo:* fast, but not extremely so).

*Mesto.* Mournful.

*Moto, con.* With motion.

*Non tanto, non troppo.* Not too much (*e.g. Allegro non troppo*)

*Ongarese, All'.* In Hungarian style.

*Pesante.* Heavily.

*Quasi.* As if, or almost: *e.g. Allegro quasi presto* — *allegro,* almost *presto.*

*Risoluto.* Resolutely, with decision.

*Scherzando.* Playfully.

*Scorrevole.* Freely flowing.

*Sempre.* Always, *e.g. sempre pesante* — always heavily.

*Semplice.* Simply.

*Soave.* Suavely, gently.

*Sostenuto.* Sustaining the tone or slackening the tempo, *e.g. allegro sostenuto* — somewhat slower than *allegro.*

*Spiritoso.* Spirited, lively.

*Teneramente.* Tenderly

Certain other terms relate to the dynamic level or to tempo changes. The most commonly used are these:

Dynamic level increasing from very soft to the loudest possible.

| *Pianississimo* | *pianissimo* | *piano* | *mezzo-piano* | |
|---|---|---|---|---|
| (abbr) ppp | pp | p | mp | |
| | *mezzo-forte* | *forte* | *fortissimo* | *fortississimo* |
| | mf | f | ff | fff |

"*Piano*" (p) is the Italian term for soft: the endings make superlative and double-superlative degrees: similarly with "*forte*" (f), the Italian term for loud (literally, strong). The word "*mezzo*" signifies "medium."

The terms "*crescendo*" and "*diminuendo*" are frequently used, and denote a growing and a diminishing in dynamic level, respectively.

The most common terms relating to the change of tempo are these:

*Accelerando.* To accelerate, or speed up. Often preceded or followed by "poco a poco," meaning wherever used, "little by little."

*Meno mosso.* Less motion, more slowly.

*Piu mosso.* More motion, faster.

*Ritardando, rallentando.* Gradually slackening the speed. Abbreviated *rit.* and *rall.*

Most terms used in the above situations are derived from the Italian due to the fact that in the early Baroque era, when these terms first gradually came into use, most composers were trained in Italy. Hence Italian became the language most common among musical performers and was readily understood by them. Since Beethoven, German has appeared as a nationalistic substitute for Italian, and the same is true of French since Debussy, possibly somewhat before him. Some American and English composers use English terms as well as the Italian ones. Certainly there are no substitutes for the dynamic abbreviations so commonly used.

# Appendix II: Bibliography

## GENERAL REFERENCES

EINSTEIN, ALFRED. *Music in the Romantic Era.* New York: Norton, 1947.
GROUT, DONALD J. *A History of Western Music.* New York: Norton, 1962.
LANG, PAUL H. *Music in Western Civilization.* New York: Norton, 1941.
McKINNEY, H. and ANDERSON, W. R. *Music in History.* New York: American Book, 1957.
SCHOLES, PERCY. *The Oxford Companion to Music.* New York: Oxford, 1955.

## BAROQUE PERIOD

DAVID, H. and MENDEL, A. *The Bach Reader.* New York: Norton, 1945.
MILES, R. H. *Johann Sebastian Bach.* Englewood Cliffs, N. J.; Prentice-Hall, 1962.
SPITTA, P. *Johann Sebastian Bach.* New York: Dover, 1951.
TERRY, C. S. *J. S. Bach.* New York: Oxford, 1933.

DEUTSCH, OTTO. *Handel: A Documentary Biography.* New York: Norton, 1955.
FLOWER, N. H. *George Frederick Handel.* New York: C. Scribners, Cassell & Co., 1923.
WEINSTOCK, H. *Handel.* New York: Knopf, 1946.

PINCHERLE, M. *Corelli, His Life, His Music.* New York: Norton, 1956.
PINCHERLE, M. *Vivaldi.* New York: Norton, 1957.

## CLASSIC PERIOD

BURK, J. N. *The Life and Works of Beethoven.* New York: Modern Library, 1946.
SULLIVAN, J. W. N. *Beethoven, His Spiritual Development.* New York: Mentor, 1947.
TURNER, W. J. *Beethoven: The Search for Reality.* London: Dent, 1933.

GEIRINGER, K. *Haydn, A Creative Life in Music.* New York: Norton, 1946.
BREVET, M. *Haydn.* London: Oxford, 1926.

BIANCOLLI, L. *The Mozart Handbook.* Cleveland: World, 1954.
BURK, J. *Mozart and His Music.* New York: Random House, 1959.
EINSTEIN, ALFRED. *Mozart, His Character, His Work.* New York: Oxford, 1951.
TURNER, W. J. *Mozart, The Man and His Works.* New York: Tudor, 1946.

DEUTSCH, O. E. *The Schubert Reader.* New York: Norton, 1947.
EINSTEIN, ALFRED. *Schubert, A Musical Portrait.* New York: Oxford, 1951.
FLOWER, N. H. *Franz Schubert, The Man and His Circle.* New York: Tudor, 1928.

## EARLY ROMANTIC PERIOD

BARZUN, JACQUES. *Berlioz and the Romantic Century.* (2 vols.) New York: Columbia University Press, 1950.
BERLIOZ, H. *Memoirs.* New York: Knopf, 1948.

GIDE, ANDRÉ. *Notes on Chopin.* New York: Philosophical Library, 1949.
WEINSTOCK, H. *Chopin: The Man and His Music.* New York: Knopf, 1949.

STRATTON, S. S. *Mendelssohn.* London: Dent, 1934.

SCHAUFFLER, R. H. *Florestan: The Life of Robert Schumann.* New York: Holt, 1946.
SCHUMANN, ROBERT. *On Music and Musicians.* New York: Pantheon, 1946.

## MIDDLE, LATE AND POST-ROMANTIC PERIOD

GEIRINGER, K. *Brahms, His Life and Work.* New York: Oxford, 1947.
NIEMANN, W. *Brahms.* New York: Knopf, 1947.

SITWELL, S. *Liszt.* New York: Philosophical Library, 1956.
SEARLE, H. *The Music of Franz Liszt.* London: Dent, 1954.

MAHLER, ALMA. *Gustav Mahler: Memories and Letters.* New York: Viking, 1946.
NEWLIN, D. *Bruckner, Mahler and Schönberg.* New York: King's Crown, 1947.
NEWMAN, E. *Strauss.* London: John Lane, 1908.
STRAUSS, R. *Recollections and Reflections.* London: Boosey & Hawkes, 1953.

ABRAHAM, G. *Music of Tchaikowsky.* New York: Norton, 1946.
BOWEN, C. D. *Beloved Friend.* New York: Random House, 1937.
SHOSTAKOVICH, D. et al. *Russian Symphony: Thoughts About Tchaikowsky.* New York: Philosophical Library, 1947.
WEINSTOCK, H. *Tchaikowsky.* New York: Knopf, 1946.

GATTI, G. *Verdi: The Man and His Works.* New York: Putnam, 1955.
HUSSEY, D. *Verdi.* New York: Pellegrini & Cudahy, 1949.
TOYE, F. *Giuseppe Verdi: His Life and Works.* New York: Knopf, 1946.
WALKER, F. *The Man Verdi.* New York: Knopf, 1962.

BURK, J. *Letters of Richard Wagner.* New York: Macmillan, 1950.
NEWMAN, E. *The Life of Richard Wagner* (4 vols.). New York: Knopf, 1933-46.
——— *Wagner as Man and Artist.* New York: Tudor, 1948.
SHAW, G. B. *The Perfect Wagnerite.* New York: Brentano, 1916.

## RUSSIAN NATIONALIST AND CONTEMPORARY COMPOSERS

ABRAHAM, G. *Eight Soviet Composers.* New York: Oxford, 1943.
CALVOCORESSI, M. D. *Modeste Moussorgsky.* Fair Lawn, N.J.: Essential Books, 1956.
LEYDA, J. and BERTENSSON, S. (eds.). *The Moussorgsky Reader.* New York: Norton, 1947.
NESTYEV, I. V. *Serge Prokofiev.* New York: Knopf, 1946.
RIMSKY-KORSAKOFF, N. *My Musical Life.* New York: Knopf, 1942.
SEROFF, V. *Dmitri Shostakovitch.* New York: Knopf, 1947.
——— *The Mighty Five.* New York: Allen, Towne & Heath, 1956.
——— *Rachmaninoff.* New York: Simon & Schuster, 1950.

# Bibliography

### IMPRESSIONISM

SEROFF, V. *Debussy, Musician of France*. New York: Putnam, 1956.
THOMPSON, OSCAR. *Debussy, Man and Artist*. New York: Dodd, Mead, 1937.

SEROFF, V. *Maurice Ravel*. New York: Holt, 1953.
DEMUTH, N. *Ravel*. London: Rockliff, 1951.

HUTCHINGS, A. *Delius*. London: Macmillan, 1948.

### CONTEMPORARY PERIOD

BRODER, NATHAN, *Samuel Barber*. New York: G. Schirmer, 1954.

FASSETT, A. *The Naked Face of Genius: Béla Bartók's American Years*. Boston: Houghton-Mifflin, 1958.
HARASZTI, A. *Béla Bartók: His Life and Works*. Paris: Lyrebird Press, 1938.
STEVENS, H. *The Life and Music of Béla Bartók*. New York: Oxford, 1953.

REDLICH, F. *Alban Berg*. New York: Abelard-Schuman, 1957.
REICH, W. *Alban Berg*. Vienna: H. Reichner, 1937.
—— *A Guide to Alban Berg's Opera, Wozzeck*. New York: League of Composers, 1931.

BERGER, A. *Aaron Copland*. New York: Oxford, 1953.
SMITH, J. *Aaron Copland*. New York: Dutton, 1955.

VLAD, R. *Luigi Dallapiccola*. Milan: Suivini-Zerboni, 1957.

COWELL, H. and S. *Charles Ives and His Music*. New York: Oxford, 1955.

MILHAUD, D. *Notes Without Music*. New York: Knopf, 1953.

ARMITAGE, M. (ed.) *Schönberg*. New York: G. Schirmer, 1937.
LEIBOWITZ, R. (Tr. Newlin) *Schönberg and His School*. New York: Philosophical Library, 1949.
NEWLIN, D. *Bruckner, Mahler and Schönberg*. New York: Columbia University Press, 1947.
STUCKENSCHMIDT, H. H. *Arnold Schönberg*. New York: Grove Press, 1960.
WELLESZ, E. *Arnold Schönberg*. New York: Dutton, 1925.

SCHREIBER, H. and PERSICHETTI, V. *William Schuman*. New York: G. Schirmer, 1954.

LEDERMAN, M., ed. *Stravinsky in the Theater*. New York: Pellegrini & Cudahy, 1949.
MYERS, R. *Introduction to the Music of Stravinsky*. London: Dobson, 1950.
STRAVINSKY, I. *Igor Stravinsky: An Autobiography*. New York: Steuer, 1958.
STRAVINSKY, I. and CRAFT, R. *Conversations with Igor Stravinsky*. New York: Doubleday, 1959.
STRAVINSKY, I. and CRAFT, R. *Memoirs and Commentaries*. New York: Doubleday, 1960.
STROBEL, H. *Stravinsky: Classic Humanist*. New York: Merlin Press, 1955.
TANSMAN, A. *Igor Stravinsky: The Man and His Music*. New York: Putnam, 1949.

MOLDENHAUER, HANS. *The Death of Anton Webern*. New York: Philosophical Library,

619

## General Readings in Art, Aesthetics, History and Theory

Abraham, G. *This Modern Music.* New York: Norton, 1952.

Bauer, M. *Twentieth Century Music.* New York: Putnam, 1947.

Chase, G. *America's Music from the Pilgrims to the Present.* New York: Mc-Graw-Hill, 1955.

Chavez, C. *Toward a New Music.* New York: Norton, 1957.

Copland, A. *Copland on Music.* Garden City: Doubleday & Co., 1960.

—— *Music and Imagination.* Cambridge: Harvard Univ., 1952.

—— *Our New Music.* New York: Whittlesey House, 1941.

Dallin, L. *Techniques of Twentieth Century Composition.* Dubuque: Wm. C. Brown, 1957.

Debussy, C. *Monsieur Croche, Dilletante Hater.* New York: Vilny, 1928.

Dewey, J. *Art as Experience.* New York: G. P. Putnam's Sons, 1934.

Dorian, F. *The History of Music in Performance.* New York: Norton.

—— *The Musical Workshop.* London: Secker & Warburg, 1947.

Edman, I. *Arts and the Man.* New York: Mentor, 1949.

Eisler, H. *Composing for the Films.* New York: Oxford, 1947.

Fleming, W. *Arts and Ideas.* New York: Holt, 1955.

Graf, M. *Modern Music.* New York: Philosophical Library, 1946.

Grosser, M. *The Painter's Eye.* New York: Mentor, 1955.

Hindemith, P. *A Composer's World.* Cambridge: Harvard Univ., 1952.

Hunter, S. *Modern American Painting and Sculpture.* New York: Dell, 1959.

—— *Modern French Painting.* New York: Dell, 1956.

Kerman, J. *Opera as Drama.* New York: Vintage, 1959.

Kolodin, I., ed. *The Composer as Listener.* New York: Collier Books, 1962.

Krenek, E. *Music Here and Now.* New York: Norton, 1939.

Langer, S. *Philosophy in a New Key.* Cambridge: Harvard Univ., 1951.

Mellers, W. *Romanticism and the Twentieth Century.* Fairlawn, N.J.: Essential Books, 1957.

Newmeyer, S. *Enjoying Modern Art.* New York: Mentor, 1955.

Norman G. and Shrifte M. *Letters of Composers.* New York: Knopf, 1946.

Peltz, M. *Introduction to Opera.* New York: Barnes & Noble, 1961.

*Reihe, Die, No. 1: Electronic Music.* Bryn Mawr: Presser, 1957.

Robertson, A. *Chamber Music.* Baltimore: Pelican Books, 1957.

Sachs, C. *The Commonwealth of Art.* New York: Norton, 1946.

Santayana, G. *The Sense of Beauty.* New York: Collier, 1961.

Sargeant, W. *Jazz, Hot and Hybrid.* New York: Dutton, 1948.

Schönberg, A. *Style and Idea.* New York: Philosophical Library, 1950.

Sessions, R. *The Musical Experience of Composer, Performer, Listener.* Princeton: Princeton Univ., 1950.

Slonimsky, N. *Music of Latin America.* New York: Crowell, 1945.

Stravinsky, I. *Poetics of Music.* Cambridge: Harvard Univ., 1947.

Thomson, V. *The Art of Judging Music.* New York: Knopf, 1948.

Vaughan Williams, R. *The Making of Music.* Ithaca: Cornell Univ., 1955.

—— *National Music.* London, 1934.

Walter, Bruno. *Of Music and Music Making.* New York: Norton, 1960.

# Index

# Index

# Index

# Index

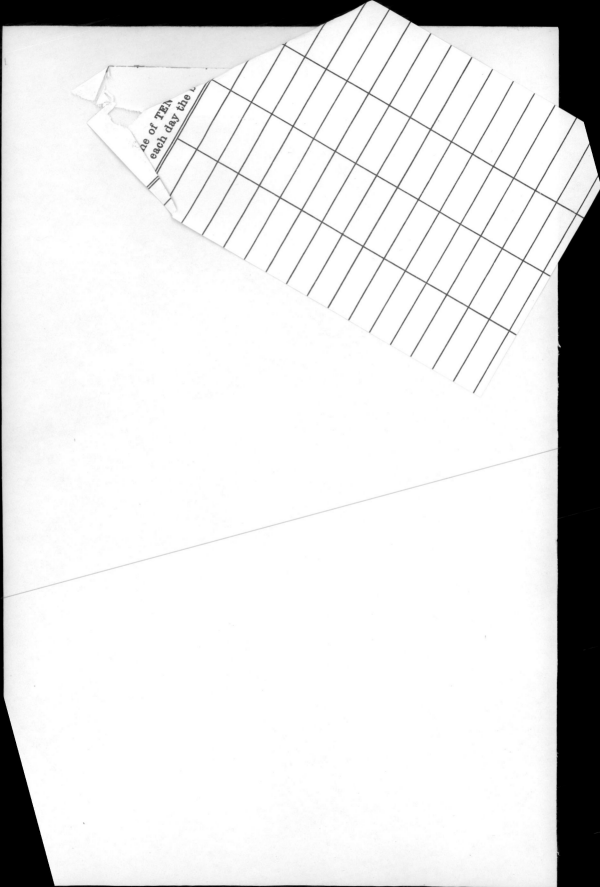